Fundamen
of Human
and Cogni

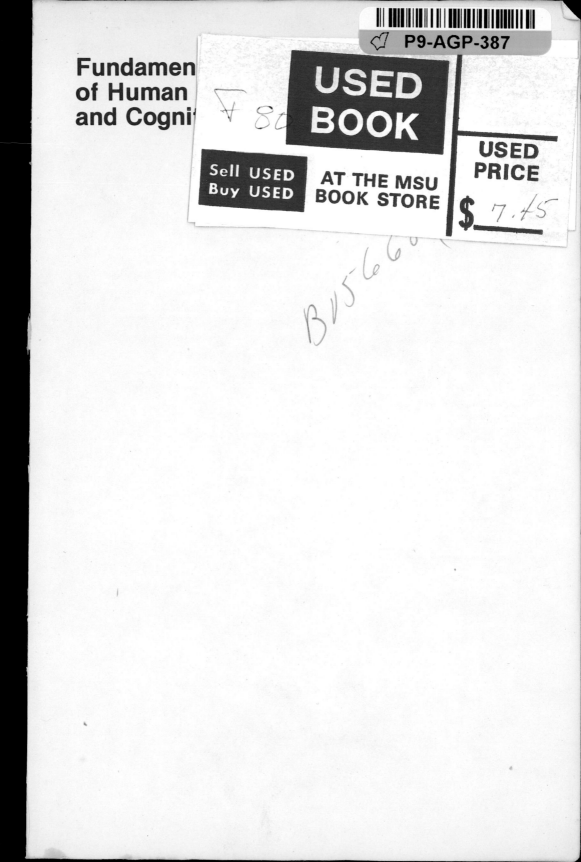

Fundamentals of Human Learning, Memory, and Cognition

Henry C. Ellis
University of New Mexico

Second Edition

Wm. C. Brown Company Publishers
Dubuque, Iowa

Fundamentals of Psychology Series

Fundamentals of Scientific Method in Psychology
Malcolm D. Arnoult

Fundamentals of Human Learning, Memory, and Cognition
Henry C. Ellis

Fundamentals of Learning and Motivation
Frank A. Logan

Frank A. Logan
General Editor
University of New Mexico

Copyright © 1972, 1978 by Wm. C. Brown Company Publishers

Library of Congress Catalog Card Number: 77-79556

ISBN—0—697—06623—1

Printed in the United States of America

This book is dedicated to my wife, Florence, and to
our children, Joan, Diane, and John

Contents

3 Verbal Learning   43

4 Memory I: The Processing of Information   77

7 Language   159

Foreword

There is no single best way to introduce students to as diverse and complex a subject matter as psychology. The special needs and interests of both student and teacher help determine the course content and organization. The Fundamentals of Psychology Series is designed to better enable the approach that I have found to be most effective.

That approach is to restrict the course content to a relatively small number of topics so as to cover them in greater depth than customary. Of course, this implies that other topics are omitted or mentioned in a very cursory manner. But my conviction is that students are richer for having explored a few topics sufficiently to begin to comprehend the concepts and to appreciate their roles in understanding behavior.

Accordingly, while this series is intended for beginning students, its goal is to lead them further into each topic than is typical of introductory texts. This very feature may make the series also valuable in more advanced courses where the teacher wants to begin with a review of the fundamentals before proceeding to more specialized content. In either event, we hope students will find the series interesting and challenging.

Frank A. Logan

Preface

The purpose of this book is to portray the fundamental principles of human learning, memory, and cognition. It is written with the belief that students can be introduced to the psychology of human learning, memory, and cognition through a coherent oversimplification so that the fundamental principles are revealed in bold relief. Emphasis, however, on the fundamentals means that many subtleties, details, and important qualifications are left untouched. General principles are described and are portrayed as truths even though they may be inaccurate in certain details or require considerable qualification.

In some sense this process characterizes much of teaching. Students are first presented with major generalizations and principles and subsequently begin to learn about their exceptions, qualifications, and limitations. On occasion the complexities of a principle are at least partially described; however, in the main the fundamental principles are presented without discussion of all their potential ramifications. The principal justification for this approach is that students can more readily acquire a coherent picture of an area and will have an organizational framework for integrating new facts, concepts, and principles in human learning, memory, and cognition in their subsequent education.

The book is written with the conviction that the principles of human learning, memory, and cognition should be introduced in such a way that students see their direct pertinence to and potential impact upon human affairs. Illustrations of practical applications are liberally provided, with the hope that students will gain a fuller and richer understanding of the principles when they can relate them to their personal experiences. These illustrations cannot, of course, perfectly reflect principles derived from laboratory settings, but they can approximate them and thus hopefully lead students to think of other illustrations as well as of potential exceptions.

This book is one of a series of "Fundamentals of" books produced by the same publisher. It is, therefore, intended to be compatible with others in the series, but an understanding of this book does not depend upon reading any of the other books. This book shares with the others in the series the assumption that fundamental principles and concepts of psychology can be more readily grasped by students when these principles and concepts are related to familiar everyday experiences.

This book attempts to bridge the gap between the old and new topics in human learning, memory, and cognition. The traditional and more well-developed topics must be related to the newly developing areas. The psychology of human learning, memory, and cognition is rapidly changing, and an effort is made to convey this portrait of a rapidly expanding area of knowledge. Theoretical developments are in a rapid growth period, and cognitive and information-processing views of behavior are emphasized where they seem most appropriate. Where possible the continuity among theoretical approaches is emphasized as well as their distinctive characteristics. Finally, in no sense can this book be regarded as a final description; rather it must be viewed as a momentary state-of-the-science report.

This book deals with the wide range of topics encompassed by human learning, memory, and cognition whose scope ranges from simple learning (conditioning) to the complex processes of memory, concept learning, thinking, and problem solving. Chapter 1 describes the objectives and scope of the book. Chapter 2 provides an introductory statement of the elements of conditioning. Many features and details of conditioning processes are excluded and only the most fundamental features are described. The justification for including a chapter on conditioning is that some conditioning concepts, especially those of discrimination and generalization, are still used in accounts of more complex behaviors found, say, in concept learning. Thus it is in some sense desirable that students have the opportunity to see how these concepts were initially developed in the context of conditioning. If students have already been exposed to conditioning this chapter may then be easily bypassed.

Chapter 3 deals with verbal learning and some topics of memory. Chapter 4 introduces memory from the viewpoint of information processing. Chapter 5 continues the discussion of memory, emphasizing organizational processes, forgetting, and models of memory. Topics which logically follow the development of memory are concept learning, language, thinking and problem solving, attention and perceptual learning, and motor skills learning, chapters 6, 7, 8, 9, and 10, respectively. Transfer is discussed in chapter 11 and the discussion focuses on the effects of prior learning on new learning. In chapter 12, the final content chapter, individual differences in learning and in memory are examined.

The material in each chapter is not described in isolation from other related areas, but reflects in some way the principles and concepts described in earlier chapters and on occasion anticipates subsequent issues. At an elementary level the student is presented comparisons of S-R associative and cognitive conceptions of behavior and indications of advantages and limitations of each are discussed.

As with other books in this series, each major chapter ends with a set of examination items and explanatory answers. Students may use these items not only for review, but also for feedback in gauging their own comprehension of the material. This, however, is not their only purpose, for it is hoped that the test items will stimulate students to raise new questions and to engage in additional thinking about the issues. Some of the questions are relatively straightforward, whereas others present issues from a somewhat different perspective, hopefully to encourage students to stretch their imagination.

At the end of the book is the glossary describing the major technical terms defined in this book. The definitions are brief and do not, of course, provide all of the potential meaning of the terms. The Glossary provides a convenient refresher for students but should not be relied upon exclusively. The understanding of technical terms and concepts comes when students can *use* the terms in the appropriate context. A list of suggested readings which will enable students to explore more deeply particular areas is also provided. Finally, a list of references by chapter is given. No formal references are cited in the book, and few experiments are presented. The references, however, provide representative materials which will allow students to explore particular topics in the original literature.

Henry C. Ellis

Acknowledgments

I am indebted to many persons for assistance in the preparation of the second edition of *Fundamentals of Human Learning, Memory, and Cognition.* I am again indebted to Prof. Frank A. Logan for his helpful suggestions and encouragement. I would also like to thank Prof. Harold Delaney for his thoughtful comments and suggestions and for his assistance in preparing the chapter on individual differences. I would also like to thank Prof. Brian Babbitt, Missouri Southern College, for his assistance in preparing the attention section of Chapter 9, and to Prof. Charles Grah, Austin Peay State University, for his assistance in preparing test items for Chapter 12. My grateful acknowledgments goes also to those colleagues who provided useful comments based on their reading of part or all of the text or who provided student feedback, particularly to Profs. Burton G. Andreas, State University of New York at Brockport; William F. Battig, University of Colorado; Terry C. Daniel, University of Arizona; James Devine, University of Texas at El Paso; Douglas P. Ferraro, University of New Mexico; John P. Gluck, University of New Mexico; Judith Goggin, University of Texas at El Paso; Robert Haygood, Arizona State University; Reed Hunt, University of North Carolina, Greensboro; John Jahnke, Miami University; Kenneth Kleinman, Southern Illinois University at Edwardsville; Philip Meyer, University of South Dakota; Raymond Miles, University of Colorado; Frederick J. Parente, Towson State University; Ronald W. Shaffer, Western Washington State College; B. Charles Tatum, Cornell College and William J. Tomson, University of Michigan at Dearborn.

I would also like to thank Edward Bowers, Jr., Don Rivers, and David Smith, my editors, for their encouragement, support, and patience, and Richard Crews, Publisher, who has done everything possible to make my association with Wm. C. Brown Company an enjoyable experience. In addition, I would like to thank Mrs. Karen Gilligan for her excellent work as production editor.

Finally I am grateful to Eleanor Orth, Elna Parks, and LaNelle Ruebush for their typing skills.

Introduction to Human Learning, Memory, and Cognition

Humans learn, remember, and think. They also plan, solve problems, and use language. Probably the most interesting feature of human behavior is that we *learn* to modify our behavior when confronted with new situations. Of equal importance is our learned proficiency to generalize in new situations on the basis of prior learning and to develop concepts and strategies in coping with both current and forthcoming events. This flexible, adaptive character of human behavior thus emphasizes the fundamental significance of *learning* in the understanding of human behavior.

Learning plays a central role in contemporary psychology. Most human behavior can be said to be influenced by learning, particularly by the time one reaches adulthood. At birth the infant possesses a few basic unlearned responses such as crying, eating, and elimination. Yet even these responses come to be modified by the learning process. For example, the child learns to expect food at particular times and not at others; he subsequently learns that a crying response may or may not receive attention by the parent, depending upon particular circumstances; and he ultimately becomes toilet trained.

The most significant learning for the human being is language. Language is a basic tool for thinking, problem solving, and other more complex symbolic activities. The acquisition of knowledge and skills is heavily dependent upon the use of language. Indeed, the possession of language enables us to plan for the future, facilitates our learning of concepts and principles, and enables effective communication.

The importance of learning is reflected in its scope and generality as seen in its influence on other topics in psychology. For instance, your personal feelings and attitudes are the products of an extensive learning history. Thus, the social psychologist studying attitudes is, in fact, studying one outcome of the learning process. Similarly, you learn to interpret events in the world in uniquely individual ways or, alternatively, in ways typical of your particular culture as the result of certain experiences. Your likes and dislikes, prejudices, opinions, values, all of which reflect your particular life style, are the result of a long history of learning experiences. Moreover, your skill in organizing and remembering events, in problem solving and thinking, and in generalizing to new situations is in large part the result of the way in which you have learned to respond in tasks requiring memory, problem solving, thinking, and transfer.

More complex problems such as mental illness and crime can in part be understood as the result of individual learning histories. It is widely agreed that many disorders of behavior can be understood as the result of learning where neurological or biochemical influences are known not to be present. Just as many of us learn to be effective in coping with environmental and interpersonal problems, others learn to function in maladaptive, less effective ways in coping with daily events. Indeed, some current forms of therapy employ procedures derived from principles of learning on the assumption that therapy is a form of learning itself.

Finally, many efforts at improving the quality of education are based upon our current knowledge of principles of learning. To the extent that the *conditions* which affect learning and the *principles* of learning are understood, teachers are better able to bring about changes in educational practices directed toward more effective learning of knowledges and skills. In the past decade a rapidly growing technology of learning has emerged which has developed largely from the extension and application of fundamental principles of learning. This technology—reflected, for example, in developments such as programmed learning, computer-assisted instruction, and individualized instruction—represents a systematic effort to apply knowledge about the psychology of learning to pressing problems of education. Thus the study of human learning is not an isolated or restricted activity, but involves a serious attempt to cope with some of the important practical problems of everyday life.

Objectives

The objectives of this book are to examine the fundamental principles of human learning and cognition and to explore some of their practical implications. This book examines the range of processes going from simple learning (conditioning), verbal learning, and memory, to concept learning, perceptual learning, problem solving, thinking, language, and motor skills learning and transfer. The focus of this book is on the most basic, *fundamental principles* of human learning, memory, and cognition. These principles have been developed largely from laboratory studies of human performance in highly controlled experimental situations. Topics such as instrumental learning, conditioning, and motivation receive less attention. Thus no attempt is made to cover the full range of the psychology of learning in great detail. The emphasis is on those topics that are central to the understanding of human learning, memory, and cognition.

This book is written with the belief that the principles of human learning, memory, and cognition should be introduced in such a way that the student sees their pertinence to human affairs. Thus, although the principles are initially described somewhat formally, their applicability to human affairs is given considerable attention. Illustrations of practical application and implication of the basic principles are liberally provided, with the expectation that students will gain a clearer understanding of these principles when they can relate them to personal experience.

Scope of Human Learning and Cognition

As a topic in the psychology of learning, human learning may refer simply to any class of learning situations that involves humans. Thus in a larger sense the study of human learning involves the broad range of topics from simple human conditioning to complex processes involving concept learning and problem solving. Sometimes the meaning of the term is restricted principally to those processes involving the acquisition of skills and knowledge, transfer, and memory. Thus, for example, the acquisition of verbal skills such as language would be an instance of human learning. Similarly, learning to drive, to read, or to become proficient in some athletic skill would also represent instances of human learning. At a somewhat more restricted level, the term *human learning* sometimes refers to those learning situations and principles that are *characteristically* human, providing one basis for distinguishing between principles of human learning and principles of learning derived from the study of lower animals. This book emphasizes, however, the integrated character of learning and the generality of its principles.

The distinction between learning and cognition is to some extent arbitrary. *The term "cognition" emphasizes the symbolic, mental, and inferred* (not directly seen) *processes of humans.* Thus the sharpening and refining of abstract concepts such as "freedom" and "justice," the search for a solution to a problem, and the use of strategies in games are said to be instances of cognitive processes because they presumably involve mental or symbolic processes on the part of the learner. *Cognition* means knowledge; thus "cognitive psychology" is concerned with how humans acquire, store, and use knowledge.

Cognition thus typically refers to the class of processes involving such activities as thinking, reasoning, knowing, problem solving, and conceptual learning. More generally, reference to cognitive processes implies an active role of the human in learning situations, use of strategies, and ways in which the learner might organize materials in order to learn and retain them more efficiently. Since it is difficult to think of any human learning situation in which the human is not in some way actively responding, organizing, and reorganizing the material, human learning almost always involves some kind of cognitive activity. Even in conditioning and in verbal association formation, processes that are relatively less complex in the range of processes to be described, the learner may play an active role. Therefore, this book makes no attempt to distinguish sharply between human learning and cognition. Cognitive processes are intertwined with human learning, and thus the topics are jointly treated in this book.

A Traditional Definition of Learning

Although you will develop a definition of learning in reading this book, it is useful to define learning in a general way now so that you may have a working definition of the concept. Learning is a hypothetical process that is not directly seen, but is inferred from behavioral changes of the individual. Not all behavioral changes, however, allow the inference of learning. Only those changes in behavior which can be attributed to practice variables represent "learning." Performance changes due to drugs, maturation, fatigue, and motivation are not changes attributable to learning.

Learning is a relatively permanent process that is inferred from performance changes due to practice. Thus skill in reading, which obviously results from practice, is an instance of learning. Similarly, improvement in athletic skills such as golf and tennis are instances of learning because these are changes which can be attributed to practice conditions. In contrast, performance changes due to drugs or fatigue are not changes attributable to learning because the resulting behavioral changes are temporary in nature and do not depend directly upon practice. Extended practice may, of course, produce fatigue; changes in performance due to fatigue do not, however, represent learning.

Fatigue produces a temporary decrement in your performance, and hence such performance changes are distinguished from those due to learning. Drugs such as alcohol and marijuana can produce a temporary high, but the behavioral changes are short-lived rather than permanent. This does not deny, however, the fact that one can learn to behave in somewhat characteristic ways when under the influence of drugs or while one "thinks" he is under the influence of a drug. Such behavior is likely to depend upon the setting or context in which drugs are used. For instance, it is known that some individuals can experience a high while sitting in a darkened room full of incense listening to exotic music so long as they *believe* they are smoking marijuana. In such experiences, individuals have been given control (placebo) cigarettes without the knowledge that they contain no marijuana. Such findings point out the role of contextual stimuli and suggestion in influencing the manner in which we react to events. In a similar vein, behavioral changes that result from maturation are not attributable to the process of learning since maturational changes will occur despite special practice conditions.

A Definition of Memory

Information that is learned may be used or applied at some later date. Obviously, if information is to be used it must be stored and it must also be accessible at the time needed. Thus *memory* refers to storing information and to accessing or retrieving information. More generally, *memory encompasses three basic processes: encoding, storage, and retrieval.* These processes are described in detail in later chapters, but we shall establish basic definitions here. *Encoding* refers to arranging information so that it can be placed in storage. The process of encoding includes modification of information such as selecting certain features for storage. For example, when you read a book you do not remember the words or sentences verbatim (except in very rare cases); rather you try to get the gist or the main ideas which you encode. *Storage* refers to storing information in the memory system. The fact that we can remember information for days, weeks, or years implies that information is stored. *Retrieval* refers to the process of accessing or getting at the stored information. Information may be stored in memory, but storage is no guarantee that we can get at the information. All three processes are part of memory, and thus it follows that a failure in any one of the processes can lead to a failure in memory.

What Is Learned?

The study of learning leads inevitably to the question, What is learned? a question which has generated much theoretical debate. Some psychologists have viewed learning as the formation of associations between events, in which the events are called stimuli and responses. In general a stimulus-response association is said to be formed if we learn when and/or where to execute a response. For example, if you learn to turn right at the corner of Jefferson Street and left at the intersection of Washington and Adams Streets in order to go to the nearest grocery store, you can be said to have learned an association because you are making particular responses in the presence of particular stimuli.

In contrast, other psychologists have argued that what we learn is an association between stimuli themselves. The idea is that a stimulus-stimulus association is learned, which means that we learn to expect a particular stimulus whenever a particular stimulus event occurs. In essence we learn the significance or meaning of stimuli rather than learn to make particular responses. That is, instead of learning a stimulus-response association when learning how to go to the grocery store, what we actually learn is the location of the store. By learning the place of location of the store we are learning a "cognitive map" or general idea about how to get to the store.

Thus a stimulus-response or S-R theory of learning emphasizes responses, whereas a stimulus-stimulus or S-S theory emphasizes that we learn ideas, knowledge, or cognitions.

A Cognitive Approach to Learning

Although the S-S approach emphasizes ideas or cognition, the approach is still couched within an associationistic framework. In more recent years, the trend toward cognitive (but nonassociative) and information-processing conceptions of learning, memory, and complex processes has strengthened enormously. The view which has come to be prevalent is that the human is an active processor of information rather than a passive organism in which associations become stamped in via repetition. Mental processes such as abstraction, reasoning, organizing, thinking, searching one's memory, and the like, are seen as fundamental cognitive processes which are not easily reduced to associations. If we consider our example of learning about going to the grocery store again, a cognitive view which is nonassociative would emphasize that what we actually learn is a *plan* about going to the store—a mental structure, schema, or pattern—which cannot be adequately described as simply as the learning of S-S associations. From the perspective of modern cognitive psychology, the study of learning is the study of how we acquire knowledge (and skills), not how we acquire associations. Thus cognitive psychology is similar to S-S theory but abandons the notion of association formation as the unit of what is learned. We will have occasion to see how these different views have operated, although this book will view most of human learning and memory within the framework of cognitive psychology.

Summary

In this book we are concerned with the broad range of events encompassed by the topics of human learning, memory, and cognition. These topics play a significant role in psychology today and are basic to your understanding of a wide range of human behavior. The focus will be on the fundamental principles of human learning, memory and cognition, with considerable emphasis on the practical application of these concepts to daily affairs.

Learning was defined as a relatively permanent change in performance which is the result of practice. Such a definition distinguishes between performance changes due to practice and changes due to maturation, fatigue, and drugs. Memory was seen to encompass the processes of encoding, storage, and retrieval. Human learning and cognition were not sharply distinguished since the processes were viewed as highly interrelated. The term *cognition* was seen to emphasize the symbolic mental activity of humans.

Before you can apply concepts and principles of learning for your own benefit, you must first have some understanding of the basic principles. The emphasis in this book, therefore, is first on an examination of the basic principles and generalizations in each topic area and then on discussion of how these principles are applicable. Emphasis is placed both on how these concepts may assist in your personal effectiveness as a learner, thinker, and problem solver and on how you might assist others in the teaching-learning process.

To the Student

A list of multiple-choice, true-false, and discussion items are presented at the end of this chapter and of all other chapters. The answer to each multiple-choice and true-false item is also given along with a brief explanation. These items sample the content of the chapter and thus provide some index of your comprehension of the material. The questions are not, however, exhaustive of the content of the chapter and hence should not be relied upon exclusively for study and review. Some questions tap the factual information of the chapter, whereas others attempt to apply concepts and principles to new situations not directly described in the text. Thus, the questions sample the types of questions found on typical examinations. In preparation for examinations, a good practice is for you to make up several test items of your own.

Multiple-Choice Items: Introduction to Human Learning, Memory, and Cognition

1. The definition of learning emphasizes that learning is
   a. a transient, nonpermanent process
   b. directly observable

- c.   a hypothetical process
     d.   due to maturational changes
2.   The definition of memory emphasizes that memory is
     a.   a matter of retention
     -b.   a three-stage process
     c.   knowledge
     d.   unrelated to learning
3.   The definition of cognition emphasizes that cognition is
     - a.   symbolic or mental activity
     b.   concrete rather than abstract
     c.   skill learning
     d.   association formation

True-False Items: Introduction to Human Learning, Memory, and Cognition

T 1.   The concept of cognition emphasizes the active role of the learner.
F 2.   Learning and cognition are quite separate processes.
T 3.   The current prevalent view of learning is that humans are active processors of information.

Discussion Items: Introduction to Human Learning, Memory, and Cognition

1.   How might you describe the process of learning addition and subtraction as a process of stimulus-response association? as a stimulus-stimulus or cognitive process?

2.   How would you describe the information learned in this brief chapter in terms of encoding, storage, and retrieval? (After you have read chapter 4, Memory I, answer this question again.)

Multiple-Choice Answers: Introduction to Human Learning, Memory, and Cognition

1.   (c)   We can observe a person studying some material or practicing some skill, that is, we can observe changes in performance but not learning itself. Learning is a hypothetical process not directly observable.

2.   (b)   Memory is a three-stage process involving encoding, storage, and retrieval.

3.   (a)   *Cognition* refers to symbolic or mental activity of the learner; *cognition* means to gain knowledge.

True-False Answers: Introduction to Human Learning, Memory, and Cognition

1. (True)   The idea of cognition or cognitive processes emphasizes the active rather than the passive role of the learner.

2. (False)   Learning and cognition are related and overlapping concepts. Cognitive processes play an important role in the learning process.

3. (True)   Most psychologists do view learning as the active processing of information.

Elements of Conditioning

2

Psychologists generally agree that the simplest form of learning is conditioning. This by no means implies that conditioning is an uncomplicated process or that all of its aspects are thoroughly understood. What is meant is that conditioning, as one form of learning, is readily observed in lower organisms and thus appears to be phylogenetically a more elementary form of learning than processes such as concept learning, thinking, and problem solving. Sometimes it is implied that an understanding of conditioning requires fewer assumptions and principles than does the presumably more complex phenomena of memory, concept learning, and thinking. Conversely, the implication is that an understanding of more complex human learning requires *additional* principles beyond those developed in the study of conditioning.

Related to this second meaning is the assumption held by some psychologists that principles of learning are hierarchically organized, beginning with conditioning as the simplest and going to concept learning and problem solving as the most complex. These more complex forms of learning are thought by some authorities to depend upon simpler types of learning that involve associative principles. The basic idea is that a classification of types of learning produces a hierarchy of types going from the simplest to the most complex, and that more complex types of learning build upon or are composed of simpler elements of learning. Today, many psychologists reject the assumption of a hierarchical classification of types of learning, despite the fact that virtually all accept the assumption that conditioning is the most elementary form of learning.

Conditioning and Human Learning

Any discussion of conditioning in a volume devoted to human learning and cognition should describe its relationship to other areas of learning. The usefulness of beginning with an elementary chapter dealing with principles and concepts of conditioning is twofold: First, there is a considerable body of knowledge about conditioning with human subjects. Thus human conditioning is properly one aspect of any study of human learning. This statement does *not* mean, however, that conditioning is representative of the broad domain of human learning activities that are considered in this book. All that is meant is that conditioning is one class of learning processes among several kinds characteristically observed in humans.

The second reason for briefly examining conditioning concepts and principles is that they have been extended to many aspects of more complex human learning, especially in the areas of verbal learning, transfer, memory, and concept learning. Despite their extension, it must be emphasized that a large number of psychologists question what they regard as an uncritical extrapolation of concepts and principles of conditioning to explain more complex forms of learning. Some authorities believe that dependence upon conditioning principles for explanatory concepts, while valuable in a few instances, has prevented psychologists from focusing on important features of human learning not readily handled by conditioning principles. Others have emphasized what they regard to be the essential dichotomy of principles of animal versus human learning and have taken the view that an understanding of human learning will emerge only when principles are developed at this level of analysis.

This book adopts neither the extreme of ignoring conditioning principles, nor the unrealistic position of saying that all forms of learning are reducible to conditioning principles. Occasionally we will have opportunity to examine explanations of complex human learning derived from conditioning principles. We shall indicate where such principles appear useful and reasonable, while at the same time we shall indicate where additional principles developed within the context of characteristically human research appear necessary for a full understanding of human learning.

It is reasonable to assume that a comprehensive understanding of human learning will require the development of concepts *specific* to human learning situations. This belief is shared by a large number of psychologists who emphasize the cognitive, purposeful, and organizational character of human learning. Nevertheless, this belief need not carry with it the assumption that we can or should disregard what has been gained from studies of simpler learning. One objective of this book is thus to introduce the student to developments in human learning that appear to require distinctly cognitive conceptions, while retaining those concepts that derive from studies of simple associative learning when they have integrative usefulness. The focus will be on the generality of principles and the still integrative and unifying character of the concept of learning across the broad range of topics included under this process.

Basic Conditioning Procedures

Three basic procedures are employed in the study of conditioning proc-
esses. One is |classical| conditioning, which refers to procedures devel-
oped by the Russian physiologist Pavlov. The second refers to(instrumental)
conditioning, sometimes referred to as instrumental learning. The third
is |operant| conditioning which is similar to many features of instrumental
conditioning, and therefore for the purposes of this text the two are
treated as if they were the same procedure. This chapter provides only
a very brief introduction to the topic of conditioning and interested
readers should refer to any of a number of texts which are almost entirely devoted to the topic. (Suggested for a systematic introduction to
conditioning principles is Frank Logan's *Fundamentals of Learning and
Motivation,* a companion volume in this series.) Since many of the
procedures were first developed with animals, these procedures in their
original context are described first and illustrations of human conditioning follow.

Classical Conditioning

Classical conditioning refers to a set of training procedures in which one
stimulus comes to substitute for another in evoking a response. These
procedures are called classical because of their historical priority as
developed by Pavlov.

The procedures characteristically employed by Pavlov involved
placing a laboratory animal, such as a dog, in a restraining harness before training. A small opening was made in the dog's cheek so that saliva
could be collected and measured during the training session. The experimenter, not visible to the animal, sounded a tuning fork and then
presented food powder to the animal. The food powder would, of
course, automatically elicit the response of salivation, whereas the sound
had no initial effect on the animal's behavior. After a number of pairing
trials of food powder and sound, the sound was presented by itself and
the animal was observed to salivate. Thus an initially neutral event, the
sound, acquired the capacity to elicit a response by virtue of being paired
with the food powder.

Pavlov called the food powder an *unconditioned stimulus* (UCS),
which means simply that a given stimulus has the capacity to produce a
response at the beginning of an experiment. The UCS may possess some
innate biological capacity to produce a response in the sense of being unlearned, or it may have acquired this capacity as a result of learning
that occurred before the animal was brought to the laboratory. The response elicited by the UCS, which in this instance is salivation, is called
the *unconditioned response* (UCR). Pavlov referred to the sounds of the

tuning fork as a *conditioned stimulus* (CS), which is any initially "neutral" stimulus that acquires the capacity to elicit a response as a result of CS-UCS pairing. The salivary response produced by the tuning fork is called a *conditioned response* (CR) to emphasize that it is a learned response dependent upon the presentation of the CS. The CR can be preparatory in the sense that salivation is preparatory for eating.

Are the UCR and the CR the same response? In a qualitative sense they can be regarded the same since in our example they were both salivary responses. Otherwise, they are different responses, especially because their *quantitative* features usually differ. For example, the magnitude of the CR is usually less than the UCR.

Other classical conditioning procedures have been developed. Pavlov's procedures are referred to as classical *appetitive* conditioning because the UCS (food) is an emotionally positive stimulus. Procedures that are called classical *defense* conditioning are widely used and involve presentation of an emotionally negative or aversive stimulus such as an electric shock. The conditioned galvanic skin response (a change in the electrical resistance of the skin) and conditioned finger withdrawal, both of which employ shock as an UCS, are examples of this class of conditioning.

A typical example of classical conditioning with humans is eyelid conditioning. A puff of air delivered to the eye will automatically elicit an eye-blink response; here, obviously, is the UCS-UCR sequence. If the puff of air is paired with a tone over a series of presentations, the tone alone will come to elicit the eye blink.

Instances of human classical conditioning are numerous. For instance, you can become conditioned to pictures of food in that advertisements portraying delicious steak dinners may elicit a salivary response even though you may not be hungry. Similarly, we become somewhat temporally conditioned to expect food at particular times and not at others. Human salivary responses can be easily conditioned in the laboratory by pairing the presentation of candy and a tone; the tone alone will eventually elicit salivation after a series of training trials.

Words and symbols also serve as conditioned stimuli for humans. The phenomenon of *semantic* conditioning has been well explored and indicates that word stimuli when paired with UCS can come to elicit a wide range of responses. Such findings help to explain why particular words and symbols can become such strong emotional stimuli for humans. Merely thinking, as well as saying, a word can come to function as a conditioned stimulus. Many people react immediately when labeled in a derogatory fashion; the label has come to serve as a conditioned stimulus. Similarly, certain political concepts such as "socialism," "communism," and "fascism" may elicit strong emotional responses from individuals who may favor the concept or who alternatively look at it with abhorrence. Indeed, the generality and applicability of conditioning principles have been widely recognized in literature as seen, for example, in Aldous Huxley's *Brave New World*.

An Application

Some commercial devices for controlling bed-wetting use principles derived from classical conditioning. Exhortations to the child "to grow up" or "to control yourself" are essentially worthless and merely tend to increase the child's feelings of anxiety and inadequacy. What is important is to get the child to awaken to the stimuli which stem from bladder tension; unfortunately, these stimuli are relatively weak and go unattended in the child who bed wets. The typical commercial device consists of a pad on which the child sleeps; the pad is so constructed that when moisture (urine) hits the pad it completes an electric circuit and activates a noisy doorbell. The sound wakes the child who then goes to the bathroom to complete urination. After a number of such trials, the child begins to awaken to the stimulus of bladder tension alone. Such cures are reported to be effective in many instances.

Time Relationships

There are several ways of presenting the conditioned stimulus (CS) and the UCS in classical conditioning experiments, and these procedures determine the type of conditioning experiment. These procedures are outlined in figure 1 which shows the temporal relationships between the UCS and CS. The top line represents the CS presentation. The bump or rise in all lines represents the period in which the CS or UCS is presented. The other four lines represent various UCS presentations and show their relation to the CS.

Let's consider the first example, simultaneous presentation of CS and UCS. Line *CS* represents a line made by a pen tracing on a piece of paper as it moves across the paper with the passage of time. The period of onset of the CS is represented by the rise in the line; offset of the CS is represented by return of the line to its original position. Thus, the line representing simultaneous conditioning means that both the CS and UCS come on and go off together, a procedure which produces very little learning. The line representing delayed conditioning indicates a delay between the onset of the CS and the onset of the UCS. The line representing trace conditioning indicates that the CS goes off before the UCS comes on. This procedure is called *trace* because any conditioning which occurs depends upon some trace of the CS in the nervous system since the CS is not actually present. Finally, the line representing backward conditioning indicates that the UCS goes off before the CS comes on.

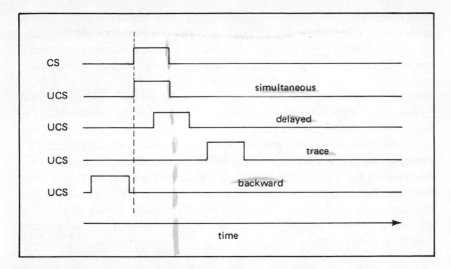

Figure 1. The four principal classical conditioning procedures which differ in respect to the temporal relation between the CS and the UCS.

Generally trace and delayed conditioning procedures produce conditioning superior to that of backward and simultaneous procedures.

Operant (or Instrumental) Conditioning

In the Pavlovian conditioning situation, the organism is *relatively* passive. The experimenter decides when to administer the stimuli and awaits the virtually inevitable response of the organism. The organism, of course, has no control over when these events occur. In contrast, *operant conditioning* is a situation in which the organism has greater control over events. The response that the organism comes to make is necessary in order to obtain reward.

Consider the following situation. A very young child is placed in front of a device which has a small lever. The device is so arranged that when the child presses the lever she receives a piece of candy. The task of the child is thus to discover what response will lead to the reward of obtaining candy. Initially the child will make a variety of responses, including looking at the device, exploring the device with her hands, and touching the lever. If the child is very young, the experimenter may employ the procedure of *successive approximations* and reward responses that approximate pulling the lever such as approaching or touching it. Eventually, however, the child will pull the lever firmly and be rewarded by receiving the candy. The child quickly catches on to this arrangement and learns that she must pull the lever in order to obtain reward.

A similar arrangement is used in studying operant conditioning in lower animals. An animal is placed in a square chamber that is sound deadened. The chamber itself is sometimes called a Skinner box after the psychologist B. F. Skinner. The interior of the chamber contains a small bar or lever which the animal must learn to press and a food mechanism for delivering reward in the form of food pellets to the animal. When the animal is initially placed in the chamber he will most likely explore the walls, corners, and other features of the chamber. The vigor of his exploration is dependent in part on how long he has been deprived of food. As in the previous example, the experimenter may employ successive approximations by first rewarding the animal as it approaches the bar, subsequently as the animal places his paw on the bar, and finally as the animal presses the bar. As the animal acquires the bar-pressing response, he will approach a fairly steady rate of bar pressing, at which time it is concluded that acquisition of the response has been established.

Operant and Instrumental Conditioning Distinguished

Sometimes psychologists make a distinction between operant and instrumental conditioning. The distinction is essentially a procedural one and lies in the manner in which the trials are administered during training. *Instrumental* conditioning refers to situations in which there are discrete trials. A trial is completed, the subject is removed from the apparatus, and another trial begins. Thus, the experimenter controls the sequence of trials. For example, consider a simple discrimination-learning task in which a subject must learn in which arm of a Y-shaped maze he will obtain reward. At the end of each trial the experimenter removes the subject from the apparatus and returns him to the start box for some specified period and then begins the next trial.

In contrast to discrete trial procedures, the subject may be allowed to respond freely, controlling or regulating his own rate of responding. For example, in the Skinner box the animal may be allowed to respond freely, thus defining a class of operations known as *operant* conditioning. The distinction between operant and instrumental conditioning *is of no great importance for our purposes,* and the two terms may be used interchangeably at an elementary level. At a more complex level, psychologists may choose to make this distinction depending upon particular assumptions they may wish to make about these procedures.

Variations in Operant (Instrumental) Conditioning

Just as there are procedural variations in classical conditioning, there are several variations in procedures used in instrumental and operant conditioning. So far we have described only one procedure, that of simple *reward* training.

We can modify the task just described by placing a light on the wall of the chamber so that the animal can easily see it. Then we can arrange the situation so that when the light is on and the animal presses the bar he obtains food. When the light is off, however, a bar-pressing response does not lead to food reward. When the animal is consistently rewarded in the presence of the light and not rewarded when the light is off, the animal will come to discriminate *when to respond.* This procedure describes the basic procedure of *discrimination* training, which is essentially an extension of reward training, but with a discriminative stimulus or cue present.

In general, operant (or instrumental) conditioning situations can be arranged so that discriminative cues are either present or not. In addition, the experimental procedures may use either reward or punishment. For instance, we may reward an animal with food when he makes the appropriate response or we may punish an animal by applying electric shock. Finally, the response to be learned may be one that is produced or one that is withheld. When a response is withheld, the organism is learning not to make a response. Variations in any one of these three general conditions (cue present or not, reward or punishment, and response produced or withheld) produce several kinds of instrumental learning paradigms. Let us consider one further example.

Consider the arrangement in which an animal is placed in a compartment or chamber, the floor of which consists of a metal grid through which current may be passed. Periodically the animal is shocked, and his task is to learn to turn a wheel in order to escape the shock. When the grid is first charged, the animal moves about quite vigorously trying to escape the shock. As soon as the animal touches the wheel the experimenter turns off the current. Fairly rapidly the animal will learn that turning the wheel is instrumental in escaping from shock and will come to respond almost instantly when the shock is presented. This procedure describes the basic paradigm of *escape* conditioning in which a response comes to be produced in order to escape the aversive event.

Verbal Operant Conditioning

Operant procedures have also been applied to verbal conditioning. For example, in laboratory settings a human subject is required to emit words from certain response categories such as nouns, verbs, adjectives, and pronouns, and the experimenter arbitrarily decides to reinforce one class of these responses and not the others. Subjects may simply be asked to say words, or to construct sentences, or even to tell stories. The basic procedure is to get the subject to make verbalizations of some kind and then to selectively reinforce one class of responses. With such procedures, the response or response class that is selected for reinforcement will strengthen, that is, increase in probability.

A wide variety of reinforcers have been used in these experiments.

Sometimes the experimenter may simply say um-hum immediately following a word of the correct class. Other verbal responses such as good, fine, or all right can serve as reinforcers. In addition, lights and buzzers may also be used; however, the effectiveness of such stimuli depends upon how much information they convey to the subject.

A theoretical issue with such procedures is whether the human subject must be aware of the response-reinforcement contingency in order for verbal conditioning to occur. Conscious awareness of the relationship or contingency is usually defined as the ability of the subject to verbalize the contingency, that is, to state that the experimenter reinforced a particular class of responses. The evidence indicates that subjects who are aware, as defined by some set of operations, do verbally condition faster than unaware subjects. Nevertheless, awareness does not appear to be necessary for verbal operant conditioning to occur.

The fact that verbal responses can be controlled by operant procedures has general implications for the control of human behavior. One implication is that our verbal behavior is at least to some extent under control of external reinforcing events. Another implication is that such procedures are applicable to speech and behavior disorders in that it is possible to change the type and frequency of verbal responses emitted by humans by careful control of reinforcement contingencies. We will discuss the application of conditioning principles at the end of this chapter.

Classical and Instrumental Conditioning Compared

A comparison of classical and instrumental (operant) conditioning is presented in Table 1. These comparisons emphasize that the distinctions between the two forms are principally procedural.

The response-reward sequence clearly differs with the two types of conditioning. In classical conditioning the UCS, which may be regarded as a reinforcing stimulus, produces the particular response of interest. Food powder elicits salivation; electric shock applied to the finger produces finger withdrawal; a puff of air to the eye produces an eye blink. Regardless of whether the stimuli are emotionally pleasant or aversive events, they precede the response. Thus we prefer to identify the UCS as a reinforcing stimulus, about which we will say more later, rather than to use the more familiar term *reward*. In contrast, the response must be produced prior to obtaining reward in instrumental (or operant) conditioning. The animal must press the bar to obtain food; the child must say please before obtaining the candy; the student must complete the assignment before being given a reward in the form of a free period.

In classical conditioning the response is produced by a specific discrete stimulus. In instrumental conditioning no specific stimulus is identi-

TABLE 1 Comparison of Classical and Instrumental Conditioning

Comparison	Classical Conditioning	Instrumental Conditioning
1. Response-reward sequence	1. UCS precedes response	1. Response is prior to reward
2. Role of stimuli	2. Response produced by a specific stimulus	2. No specific stimulus produces a response
3. Character of response	3. Response is elicited	3. Response is emitted
4. Observed changes	4. Effectiveness of formerly neutral stimulus on magnitude of a response	4. Change in speed, force, frequency of response
5. Involvement of nervous system	5. Usually involves autonomic nervous system	5. Usually involves somatic nervous system
6. What is learned	6. Emotions such as fears, attitudes, feelings	6. Instrumental (goal-seeking) behavior

fiable; therefore we cannot conclude that some particular stimulus evokes a response. Many stimuli may be present in instrumental conditioning, but none can be said to elicit the response directly. Thus, sometimes the response in instrumental conditioning is said to be *emitted,* whereas the response in classical conditioning is said to be *elicited* by a specific stimulus. A blast of air to the eye or a tap on the knee will elicit or produce the response directly. But consider learning to dance, which is an instance of instrumental learning. We cannot say that the sound of the music elicits the response of dancing because music doesn't force the response. All we can say is that music as a stimulus may set the occasion for the response of dancing.

The observed change in classical conditioning is essentially that of stimulus substitution. A formerly neutral stimulus, the CS, acquires the capacity to substitute for the UCS. With repeated CS-UCS pairings, a response elicited by the UCS becomes elicited by the CS with increasing strength. In instrumental (or operant) conditioning what is observed is characteristically a change in the frequency of a response emitted, in its speed, or in its force.

Classical conditioning characteristically involves the autonomic nervous system, whereas instrumental conditioning involves the somatic nervous system. This distinction is not always perfect since both components of the nervous system may be involved in either conditioning situation. In fact, one recent application of conditioning procedures which is of potential medical importance concerns the use of operant (instrumental) conditioning to facilitate the control of heart rate and blood pressure, behaviors under the primary control of the autonomic nervous system.

Finally, classical conditioning typically involves the learning of emotional responses such as fears and hopes, and the learning of attitudes, opinions, feelings, and expectations. In contrast, operant conditioning involves the acquisition of goal-directed instrumental responses.

Despite the procedural differences, differences associated with nervous system involvement, and types of responses learned, there appears to be considerable evidence for regarding both types of conditioning as involving fundamentally the same processes. For example, they both obey the same laws or principles, which we shall describe shortly. As just noted, many autonomic responses formerly regarded as subject only to classical conditioning procedures have been shown to be instrumentally conditioned. Thus, we can regard these two types of conditioning as procedurally differing operations that nevertheless appear to reflect some common set of underlying processes.

Concept of Reinforcement

The view that behavior is dependent upon its consequences has occupied a central position in the psychology of learning since the early experiments of Edward Thorndike. It was Thorndike's belief that learning was fundamentally dependent upon rewards and/or punishments that closely followed the response that was produced. Indeed, our description of instrumental learning emphasized that the rewarded responses become learned, whereas nonrewarded responses fail to become learned.

Psychologists frequently employ the term *reinforcement* rather than reward. Reinforcement is theoretically a more neutral term and refers in general to the process by which some response tendency comes to be strengthened. Moreover, it is somewhat more convenient to discuss classical and instrumental conditioning jointly with this concept, particularly because it is a bit awkward to use the ordinary concept of reward in classical conditioning.

Positive and Negative Reinforcers

A *reinforcer* is any event which, when occurring in close temporal relationship to a response, increases the *likelihood* that the *response* will be *repeated* in the future. We know that many events can serve as reinforcers. Obviously, food to a hungry organism can serve as a reinforcer. For some individuals praise may serve as a reinforcer; however, not all individuals are affected by praise in this fashion. Teachers frequently discover that praise may work for middle-class children, whereas it may not function for lower-class students who may in fact lose status among their peers if they receive teacher praise. Praise from the teacher may cause such children to lose face among their friends and thus inadvertently produce undesirable behavioral by-products in the classroom.

A vast number of events can serve as reinforcers. We cannot however always identify a particular reinforcing event in advance of a learning situation. At a functional level, however, we can identify any event as a reinforcer if it acts like one, namely, that it serves to increase the strength of a particular response.

In instrumental conditioning we can distinguish between positive and negative reinforcers: *Positive reinforcers* are any events which strengthen a *response* when they are *presented*. Thus food, candy, praise, and money are said to be positive reinforcers if their presentation following a response tends to strengthen that response.

In contrast, *negative reinforcers* are any events which *strengthen* a *response* when they are *terminated* or *removed*. Negative reinforcers are emotionally aversive events which we are desirous of removing or avoiding. For example, electric shock is a negative reinforcer in instrumental learning if we learn a response in order to escape or avoid the shock. In our description of escape learning, shock served as a negative reinforcer because the animal learned a response in order to terminate the shock. Similarly, if children work hard in order to avoid possible sarcasm or ridicule from parents, they can be said to learn as a result of negative reinforcement.

Our learning is under control of both positive and negative reinforcers and both factors may be present on a given occasion. High school students may, for example, try to obtain high grades in order to be admitted to a university, receive notice from their friends, or even receive an increase in their allowance from their parents. They may also study diligently in order to avoid parental nagging, teacher disapproval, or fear of the long-term consequences of not being admitted to a university. It is not always easy to disentangle both elements in everyday learning.

Why Do Reinforcers Work?

It is clear, of course, that the principle of reinforcement is empirically valid. Responses that are followed closely by reinforcing events tend to be strengthened. Indeed, this statement is roughly comparable to Thorndike's classical law of effect. At a descriptive level the principle simply states that reinforcers work. This, of course, does not tell you why they function as they do.

Several theories have been advanced to explain the operation of reinforcers upon behavior. A long-standing theory first formalized by Clark Hull was the *drive-reduction hypothesis*. This notion stated that reinforcers work as they do because they reduce some prevailing drive of the organism. A hungry organism has the hunger drive reduced by food; a thirsty organism reduces the thirst drive by water. The basic idea was that a reinforcing agent modified some metabolic state of the organism.

Although this theory had considerable appeal at the time of its formulation, its generality was subsequently shown to be limited. For instance, animals will learn responses when they are given a nonnutritive substance such as saccharine. Saccharine cannot be regarded as drive reducing, despite its sweet taste, indicating that the drive-reduction theory cannot readily handle this kind of result. Other experiments have indicated that the drive-reduction interpretation simply cannot handle all the facts. We do not as yet have an all-inclusive theory of reinforcement. The best we can conclude is that several theories appear to be necessary in order to account for the facts. Nevertheless, despite the fact that we do not have a complete theoretical account of reinforcement, the empirical law of reinforcement still holds.

Secondary Reinforcing Events

Psychologists distinguish between primary and secondary reinforcing events. Primary reinforcers refer to events such as food and water and are closely tied to biological needs of the organism such as hunger, thirst, and pain avoidance. Secondary reinforcers refer to events that function so because of learning. Money and praise may function as secondary reinforcers but do so because humans learn to regard them in this fashion. *Stimulus events which are initially neutral to the organism may acquire secondary reinforcing properties as a result of being associated with primary reinforcing events.* Regardless of whether we are dealing with primary or secondary reinforcers, they both act the same way in the principle of reinforcement. As we saw in the section on verbal operant conditioning, verbal responses can act as secondary reinforcers.

Responses as Reinforcers

So far we have described reinforcers largely as if they are *stimulus events* or objects. Food, water, money, and candy are all stimulus events that may reinforce behavior. Reinforcing events may also be *responses,* a point emphasized by David Premack. His view is that organisms are reinforced by being allowed to engage in behaviors which they prefer. More formally, Premack contends that *high-probability responses,* which are responses we most frequently emit (and hence, presumably prefer), may serve to reinforce *low-probability responses.* The appropriate contingency is to arrange high-probability responses so that they *follow* low-probability responses. The sequence is critical if a low-probability response is to be strengthened.

This principle can be easily illustrated. Suppose, for example, that a child wishes to eat dessert and is uninterested in the meat or vegetables. You may say, "Eat your meat and vegetables and then you may have dessert." Eating dessert is a high-probability response; eating meat and vegetables is the lower probability response. The sequence is arranged so that the high-probability response can occur _only after_ the low-probability response has occurred. Similarly, the child may be told that she can play outside after she has picked up her toys. Thus playing outside is made contingent upon picking up the toys. Similarly, you arrange such a contingency when you insist on doing your homework before you watch television or attend a film. In this fashion humans may come to control their own behavior. (For a discussion of self-control see Frank Logan's _Fundamentals of Learning and Motivation._)

The principle is most effective when the low-probability behavior required represents a reasonable amount of activity for the child as distinct from some endless task. Thus you can require too much behavior, making the principle far less effective. The low-probability behavior should represent some reasonable task not too difficult for the child, ideally one that can be completed without much frustration. Systematic use of the principle will allow you to make greater behavioral demands on an organism as learning progresses.

The principle is a very practical one in that it allows you to identify a reinforcer for a particular individual. Knowing what is reinforcing for an individual allows you to plan learning sequences far more efficiently than if you simply assume that some activity is reinforcing. This principle is receiving considerable application in kindergartens and schools, where children may contract to do a certain amount of work which when completed is followed by reinforcement in the form of some activity of their own choosing. What is sometimes arranged is a _reinforcement menu_ in which the child, following completion of some task, goes to a particular room where he may choose from a variety of games and activities including, for example, pinball machines, chess, and interaction with his peer group.

Schedules of Reinforcement

It is not essential to reinforce every response for learning to occur. When reinforcement is given less than 100 percent of the time, the procedure is called _partial_ reinforcement. There are various ways of scheduling reinforcement. One way is to arrange it so that the first response to occur after a designated time interval following the last reinforcement, say one minute, is reinforced. This is called a _fixed-interval_ schedule. Under this schedule the rate of operant responding is characteristically low immediately after reinforcement, but an increase in response rate occurs toward the end of the time interval. Another arrangement is to

reinforce the organism for a set number of responses, say, one reinforcement for every five responses emitted. This is called a *fixed-ratio*
schedule. In general, the output of responses is very high under this
schedule and the rate of responding is relatively stable. A fixed-ratio
schedule is analogous to being paid for a particular amount of work
accomplished rather than being paid, say, at the end of a specific time
such as a week. Pay is tied to doing so many things, that is, making a
certain number of responses.

Schedules may be varied as well as fixed. With a *variable-interval*
schedule the learner is reinforced after differing intervals of time which
vary in an irregular fashion. For instance, reinforcements might come
after such irregular intervals as 10, 30, 50, 70, 90, and 180 seconds.
A variable-interval schedule produces a steady rate of responding.
Similarly, with a variable-ratio schedule the learner is reinforced after
varying ratios of responding. For example, ten responses may be required for reinforcement and then only three responses be required.
Hence the ratio varies.

The way reinforcement is scheduled can have a powerful effect on
behavior. For example, knowledge of the effects of fixed-interval schedules can enable you to predict certain kinds of behavioral outcomes.
Since the rate of responding is relatively low immediately following reinforcement and does not speed up until the end of the interval is approached, you might readily infer that this schedule is nonoptimal for
maintaining, say, work output in a classroom setting. For instance, if
students are simply told that they have thirty minutes to complete a
classroom assignment which many can complete in half the time or
less, some of the students will then dawdle before settling down to work.
Indeed, a few will engage in other behavior such as pestering their
neighbors and will wait until the last few minutes before going to work.
In short, a fixed-interval schedule can allow for inattention, classroom
disruption, and other undesired behaviors.

Basic Principles of Conditioning

The study of classical and operant or instrumental conditioning has
yielded several basic principles which are observable in the various
forms of conditioning. In this section we shall outline the salient aspects of each of these principles and indicate in a limited fashion how
these principles are applicable beyond the immediate context in which
they emerged. These principles can best be regarded as basic empirical
generalizations about conditioning phenomena.

Acquisition

We have already described the process by which responses are acquired in classical, instrumental, or operant conditioning. In classical condi-

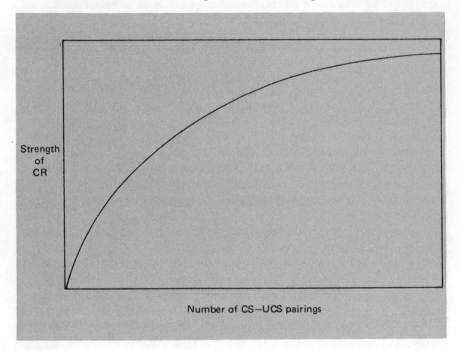

Figure 2. Hypothetical function showing strength of CR as a function of CS-UCS pairings.

tioning we noted that the CS *acquires* the capacity to elicit the CR. In instrumental or operant conditioning, the response that receives reinforcement is gradually strengthened, while other responses fail to gain strength. In classical conditioning the strength of the CR is a function of the number of CS-UCS pairings as shown by the curve in figure 2. This curve is a hypothetical function showing that the strength of the CR gradually increases with the number of CS-UCS pairings. If the particular response was salivation, this curve then reflects the fact that the *amount* of salivation increases on test trials (when the CS is presented alone) as a result of the number of tone-food powder pairings.

Similarly, in instrumental conditioning the strength of the response as measured, say, by the speed of responding increases as a function of the number of reinforced trials.

Finally, the acquisition of CRs is dependent upon several variables in addition to the number of CS-UCS pairings and the number of reinforced trials. Classical conditioning is dependent upon both CS and UCS intensity, with more rapid conditioning occurring with increased stimulus intensity.

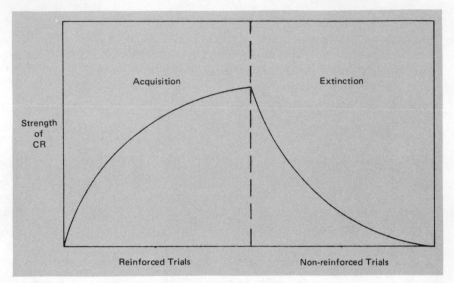

Figure 3. Graphic portrayal of acquisition and extinction of a conditioned response.

Extinction

Once an instrumental or operant response such as bar pressing at a fairly steady rate has been acquired, we may then remove the reinforcement. When we do, the organism will continue to respond briefly, followed by a gradually diminished rate of responding, a process called *extinction* of the responses. *Extinction is thus the reduction in response strength following removal of the reinforcement.* Similarly, in classical conditioning repeated presentation of the CS alone will lead to a reduction in response strength.

Figure 3 illustrates both acquisition and extinction of a CR. The left half of the figure portrays acquisition of a CR as a function of number of reinforced trials and the right half portrays extinction of that same response. The figure portrays extinction going to zero responding. In actual practice, the extinction of a CR is defined usually in terms of no responding for some conventionally agreed time interval.

Resistance to extinction, that is, the tendency to continue responding during the extinction period, is dependent upon both factors that were present during acquisition and factors present during the extinction session. One important factor is the variability in the training conditions; another is punishment.

Partial Reinforcement

The manner in which reinforcements are presented during acquisition affects performance in subsequent extinction. In operant conditioning, reinforcement variability can be introduced by reinforcing some but not all of the responses. Similarly, in instrumental conditioning we may administer *partial* reinforcement, which is to give the reinforcement only on some of the trials. A general principle is that *partial reinforcement increases resistance to extinction,* a principle so general that it is known as the *partial reinforcement effect.*

Consider a hypothetical gambling situation. Suppose that in one situation a slot machine is rigged so that every time you play the machine you are rewarded. This, of course, is an instance of continuous reinforcement. In another, however, the arrangement is that you are reinforced irregularly for only 25 percent of your responses. Now let us imagine that following extended training in these two settings an extinction session is introduced; in neither case are you rewarded for playing the machine, although you are unaware that the rules of the game have changed. What happens? You are likely to persist playing the machine for a much longer period of time following partial reinforcement than following continuous reinforcement.

Human instances of partial reinforcement abound. For example, if you are denied the opportunity to use the family car after regular use, the denial can be a frustrating experience. If you are regularly denied this opportunity, you may gradually extinguish requesting use of the car. On the other hand, if your experience is of occasionally being told yes between periods in which you are refused, you then learn to persist in your requests. In effect, since you never know when you will be reinforced, you are more likely to persist in making responses. Consider another example in the area of child training. One reason that children may resist going to bed at a regular time is that parents have been inconsistent. If a child cries and demands to stay up past regular bedtime and the parent allows this on some occasions, the child then learns that crying and demanding behaviors get reinforced. Regardless of whether a particular behavior is viewed as desirable or undesirable if it is partially reinforced it then becomes more difficult to extinguish.

Effects of Stimulus and Response Variability

Partial reinforcement in instrumental conditioning represents the general case of reinforcement variability. In general, the more variable the conditions of reinforcement during acquisition, the greater the resistance to extinction. In a similar vein, organisms that are trained in situations in which the stimulus context is more *variable* show greater *response persistence* during extinction. The principle of stimulus variability helps to explain why certain habits are extremely difficult to extinguish. Consider, for example, the difficulty reported by many individuals who attempt to quit smoking. The smoking response is one that is likely to have developed in a great variety of stimulus situations. The various conditions in which a person might smoke a cigarette include when one awakes, after breakfast with coffee, on the way to work, at lunch, upon arrival at home, at a party, and so forth. The occasions for smoking are almost infinite. Thus the response of smoking can become tied to a large number of environmental (as well as internal) stimuli, providing a large number of habits to be extinguished.

Likewise, response variability leads to greater resistance to extinction. This principle can be understood if it is assumed that with greater response variability a greater number of *different* habits are being strengthened during acquisition. Thus, during extinction as one response is extinguished, other responses remain available, allowing for prolonged response persistence.

Spontaneous Recovery

A third conditioning principle is that a response that has undergone extinction is subject to spontaneous recovery. For example, if we remove an animal from an operant chamber for some period of time after having extinguished a bar-pressing response and then return the animal to the chamber, we will observe the temporary resumption of bar pressing at a rate above that of the extinction criterion. This temporary resumption of responding after extinction is designated *spontaneous recovery of responses* and indicates that the habit tendency *is still present even though the response was previously extinguished.*

Generalization

So far our discussion of conditioning has emphasized that learning is fairly specific to the particular events that occur during training. Nevertheless, learning in one situation or context can *generalize* to another. Your learned dislike of sixth grade arithmetic may generalize to a fear of mathematics in subsequent grades. Similarly, your fear of a particular teacher of mathematics may generalize to a fear of other teachers or to mathematics in general. Likewise, your liking of one person may generalize to other individuals who possess similar traits.

The basic principle of stimulus generalization notes that whenever a response *is learned in one stimulus situation,* other stimuli similar to those in the training situation *acquire some tendency to produce that response.* For example, in a classical conditioning paradigm in which an animal learns to salivate to a CS of a particular tone, say 1,000 cycles per second (written as 1,000 hertz or Hz), he also acquires some tendency to respond to other tones. Moreover, the greater the similarity of these tones to the CS, the greater is the likelihood that the animal will respond.

This tendency to respond to similar stimuli is called *stimulus generalization.* Its basic importance is that it stresses that learning is *not* entirely *specific* to the situation in which responses are acquired. The principle is important in that it provides for flexibility and generality in learning, emphasizing that our learning is not always bound to specific stimulus events. Indeed, the principle of stimulus generalization underlies our learning of many simple concepts and provides the basis for much of what is called *transfer of training.* These issues are described in subsequent chapters.

There are actually two principles involved in the concept of generalization. One is the principle of *stimulus generalization* just described and the other is the principle of *response generalization.* This second principle refers to the fact that responses *similar* to the learned response also have some tendency to occur, especially during the early stages of conditioning. If the learned response is momentarily unavailable, another similar response may be emitted. For example, in learning to pronounce a new word you may be unable to produce the correct pronunciation, but still be able to produce some approximate pronunciation of the word, one that is highly similar to the correct pronunciation.

We have already noted that the amount of generalization depends upon the degree of similarity between two stimulus events. The greater the stimulus similarity, the greater will be the probability of generalization. The factors that affect resistance to extinction also affect the degree of generalization. In general, the greater number of different stimuli present during acquisition, the greater is the likelihood of generalization. Similarly, the larger the number of different responses practiced during acquisition, the greater will be the likelihood of generalization. Finally, the more variable the conditions of reinforcement during acquisition, the greater is the likelihood of generalization.

Discrimination

Although generalization can be adaptive in the sense that it provides for flexibility in behavior, for transfer, and for ability to form simple concepts, unlimited generalization can also lead to inappropriate behavior. Two people may look alike, hold the same occupation, live in the same neighborhood, and yet hold quite different beliefs about important features of life. Inappropriate generalization to similar stimuli can thus form the basis of much human error. Fortunately, however, humans also come to discriminate among environmental stimuli, which is to say that we can learn to respond differently to highly similar stimuli.

The process of learning to respond differently to similar stimuli is called *stimulus discrimination*. This process occurs when responses in the presence of one stimulus are reinforced, while responses produced in the presence of another are not reinforced. The differential reinforcement of responses made to different stimuli is the basis by which discrimination learning occurs.

Consider, for example, our illustration of classical conditioning in which a salivary response becomes conditioned to a CS of 1,000 hertz. Other tones, we noted, also acquire some capacity to elicit the CR through the process of stimulus generalization. This generalization tendency can be weakened, however, by training that employs differential reinforcement of the response tendency in the presence of different stimuli. If we continue to pair the CS and UCS, the CS will continue to elicit the response. By presenting similar stimuli, such as tones of 600 and 1,400 hertz *without* the UCS (food powder), the organism will gradually come to respond principally to the CS and with much less magnitude to stimuli similar to the CS.

We can also arrange for a discrimination to be acquired in the instrumental or operant conditioning paradigm, a procedure which was described earlier in this chapter. Recall that an animal could be trained to press a bar in the presence of light and not to press when the light was off. In this example, reinforcement of bar pressing was made contingent upon the presence or absence of the light.

Stimulus discrimination is a basic feature of virtually all learning and is evident in many everyday experiences. We learn, for example, that it is generally more reinforcing to stop in the presence of a red light and to go in the presence of a green light. Similarly, young children learn to discriminate between letters of the alphabet that are perceptually similar. In school, they learn that $3 + 3$ is a stimulus for the response 6, but that 3×3 is not. The discrimination of speech sounds, of letters and words, of symbols, of numerals, and of people are instances of a whole range of events for which we must acquire discriminations. As adults we acquire more complex and sophisticated discriminations. The skilled wine taster, for example, learns to discriminate among an ordinary red table wine, a good California Cabernet Sauvignon and a 1928 vintage Chauteau Lafite Rothschild as a taste for French wines is acquired.

The concepts of generalization and discrimination have received extensive use in accounting for more complex human learning phenomena, particularly in the areas of verbal learning, transfer, and concept learning. The learning of simple concepts can be regarded as involving the processes of generalization and discrimination. For instance, learning color and shape concepts involves generalizing among the class of instances that belong to the concept while discriminating among the conceptual categories. We can only allude to the applicability of generalization and discrimination at present, and we will discuss these issues in subsequent chapters.

Conditions Which Affect Discrimination

We noted earlier that stimulus discrimination is the process by which you learn to respond differentially to somewhat similar stimuli. An obvious factor, therefore, that influences stimulus discrimination is the *similarity* of the stimulus events. In general, *the greater the similarity of stimuli, the more difficult it is to learn to discriminate the stimuli.*

The failure to learn discriminations with reasonable ease is frequently the result of inconsistent reinforcement of responses made to similar stimuli. Consider a simple example. Many children enjoy a snack upon arrival at home after a day at school. The mother may allow a snack if the child asks for it shortly after arrival at home. If the child waits too long so that the dinner hour is approaching, the mother may veto the snack. Thus, the mother's basic task is that of teaching the child a temporal discrimination of asking for a snack within, say, a half hour after arriving at home. If the mother, however, allows the child to have a snack on some occasions even when dinner will shortly be served, the child will have difficulty in learning this discrimination. Thus the *consistency* of differential reinforcement of responses made in the presence of different stimuli is fundamental for discrimination learning.

Another essential feature in developing discriminations is getting the learner to attend to or focus on the essential or *relevant* dimensions of the stimulus. Many stimuli in our environment are quite similar and yet call for different responses. The letters *b* and *d* are physically similar; thus effective discrimination of these events can occur only when the relevant features of these stimuli are attended to by the child. Two individuals may be very similar in many of their attitudes and personality traits and yet be different in other critically important ways. If you have learned to respond to their similar characteristics, you may stereotype the individuals by placing them in the same category, thus making it much more difficult to detect their distinctive characteristics. This is simply to say that a learned tendency to respond to similar stimuli in the same way makes it more difficult to establish a discrimination.

Differentiation

The fact that humans can discriminate among stimuli was seen as a process that can work against unlimited generalization tendencies. Generalization is, of course, adaptive when the behavior is appropriate. As we saw, discrimination is important in a variety of situations if you are to function most effectively. We learn, however, not only to *discriminate* among stimulus events but also to *differentiate* among responses.

Response differentiation refers to the process whereby somewhat *similar responses* are *differentially reinforced*. In this fashion one response becomes strengthened and others are gradually weakened. The process of response differentiation emphasizes that responses can become shaped or more precise in the course of learning.

Let us first consider a laboratory illustration of response differentiation. In this illustration an animal has learned to bar press in order to receive a food award. We now arrange the task so that we reward the animal *only* when he makes a bar press of a specific force. Responses with less force are never reinforced and responses equal to or greater than the criterion force always receive reinforcement. With this arrangement the animal will come to bar press at or above some specific force, which means that he has *differentiated* this response (actually response class) from others.

Response differentiation is such a frequent part of learning that you may fail to notice its regular occurrence. Parents shape the speech behavior of children when they encourage a child to pronounce a word in one way rather than another. Thus proper pronunciation and articulate speech are the outcome of a long history of response differentiation. Similarly, many athletic skills require that a response be executed with a particular force or a particular speed. Again, the development of these response properties is a matter of response differentiation. Learning skills such as swimming, diving, tennis, and golf all involve the differentiation of responses, that is, the acquisition of a particular response or response class most likely to achieve satisfaction and the corresponding elimination of irrelevant, nonreinforced responses. As we will subsequently see, the process of response differentiation is relevant to processes in motor skills learning. Let us now turn our attention to two areas in which conditioning principles have been applied: therapy and education.

Application of Conditioning Principles

Psychologists have not been content just to describe the fundamental principles of conditioning, but have also attempted to extend or apply these principles to the understanding of much more complex events. In recent years, conditioning principles have been employed in accounts of social learning and developmental processes, in personality theory and therapy, and in application to individual and classroom learning situations. The past twenty years have witnessed new developments in educational technology, such as programmed instruction and computer-aided instruction, which are based upon assumptions about the learning process derived from studies of operant conditioning. In a similar vein, behavior modification approaches to therapy have conceptualized the therapeutic process as one that can be understood in terms of conditioning principles. In this section we shall briefly outline certain features of the way in which principles of conditioning have been applied to problems of therapy and education.

Conditioning Principles and Behavior Therapy

There are many approaches to therapy. One approach is directly based upon the principles of conditioning which are applied to the treatment of behavior disorders. This approach has been most extensively applied to the less severe behavior disturbances (neurotic behavior), but has also been applied to more severe disturbances such as the psychoses.

The basic assumption underlying conditioning therapy is that maladaptive behaviors are learned behaviors and that such learning occurs in accordance with the same principles under which other learning occurs. This is simply to say that if adaptive behavior is acquired in accordance with principles of learning, then it is reasonable to assume that many maladaptive behaviors may also be learned. In other words, given that behaviors become strengthened through differential reinforcement, the principles should be applicable regardless of the adaptive or adjustive character of the behavior.

Given these assumptions, behavior disorders are thus viewed as *learned events*. In effect, we can learn to become "sick." Therefore, one of the principal tasks of the therapist is attempting to reduce or eliminate the undesirable behaviors by extinguishing such behaviors. The basic idea is to ensure that the maladaptive behaviors are no longer reinforced. For example, a hospital patient who hallucinates is no longer allowed to have the hallucinatory behavior reinforced. Such reinforcement may occur when attendants or others ask the patient about his hallucinations. Therapists employ *extinction* of the responses as one aspect of therapy, but also emphasize a second way of weakening responses through *counterconditioning*. Here maladaptive behaviors are weakened by strengthening incompatible or competing responses. If anxiety is the characteristic response to a particular situation, the therapist attempts to strengthen responses incompatible with anxiety such as relaxation responses. Relaxation is nevertheless just one possible response that may be strengthened. The basic principle of counterconditioning is that *an incompatible response or class of responses is to be strengthened*.

Behavior modification approaches to therapy have been applied to a wide variety of disorders such as phobias, alcoholism, overeating, sexual disorders, and speech disturbances. Mental hospital patients long hospitalized have responded to therapy using these general procedures when other approaches have failed.

Some Techniques of Behavior Therapy

A variety of techniques and approaches have been used in behavior therapy. One technique is *systematic desensitization* which involves three somewhat separate sets of operations. The patient is first trained in deep muscle relaxation. This is followed by a ranking of stimulus events as to degree of eliciting anxiety. The therapist and the patient jointly work out a hierarchy of anxiety-eliciting stimuli. A hierarchy might include numerous items such as getting back an examination in class, studying the night before an examination, hearing an instructor announce an examination, and so forth. The third step is desensitization proper. The patient is induced to relax thoroughly and to imagine those items in the hierarchy that elicit anxiety. When the patient indicates that an item does produce slight tension or discomfort, he is instructed to stop visualizing the scene and relax. The objective is to gradually de-sensitize the patient to what were originally anxiety-provoking stimulus situations.

Another technique is *implosion therapy* which is similar to system-atic desensitization. Here the patient attempts to imagine or visualize the fear-inducing stimuli at the suggestion of the therapist. For instance, a person suffering from snake phobia might imagine walking over a group of snakes. Since no actual punishment in the form of snakebite occurs, the assumption is that the fear of snakes will gradually extin-guish. Another technique is *aversion therapy*. For example, in dealing with an alcoholic the therapist attempts to condition the taste and smell of alcohol with some aversive consequence such as nausea and vomiting produced by drugs. Eventually, the alcoholic is expected to refrain from drinking since the cues associated with alcohol produce negative emotional reactions. Many other varieties of behavior therapy have been developed. Lack of space limits our consideration to only a few in this section.

Behavior therapists have sometimes been criticized by more tradi-tional therapists who contend that behavior modification is essentially a superficial approach to behavior disorders because it deals only with surface behavior rather than with the root causes of the disorders. Pre-sumably, whatever is producing the conflict may still remain unresolved. Behavior therapists counter by contending that it is necessary to elimi-nate the maladaptive behaviors if successful therapy is to occur. Moreover, success in eliminating some maladaptive behavior such as fear of crowds may lead to additional changes such as growth in self-confidence.

Resolution of the arguments over the merits of behavior modification approaches to therapy is not possible within the scope of this book. The important point to note is that principles of conditioning are receiving extensive application in the treatment of behavior disorders.

Conditioning Principles and Programmed Instruction

The teaching process can be regarded at least in part as the task of arranging instructional experiences so as to maximize learning outcomes. It therefore follows that principles of conditioning, as well as human learning and cognition, have relevance to practical problems of education. Principles of conditioning and learning carry no special implications about what topics should be taught, but they do have implications about *how* teaching should be conducted for the purpose of maximizing learning. The potential application of principles of instrumental or operant conditioning to educational practices was most clearly recognized by B. F. Skinner in the midfifties. This recognition led Skinner to embark upon a program for the expansion and use of these principles to problems of individual instruction, which led to the instructional technology of *programmed instruction.*

Programmed instruction is a way of presenting educational materials to students in a step-by-step fashion. The student is presented a small amount of information and asked to respond to a question or problem. Each step is called a *frame,* and a frame has a *stimulus* component in which the information is presented, a *response* component in a place in which the learner responds, and a *confirmation* component in which the student is given feedback or knowledge of results. Figure 4 is an example of two frames from a sequence designed to teach the concept of learning. The learner proceeds through a series of frames until he acquires a full understanding of the concept of learning. At each step enough information is presented so that the learner's response is likely to be correct. The objective of the frame is to guide the student toward making the correct response.

Programmed instruction makes use of certain basic principles of instrumental or operant conditioning. First, from our earlier discussion it is clear that the learner must be *active* if learning is to occur. The important point is that the learner must respond in some manner; learning is not a passive process. The sequence of frames keeps the learner actively responding at each step.

The second principle is that responses must be reinforced if behavior is to be changed. In this instance, the confirmation of the learner's response to each frame can be regarded as somewhat analogous to reinforcement. While there is current doubt about simply equating reinforcement with confirmation, the desirability of producing some form of immediate feedback for the learner is clearly recognized. Thus, the learner is given immediate knowledge of results regarding the adequacy of each response he makes.

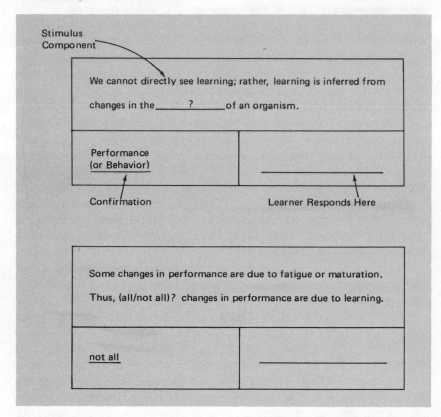

Figure 4. Example of two frames in a programmed learning sequence designed to teach the concept of learning.

The learner is led through a series of frames in which his concept is gradually sharpened and refined. The learner is not simply emitting responses, but is responding to carefully written items that are designed to lead the student to learn a concept.

Each student sets his own pace; therefore in this sense working through the program is analogous to a free operant situation since the learner is responding at his own rate. It is this feature which is characteristic of much individualized instruction.

We can only briefly refer to these features of programmed instruction. Their general significance is that they represent the emergence of an instructional technology which is derived from studies of simple learning.

Keller Plan: Personalized Instruction

An important extension of the operant conditioning-programmed learning approach is the plan developed by Fred Keller in 1968. He described a plan by which an entire course such as introductory psychology can be programmed and taught, with lectures being optional for the student. In this plan a course is divided into a number of units, each unit covering a particular topic. The student studies a given unit and as soon as she feels prepared, she takes a quiz covering the topic. If she passes, she continues on to the next unit. A passing level of achievement is typically set high, say at 90 percent achievement or better, because the material is broken down into easy-to-master units. If the student does not pass, a diagnosis is made of her deficiencies, and the student again takes the quiz after reviewing the unit. No penalty is given for failing the quiz; the student repeats a quiz until she actually masters the unit. Then the student continues to the next unit. Experimental tests of the plan reveal that it has been successful. The reasons for its effectiveness are probably due to the same features as in programmed learning: actively responding, receiving feedback, proceeding at the student's own rate, and going on to new materials only after prior material is fully mastered.

Summary

This chapter has portrayed some of the fundamental elements of conditioning. Conditioning was described as the simplest form of learning. Three types of conditioning were described: classical and instrumental, or operant. In classical conditioning, a conditioned stimulus comes to elicit a conditioned response as a result of repeated presentations of both an unconditioned and a conditioned stimulus. Instrumental and operant conditioning are similar in that a response must be emitted before it is reinforced. They differ in that instrumental conditioning involves a discrete trial procedure, the trials being controlled by the experimenter, and the operant situation a procedure in which the organisms respond freely.

A reinforcer was seen as any event that increases the probability of a response. Reinforcers are either positive or negative; positive reinforcers strengthen a response when they are *presented,* whereas negative reinforcers strengthen a response when they are *removed.* Reinforcers may be responses as well as stimuli in that high-probability responses may serve to reinforce weaker responses. Reinforcers may be primary or secondary; secondary reinforcers for humans are usually verbal or symbolic in nature.

Six principles of conditioning were described: acquisition, extinction, spontaneous recovery, generalization, discrimination, and differentiation. Some of the important factors that affect extinction, generalization, and discrimination were described. In particular, the role of partial reinforcement and variability was given emphasis. These principles have been extended and applied to more complex human learning situations. Examples of this application were seen in the areas of therapy and programmed instruction.

Multiple-Choice Items: Elements of Conditioning

1. A basic procedural difference between classical and instrumental conditioning is that in classical conditioning
   a. the response precedes the reinforcement
   b. the CS is never defined
   c. the response follows the reinforcing stimulus
   d. the response is not specific to the stimulus
2. In the delayed conditioning procedure the UCS
   a. is delayed and onset occurs after the CS offsets
   b. is delayed and overlaps with the CS
   c. occurs before presentation of the CS
   d. completely overlaps the CS
3. Rewarding a person for behaving in a progressively more appropriate or desirable fashion is called
   a. stimulus discrimination
   b. fixed-interval schedule
   c. response generalization
   d. successive approximations
4. A reinforcer is any event which
   a. increases the probability of a response
   b. brings about drive reduction
   c. increases physiological well-being
   d. produces systematic changes in the nervous system
5. Negative reinforcers are events that serve to
   a. strengthen a response when they are presented
   b. weaken a response when they are removed
   c. strengthen a response when they are removed
   d. punish a response
6. A teacher dismisses her class when the students become rowdy. She observes during the semester that the students become pro-

gressively rowdier. This occurs because she is
  a. punishing the students' behavior
  b. reinforcing the students' behavior
  c. using a fixed-interval schedule of reinforcement
  d. using spontaneous recovery

7. The concept of superstitious behavior can be understood as the result of
  a. accidental contingencies of reinforcement
  b. stimulus generalization
  c. successive approximations
  d. extinction

8. An operant discrimination is established with a three-phase sequence. Select the correct sequence.
  a. present a stimulus, wait for response to be elicited, provide reinforcement
  b. wait for response to be emitted, provide reinforcement, present a stimulus
  c. present a stimulus, wait for response to be emitted, provide reinforcement
  d. wait for response to be emitted, present a stimulus, provide reinforcement

9. Receiving a paycheck once a month is most analogous to which schedule of reinforcement?
  a. fixed interval
  b. fixed ratio
  c. variable interval
  d. variable ratio

10. If a three-year-old child almost always asks her father for candy and rarely asks her mother, the process of ——— has occurred.
  a. response differentiation
  b. stimulus discrimination
  c. stimulus generalization
  d. variable-interval reinforcement

11. The principal objective of programmed learning is to
  a. raise the I.Q. of slow learners
  b. replace teachers
  c. teach primarily very complex subject matter
  d. make learning more effective

12. The principal assumption underlying the application of conditioning principles in therapy is
  a. the medical model of mental disorders
  b. reliance on willpower of the patient
  c. stress on the patient's gaining insight
  d. belief that many mental disorders are the result of learning

True-False Items: Elements of Conditioning

1. Conditioning principles can be extrapolated to explain all forms of more complex human learning.
2. Classical conditioning involves the process of stimulus substitution.
3. In instrumental conditioning the response occurs after the reinforcement.
4. The basic difference between operant and instrumental conditioning is that the response is freely available in operant conditioning.
5. Looking in your refrigerator for a snack is an instance of an operant response.
6. Negative reinforcers lead you to cease making a response.
7. If you assume that nursery school children like to run and scream but rarely clean up the play area, then allowing them to run and scream *after* they clean up the play area will tend to strengthen cleaning-up responses.
8. The basic procedure for extinguishing a response is to make sure that no reinforcement follows emission of the response.
9. The extinction of responses learned in various environmental settings is relatively easy.
10. A young child erroneously calling the milkman "Daddy" is an instance of discrimination.
11. The loudness with which you characteristically talk and the skill with which you characteristically write are learned response properties. Such learning represents instances of response differentiation.
12. The application of conditioning principles to therapeutic procedures assumes typically that the behavior disorder being treated developed as a result of learning.

Discussion Items: Elements of Conditioning

1. Compare and contrast the major features of classical and instrumental conditioning.

2. How might you use the basic principles of instrumental (or operant) conditioning to teach yourself better study habits? to reduce excessive watching of television?

3. What implications do the notions of stimulus, response, and reinforcement variability have on acquisition of behaviors? on maintaining behaviors?

4. What principles of conditioning might account for the difficulty many people report in eliminating the smoking habit? On the basis of conditioning principles, outline a program for the reduction or elimination of smoking behavior.

5. How might you teach someone to become more self-assertive using conditioning principles? Let assertiveness mean being able to defend your position, stand up for your rights, and so forth, *without* being abrasive or obnoxious.

Multiple-Choice Answers: Elements of Conditioning

1. (c) In classical conditioning the UCS, or reinforcing stimulus, precedes the response. In contrast, the response occurs prior to reward in instrumental conditioning.

2. (b) Delayed conditioning simply means that the UCS follows the onset of the CS, but also overlaps its presentation.

3. (d) Successive approximations is rewarding someone for behavior which approximates the desired behavior, moving progressively closer to the desired behavior until only the desired behavior is rewarded.

4. (a) A reinforcer is any event which increases the probability of some response or responses. Reinforcers may do other things, but an increase in response probability is the defining characteristic.

5. (c) A negative reinforcer is any event that increases the probability of a response when the reinforcer is terminated or removed. For example, if a child learns in order to terminate or avoid some aversive event, he learns because of a negative reinforcing contingency.

6. (b) The behavior of rowdiness is strengthened because it is being reinforced by the teacher in the form of class dismissal.

7. (a) Superstitious behavior is learned like any other behavior, namely, it gets reinforced. In this case, the superstition is acquired under accidental reinforcement contingencies. For instance, not walking under a ladder gets reinforced if no unpleasant results follow.

8. (c) A positive or discriminative stimulus is presented in learning an operant discrimination. If the response is emitted in the presence of the stimulus, it is followed by reinforcement.

9. (a) Receiving a paycheck once a month is an example of fixed-interval reinforcement. The reinforcement occurs after a fixed interval of time.

10. (c) The child has learned in this example that father is more likely to set the occasion for reinforcement than mother. Hence, the child has learned to discriminate the stimulus father from the stimulus mother.

11. (d) Programmed learning focuses on making learning more effective, which means increasing the achievement level of the learner and/or reducing the time to learn a specified amount of material.

12. (d) The assumption that many mental disorders are the result of the learning process is basic to conditioning therapy.

True-False Answers: Elements of Conditioning

1. (False)   Although conditioning principles appear useful in explaining some forms of more complex learning, it appears that additional principles are needed to account for the more complex phenomena of memory, concept learning, and problem solving.

2. (True)   In classical conditioning a formerly neutral stimulus, the CS, comes to elicit a response that initially was produced only by the UCS.

3. (False)   The contingency is just the reverse. The reinforcement must follow the response if learning is to occur.

4. (True)   In operant conditioning no constraints are placed on the organism's responding within the time limit allowed for responding.

5. (True)   As long as you are free to look in the refrigerator whenever you choose, looking is an operant response. It is no longer a free operant, however, if you are permitted, say, to look only once a day.

6. (False)   Negative reinforcers actually strengthen a response when the negative reinforcer is removed or terminated. For example, you may work hard around the house in order to avoid nagging from your parents. In this case the response of working is strengthened because it prevents the occurrence of nagging.

7. (True)   This is the case because you are arranging for high-probability behavior (running and screaming) to follow low-probability behavior (cleaning up), a contingency which strengthens low-probability behavior.

8. (True)   This statement is simply the principle of extinction.

9. (False)   Responses learned in various settings are much more resistant to extinction because the learned habit is tied to many stimuli.

10. (False)   This example illustrates generalization, in which the child responds to another adult male as if he were daddy.

11. (True)   Properties of responses such as loudness, speed, force, and so forth, are learned as the result of differential reinforcement.

12. (True)   Conditioning therapy assumes that the maladaptive behavior is learned in accordance with the same principles in which adaptive behavior is learned.

Verbal Learning

3

Most human learning involves verbal processes. Learning a foreign language, solving a problem in mathematics, and associating names and dates are all situations that involve what is known as verbal learning. Learning to understand the meaning of an abstract document such as the Bill of Rights and learning to understand the meaning of an unfamiliar word also constitute everyday tasks that involve verbal learning.

The fact that we use language in so much of everyday learning may make this activity seem commonplace or even unimportant. Nevertheless, the fact that we engage in verbal learning activities provides us with powerful ways of dealing with our environment. Language can serve to reward or punish behaviors and thus can have motivational effects. The effects of saying good or bad or even saying very little, are obvious examples. Similarly, language is used for communication purposes and operates in the development of concepts from the most elementary to the most complex. Language, or verbal behavior, is clearly tied up with thinking and symbolic activities and serves to mediate a variety of events. For example, by saying to yourself "I should study tonight and tomorrow night for the test, and then see the film" you are able to mediate behavior verbally in order to secure a successful outcome.

The systematic study of human learning began with verbal learning, and the principal issue was the formation and retention of verbal associations. Consider the question, How is it that the majority of humans when asked to think of an association for the word *table* think of the word *chair* as the most dominant associate? In turn, why are words such as *door* and *dog* less frequently given as associates? A long-standing view is that events and things tend to become associated because they are experienced together frequently. The basic idea is that if events A and B occur together—that is, contiguously—then A will on some future date tend to evoke B, and if they occur together frequently, they will then become strongly associated. Thus, according to this classic view, *table* and *chair* are likely to be strong associates because of the frequency with which they have occurred together in the past. In turn, *table* and *door* will be weaker associates because they have occurred together less

43

frequently. Although this account involving frequency and contiguity is a classical one and is partly true, we will subsequently see that it does not represent a completely satisfactory explanation.

In the preceding discussion two important concepts have been introduced: *contiguity* and *frequency*. By *contiguity* is meant that events overlap or are close together in space or in time. If a book and a coffee cup are next to each other on your desk, they are spatially contiguous. If your eye blinks following a blast of air, the two events are temporally contiguous. *Frequency,* of course, refers to how often two events occur contiguously. The concepts are important because they are the long-standing principles that presumably govern the development of associations. Moreover, it was an interest in the *laws of association* that provided the background for the early study of verbal learning.

Scope of Verbal Learning

Verbal learning is any learning situation in which the task requires the learner to respond to verbal material such as words or to respond with verbal responses. It includes a wide variety of learning situations ranging from the association of nonsense verbal materials to the solution of complex verbal problems. For example, a learner might be required to associate a list of unfamiliar verbal materials such as XUJ and BAL as an instance of a relatively simple task. In contrast, the human learner might be presented with a verbal analogy such as *Toulouse* is to *Lautrec* as *Rimsky* is to _?_ , the answer being *Korsakov*. In this case the solution to the analogy would be aided if the person recognized that Toulouse-Lautrec is the name of a famous French painter. Therefore, one might anticipate that Rimsky would be the first part of the double name of another well-known artist, in this case a composer. The analogy might be solved, however, if you recognized that Toulouse-Lautrec was someone's name even though you cannot identify him as a painter, an artist, or even as French. Recognition of the name as a name could lead you to search your memory for the class of events that include double names beginning with Rimsky.

From the preceding example it is clear that verbal learning involves complex processes such as problem solving, thinking, and concept formation. For the sake of convenience, however, these topics will be discussed in subsequent chapters. This chapter focuses on relatively simple kinds of verbal learning, principally those that involve the memorization of serial lists and lists of pairs of verbal materials. Keep in mind, however, that even these relatively simple tasks, which may appear to you to be no more than *rote* learning, almost always involve some kind of more complex activity on the part of the learner. This activity usually involves an attempt by the learner to use certain strategies, to organize or group the verbal materials in certain ways, or to code the materials, sometimes through the use of mnemonic or other devices. Thus verbal learning involves *cognitive* activities.

The study of verbal learning was first systematically begun by Hermann Ebbinghaus, a German psychologist, in 1885. Ebbinghaus was interested in the conditions under which humans learn to form associations and in the way in which associations are forgotten over time. Prior to this time it was generally believed that such complex processes did not lend themselves to experimental investigation and that it was not possible to measure such processes. Ebbinghaus was able to demonstrate, however, that it was possible not only to measure human memory in a precise, quantitative way, but also to examine experimentally the conditions of human learning and memory.

Ebbinghaus was strongly influenced by the thinking of a group of philosophers known as British associationists. This group of philosophers is represented by such men as John Locke, David Hume, George Berkeley, James Mill, and John Stuart Mill, to mention a few. Two features of British associationism are noteworthy: One is the belief that our knowledge arises directly from *experience*. Humans have no innate or inborn ideas but have instead gained knowledge through experience with the world. The beginning of our knowledge occurred with the acquiring of simple ideas through experience. A second feature of British associationism, as implied by the name, is that simple ideas can become linked together to form more complex ideas by *association*. These philosophers did not, however, study the formation of associations, and it remained for Ebbinghaus to initiate the experimental study of association formation.

In order to examine association formation in a way that he felt was largely free of past experiences of the learner, Ebbinghaus developed the nonsense syllable. The nonsense syllable is a verbal unit consisting of a consonant-vowel-consonant combination, such as XOB. The use of familiar words or sentences as learning materials for adult humans would obviously be unsatisfactory *if* the objective of the psychologist was to study the learning process from scratch, that is, uninfluenced by past learning experiences. We now know, however, that nonsense syllables are not free from the influence of past learning because they are known to possess associative properties and they vary in their meaningfulness. As a result, studies of verbal learning today use a wide variety of materials including words, sentences, and paragraphs.

Procedures and Materials in Verbal Learning

Various materials are used in the study of verbal learning. At the simplest level, single letters may be used. Three-letter nonsense syllables, called *trigrams,* may be used. Trigrams may be either consonant-vowel-consonant (CVC) combinations or consonant-consonant-consonant (CCC) combinations. The term *trigram* has come to replace the term *nonsense syllable* because it is more convenient to refer to the meaningfulness of trigrams. Trigrams vary in associative properties such as association value. In order to determine association value, human subjects are shown trigrams one at a time for a brief period and asked if they have an association to the trigram. The percentage of subjects having an association to a verbal item defines its association value. For example, the trigram BAL has an association value of 100 percent, meaning that for all subjects it had an association. In contrast, YIW has an association value of only 7 percent. An extensive scaling of the 2,480 possible CVCs was conducted by the psychologist James Archer in which he asked each subject whether the item was a word, sounded like a word, reminded him of a word, or could be used in a sentence. He then determined the meaningfulness of the items by calculating the percentage of subjects who regarded each CVC as meaningful.

Other associative properties of verbal materials are known. For example, we can measure the number of associations that subjects give to verbal units, and we can have subjects rate the pronunciability and familiarity of verbal materials. When individual words are used, a useful measure has been the average number of associations given to the word in a fixed time period, a measure that defines meaningfulness. The meaningfulness of two-syllable words, including a small number of artificial words, has been described by Clyde Noble. Examples of artificial words are *gojey* and *neglan* which average only one association in a 1-minute period. You might try this with a friend by asking him to write all the associations that come to mind for these artificial words in a 1-minute period. Highly meaningful words such as *office* and *wagon* average about eight written associations in the same period.

Groups of words and sentences are also used in studies of verbal learning. When we deal with groups of words we become interested in the interitem associative connections among the words. Words such as *summer, swimming,* and *warm* are interrelated and yet do not belong to the same type of class as do *orange, apple, banana* and *lemon.* Finally, when we deal with sentence learning, we are concerned with specifying grammatical properties of the sentence. Thus a wide variety of materials are used in studies of verbal learning and that one important feature of these studies is the *measurement* and *control* of their various properties.

Let us now examine some ways in which we study verbal learning. Four basic procedures have been developed: (1) serial learning, (2) paired associate learning, (3) free recall, and (4) recognition learning.

Serial Learning

In serial learning the verbal units are presented in the same order from trial to trial. A familiar example of serial learning is learning to recite the alphabet. Another obvious example is learning the days of the week as well as the months of the year. The fact that you can recite the days of the week, the months of the year, or the alphabet in perfect order is the final result of learning a serial task. Thus, any task which requires you to learn a series of verbal responses in a particular order represents an instance of serial verbal learning. While these examples may strike you as relatively simple kinds of learning, many of our everyday tasks require responding in a particular serial order. The grammatical structure of the English language determines in part the particular serial order of the sentences that you speak and write. Certain word types have a high probability of being followed by other word types; for example, verbs usually follow nouns, thus imposing a particular order. The learning of geological ages in their proper chronological order is another instance of serial learning; the particular sequence is important because each age implies particular changes and characteristics. Other tasks not exclusively verbal in nature but involving *motor* components also involve serial learning. A simple example is tying your shoe. Another is starting a car, where a particular sequence of responses must be made. Many tasks involve *both* verbal and motor components. A simple example of serial learning that involves both is learning the combination of a lock. In this instance you must learn the correct sequence of numbers and you must be able to turn the dial (motor component) in a precise and careful fashion.

In laboratory studies of serial learning, verbal units such as words are presented one at a time in a fixed order. Each word serves as a cue for recall of the next word in the list; when the learner can recall the entire list, learning is completed. In serial learning studies it is typically the case that more errors are made with items in the middle of the list and fewer errors are made at the beginning and end of the list. Why is it that items in the middle of a series are more difficult to learn than items at the beginning or end? Although we lack a complete account of this effect, two factors appear to be important. First, the items in the beginning and end positions are more discriminable to the learner since it is easy to recognize the beginning and end of the list. There is more uncertainty on the part of the learner in locating the last item compared with the first, but items in both positions are more discriminable than items in the middle. Second, the middle items are subject to greater interference, in that confusion among these items is more likely to occur.

Paired Associate Learning

In paired associate learning, the task of the learner is to learn to associate pairs of items, one member of the pair being the stimulus item and the second member being the response term. With this procedure the experimenter designates which item serves as the stimulus and which item serves as the response, in contrast to serial learning in which an item can serve both functions.

A familiar example of paired associate learning is the learning of foreign language vocabulary. Each foreign word is paired with its English equivalent, and the task of the learner is to learn to produce the foreign word when presented with its English equivalent. The procedure of learning foreign language vocabulary by the use of flash cards represents one instance of paired associate learning. More generally, any procedure that requires you to associate specific responses to specific stimuli constitutes paired associate learning. It must be cautioned that most aspects of foreign language learning are not paired associate in nature. Those features of language learning involving grammar and sentence construction involve other aspects, which will be described in a later chapter.

An example of paired associate learning in which different common words are used both as stimulus terms and as response terms follows.

Stimulus	*Response*
Dog	
Dog	Bicycle
Cigar	
Cigar	Tree
Television	
Television	Coat
Orange	
Orange	House
Car	
Car	Apple

The pairings are completely arbitrary in this list, and no *necessary* associative connection exists between the stimulus and response terms. The subject's task is to learn to associate each response with its stimulus word so that when he sees the stimulus word alone he can produce the correct response. This procedure is the paired associate *anticipation* method. Using the list shown here, the subject is first shown the stimulus term *dog* and is then shown the stimulus-response pair, *dog-bicycle*. He is next shown *cigar* and then the pair *cigar-tree,* and then the remaining pairs. The words are presented for a constant duration, usually 2 seconds for the stimulus and 2 seconds for the stimulus-response pair. After the learner sees the entire list once, it is repeated for successive trials, and the learner attempts to anticipate the correct response while each stimulus is present.

A moment's reflection may lead you to see that a person is likely to make linkages or connections in the pairs just described. For instance, the pair *dog-bicycle* may be verbalized as "A dog riding a bicycle." Moreover, we may have a clear image of a dog riding a bicycle. The principal point to note is that paired associate learning is far more than simple rote learning and involves a number of processes. Of particular importance is that the human is not passively acquiring stimulus-response associations as such, but is actively engaged in organizational, coding, and mediational processes in the effort to learn the task. This brief discussion alerts you to some of the complexities of a standard verbal learning task. We will explore these processes in greater detail later.

Free Recall

In free recall the subject is presented a series of verbal items one at a time and required to recall the items without regard to order. The order of presentation of the units on each trial is varied and the learner is free to recall in any order chosen. Hence the term *free recall,* or *free recall learning* as it is sometimes called.

The units can be presented singly in several ways. The experimenter presents the materials at a steady rate. Frequently a memory drum or projector is used and the exposure time such as 2 seconds is fixed for each item. An alternative procedure is to present the subject with the complete list, give her a study interval, and then test for recall. An apparent limitation of this last procedure is that it does not permit control of the study time for each unit.

Methodologically, the free recall procedure is the simplest procedure to study verbal learning in that it is less structured by the experimenter. As an example, you would be presented a set of words, singly, such as the ones listed here, and asked to recall as many as you can. You would be given successive presentations of the list until you could recall all items or until you reached some arbitrary criterion. When repeated trials are used, the procedure is known as multitrial free recall learning. Imagine that you are presented these sixteen items:

apple	tea	elephant	soda
lion	potato	spinach	pear
coffee	orange	milk	cow
cabbage	seal	lemon	carrot

After the first few presentations, perhaps even on the first, you would probably notice that the verbal materials can be classified into four categories: vegetables, fruits, beverages, and animals. In turn, this could affect the *order* of recall of the items, in that during recall you would tend to report one category first, then another, and so on. *This clustering in the order of recall is taken as evidence that humans organize events in memory.* Indeed, one of the basic reasons for using the free recall procedure is to study organizational processes.

The preceding example is a simple one in that the categories are fairly obvious. We can, however, increase the difficulty of detecting the categories and study the ways in which humans try to organize materials when the cues for organization become extremely subtle or are not actually present in the list. In general, human subjects are sensitive to the cues present in preorganized lists and reorganize the list as presented by the experimenter in accordance with the cues, rules, or categories present in the list. What about lists that have no evident structure of preorganization? Even where the experimenter makes no effort to preorganize the list, the learner attempts to organize the material in some fashion. This finding has been demonstrated by Endel Tulving, who found that there were significant consistencies in the order in which subjects recalled items from trial to trial, even though the order of presenting the items varied randomly. Tulving calls this *subjective organization,* emphasizing that humans impose their own organization in order to recall the items.

The results of free recall studies lend powerful support to the importance of the learner as a decision maker. The learner is clearly not passive, but is actively involved in seeking and trying strategies, looking for grouping rules, and imposing structure or organization in learning tasks, even those that involve relatively meaningless material. As a result, the free recall procedure has become extremely popular in recent years in the attempt to discover what the subject does in learning activities. The free recall procedure is important because it permits investigation: (1) of how the learner organizes the material, (2) of the cues (for example, conceptual categories) that the learner detects during learning and uses during recall, and (3) of the strategies the learner uses in retrieving items from memory.

Recognition Learning

The procedure of recognition learning has received increased use in recent years: *In recognition learning, the learner is shown the items in a study phase and then is tested for recognition on subsequent trials.* Recognition learning is similar to free learning during the study phase but is different during the testing phase. During testing the learner is presented with a series of items and asked to recognize them saying "yes" or "no," or "old" or "new" when he looks at each item. The series of test items consists of both old items that the subject has seen and new distractor items that are similar to the old items, in the sense of being from the same class. Recognition learning does *not,* therefore, require the learner to recall or produce the items but only to recognize them in the sense of identifying them as old (previously seen in the set of items) and new (not previously seen).

Instances of recognition learning are quite common in our everyday experience. Learning to recognize the faces of people is an obvious instance. Becoming familiar with particular landmarks along a highway or along a route that you frequently drive or walk is another instance. *In essence, recognition learning is the process by which we become able to distinguish familiar from unfamiliar events in our environment.* It is very similar to the process of *discrimination learning,* the critical difference being that discrimination learning involves making specific responses in the presence of the stimuli. Recognition learning, in contrast, does not require the learner to make specific responses of any kind but merely requires him to indicate whether an item is old or new.

Recognition learning can be illustrated as follows: A subject is shown a series of items singly such as these words:

happy	cringing	related	angry
slowly	pretty	increasing	changing

Then he is shown a test sheet and asked to indicate which items were ones seen in the list and which items were not in the list. The test sheet contains the items the subject saw plus a set of distractor items as well. The distractor items are frequently synonyms of the words seen, or associates of the words, and new distractor items are used in each test with repeated-trial recognition learning experiments. An example of the test sheet would look like this; half of the items are old and half are new.

increasing	crawling	furious	related
unstable	slowly	cringing	enlarging
frightened	changing	happy	angry
pretty	delighted	coupled	attractive

Two kinds of recognition tests are used: (1) *single-item* tests and (2) *multiple-item* tests. In the *single-item* procedure, each item is shown one at a time and the subject is asked to say "old" or "new" to each item. Sometimes the subject is asked to rate his confidence in how old or new the item is so that the experimenter can obtain an estimate of "memory strength" for the items independent of the particular subjective criterion the subject has. The principal point to note is that with a single item procedure, which gives a measure of the number of correct recognitions (called the hit rate), no direct control over the subject's criterion or response bias is present. For example, one person might be very conservative and therefore reluctant to say "old" or "yes" in the recognition test. Another person might be willing to say "old" frequently and thus get a higher recognition score just by virtue of his response bias. Normally, if a single-item procedure is used, the measures have to be corrected or transformed by complex procedures derived from signal detection theory. In the *multiple-item* procedure, the subject is shown each item learned along with one or more distractor items. In general, the more similar the distractor items are to the old items, the more difficult is recognition learning.

On the basis of the preceding discussion, you may perhaps have tentatively decided that a multiple-choice examination is like a recognition learning experiment involving, unfortunately, only one trial. This is precisely the case in that multiple-choice examinations usually present four or five choices for each question and your task is to recognize the correct item. The student frequently asks the question, Should I answer (guess?) all questions even though I don't know the answer to all of them? The answer to this question hinges on whether your instructor uses what he calls a "correction for guessing." If he does not, then your best and only strategy is to answer all questions even if you have to guess on some. With a four-item choice you have a one-fourth chance of getting the answer correct by guessing, and since there is no penalty for guessing, you have nothing to lose. Suppose, however, that he imposes a "guessing penalty." If you can narrow your choices by crossing out one or more obviously wrong answers it is still to your advantage to guess. Finally, if your instructor tells you to answer all questions, then it is obviously to your advantage to do so since presumably no guessing penalty will be used.

Associationism and Verbal Learning

The classical approach to the study of verbal learning stems from association theory. Principles which emphasize contiguity of experience and frequency of experience are paramount in the associative approach. The methods of serial and paired associate learning are the predominant methods of associationists. Their basic objective is to determine the variables that affect verbal learning. Variables regarded to be of major importance are task variables such as meaningfulness of items, familiarity of items, frequency of experiencing items, and similarity among items. During the heyday of classical verbal learning research these factors were studied extensively, and little emphasis was paid to the role of the learner and the importance of cognitive processes. The study of serial and paired associate learning was frequently regarded as the study of habit or association formation, somewhat like that in conditioning. Verbal learning was thought of as rote learning without much if any meaningful activity on the part of the learner. In this section we shall briefly examine this traditional approach to verbal learning. This approach and the now dominant cognitive approach to verbal learning will be contrasted subsequently.

Meaningfulness and Verbal Learning

The study of the effects of meaningfulness on paired associate learning is squarely in the tradition of the associative approach. Verbal units have associations, and Clyde Noble suggested that one way to study meaningfulness is to measure the number of associations given to a word or to any verbal unit. *Meaningfulness* can be defined thus in terms of the number of associations elicited by a verbal unit, with more meaningful items eliciting more associations. Let us now consider the effects of meaningfulness in paired associate learning as illustrative of the associationistic approach.

In paired associate learning we can vary independently the meaningfulness (M) of the stimulus and response terms. In this manner we can determine the relative importance of the two. The typical finding is graphed in figure 5, which shows acquisition curves for paired associates for four conditions involving all combinations of low- and high-stimulus M and response M. The figure shows a number of relationships. Clearly obvious is that the most rapid learning occurs when *both* stimulus M and response M are high *(H-H)*, whereas the slowest rate occurs when both are low *(L-L)*. The difficulty in learning increases in the order *H-H, L-H, H-L,* and *L-L*. The first letter of the sequence designates stimulus M; the second letter, response M.

More important is the fact that the effect of stimulus M depends upon whether response M is low or high. Specifically, the figure reveals that *variations in stimulus M produce a much greater effect on learning when response M is low than when it is high.* You can confirm this for yourself by noting that the difference between the curves for *H-L* and *L-L* conditions is much larger than the difference between the *H-H* and *L-H* conditions. When the effect of one or more factors on performance depends upon the values of another factor, we have what is called an *interaction,* in this instance, stimulus M and response M interact in their effect on the learning of paired associates. The figure shows another interaction in that *the effect of response M on learning is greater when stimulus M is low than when it is high.* You can see this by noting that the difference between the curves for *L-H* and *L-L* is greater than the difference between *H-H* and *H-L.* If you ignore, however, the complication of the interaction, *response M has a larger overall effect on learning than does stimulus M.*

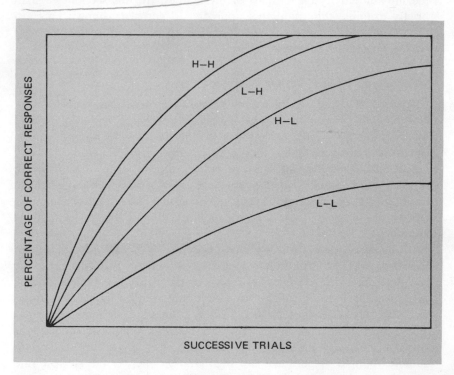

Figure 5. Paired associate acquisition curves for all combinations of low- and high-stimulus meaningfulness and low- and high-response meaningfulness. The first letter designates stimulus meaningfulness and the second letter designates response meaningfulness. For example, *H-L* means high-stimulus meaningfulness and low-response meaningfulness.

But how does meaningfulness affect paired associate learning? What kind of theory can handle this finding? The classical attempt to explain these results stemmed from *association probability theory*. The basic idea is that the more associations elicited by members of a pair, the greater the likelihood that an association from a stimulus and a response will link up in some manner. Moreover, if the stimulus and response terms elicit many associations they could then conceivably elicit a common association, making the linkage easy. A variety of possibilities would exist according to this theory. Consider, for example, the task of associating *cow* and *dog*. Since they both are animals, the link between the two is easy if the learner thinks of animals as a common associate. Plausible as association probability theory may seem, it runs into difficulty on several accounts. First is that the greater the number of responses that are attached to a stimulus in a training procedure, the poorer is performance in a second task using these stimuli, a phenomenon known as the *interference paradox*. Other difficulties arise with this theory, in particular its difficulty in handling certain transfer of training findings. Suffice it to say that association probability runs into difficulty on several grounds and lacks sufficient power and generality to be a comprehensive theory in accounting for the effects of meaningfulness.

The second and more generally accepted theory today emphasizes *encoding* of integrated units. This second theory is a much more cognitive type of theory in that it emphasizes the activities of the human. Here you will get a brief glimpse of a shift from associative to cognitive theories, although the break is not radical. The theory stems from two principles, one dealing with response learning and the other emphasizing stimulus learning.

On the response side, the theory emphasizes that response M exerts its effect in learning because more meaningful responses can be treated as a *unit* by the learner. More meaningful responses are more integrated, or "unitized," and hence can enter into association formation more readily. Words such as *table, chair, love,* and *psychology* are obviously familiar and highly practiced words. You have already learned how to pronounce them and they function, therefore, as integrated units. On the other hand, verbal units such as REH, ZQJ, and GXC are much less familiar and require considerable practice before they become integrated as a unit.

A quite similar kind of explanation accounts for the effect of stimulus M in paired associate learning. Here stimulus M is seen to exert its effect via the stability of perceptual-recognition responses made to stimuli. The basic idea is that for a stimulus term to function reliably in evoking a given response, the stimulus must eventually be perceived in a relatively consistent fashion over successive trials. This theory contends that the learner makes some kind of *identifying* response to a stimulus term, a response that is implicit and serves as some kind of representation of the actual stimulus term. It is not so important to know what this representation or implicit response is so long as one learns to respond to each stimulus term in some consistent or reliable fashion. Unless the learner can respond to each stimulus consistently, he cannot treat the stimulus of the moment as he did when he previously saw it and hence cannot associate the stimulus and response terms except by chance. The assumption is that high-meaningful stimuli are more likely to be consistently encoded as intact units than are low-meaningful stimuli. The word *cow* is likely to be encoded as "cow" with a clear representation; in contrast, the syllable XFL does not produce immediate or clear unitary encoding for most people and may be variably encoded on successive occasions.

Similarity and Verbal Learning

Similarity is another factor which exerts considerable influence on verbal learning. Moreover, the effects of similarity depend on the kind of verbal learning task; in some cases, similarity aids learning and in others it hinders learning. Before we examine these effects we need first to look at what is meant by similarity in verbal learning.

Formal similarity of verbal materials is defined by the number of common or overlapping letters that are used in constructing a list of items. The greater the number of common elements the greater the similarity of the items. The two lists of trigrams here represent lists high and low in similarity:

High Similarity	*Low Similarity*
TRM	RFG
THR	KJC
TRH	DPZ
TMR	VMX

Words can also vary in *meaningful similarity,* in that a list high in similarity would consist of synonyms such as productive, hard-working, efficient, ambitious, driving, and so forth, whereas a low-similarity list would consist of unrelated words. Words may be *conceptually similar* in that they belong to the same category or represent instances of the same concept. If the list contained the items Phoenix, Tucson, Albuquerque, El Paso, and Las Vegas, you would recognize them as cities in the southwestern United States.

As just noted, the effects of similarity depend upon the nature of the learning task. In *free recall,* both meaningful and conceptual similarity facilitate learning. If the items in a free recall experiment can be categorized or classified conceptually, we find that such words are recalled more readily than if the words belong to different categories. Both meaningful and conceptual similarity produce their effect on recall because when the items are highly similar and thus easily classified into a category the learner can recall the various items by recalling the category name. Moreover, when the items are conceptually or meaningfully related, the likelihood that one instance of a category will produce recall of another instance is increased. For example, if the category class is American automobiles, then recall of one instance, Chevrolet, can lead to the association of Buick, as well as to many others.

In *paired associate* learning, similarity produces mixed effects on the rate of learning. If the response terms are made increasingly similar along meaningful or conceptual dimensions the response learning stage is achieved faster even though overall rate of learning is reduced. This is simply to say that response similarity aids response learning, but interferes with associative learning. Increasing the formal similarity of the stimulus terms in a paired associate task greatly increases the difficulty of learning. That this should happen does not seem too surprising. When the stimuli are highly confusable, or difficult to distinguish, you are unable to be sure on each trial exactly which stimulus term is appropriate. More generally, it is simply more difficult to acquire stable identifying responses to stimuli that are highly similar, and thus learning is retarded.

This discussion further implies that what determines the difficulty of learning is not so much a matter of features or properties of a single stimulus, but rather properties of the entire stimulus set. In other words, it is not simply the characteristics of the individual items, but also the *structure* of the set that determines how we learn.

Stage Analysis of Verbal Learning

During the 1950s and early 1960s psychologists examined verbal learning in great detail and began to identify various stages or components of the verbal learning process. Their approach was to try to understand the fundamental features of various learning situations by analyzing them into their simplest processes. The paired associate task was seized upon as the vehicle for this analysis, and psychologists subsequently identified a variety of processes operating in paired associate learning. Initially, the component analysis effort was decidedly associationistic in flavor. Yet in the very analysis of this task which was thought to be the prototype of rote learning, it was discovered that if at all possible the human plays a very active role in processing the information being presented. Let us briefly examine a few of these processes.

Response and Associative Learning

What must you do in order to learn a list of paired associates? First, you must learn the responses to the point that you can recall them, and second, you must hook up the responses to the stimuli. The first stage, in which the responses become integrated so that they are available for recall, is the *response learning stage*. The second stage, which requires hooking up particular responses to particular stimuli, is the *associative stage*. If the responses are low in meaningfulness or are difficult to pronounce, then much of your effort will be devoted to response learning, that is, to integrating the responses into available units. This must be achieved to some reasonable level before associative learning can take place. The responses do not have to be fully integrated before some associative learning begins to take place; nevertheless, before association formation can occur *some* kind of response must be available.

Stimulus Discrimination

Now let us take a look at processes that operate on the stimulus side of paired associate learning. Discrimination among stimuli is a basic process in paired associate learning. We have already noted that the learner must reliably distinguish among the stimulus terms if he is to associate specific stimuli with specific responses. Moreover, the greater the similarity of the stimuli, the more important this process becomes. On the other hand, if the stimuli are already highly distinctive, then discrimination plays only a small role. But what does it mean to say that a person discriminates among stimuli? At a fundamental level it simply means that you can respond differently in the presence of different stimuli, despite the fact that the stimuli may possess many common features. Identical twins appear very much alike, and yet you know of instances where you can reliably distinguish between them. The cockpit of a commercial airliner contains many dials and panels which look quite similar, yet the trained pilot can quickly discriminate them. Burgundy and chianti may taste similar to you when you initially experience these two red wines, yet with experience you can readily tell the difference even if you are blindfolded.

Stimulus Selection

But we do not always deal with stimuli "just as they come." Humans engage in *stimulus selection,* that is, they use only a portion of an experimenter-presented stimulus as distinct from the entire stimulus. The experimenter-presented stimulus is the *nominal* stimulus, whereas the *functional stimulus* is that part which the subject uses to cue a response. For example, in a paired associate task the stimuli that are actually presented by the experimenter, such as XOL, KUF, and TAZ, are the nominal stimuli. What the learner chooses to use constitutes the functional stimuli. With these trigrams the learner may select and use only the first letter of each so that the functional stimuli are X, K, and T.

What functional stimulus selection does is to enable more efficient learning. You do not have to attend to and recognize the entire stimulus unit, but only a portion of the stimulus. In this fashion, redundant information can be ignored so as to facilitate learning. Stimulus selection is such a frequent and routine process that you may not be aware of its operation. You need not, for example, see an entire person in order to identify him; you need only see his face. Moreover, you can identify some of your close friends even if you see only a portion of their face. As an exercise you might have someone cover up portions of a photograph of someone you know and see how much "loss" you can take and still identify the person.

The fact that we respond to fewer than all of the cues present, which is to say that we learn to ignore redundant information, is quite evident from the behavior of skilled readers. Fast readers do not look at each individual word and ignore much unnecessary information. Words such as *the, an,* and *of* tend to be ignored by fast readers because they pick up the meaning of each sentence from less than the total sentence. They have learned to respond to subtle grammatical cues which will do the job of cueing their reading. Similarly, when we read someone's poor handwriting, we can guess the words on the basis of the likely sequence of letters in the English language.

The more general significance of the stimulus selection process is that it emphasizes the learner as an active processor of information as distinct from a relatively passive organism. Thus we can already begin to see a shift from an associative rote conception of paired associate learning to a more cognitive conception of what is being processed.

Stimulus Coding

In addition to stimulus discrimination and stimulus selection, humans will *code* stimulus input. *Stimulus coding is the process in which you change or transform a nominal stimulus into some new state or representation.* For example, if the stimuli in a learning task consist of the geometric figures △ , ○ , and □ , you will readily code these stimuli as "triangle," "circle," and "square." It is not necessary that you say these words aloud; implicit or subvocal verbalization may serve to code the stimuli. Moreover, codes may involve mental images as well as be verbal. Except perhaps for the simplest kind of stimuli, our performance seems not to depend directly upon the physical properties of nominal stimuli, but upon the manner in which we code the stimuli.

Transformations of nominal stimuli into some representation may be of the one-to-one variety, involving a particular transformation of each nominal stimulus as in the example just given, or they may be of a several-to-one arrangement in which two or more nominal stimuli receive the same transformation. We also distinguish between *substitution coding,* which is the replacement of the stimulus input with a new representation, and *elaboration coding,* which requires the storage of additional information with the unit to be remembered. An example of the latter would be changing the trigram FAV into favor.

We frequently code stimulus events by giving them shorthand verbal labels. For example, the student union building becomes the SUB; the University of Southern California becomes USC; International Business Machines becomes IBM. We also code unfamiliar visual patterns by giving them verbal labels.

The coding of stimuli does not always improve our ability to learn paired associates. Consider the anagrams RELABV and RELASN which as stimulus terms in a paired-associate list would require some effort to discriminate. By coding (transforming) them into VERBAL and LEARNS they can be more readily discriminated than in their initial state. If, however, it requires more effort on your part to code the stimuli than it does simply to discriminate them as they exist then coding will not facilitate learning.

How Are Associations Formed?

Let us now turn our attention to *how* we form associations. We have described some of the important factors that influence association formation, but we have not yet touched on how associations are formed. The answer to this question is complicated by the fact that the study of association formation in humans typically involves associations that they have already learned. If, for example, you are asked to pair such words as *boy-girl* and *table-chair,* your already existing associations will help you learn the pairs. If there is no direct connection between the items, then we frequently use mediating associations to help us link the terms. Thus, the study of association formation from scratch is difficult to achieve with human subjects.

We obviously learn associations by bringing to bear our rich associative networks in linking stimuli and responses. But can association formation take place without these links? Can two things be associated just because they occur contiguously, without any mediation linkages or intent on the part of the learner to learn? The answer appears to be yes. Simply by pairing unrelated words in a verbal discrimination task (a task in which the learner must learn which word in each of a list of pairs is correct), Norman Spear and colleagues demonstrated that some association between the pairs developed on the basis of contiguity. In effect, even though the learners did not have to process the pairs at a deep level, a limited amount of learning still took place via contiguity.

Everything that has been said so far implies that associations are formed gradually. Presumably, repeated presentations or trials are necessary for association formation to occur. According to this view, association formation is a gradual and continuous process which takes place over repeated trials. In contrast to this gradual or *incremental* view is the notion that associations are formed on an *all-or-none* basis. This latter view emphasizes that once an association is formed, it develops full associative strength. In other words, it develops maximum strength or none at all.

Common experience tends to support the incremental view. As we reflect on our everyday learning experiences, they seem to be gradual in nature, taking place over several or many trials. Yet this apparently gradual nature of association formation may hide or cover up the fact that single pairs are learned in an all-or-none fashion. For example, single pairs can be learned on an all-or-none basis despite the fact that an ordinary learning curve for paired associates is gradual in nature.

At present we are unable to give a definitive answer to this question. Indeed, the issue of incremental versus all-or-none conceptions of association formation turns out to be far more complicated than it was originally thought to be. At present it can be said that some results regarding association formation are best viewed as evidence for an incremental view, whereas others seem consistent with an all-or-none view. Like theoretical problems in other areas, such as physics, we will have to be content with two views of the process. For example, in physics we have two theories of light, one regarding light as a wave propagation process and the other regarding light as consisting of units or quanta of energy. Under certain circumstances the wave conception best handles known findings and under other circumstances the quantal conception does a better job.

Are associations learned in both directions? We commonly describe association formation in terms of recalling the responses to the appropriate stimuli. These are called *forward associations* in that the direction is from stimulus to response. In contrast, a *backward association* is assumed when you can recall a stimulus when presented the response as a cue.

It is quite clear that we do form backward associations in the course of learning paired associates. People do learn the reverse relationships, even though the backward association is usually weaker. For instance, in learning the vocabulary of a foreign language, you not only learn the pairs in a forward direction, but you also learn the reverse association to some extent.

Cognitive Approach to Verbal Learning

Throughout the scientific study of learning and memory associationistic and cognitive views of behavior have developed. We have already seen that associationism views learning as the acquisition of associations between stimuli and responses. Experimental issues were directed at the determination of factors which affect the relative strength of associations, and the principal interest was on acquisition or learning itself. The elicitation of a response depends, theoretically, on the strength of the associative connection or bond, and the strengthening of associations is a matter of such factors as frequency, contiguity, and/or reinforcement. During the heyday of associationistic and behavioristic conceptions of learning, roughly from 1925 through 1955, the concept of memory was relegated to a relatively minor role. Basically, memory was thought to refer to the system that retains the products of learning, associations, and the study of memory focused largely on the study of the fate of learned associations. Accordingly, memory was thought to be a secondary process which could be derived from principles of learning. Thus any interest in memory tended to focus on forgetting, which was regarded as the loss of associative strength during some retention interval.

But very early in the history of psychology objections to this associationistic conception of learning and memory appeared. Alternative cognitive conceptions were developed by the Gestalt psychologists such as Wolfgang Kohler and Kurt Koffka. According to Gestalt theory contiguity and frequency of experience are important *only* insofar as they allow for the operation of *organizational processes*. Associations are not learned by some stamping-in process via repetition. For example, Kohler argued that associations of word pairs such as *bicycle-dog* are not learned by frequency and contiguity, but are formed on the basis of mental images that are aroused by the word pairs. In turn, the images allow the pair to be organized as a unitary kind of experience. Thus what is learned and retained is some kind of organized unit or whole experience, not a stimulus-response association.

The second important assumption of Gestalt psychologists is that learning and memory are active processes. Learning involves an active person using images, strategies, organizational processes, and the like. Likewise, memory is thought not to be the passive registration and storage of information, but is thought to involve coding and retrieval processes. Information in memory is thought to change dynamically over time, and changes in memory are regarded as qualitative as well as quantitative. The learner is seen as organizing information in some meaningful fashion; he devises strategies and plans, he uses images and other mnemonic devices, he thinks, hypothesizes, and makes decisions. Gradually, over a number of years, many psychologists have accepted and adopted these assumptions about learning and memory as they have recognized the reality of the active learner. With this approach, however, there has been no abandonment of the objectivity of the associationistic and behavioristic traditions. In this section we shall examine some representative instances of verbal learning research which are influenced or directed by the cognitive approach.

Clustering in Free Recall

We have noted that in free recall humans rearrange the order in which materials are presented. When you are presented with a series of words and required to recall them, your recall order or output of the words can differ from the input in which they are presented. This effect is called *clustering* in free recall and is one kind of evidence for organizational processes in verbal learning.

Sometimes we may cluster or organize verbal materials simply by associating one word with another. If the materials presented contain mutual associates, we then tend to recall them as such. This process is called *associative clustering*. For example, the pairs *boy-girl, night-day, green-grass, nose-smell,* and *dog-fight* are likely to be recalled together even though the items were presented in a scrambled order.

Another kind of clustering is *category clustering*, in which the recall of items is related to specific conceptual categories in the list. Things that can be classified in some way tend to be recalled together. In the examples just given, recall of *night* and *day* together might occur because they are frequent associates, but also might occur because they are words belonging to the concept time of day. In contrast *rose* and *smell* are not members of the same concept, but are clearly recalled because they are associatively related. In category clustering the order of a person's recall of a list of words might appear as follows: *bean, potato, lettuce, celery, gold, silver, lead, iron, robin, bluebird, finch, jay, elephant, lion, monkey,* and *gazelle.* This would show complete clustering; however, clustering is usually not this complete or perfect. Clustering can occur even though the words are randomly presented at input. As another example, if asked to recall all the names of people you know, you may tend to recall close friends, then relatives, and finally acquaintances.

Subjective Organization

Humans also impose their own organization on verbal lists when no evident organization or structure is present; this procedure is called *subjective organization.* This phenomenon was clearly demonstrated by Endel Tulving who found that in repeated free-recall trials of a list of completely unrelated words each subject gradually recalled the list in a progressively more consistent fashion. Subjects did, of course, differ from each other; what is important is that a given subject became more consistent with respect to her own recall order.

Coding

The process of changing or altering information to be remembered is called *coding.* More generally, coding refers to the *rearrangement* of information so as to facilitate its retention. For example, if you were given the relatively meaningless syllables BYO, CIE, and IPL, you might code these as BOY, ICE, and LIP. Coding processes may also involve *elaboration* of information. Here some additional information is imposed on the information to be learned. For example, the syllable LOC might be elaborated and stored as words such as *lock* or *location.* Such transformations are instances of what are called natural language mediators because the human uses language to make the information more meaningful. Another instance of coding is seen in the simplication or reduction of information. For instance, George Miller has shown that humans can retain long sequences of information such as binary digits by "chunking" the digits into groups and coding each group of digits. For example, 000 can be coded as 0, 001 as 1, 010 as 2, 011 as 3, and so on. Thus a string of 21 binaries could be coded as a chunk of only 7 digits.

Once you code information, however, you are faced with the task of *decoding* the coded information back into its original form during recall. For instance, a typist must decode shorthand into English words and sentences. If the task of decoding is very difficult, you are better off learning and retaining the information as presented. For example, students sometimes memorize vast amounts of information by use of mnemonic codes and are then unable to remember what information the code represents. Therefore, in general fewer or less complex coding rules make your task of decoding much easier.

Natural Language Mediation

We just noted that one type of coding is called natural language mediation. In this situation humans use their own language in learning materials. This clearly illustrates the cognitive approach to verbal learning because the learner is seen as an *active agent* in processing the information. When given relatively meaningless information to memorize, the human can organize the information by using words, phrases, or sentences to help bring meaning to the material. For example, if asked to learn the pair of words *car-apples,* a person might actually store the pair in the form of a sentence such as A bag of *apples* is in the back seat of the *car.*

Mental Imagery

Our ability to use mental images is a powerful factor in verbal learning. For instance, when paired-associate word pairs are learned, the use of mental images or pictures greatly facilitates learning. By *mental images* is meant the kind of pictorial representation or arrangement which humans can construct on the basis of their own self-instructions, as when you visualize sitting down to a juicy steak dinner or on instructions from someone else conjure up a mental picture of some event or thing.

Mental imagery has been studied in two general ways. One way has been to instruct humans to construct mental images while learning verbal materials. The typical procedure is to instruct a subject just prior to learning a list of paired associates "to try to think of a mental picture that will relate the two words that must be associated." The second procedure is to vary the *imagery value* of the words or verbal units in a learning experiment. The imagery of verbal materials is measured very much like meaningfulness; subjects are asked to rate the materials in their ease of generating imagery. Even without imagery instructions, *humans learn high-imagery pairs faster than low-imagery pairs.*

Imagine that you are learning a set of paired associates in which three of the pairs are *dog-bicycle, black-butter,* and *candy-cigar,* and that you are instructed to construct a mental image or picture that will group or relate each pair. With the first pair you might visualize a picture of a dog riding a bicycle in a circus, or a dog running beside a boy riding a bicycle, or any of a number of possible images. A plate of black butter might come to mind with the second pair, unpleasant as that might be, and a picture of a candy cigar or a picture of a candy and cigar counter in a local drug store might arise with the third pair. All of these would serve to relate both words in the same picture and thus would facilitate learning.

As we noted earlier, the imagery value of verbal materials determines their ease of learning. In paired associate learning we can vary independently the imagery value of the stimulus and response terms, just as we vary meaningfulness. In this case, imagery value of both stimulus and response terms facilitates learning. In addition, however, *stimulus imagery is a more important factor than is response imagery in affecting rate of learning.* This fact is of interest because it contrasts with the effect of meaningfulness on the rate of verbal learning, where response meaningfulness was seen to be more important than stimulus meaningfulness. We will return to the matter of how imagery and meaningfulness are related shortly.

Imagery Theory

Why does stimulus imagery exert such a powerful effect on learning? Allan Paivio has proposed a conception in which the stimulus term is viewed as a "conceptual peg" to which the subject hangs his response during learning. The response term is recalled during testing by way of the conceptual peg. The more likely a stimulus term arouses an image, then the better able the learner is to recall or retrieve the appropriate response.

The more general explanation of the effects of imagery in studies of verbal learning and memory is that images may serve as alternatives to, or jointly with, verbal codes as a way of representing information in memory. If you represent some information by way of *both* image and verbal codes the representation would then be more powerful. This idea is called the *dual-coding theory* as outlined by Allan Paivio. The basic notion is that we have two coding systems, one dealing with verbal linguistic information and the other dealing with nonverbal information designated image codes. The verbal and image systems may interact, one influencing the other, but the two systems are different in certain critical ways.

Although there is a good deal of evidence which appears to favor the dual-coding theory, the idea has been recently subjected to critical analysis. There is no question, of course, that instructions to image do enhance memory, and it is true that the high-imagery materials are more readily learned than low-imagery materials. The question is, Is it necessary to assume that there are pictures or mental images actually in memory to account for the effects of imagery instructions? Perhaps not. It does not on logical grounds appear reasonable to assume that we store pictures since we would need an almost unlimited memory storage system to store all the visual scenes that we daily perceive. It can also be argued that we don't keep picturelike information, a sort of raw sensory information, in our long-term memory, but rather convert the pictorial information to some sort of verbal propositional information which is stored. John Anderson and Gordon Bower have argued along these lines, contending that imagery instructions lead to a deeper, more conceptually based analysis of the information. Lest you be confused, let us reemphasize that there is no doubt about the effectiveness of imagery as a factor in verbal learning and memory; the conflict lies rather in the *interpretation* of imagery effects in learning and memory.

Imagery Techniques

Two widely known techniques of imagery are the *method of loci* and the *pegword method*. The method of loci was known to the ancient Romans and is illustrated by the following story. According to history, a Greek poet, Simonides, was commissioned to read a poem at a banquet in honor of a Roman nobleman. After reading the poem, Simonides was called outside the banquet hall. During his absence the roof of the hall caved in, and all persons at the banquet table were killed, crushed beyond recognition. Simonides was nevertheless able to identify each person for purposes of separate burial because he was able to recall the *place* of each guest reclining at the table. This unusual feat of memory resulted from Simonides' being able to form a mental image of the place where each person had reclined so that a compound image of person-place was stored in memory. This procedure is called the method of loci (location) because it requires the development of an image which is tied to some location in a spatial framework. The information is recalled by mentally moving through the locations of the spatial image.

You can try out the method of loci by remembering a series of items such as a grocery list: Suppose your task is to remember a list of items such as oranges, hot dogs, bread, milk, and potatoes. The method involves constructing a mental image in which each item is located in a particular place. You can achieve this by imagining that you are taking a walk through familiar surroundings such as the walk from home to the store. Assume in your walk that you pass a grove of trees, a fence, a truck, a house with a large porch, and a newly plowed field. You would then imagine scenes as follows, in which each item on the list is related to places you pass: oranges hanging on the trees in the grove, hot dogs draped over the fence, a truck loaded with loaves of bread, milk cartons sitting on the porch, and potatoes in the field.

Another approach to remembering information using imagery is the pegword method which is a plan for memorizing. The method requires knowledge of a little series: one is a bun, two is a shoe, three is a tree, four is a door, five is a hive, six is sticks, seven is heaven, eight is a gate, nine is a line, and ten is a hen. You then use the series to learn any set of items by imagery. Suppose the items consist of words such as *pencil, boy, dog, bicycle,* and so forth. You would then construct images as follows: a pencil lying on a bun, a boy tying his shoe, a dog sleeping by a tree, a bicycle being carried through a door, and so forth.

Motivation and Verbal Learning

What is the role of motivation in verbal learning? We know in the case of animal learning that motivation is necessary for performance, but not for learning. Although motivational variables have been studied extensively in animal learning, much less attention has been given motivational variables in human learning.

Let us note why this has been the case. In studies of animal learning it is usually essential to deprive the animal of food or water in order to get him to perform. Such is not the case with human subjects. Usually, the instructions are sufficient to motivate the subject to perform the task. Moreover, the subject usually arrives at the laboratory setting with at least a fair amount of motivation. By the time the subject has received the instructions, motivation is usually at such a level that it is difficult to produce large changes in motivation otherwise. Thus, it is not because of disinterest in motivation that it has not been extensively studied in verbal learning, but because the learner is typically well motivated in laboratory studies of learning.

Intentional versus Incidental Learning

Consider the issue of intentional versus incidental learning. Psychologists have long pondered the question of whether intent to learn is essential for learning. The answer is no! *Regardless of our intentions, we learn something about those things to which we are exposed.* Indeed, there is no reason to maintain the distinction between the two kinds of learning, which really amount to two kinds of instructional operations in verbal learning tasks. If differential responses are made to stimuli, they will be learned without regard to intent. If differential responses are not made, then learning will not occur.

Anxiety

Motivational factors do affect performance as has been shown in studies of the effects of anxiety on verbal learning. Where the task is fairly complex or difficult, motivation in the form of anxiety actually interferes with performance. *As the task becomes more complex, less motivation is necessary for achieving optimal learning.* This simply emphasizes the point that you can be too motivated for effective performance, an all too frequent occurrence on the part of the student.

Frequently a student complains that he is doing poorly in a course despite the fact that he likes the course and is highly motivated. Leaving out matters of intelligence and good study habits, the likely possibility is that the student is too highly motivated for efficient performance. A high motivational state may act to energize many responses so that the student becomes confused. In studying, he may fail to think through relationships even though he has memorized many facts. In the test situation, he may have difficulty, therefore, in distinguishing between subtle alternatives that he faces in the usual multiple-choice test.

Anxiety affects not only your studying, but also your performance in the classroom. Highly anxious students tend to think more about irrelevant details of the class such as a crack in the wall, a mark on a desk, the instructor's dress, manner, or appearance, and what other people are doing. Consequently, such students think less about the topic of discussion and hence learn less. What high anxiety appears to be doing is producing a general energizing effect so that a large number of irrelevant environmental stimuli gain the student's attention. Thus, you may find your attention wandering from the lecturer during the classroom period if you are in an anxious state.

Handling Anxiety

Everyone gets anxious at specific times. Moreover, a little anxiety is useful because it can serve to energize performance. Therefore, the problem is not so much the matter of avoiding anxiety, which is virtually impossible, but of handling or coping with anxiety. The problem is one of dealing with anxiety so that it does not cripple our everyday performance in learning situations.

Consider first anxiety in test-taking situations. It is normal to be a little anxious just before taking a test, especially if you are unfamiliar with the instructor's tests. Suppose, however, that you characteristically become quite anxious prior to and during a test so that your performance is poor. What can you do? One approach that I have used with students is to give them practice tests which they must take in the regular classroom at some period when the classroom is not being used. In some instances, I have arranged for a faculty colleague to prepare a practice test typical of one students are likely to receive. In other cases students have made up their own tests. The logic of this approach is to have students practice taking tests in the very environment that they will take the real test. The test must be taken during the same amount of time allotted for the classroom period, and the test is graded immediately so that students can check their performance. *If,* under these circumstances, students can perform well, they tend to reduce their anxiety about test taking.

Consider anxiety in the classroom. This may be the result of general anxiety that you possess or of anxiety specific to certain features of the class, such as the instructor asking questions of students. As we noted, if you are anxious, you tend to think about other things than the lecturer's topic. You may tend to daydream about other events.

A little daydreaming is normal, but you can see that daydreaming in the classroom is quite nonproductive. What you must do is learn to recognize when you are daydreaming and redirect your attention to the lecture. Sometimes this can be accomplished by verbal self-instruction in which you occasionally monitor your thinking in the classroom; if you discover that you are daydreaming, you refocus your attention on the lecture. This requires that you develop the habit of occasionally "looking at" what you are thinking. Another approach is to reward yourself when you have carefully attended to and thought about the lecture. For example, you may schedule a coffee break after class *only if* you have listened attentively and thoughtfully in class.

There are many specific things you can do in handling anxiety. Regardless of what approach you take, the effectiveness of any approach must be viewed in terms of the extent to which you can avoid paying attention to distracting, irrelevant stimuli and the extent to which you can attend to the main issues of the class.

Summary

This chapter has described the major procedures and approaches for studying verbal learning. The study of verbal learning began with an effort to understand how humans form and retain verbal associations. Verbal learning was seen, however, to be a much more complex process than originally conceived and is currently viewed as composed of several processes. The laboratory study of verbal learning has typically employed four types of procedures: serial learning, paired associate learning, free recall, and recognition learning. Each procedure taps somewhat different processes in verbal learning and hence there is no single procedure for studying verbal learning.

The classical approach to the study of verbal learning stemmed from association theory. Factors such as meaningfulness and similarity were extensively studied and found to be major variables in verbal learning. Stage analysis was shown to analyze verbal learning into its fundamental component processes such as response learning, associative learning, and stimulus discrimination. Finally, we examined the cognitive approach to verbal learning. What is characteristic of the cognitive approach is the emphasis on organizational processes and the view of the learner as an active processor of information. Important organizational processes included clustering in free recall, subjective organization, coding, natural language mediation, and imagery.

Motivation in the form of anxiety was seen as an important factor in affecting performance in verbal learning tasks. In general, we saw that as a task increases in complexity, less motivation is necessary for efficient learning. Practical procedures for the reduction of excessive anxiety during test taking are known. One such procedure requires students to practice examination taking as part of their regular study procedures. Controlling anxiety in the classroom was seen as dependent upon your ability to focus and maintain your attention on the topics under discussion and to develop habits of monitoring your classroom thinking so as to avoid daydreaming.

Multiple-Choice Items: Verbal Learning

1. The study of verbal learning began with an interest in which issue?
   a. how information in memory is retrieved
   b. how ideas are associated
   c. differences in recall and recognition
   d. how imagery affects learning
2. Learning the geological ages in order would be an example of
   a. paired associate learning
   b. recognition learning
   c. free recall learning
   d. serial learning
3. Free recall is an especially useful procedure for studying
   a. the memorizing of sequences
   b. organizational processes
   c. one-trial learning
   d. association formation
4. The phenomenon of subjective organization indicates that humans
   a. impose some kind of structure on materials to be learned
   b. do better on cued than on noncued tests of recall
   c. will rote learn materials
   d. may store information in memory that is not always accessible
5. The classical or earliest approach to the study of verbal learning stemmed from
   a. cognitive psychology
   b. stage analysis
   c. associationism
   d. information processing
6. Variations in stimulus meaningfulness produce a greater effect on paired associate learning when the responses are
   a. low in meaningfulness
   b. high in meaningfulness
   c. moderate in meaningfulness
   d. high in meaningfulness and imagery value
7. Which process will become increasingly important if the learning

task contains highly confusable stimuli?
  a. stimulus discrimination
  b. response learning
  c. association formation
  d. coding
8. The process of responding to only one part of a nominal stimulus
    rather than to the entire stimulus is called
  a. encoding
  b. stimulus coding
  c. mediation
  d. stimulus selection
9. The cognitive approach to verbal learning has stressed the im-
    portance of
  a. associations
  b. contiguity
  c. frequency
  d. organization
10. The process of category clustering in free recall is one instance of
    the more general process in human learning and memory called
  a. subjective
  b. mediational
  c. organizational
  d. imagery
11. Changing an item into something different for purposes of learning
    and memory is called
  a. generalization
  b. coding
  c. free recall
  d. stimulus selection
12. The dual-coding theory emphasizes that we have
  a. verbal and motor codes
  b. verbal and linguistic codes
  c. sensory and perceptual codes
  d. verbal and image codes
13. The fact that humans can *link* items during learning by using new
    terms refers to the process of
  a. selection
  b. coding
  c. retrieval
  d. mediation
14. Which statement about anxiety and learning is correct?
  a. anxiety always interferes with learning

b. highly anxious students are more likely to attend to significant points of a lecture
c. any increase in anxiety is accompanied by an increase in learning
d. less motivation in the form of anxiety is necessary in learning more complex tasks

True-False Items: Verbal Learning

F 1. Since verbal learning is essentially a matter of rote (brute force) learning, it is of little consequence to human behavior.
F 2. The learning of meaningless nonsense syllables enables psychologists to study verbal association formation from scratch.
F 3. The memorization of several lines of poetry is an instance of serial learning.
T 4. In learning a serial list of verbal items, items near the middle of the list are hardest to learn and items at the beginning and end of the list are easier.
T 5. In paired associate learning, the verbal pairs are presented in a fixed order and sequence.
F 6. Learning the alphabet in the sense of learning to pronounce properly each letter of the alphabet when shown each letter alone is an instance of paired associate learning.
F 7. In free recall situations, humans can organize the material only if there are objective categories present in the list.
T 8. Both free recall and recognition learning emphasize the response learning process.
T 9. Meaningful verbal items such as words are more readily learned than, say, low-association value trigrams because the meaningful items can be more readily treated as a unit.
F 10. In paired associate learning, being able to construct a mental image of the response term is more important than constructing an image of the stimulus term.
T 11. The items San Francisco, Los Angeles, and San Diego are more likely to be recalled together than the items Seattle, Kansas City, and Atlanta because the first items are conceptually similar and hence can be easily grouped for purposes of recall.
F 12. Increasing the formal similarity of stimuli in a paired associate task increases the ease of learning the task.
T 13. Humans use all aspects of stimuli to which they are presented.
T 14. If two verbal items are jointly exposed, some associative strength

between the items may develop even though the task demands no association between the items.

F 15. Organizational processes occur in learning of sentences and paragraphs, but not in ordinary free recall or paired associate learning of lists of items.

F 16. The development and utilization of verbal links to hook up items is called verbal mediation.

F 17. Your solution of complex mathematics problems is more likely to suffer from high anxiety than the memorization of biological terms such as the structure of plants.

T 18. One way of dealing with test anxiety is to practice taking tests or quizzes.

Discussion Items: Verbal Learning

1. Why is free recall used to study organizational processes? That is, why does it lend itself to the study of organization?

2. Compare and contrast the associative and cognitive approaches to verbal learning.

3. Learning to read is much more than just a verbal learning task. Reflect for a moment on what is involved in learning to read for a beginner. How might you do a stage analysis of the beginning tasks of reading?

4. How might you use mental imagery in learning subject matter such as geology, geography, or biology? Outline a program by which you could instruct someone else in using imagery.

5. Outline a practical program of advice for someone who is typically overwhelmed with anxiety when taking a test. Outline a series of concrete things a person might do to reduce or control anxiety.

Multiple-Choice Answers: Verbal Learning

1. (b) The study of verbal learning began with an interest in how ideas are associated. This emphasis is seen in the work of Ebbinghaus and in the influence of British associationism.

2. (d) Learning the geological ages in order is a serial learning task. This is so because you must learn the material in a particular serial order.

3. (b) Free recall is especially useful for studying organizational processes because we are allowed to recall the material in any order we wish. The fact that our order of outputting items differs from the order in which they are presented and that items related by cate-

gories or associatively related may cluster are indicative of organizational processes.

4. (a) Given no apparent or predetermined structure, humans will nevertheless attempt to impose some kind of structure on materials to be learned.

5. (c) The classical approach to the study of verbal learning is associationism.

6. (a) Differences in performance due to stimulus meaningfulness have a greater effect if the responses are low in meaningfulness.

7. (a) If the stimuli in a learning task are highly confusable, which means they are difficult to discriminate, then the process of stimulus discrimination becomes more important. In contrast, if the stimuli are easy to distinguish, then the stimulus discrimination process becomes unimportant.

8. (d) Selecting or responding to only a portion of a nominal stimulus is called stimulus selection. It implies an active selection process during learning.

9. (d) The cognitive approach to verbal learning has emphasized the significance of organizational processes.

10. (c) Category clustering is one type of evidence for organizational processes. The fact that we tend to recall related items in clusters indicates that we are organizing information in memory.

11. (b) The process of coding is one of transforming, elaborating, or changing an item into something which is presumably easier to learn and place in memory.

12. (d) The dual-coding theory contends that we have two memory codes, a verbal code for linguistic information and an image code for visual pattern information.

13. (d) The linking of items by new terms or words is called mediation.

14. (d) The more complex the task, the less the motivation in the form of anxiety is necessary for optimal performance.

True-False Answers: Verbal Learning

1. (False) Verbal learning is a fairly complex affair consisting of coding and organizational processes, as well as response learning, stimulus selection, and so forth. These more complex processes are important in many aspects of human behavior.

2. (False) Even nonsense syllables can be meaningful to adults in the sense that a nonsense syllable will tend to elicit one or more associations.

3. (True) You have to learn this material in a particular order, which makes it a case of serial learning.

4. (True)   This principle holds over a wide range of verbal materials and is known as the serial position effect.

5. (False)   The position of the pairs in the list is varied from trial to trial so that particular pairs rather than positions are learned.

6. (True)   Here the task is that of learning to associate a particular response (pronunciation) in the presence of a particular stimulus (letter symbol).

7. (False)   Humans tend to organize the material in some fashion, even if readily available objective categories are not present. This process is called subjective organization.

8. (False)   Free recall does demand response learning in that recall of the responses is required; however, recognition learning requires only that the learner recognize and select the correct response.

9. (True)   More meaningful verbal materials are more easily treated as an integrated unit.

10. (False)   Just the reverse is the case. The more likely that a stimulus arouses an image, the easier it is to retrieve (get to) the response term.

11. (True)   The former items are all related in that they belong to the category of California cities; the latter three cities cannot be grouped so easily.

12. (False)   On the contrary, as the stimulus items are made more confusable (similar), rate of learning is decreased.

13. (False)   Humans frequently select and use only a fraction of the entire stimulus presented if that fraction will validly cue a response. This process is called stimulus selection.

14. (True)   Some association formation can occur simply on the basis of contiguity.

15. (False)   Organizational processes, which refer to activity by the learner in reorganizing or restructuring the materials, can readily occur in free and paired associate learning.

16. (True)   When two items are not easily associated, the learner may think of some verbal mediator which helps hook the two items together.

17. (True)   In general, anxiety is likely to interfere with more complex tasks. In this instance, we would regard mathematical reasoning as more complex than learning biological terms.

18. (True)   The effect of such practice is to familiarize yourself with examinations, making them less traumatic when you take the actual test. Moreover, practice in taking examinations may desensitize you to the aversive features of examination taking.

Memory I: The Processing of Information

The activities labeled memory are so frequent in our daily lives that we may fail to recognize their general significance. For instance, consider a block of time in your daily routine such as meeting and conversing with friends. Your conversation is likely to focus on events of the past few days, plans for the future, and highlights of the day. In discussing these events you recall the appropriate information and bring it forward in your immediate consciousness. As you prepare to describe some noteworthy event, you organize the information so that your account is, hopefully, meaningful and interesting. Thus you find yourself regularly drawing on events stored in memory and recalling them for particular purposes.

We are all familiar with the frustration of searching for a particular word in memory and not being able to come up with it. Even though you are certain you know the word, such as a person's name, you cannot recall it at the moment. The word is "on the tip of your tongue," but it does not come to mind. An especially frustrating feature of the tip-of-the-tongue phenomenon is the embarrassingly long time it may take to recall a familiar name. This is a case in which we know that the name is stored in memory despite the fact that we are unable to retrieve it. Why this process occurs and how we ultimately are able sometimes to recall an item illustrate basic problems in analyzing memory.

Consider an easy question: What is your home telephone number? For most people the answer simply pops into awareness without much evidence of thinking or search processes. On occasion, however, you may "block" if someone asks your phone number. Similarly, if you move and acquire a new phone number, you may note that the old number will be recalled unless you have had opportunity to rehearse the new number. These kinds of events require explanation in terms of principles of memory.

Consider a somewhat more difficult question: Was your bedroom doorknob in the house in which you lived when you were twelve years old on the right or left? Imagine yourself as being outside your room as you attempt to recall its location. Your recall of this involves several substages. You must first recall the house in which you lived at age twelve years; next you will probably locate your room in the house; finally, you may be able to recall the doorknob as being right or left. How this process occurs represents another instance of problems in memory. Intuitively, at least, it seems clear that recall of information involves a search process. One problem of a theory of memory is to specify the rules governing this search.

The description of memory will frequently employ the terms *retention* and *forgetting*. *Retention* refers to the extent to which material that was previously learned is still present or retained. *Forgetting* refers to that portion which is lost. Thus, retention and forgetting refer to two sides of a coin: retention to what is remembered and forgetting to what is lost. The point to note is that each process is defined in terms of the other; *forgetting* is defined as the difference between how much was originally learned and how much is retained, and *retention* is defined as how much is retained.

The preceding examples are but a few instances of the many kinds of problems in memory. The examples do emphasize that memory is not simply a passive process of storing information and reproducing it when needed. Memory involves reconstruction of events. This is simply to say that in many situations we remember rules and general principles and from these attempt to recall specific facts and details.

Encoding, Storage, and Retrieval

Our current view of memory emphasizes three processes: encoding, storage, and retrieval. Although we referred to these processes in an earlier chapter, let us look at them now with reference to the concept of memory.

For some event to be stored in memory, it must be placed in a "state" such that storage is possible. Regardless of what is stored, the material must ultimately be encoded in some fashion. These encodings may be verbal or imagelike, and they represent some kind of transformation of the nominal stimuli impinging on the individual. Encoding is the transforming of events into some state so that they can be stored and is accomplished during what we ordinarily call learning. We have discussed encoding in previous chapters, so we will only note it here.

Storage and retrieval can be understood by using a filing cabinet analogy. At an uncomplicated level memory can be considered a matter of placing things in a filing cabinet and taking things out when you want them. An item placed in a filing cabinet can be regarded as an event stored. One file clerk, however, might file items in a systematic fashion, whereas another might do so haphazardly. Items filed by either file clerk are considered to be in storage. But consider the difference when the two file clerks try to locate materials: The first clerk will generally be able to locate materials, while the second clerk will have difficulty unless, of course, an elaborate personal system for locating the materials is developed. The business of locating the materials is *retrieval*. The conceptual separation of storage processes from retrieval processes calls attention to the fact that events may be stored in memory even though they are not retrievable. More generally the distinction calls attention to two processes that until recently were treated together.

This description provides only a general understanding of the concepts of storage and retrieval. We shall explore these processes in more detail subsequently. For the moment, this description allows us to compare two major approaches to the understanding of memory: association theory and information processing.

Approaches to Memory: Associationism and Information Processing

Psychologists who study memory usually talk about memory from one of two conceptual viewpoints: either associationistic or information processing. These two terms loosely describe a constellation of assumptions and concepts used in the description of memory processes. The older approach is associationism, stemming from Ebbinghaus and Thorndike, pioneers in the study of learning and memory. The more contemporary approach is information processing, stemming initially from the work of the British psychologist Donald Broadbent.

The associationistic tradition in psychology contends that what gets learned are associations between events. It is usually assumed that stimuli and responses get associated during the course of learning and that this learning is a continuous process. The concept of association refers to some *hypothetical* process and does not imply specific events in the nervous system. It is a descriptive or functional term that in a neutral sense merely indicates that event B has some likelihood of occurrence following event A. In other words, response B has some probability of occurrence upon the presentation of stimulus A, given certain conditions. There are additional meanings attached to the concept of association, but this description characterizes its essential features for present purposes.

An associative conception of the learning process leads to looking at memory in a particular way. If learning is the establishment of stimulus-response associations, memory deals with the problem of "what happens" to these associations over the course of time and under conditions of new learning. The problem of memory becomes the problem of how associations are forgotten with the passage of time and what factors influence the forgetting of associations. From this viewpoint, memory is viewed as the consequence of learning.

The information-processing approach to memory takes a somewhat different attack on the problem of memory. Memory is viewed as dealing with the "flow of information" through the person from its initial encoding, to storage, and finally to retrieval. An important feature of information-processing approaches is the emphasis on the distinction between storage and retrieval. This distinction, however, can be incorporated into association theory. The associative position places emphasis on the storage process, that is, how events are learned, whereas information-processing approaches not only ask about how information is stored, but also focus on how information is *retrieved* from memory once it is stored. Associative conceptions of memory have, of course, been interested in recall and retrieval. It is the explicit attempt to distinguish storage and retrieval, using a conceptual language borrowed from computer technology, that characterizes information-processing approaches. Retrieval mechanisms, the business of getting things out of storage, takes on special importance for those psychologists who emphasize information-processing approaches. The focus is more on retrieval than on storage with these approaches because retrieval mechanisms are viewed as the key to unlocking memory.

It is beyond the scope of this book to do more than briefly sketch the major differences in emphasis between these two approaches. Both conceptual approaches are in a state of revision and new developments are rapidly occurring. Ultimately, some of the features of stimulus-response associationistic approaches may be translatable into information-processing approaches and vice versa. For our purposes it is important to note that these two approaches represent somewhat different ways of thinking about memory and consequently have led to different kinds of research in memory. Both approaches have, of course, advanced our understanding of memory.

Ways to Measure Memory

There are many ways in which memory can be measured. As we shall see, these different measures tap different aspects of memory processes, and the amount of retention obtained can readily depend upon the particular method of measurement. Therefore, we cannot talk about the method for measuring memory, but rather of various methods which reflect different features of the process. There are four basic methods: *recall, recognition, savings,* and *reaction time.*

Recall

A straightforward way of measuring what is retained is the recall procedure. *In recall, you are required to demonstrate what you have learned by producing the correct response(s).* Being able to produce your telephone number, the date of your birth, and a friend's name are obvious instances of recall. Answering questions on an essay examination is another instance of recall.

There is a further distinction, that of *free* and *aided* recall. Free recall simply requires that you produce the items learned in any particular order. We have already discussed this procedure in chapter 3 on verbal learning. In that chapter we noted that you are presented a series of verbal units, one at a time, and required to recall the items in any order. Free recall, therefore, emphasizes simple availability of responses, without any physical cues for recall present. In contrast, aided recall provides some sort of *contextual stimulus* to which you must respond. For example, recall in serial learning can be cued by the previous item, whereas recall in paired associate learning is cued by the stimulus terms.

Instances of free and aided recall are common in everyday experience. Recalling a list of all your relatives or close friends without their being present would be an instance of free recall. In turn, recalling the names of people sitting close to you in a class while both you and they are present in the class is an instance of aided (cued) recall. The basic difference is that aided recall has some external stimulus present to cue the response which is not present in free recall.

Humans almost inevitably create their own cues in a free recall situation. We noted this process in our earlier discussion of organizational processes in learning. The categorization of events seen in free recall is an instance in which we create our own cues for recall. Similarly, subjective organization is another instance.

In a number of cases, free recall shows retention superior to that of aided recall. Even though we may be presented stimuli to cue our responses, we may perform poorer than in simple free recall where no physical cues are present. In this case, we are simply better off to create our own cues for recall than to use those presented by the experimenter.

The recall method is also used in the study of memory for visual forms and patterns. In this instance, the subject is shown some form or pattern and is later asked to *reproduce* (draw) it as faithfully as possible. For example, the subject may be shown various geometric designs and then be required to draw the designs on subsequent trials. This variation of the recall method, called *reproduction,* has received extensive use in studies of perceptual memory and learning. One difficulty with this procedure is the problem of judging what a subject has actually drawn and scoring the drawing in a quantitative and objective fashion.

A principal feature of the recall method is that it can be relatively insensitive compared with other methods of measurement. For example, the fact that you are unable to recall a list of terms, say, in biology doesn't mean that there is no effect as a result of memorizing a list of biological terms. All of us have had experiences in which although we were unable to recall certain terms we could still correctly *recognize* them. Let us therefore consider a second method of measuring memory, recognition.

Recognition

A recognition test requires you to select items previously experienced or learned and to reject other items which are called distractor or filler items. As we noted earlier, there are two basic types of recognition tests: (1) *single-item* procedure and (2) *multiple-item* procedure. The multiple-item procedure is most common, and we will therefore consider it first.

In the *multiple-item* procedure you are shown each item learned along with one or more distractor items. If you are *required* to select one of the items in a recognition test, the procedure is called *forced choice*. This is usually done because of the advantage gained in controlling for possible differences in response bias. For example, with three choices the likelihood of getting the correct answer just by chance is one out of three. Chance probability assumes, however, that all three choices are on the average equally likely. It is usually not the case that all choices are equally likely, principally because you may know enough to eliminate at least one of the incorrect alternatives. Indeed, it is good practice when taking multiple-choice tests to eliminate those items which you know or suspect are clearly wrong and then make your selection among the remaining items, especially if the question is a difficult one.

The typical lineup in a police examination is an instance of a multiple-choice recognition procedure. A suspect is lined up with several other people, all of whom are somewhat similar in appearance. Eyewitnesses to the alleged crime are then asked to identify the suspect. The basic assumption underlying this procedure, as well as all recognition tests of this kind, is that if an item (in this case a person) is remembered it can be recognized when placed among several alternatives. On the other hand, if an item is not remembered, it can then be recognized correctly no better than by chance in the long run.

With the *single-item* procedure, each item is shown one at a time and you are asked to say "old" or "new" to each item. Some of the items are old, that is, previously experienced, and some are new. Sometimes the subject may instead be asked to say "yes" or "no," with yes indicating that he has experienced the item during some previous training session and no that he has not. Therefore, the single-item procedure is sometimes referred to as the *yes-no* procedure.

Motivational Factors and Biases in Recognition Memory

Use of a single-item recognition procedure requires an awareness of possible response biases such as a person's tendency to respond with old irrespective of the specific stimulus items presented. Assume, for example, that you are shown a series of stimuli such as advertisements from popular magazines and asked to remember them. Later you are given a recognition test in which the old items are shown singly mixed with new items. Now imagine that the instructions further state that every time you say "old" and are correct you earn one dollar. Under these circumstances you would have a strong tendency to say "old" and in fact would frequently do so even when you suspected that the items were actually new ones. You would, therefore, be unlikely to miss any of the *truly* old items, but at the same time you would tend to identify incorrectly many new items as old. Calling a new item old is known as a false alarm. This is simply to say that although you would tend to make a large number of correct recognitions (saying "old" to old stimuli), you would also tend to make many false-positives (saying "old" to new stimuli). The point is quite simple: *Motivational-incentive conditions do affect our response biases in recognition memory experiments.* And a strong bias to say "yes" in a single-item test will lead to a high correct recognition score, but can be quite misleading as an estimate of our memory.

Consider a second alternative in our illustrative experiment. If the instructions indicated that every time you said "old" and were incorrect it would cost you two dollars you would now become very conservative in making old judgments. You will say "old" less frequently and tend to reserve that response for items you are absolutely certain are old. In this case, you will miss a number of old items, but will rarely tend to identify incorrectly new items as old. The important thing to note is that your total correct recognition score, the number of truly old items called old, will be considerably different under these two alternatives, despite the fact that your memory for the items is exactly the same.

It should now be clear why consideration of response biases are necessary when recognition is used to measure memory. Forced-choice procedures automatically control for bias by requiring the subject to respond on each trial. In contrast, yes-no procedures are quite subject to bias. Some individuals may be very cautious and conservative, saying "yes" only when very sure. Others may be more liberal, saying "yes" to an item if they think that it's reasonably familiar. Consider the most extreme possibility: If you said "yes" to *all* stimuli presented in a yes-no recognition test, your correct recognition score would be perfect, but *only* because your bias was to say "yes" on every trial.

The procedures for controlling response bias in yes-no recognition tests are beyond the scope of this book. They are derived from signal-detection theory and allow separation of effects caused by decision processes, such as biases, from effects due to memory itself. For our purposes we must remember that any recognition score in a yes-no recognition test is a joint result of both our bias, or criterion for making a yes-no decision, on the one hand and our true memory of the item on the other.

Performance in multiple-item recognition tests depends upon the *number* of items in the test and upon the *relationship* between the correct item and the set of distractors. A two-item recognition test is quite easy because chance correct recognition on any item is one-half. As we increase the number of items, recognition performance decreases. Similarly, the more similar the distractor items are to the correct item, the more difficult recognition will be.

Recall and Recognition Compared

As we have noted, recognition measures usually show greater evidence for retention than do recall measures. Successful recall requires some degree of response learning since the material must be produced, not just identified. Response learning is not necessary for recognition since the correct item is always presented in the test along with distractor items. On the other hand, discrimination among items is important in recognition, especially if the items are very similar. Indeed, if we markedly increase the similarity between the distractor items and the correct items, recognition performance will then be about the same as recall performance.

Savings

The third major method is savings. The savings method can be a more sensitive method than recall because it may show some evidence for retention when none is obtained with recall. *With the savings method you first learn some task to a given criterion and subsequently relearn the task.* This procedure permits comparison of original learning and relearning in terms of a savings score based upon, for example, the number of trials or amount of time required to learn the two tasks. A measure of retention in terms of the percent saved is shown by the formula:

$$\text{Percent Saved} = \frac{\text{\# of trials to learn}-\text{\# of trials to relearn}}{\text{Number of trials to learn}} \times 100$$

For example, if you require 30 trials to learn a list of trigrams and only 15 trials to relearn the list, a savings of 50 percent is obtained. Even if the list is relearned in just one less trial, some savings would be shown.

Many of us have experienced a savings effect in memory. We note first that we are unable to recall something that we have previously learned, yet if we set about relearning it we are frequently surprised at how quickly we can pick up the material we thought we had forgotten. Although we are unable to recall the material, some residue is present enabling us to quickly relearn the material.

An impressive demonstration of the sensitivity of the savings method was shown by the psychologist Harold Burtt. Burtt read passages of Greek to a child from age fifteen months to three years. The child was read three passages daily consisting of twenty lines of iambic hexameter which were read to the child for ninety days, followed by another set of passages for ninety days more, and so on, until the child was three years of age. The child received no further reading or training in Greek until he was eight years old. At this time Burtt had the child learn the original Greek passages and compared his performance with the learning of presumably equivalent passages which the child had not experienced. The child learned the original passages faster, showing a thirty percent savings at age eight years, but no savings when he was later tested at age eighteen years. Since we have no measure of original learning in this experiment, we are unable to say much about what was actually learned in the first place. What is clear is that something was retained from this early experience that benefited the child in later relearning the material.

These findings suggest one possible implication for education. Although you may not recall certain things you have learned in school unless you use them, you can rapidly relearn them if the need arises.

Reaction Time

A measure which has become increasingly important in recent years is reaction time. Reaction time can be a very useful measure because it can be assumed that the various processes in memory require some time to perform. Thus the speed with which certain memory tasks are carried out is thought to reflect their difficulty and/or complexity. For instance, the length of time it takes you to recall the answer to the question, What did you eat for breakfast a week ago? as compared to the question, What did you eat for breakfast yesterday? can presumably reflect differences in the processes of retrieving information from long-term memory.

The usual procedure in studies using reaction time is to test for recognition or recall of well-memorized information and measure the time which elapses between presentation of the test item and the subject's response. One procedure developed by Saul Sternberg uses reaction time to study retrieval processes in memory. Subjects are given short lists of digits ranging from 1 to six and asked to remember them; thus the items are well within the subject's memory span. The subject is then presented with a test digit and asked to indicate whether the digit is a member of the original set presented. The time it takes the subject to respond is the measure taken.

Sternberg was interested in the relation between the subjects' time to respond when presented a test item as a function of the size of the memory set. Keep in mind that the number of digits in the memory set varied from trial to trial. What Sternberg found was a linear increase in reaction time as a function of size of the memory set. With each added digit in the memory set, the subjects' reaction time increased by about 38 milliseconds (38 thousandths of a second). This simply means that it took subjects 38 milliseconds longer to decide whether the test digit was in the memory set for each additional digit that was added to the memory set. This *linear* increase in reaction time suggests that the processing of information in memory scanning is a *serial* process, that is, we scan items in memory one at a time in the search for stored information. The alternative to serial processing is *parallel* processing in which we scan items in memory simultaneously. We do process information in parallel as in reading where we do not process each word in a letter-by-letter fashion. However, in the memory-scanning task our processing is serial.

Stages of Memory Storage

Let us now turn our attention to some of the fundamental stages of memory storage. Memory is not a single process but is composed of several processes and stages. We have already indicated that an important distinction exists between *storage* and *retrieval* processes. We shall now examine the stages in storing information in memory.

The process by which information is stored is currently viewed as consisting of three stages. These stages are (1) *sensory* or iconic memory, (2) *short-term* memory, and (3) *long-term* memory. These stages or phases differ in terms of what gets processed into memory. Some memory theorists contend that each stage operates in accord with different laws or principles and, therefore, occupies a different storage system. Other theorists, however, regard at least short-term and long-term memory as more or less continuous processes. Moreover, since there is some evidence that short-term and long-term memory are affected by the same variables, the notion of a continuum between the two stages, as distinct from being separate systems, is supported. We may bypass this dispute, however, and turn our attention to the three main phases of memory storage. Let us first consider sensory memory.

Sensory Memory

A stimulus continues to produce its effect upon us even when the external stimulus, such as a light or sound, is terminated. For example, if you stare at a light bulb, you will have an afterimage of the bulb for a few seconds after the light has been turned off. This persistence of the stimulus in the individual following removal of the external stimulus is called the *stimulus trace*. The trace is simply a hypothetical notion to account for the persistence of stimulation after removal or termination of the external stimulus.

Sensory memory refers to this quite brief period in which the stimulus trace persists. At this stage of memory the information that is stored is simply some sensory representation of the external stimuli that have impinged upon our receptors. This memory is sometimes called *iconic,* referring to its visual character. Obviously, the afterimage of a light disappears after a very brief period; similarly, when you press your skin you can feel the sensation fade after you remove the source of pressure.

During the sensory stage we take in far more information than we can efficiently process. Thus sensory memory is a large-capacity storage system where information is held for only a brief period of time. We can attend to only a fraction of the total amount of information received in this system. This stage represents the domain where we shift subtly from perception to memory. If sensory memory appears to be more a perceptual process than a memory process, it is only because memory begins with the reception of information which is perception itself.

Information in sensory memory decays extremely fast. Our best estimates indicate that verbal or pictorial information is retained clearly in sensory memory for less than a second, after which most of it becomes unavailable for report. In addition, the presentation of a new stimulus can erase information that is momentarily present in sensory memory. Finally, the fraction of information that we attend to and select for further processing goes to the next phase, the short-term memory system.

Figure 6 shows the basic components of the three-stage memory system. The boxes represent the storage system and the arrows represent the flow of information from various places. Information from the environment first enters the sensory information store where unless it is transferred it decays extremely fast. From this store information can go to the short-term store where it is normally maintained for a brief period, say 15 to 20 seconds, unless it enters the *rehearsal buffer,* a special function of the short-term system. Information in the rehearsal buffer does not decay, but can be maintained indefinitely by the process of rehearsal. Rehearsal at a simple level means simply the repeating of information to yourself. The last component is the long-term store where information is more or less permanently available to us. As the arrows indicate, information goes from the short-term store to the long-term store, and we may retrieve information in our long-term store for use in our working memory.

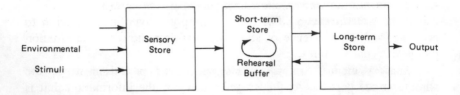

Figure 6. A schematic view of the memory system and flow of information in the system.

Short-Term Memory

How often have you looked up a number in the telephone book only to forget it by the time you start to dial the number? If you have an opportunity to rehearse the number, you usually can retain it. Without opportunity for rehearsal you are almost sure to forget the number if you fail to dial within a few seconds. This can happen if, for example, you look up the number and are then interrupted by someone before you can dial the number. This rapid loss in memory during this short period pertains to the short-term memory stage.

If information in short-term memory can be rehearsed or processed in some manner, it can then be transferred to long-term memory, a relatively permanent system. The basic difference between short- and long-term memory is that short-term memory is a small-capacity system lasting a very brief period in which information has the opportunity to be processed, whereas long-term memory is a large-capacity storage system containing information that is relatively permanent.

An important feature of short-term memory is that it is a limited-capacity system. We can process only about seven items of information at one time. In other words, our memory span is limited to about seven items or bits of information. For example, if I read aloud a series of digits in random order and ask you to repeat them, you can on the average correctly repeat up to about seven numbers.

It is obvious, however, that on some occasions you can remember much more than seven items of information. In the digit span test you may be able to chunk or group the numbers so that you can recall many more than seven. Nevertheless, your recall is now limited to about seven chunks of information. The principle still holds, but the *unit* of information has now shifted from a single item to a chunk.

This limit on how much we can process in short-term memory makes it important that we devise coding and organizational strategies for storing information. Without skills in coding things into categories, the amount of information that can be processed is quite limited. Indeed, a principal feature of people who have good memories is their capacity to code and organize information into larger chunks, enabling a much larger storage of information.

During short-term memory, information is held for a brief period. The function of short-term memory is to hold information for sufficient time so that it can be used, as in dialing a telephone number, or rehearsed and ultimately transferred into long-term storage. If it is not rehearsed or processed in some fashion, it will drop out of short-term memory. In this manner useless information does not remain in the system.

The rapid forgetting characteristically seen in short-term memory was dramatically illustrated in an experiment by Lloyd Peterson and Margaret Peterson. A CVC (consonant-vowel-consonant) trigram was read to the subject who was then instructed to count backward by threes from some predetermined number. Counting backward served to prevent rehearsal of the trigram. Subjects were tested over retention intervals ranging from 3 to 18 seconds. Despite the extraordinary short intervals used, the subjects showed a striking decline in memory, with retention being less than ten percent after 18 seconds. This finding is especially significant when it is considered that the verbal items were well within the memory span of the subjects. More generally, this rapid forgetting over 20-to-30-second intervals characterizes short-term memory.

Long-Term Memory

By rehearsing items, then, we can process information sufficiently so that it enters long-term memory. But simple rehearsal in the form of maintaining the information is probably insufficient for transfer to long-term memory. What appears to be important is *elaborative rehearsal* which involves creating elaborate codes out of the information using imagery and coding strategies so as to create a more stable set of codes. The distinction between short-term and long-term memory is not marked by a sharp, clear temporal division. Long-term memory deals with information that has entered a more permanent storage system. We must emphasize that memory in this system is relatively permanent, which is to hedge somewhat on the meaning of permanence. What is meant is that in contrast to short-term memory, where the information is present for only a fleeting period, information in long-term memory is much more accessible for a longer period of time. Some of this information is always accessible such as, for example, your mother's and father's name. Other information, such as the name of your first grade teacher, may be accessible only part of the time.

Long-term memory is not some passive process in which information taken in just sits there waiting to be retrieved when needed. Rather, information in long-term memory is continually being organized in new ways. As we learn new events, old events acquire new perspective.

The distinction between short- and long-term memory does not necessarily imply that they have different *anatomical* or physiological loci. Although some memory theorists believe that the two storage systems are located in different parts of the brain, the evidence for this kind of difference has not been unequivocally shown. B. Milner has reported an interesting case history of a brain-damaged patient with lesions in the hippocampus. The patient's immediate and long-term memory appeared to be quite normal. The patient was unable, however, to form *new* long-term memory traces, although he could perform normally on intelligence tests and other tests of brief memory. He could converse normally about topics for a brief period, but could not recall the topic of conversation for any long period of time. This kind of finding has led some memory theorists to conclude that the *loci* of the two memory systems are different; however, this type of finding does not *require* that they be regarded as systems having physically different loci. It could be that their locus is the same, but that long-term memory requires additional processes in that particular locus.

For purposes of convenience we have described memory as consisting of three different functional systems. It is not, however, necessary to think of these systems as actually separate. Indeed, we can most easily regard the memory system as continuous rather than as discrete, with information flowing continuously from one stage to another. Whether our memory system is continuous or composed of discrete stages was until quite recently an issue of much theoretical debate. The basic issue was whether short-term and long-term memory represent two distinct memory systems or, alternatively, whether they represent a continuum which functions according to the same principles. Recently, a useful way of resolving the issue of a dual storage system versus a single storage system has been proposed by Fergus Craik and Robert Lockhart in terms of a levels-of-processing approach.

Levels of Processing

The levels-of-processing approach does not require the assumption of separate storage systems in memory. The essence of this approach is that the learning of anything requires a series of processing stages which vary along a continuum of depth. The basic idea is that memory is determined by the degree or *depth* with which the information is analyzed. In the initial stages of perceptual processing stimuli are analyzed for their gross physical features such as lines, contours, and angles. At the next level of processing, information is stored in memory and the new information is matched against existing stored representation. This level is the recognition process. After a stimulus is recognized it is further processed by association and integrated with the existing information stored in long-term memory. This final stage requires that the information be organized into semantic memory, that is, memory for words and meaningful information. Thus the entire process of placing information in memory involves a series of stages in which the information is processed at progressively greater depths.

Let us consider how the levels-of-processing approach applies when you are presented with a single word such as CAR. At a superficial perceptual level you might note that the first letter is curved, the second is composed of straight lines, and the third combines both features. You might also note that the word contains three letters—a vowel between two consonants. At a somewhat deeper level you might note that the word rhymes with *bar, far,* and *tar.* At an even deeper level you would process the meaning of the word ("vehicle") and its relation to other information in memory (it makes you think of a specific car, going to work, taking a vacation, etc.). Thus the processing of information becomes progressively deeper as orthographic, lexical, acoustic, and semantic features are processed.

A main advantage of the levels-of-processing approach is that it can resolve the controversy between single and dual or multistage conceptions of memory. By adopting the levels of processing approach, a separate-stage conception of memory is unnecessary to account for the discrepancies in processing between the three stages described earlier. The three stages can now be seen as differing in the level at which information is processed, and the depth at which information is processed is what determines how well it is remembered.

Memory Processes

We noted earlier that memory involves three distinct but interdependent processes: encoding, storage, and retrieval. The process of encoding transforms information in the form of physical energy from the environment to some state suitable for memory storage. Storage is the maintenance of information over time, and retrieval refers to the means by which we access and use information in memory. In this section we shall examine encoding and retrieval in greater detail.

Encoding

We are faced daily with situations which require us to convert information into a form that is meaningful and easily remembered. This conversion or transformation requires that the information be encoded into a form which is compatible with the structure of memory. Examples of encoding operations include elaborating upon the information presented. For instance, upon hearing a story or joke you might embellish it in order to make it more meaningful or interesting. Similarly, when shown pictorial material you might attempt to construct a coherent story about the pictures. Encoding may also involve reducing information to some simpler form or state. For instance, students frequently underline key concepts and principles in a text. Similarly, our memory for everyday conversation may contain little more than the gist of the conversation plus the few details we select as important.

Selective Attention and Encoding

We simply do not encode all features of the environment. For example, ultraviolet waves exceed the limits of our visual receptors and are thus not detected. Other stimuli are potentially detectable, but we may fail to perceive them because we are simply not attending. The ability to focus selectively on some part of the environment while ignoring other aspects, called *selective attention,* is an important part of the process of encoding.

Selective attention is easily illustrated by what is known as the cocktail party phenomenon. Imagine yourself at a crowded cocktail party where your ears are bombarded with a vast array of stimulation, much of it extraneous. Besides the conversation in which you are engaged, you hear the sounds of other guests, loud laughter, music, and even the crunch of potato chips. Although it may appear that you hear and encode all extraneous stimulation, the fact is that the total amount of information almost always exceeds your processing capacity, and thus you must *select* what will be processed and what will be ignored. If, by chance, you suddenly hear your own name coming from another conversational group you may quickly attend to this conversation, trying to understand what is being said. But in the process you lose track of the immediate conversation in which you are engaged. Thus selective attention allows you to encode one conversation, but at the expense of another.

Another feature of encoding is that it may vary from time to time and from place to place. The basic idea is that our encoding of environmental stimuli is not necessarily identical on subsequent presentations of the stimuli. For instance, suppose you are standing in the checkout line of a crowded grocery store waiting your turn. You may note the person in front of you, but pay little attention if the person is a stranger. On the other hand, if the person is unable to pay for the large amount of groceries in his cart and thus delays your purchase, then you may perceive and encode the stranger in a quite different fashion. This illustrates the concept of *encoding variability* which notes that the same nominal stimuli may be encoded differently on different occasions.

Memory Codes

The importance of encoding is that it allows us to reduce information to some manageable state and/or to make the information sufficiently meaningful for storage purposes. Another area of interest is the nature of the memory code itself, that is, the nature of the stored representation in memory. Psychologists have identified at least four types of memory codes: image codes, verbal codes, symbolic codes, and motor codes.

One type of code is the *image* code in which the stored representation bears close or identical correspondence to the actual physical event or object perceived. Information in the sensory-information store is thought to be held in the form of image codes. Similarly, visual pattern information such as a face, landscape, picture, and the like, is thought to be held in an imagelike form. Those rare individuals who possess "photographic memory" are thought to hold visual image representations in memory.

A second type of code is the *verbal* or verbal-name code. We can encode the letter *A* as an image, but we may also encode it as a name. The letter *A* can appear in a variety of ways, all of which appear to mean the same thing. Whether you see *A, a,* or a, you encode them as the same letter because they refer to the same concept. Similarly, the word *car* is representative of a large number of vehicles varying in size, features, cost, and so forth. Thus verbal-name codes are important because they allow us to treat a variety of instances as a single concept.

Related to verbal-name codes are *symbolic* codes, the third type of memory code, in which an abstract word or symbol stands for some event. The peace symbol is an instance of an event which is represented in symbolic fashion.

Finally it is believed that our actions get represented in the form of *motor* codes. Everyday skilled acts such as tying your shoes, driving a car, unlocking a door, and so forth, are thought to be represented in the form of motor codes.

Retrieval

The normal person has a vast amount of information stored in memory. Indeed, it is staggering to think of the virtually limitless capacity of our memory which holds information ranging from the trivial to the vitally important. Despite the enormous amount of information which may be stored in our long-term memory, our ability to *access* this information is limited. Consider the party game called Trivia in which players are asked a number of questions dealing with trivial facts such as What is the name of Jack Benny's wife? and What is the name of Jack Benny's butler? and What kind of car did Jack Benny drive? (The answers are Mary, Rochester, and a Maxwell, respectively.) Sometimes we are amazed at our ability to recall such information with extreme ease. On other occasions we have great difficulty in recalling any fact and sit in silence. In many instances we may recognize the correct answer only after someone else has recalled it. Sometimes we may recall the first letter of the name (we know the word begins with an *m*), but we block on recalling the rest. The word is, as we say, on the tip of our tongue. Sometimes recall of the first letter then aids us in eventually recalling the rest of the letters of a particular word. All of these steps are part of the process of *retrieval,* which is the process of searching and locating information in memory.

Retrieval From the Various Stores

The process of retrieval from the sensory-information store is rather direct and automatic. Our best evidence indicates that information in sensory memory is "read" directly from the store. We apparently scan the image before it fades from memory. For instance, tennis players sometimes scan their image of where a ball hits the court to decide whether the ball is in or out. Instead of calling a ball in or out on the basis of direct visual experience, the player may scan his image and then call the shot.

Retrieval from short-term memory involves scanning information that is briefly held in memory. Search in this store is generally referred to as memory scan. Saul Sternberg has conducted studies of memory scanning which suggest that we can scan items such as digits at a rate of twenty-five to thirty items per second. Search in short-term memory is a rather direct process because the contents of short-term memory are limited and at a high level of availability, especially if they have been rehearsed.

Retrieval in long-term memory represents the most interesting aspect of retrieval because of the enormous amount of information stored. Unlike sensory or short-term memory the information is frequently not in immediate consciousness, nor is it limited to just a few items. We can generally distinguish several distinct levels in the retrieval of information in long-term memory. Here, the process of retrieval is not so automatic and can indeed require a great deal of effort.

At one level is a wide-ranging search for information relevant to some specific query. The search is usually an intelligent one, that is, an orderly and systematic tracing of clues that eventually leads to the desired information rather than a random sorting through the contents of long-term memory. For instance, if asked "Where did you have dinner four evenings ago?" you begin with your most recent dinner and work backward to the evening in question. This first level may, however, be preceded by a more general test or verification process in which you decide whether to search. If asked "Where did Abraham Lincoln dine four evenings ago?" you seem to know that the requested information is not in memory and that it is not a legitimate query. Many queries may lead to an I-don't-know response, but if sufficient incentive is provided you may attempt to dredge up the answer.

If the preliminary decision is *go,* that is, if you decide to retrieve, then the first level is accomplished. An organized search for the appropriate information can then begin. At first the organized effort of retrieval is directed at obtaining a general picture or scenario. Then a great deal of more specific information may be recalled; some of this specific information may be relevant to the query and some information may be only remotely related to the query. For example, consider the question, "What did you do for recreation three days ago?" At first you simply note that three days ago was Saturday and that you played four sets of tennis that afternoon. You then recall that you played tennis with your best friend, that you won three of the four sets, and that there was only one disagreement about scoring. After tennis you had a beer and then you went to dinner and so on.

The example shows that search of a long-term memory involves at least two stages. At the first level the search is to get a general picture, to locate the major event being queried, and you may also reject unlikely or implausible events. At this stage the broad episode is recalled. At the second stage additional information surrounding the episode is recalled and progressively greater detail begins to appear.

Working Memory

After information has been located by a search of long-term memory it must be gathered together and organized in some form, verified, and retained briefly before it can be emitted. This process of assembling and organizing the information takes place in what is called working memory. Missing or incomplete information may be noted and if it is important added information may be filled in, in order to create a reasonably coherent memory. Thus working memory is an active system where information is sifted, organized, and prepared for recall. Its function is to organize and keep information extracted from long-term memory until an appropriate response to the query which stimulated the search can be emitted.

Practice in Retrieval

We have already noted that our failure to recall some event does not necessarily mean that it isn't in storage. Events may clearly be stored in memory despite that fact that we are unable to recall the information. The fact that you can recognize certain events that you simultaneously are unable to recall indicates that things can be in storage even though you are unable to get at them.

A particularly frustrating event is to recall the answer to a test question after you have left the classroom, given that you blanked the question during the test. Most of you have probably had a correct answer pop into your awareness after you've handed in a test. Such situations further attest to the fact that information may actually be in storage, but that momentarily be unable to be retrieved.

One of the principal reasons that retrieval processes may fail even though information is in storage, is that you have failed *to practice* the task of retrieving information, that is, you have failed to rehearse the business of retrieval. What this means from a practical standpoint is that much of your study effort should be devoted to formulating and answering questions. Moreover, if the tests require that you write answers, your study habits should emphasize composing written answers, at least at a schematic level, to questions you are likely to be asked. Similarly, if you are to give an oral presentation, direct practice in giving your talk to a small group of friends is good practice. By requiring yourself to practice directly the very behaviors or kinds of behaviors required by the test situation, you rehearse the appropriate retrieval process.

Retrieval Depends Upon Organized Storage

The business of retrieving information from memory is not, of course, independent of how you store it. Obviously, if information is stored in an organized and systematic fashion, it has a better chance to be retrieved. For example, consider the fact that test questions sometimes require you to compare and contrast several theories on, say, several issues. If you have studied each theory as an isolated event, without thinking of the relationship between them, then the test will be difficult. If on the other hand you have actually compared each of the particular theories with respect to the important issues, perhaps by constructing a chart with issues across the top and theories down the side, you will then have stored the information in a much more systematic and organized fashion. Thus we see that efficient, orderly storage is necessary for good recall.

We have already seen in an earlier chapter how organizational processes influence our ability to recall materials. We noted that humans may organize materials in a number of ways as evidenced by the phenomena of associative clustering, category clustering, and subjective organization when no objective basis for organizing the materials is present. In both associative and category clustering, humans are able to use the structure inherent in the material to their advantage. This can occur in two ways: material that has some inherent structure is easier to store in memory, and well-organized material aids the retrieval process in the sense that it has a better chance to be retrieved.

Retrieval Cues

Effective retrieval depends upon the presence of retrieval cues. Earlier we distinguished between cued and free recall, noting that cued recall referred to recall in the presence of some physical stimulus, whereas free recall did not have an identifiable physical stimulus. In the most strict sense, however, all recall is cued recall. Free recall is cued by events that we are not always able to identify. At present, however, we know relatively little about the effectiveness of retrieval cues. One thing is clear: the retrieval cues, if they are to be helpful in the sense of helping us recall information that we otherwise could not recall, must be *relevant* to the way in which we stored the information in the first place. For example, if a test question asks you to compare three theories on four issues, and you had constructed a chart comparing these theories on these four issues, then the retrieval cues in the question would be directly relevant to your organized storage style.

A simple illustration of the importance of retrieval cues can be seen as follows: Suppose that a list of categorized materials is learned by a group of subjects. These categories might include animals, vegetables, minerals, plants, and so forth. Then, half of the subjects are given a free-recall test in which they are given the category labels. The remaining half is instructed to recall as many words as possible, but are not shown the retrieval cues. The first group will of course recall more words than the second group. The importance of retrieval cues is probably recognized implicitly by many instructors when they note that the way a question is written can provide the student with a good deal of information about the answer. Indeed, the student who reads a question carefully can often use informative features of the question to help cue his recall.

In summary, the long-term memory system is not simply a dumping ground of facts arranged in some random fashion. We are constantly shifting, organizing, and reorganizing our memory storage, particularly when new information is stored. If we are to store information efficiently, it must be effectively organized in some fashion. The particular organization is unique to each individual and is a result of his own individual learning history. Finally, organized, systematic storage is an important key to good recall.

Summary

In this chapter we have described some of the major characteristics of memory. The study of memory involves encoding, storage, and retrieval processes. Psychologists have used two conceptual approaches in analyzing memory, one stemming from stimulus-response associationism and the other from information-processing conceptions. Although the latter approach adopts a language derived from computer technology, the approaches are not fully exclusive or necessarily conflicting.

The measurement of retention involves the four basic methods of recall, recognition, savings, and reaction time. Recall requires the production of responses, recognition requires selection of alternatives, and savings requires relearning. Recall is usually more difficult than recognition because recall requires response learning. Recognition memory is easily influenced by motivational or incentive factors and response biases.

The basic stages of memory are sensory memory, short-term memory, and long-term memory. Sensory memory refers to the very short period in which some sensory representation of a stimulus persists after termination of the external stimulus. Short-term memory is the period in which information is stored long enough so that if it is rehearsed it may be transferred to long-term storage. If the material is not rehearsed, it will drop out of short-term memory. In long-term memory, information enters a relatively permanent storage system. Whether short-term and long-term memory represent different storage systems is thought to be resolved by the levels-of-processing approach.

Effective retrieval of information in memory depends upon organized storage. Retrieval cues aid recall, especially if the cues are relevant to the way in which the information was stored. The importance of practice in retrieval was emphasized.

Multiple-Choice Items: Memory I: The Processing of Information

1. The information-processing approach to memory views memory as a complex system in which
   a. forgetting is due to interference
   b. information flows through the various components
   c. the basic unit of information is the association
   d. all information stored is ultimately forgotten

2. If after witnessing a robbery you are asked to draw the suspect's face, your task is one of
   a. recognition
   b. recall
   c. reaction time
   d. savings

3. In a recognition memory task you are shown old stimuli (correct) and new stimuli (lures), and you may respond "yes" or "no" in making a recognition. If you respond yes to a new stimulus, this would be making a
   a. correct recognition, or hit
   b. correct rejection
   c. false alarm
   d. false rejection of an old stimulus

4. If 27 trials are required to learn a task but only 9 trials to relearn the task a week later, your savings score would be
   a. 33 percent
   b. 27 percent
   c. 9 percent
   d. 67 percent

5. The sensory memory system is
   a. large-capacity system
   b. not subject to decay
   c. equivalent to working memory
   d. uninfluenced by attention

6. Short-term memory is best regarded as
   a. uninfluenced by rehearsal
   b. representing external stimulation with high fidelity
   c. a system for forming associations
   d. a limited-capacity system

7. Human information processing is limited to about seven pieces of information. The fact that we can remember more than seven items attests to the importance of
   a. attention
   b. chunking

       c.   retrieval

       d.   associations

8.   In order for information to be transferred to long-term memory it must

       a.   be rehearsed

       b.   receive elaborative rehearsal

       c.   be attended

       d.   be perceived

9.   The idea of levels of processing basically means that

       a.   humans will process unattended information

       b.   we ignore superficial physical features of stimuli and process the more meaningful or semantic information

       c.   we ignore the semantic aspects of information and process primarily the physical features

       d.   the depth at which information is processed determines how well it is remembered

10.   In driving on a long trip you may find yourself reading the motel signs at the end of the day with great interest while ignoring other signs. This illustrates the process of

       a.   selective attention

       b.   retrieval

       c.   levels of processing

       d.   encoding variability

11.   Imagine yourself trying to recall the name of someone at a party whom you met last week. You are sure that you know the person and that her first name begins with a *J*, but you simply can't recall her name. This process illustrates a failure of

       a.   retrieval

       b.   attention

       c.   association

       d.   processing

12.   Working memory is concerned with

       a.   the large-capacity feature of sensory memory

       b.   the depth of processing

       c.   imagery

       d.   assembling and organizing information

13.   In order to emphasize retrieval processes in preparation for a test, your study habits should include

       a.   careful rereading of the text

       b.   underlining key ideas in the text

       c.   practice in answering questions likely to be asked

       d.   reading another text covering the same material

True-False Items: Memory I:
The Processing of Information

F 1. Once information is stored in memory it can be readily recalled.

T 2. If asked to recall the names of all the states in the United States, you would probably tend to recall them in clusters based on geographic regions (e.g., Maine, Vermont, New Hampshire) or on size or population (e.g., California, New York, Pennsylvania, Texas). This clustering of recall is regarded as evidence for organizational processes in memory.

F 3. Reproducing a cross-sectional drawing of some object such as a leaf structure is an instance of recognition.

T 4. The typical multiple-choice examination is an instance of the recognition method.

T 5. A forced-choice recognition procedure controls for possible differences in response bias.

F 6. Two people are shown a set of twenty advertisements, each for a brief period of time. Then they are shown these advertisements, one at a time, mixed in with eighty new advertisements and asked to correctly recognize the old items. Individual A correctly recognizes all twenty items, while B correctly recognizes only twelve items. A has a better recognition memory than B.

T. 7. Humans can typically hold about seven bits (units) of information at one time in short-term memory.

F 8. The rehearsal buffer is located in the sensory information store.

T 9. One advantage of the levels of processing approach is that it becomes unnecessary to view memory as consisting of separate storage systems.

F 10. Retrieval in long-term memory is rather direct and automatic.

F 11. We always encode the identical nominal stimulus in the same way on successive occasions.

F 12. The way we organize information is unrelated to our ability to retrieve information.

Discussion Items: Memory I:
The Processing of Information

1. What are the basic characteristics of the information processing approach to memory?

2. A real-life lineup or photographic array used by police to identify criminals is a type of recognition test. How would you go about constructing a photographic array in order to have a good test? What factors might reduce the usefulness or validity of the test?

3.   Explain how a person's biases might affect performance in a recognition test.

4.   How does the levels-of-processing approach to memory permit us to view the memory system as essentially continuous?

5.   Cite several instances of selective attention in your everyday experiences. How does selective attention affect what you might remember from an ordinary conversation? from a classroom lecture?

6.   Cite one or two instances of your failure to retrieve important information. How might you systematically go about retrieving some important piece of information from long-term memory?

Multiple-Choice Answers: Memory I: The Processing of Information

1.   (b)   Information flows through the basic components of the memory system, beginning with the sensory-information store, then to the short-term system, and finally, to long-term memory.

2.   (b)   Drawing a face is an instance of recall because you must reproduce the information.

3.   (c)   When you say "yes" to a new stimulus, you have falsely recognized that stimulus, and your response is called a false alarm.

4.   (d)   Your savings score is 67 percent. In this example 27−9/27 = 18/27 = 67%.

5.   (a)   The sensory memory system is a large-capacity system because we take in far more information than we actually process.

6.   (d)   Short-term memory is a limited-capacity system because it can process only a small amount of information.

7.   (b)   Chunking, the process of grouping items into larger units or chunks, allows us to overcome some of the limits of short-term memory.

8.   (b)   It must be rehearsed in the sense of elaborative rehearsal which means elaborating or enriching the to-be-remembered material.

9.   (d)   Levels of processing refers to the view that it is the depth at which information is processed that determines how well it will be remembered. Information processed semantically will be better remembered than information processed superficially.

10.   (a)   Concentrating on the motel signs while ignoring the others is an example of selective attention.

11.   (a)   Being unable to recall someone's name even though you know the person's name is an example of the failure of retrieval. Knowing that the person's name begins with a J is helpful because it restricts the range of names you must search.

12. (a) Working memory is where we assemble and organize information in preparation for recall.

13. (c) Practice in actually answering questions emphasizes the active role you must play in outputting information, that is, in retrieval. Here you must call upon information presumably stored in long-term memory.

True-False Answers: Memory I: The Processing of Information

1. (False) The fact that information is stored does not guarantee that it can be recalled. You may know a person's name and yet not be able to recall it, a finding which emphasizes the distinction between storage and retrieval.

2. (True) The fact that the order of output in recall is grouped in some fashion, differing presumably from the order in which the material was presented during learning, is evidence for organizational processes in memory.

3. (False) Reproducing your memory of some object by drawing it is an instance of recall. In studies of perceptual memory the recall procedure is usually referred to as reproduction or reproductive memory.

4. (True) Since the test items are presented, all you must do is select (recognize) the correct item.

5. (True) A choice must be made in every case, so possible differences in the willingness of individuals to respond to the recognition-test item is kept constant.

6. (False) With this information we cannot say anything definitive about differences in recognition because we don't know anything about possible differences in their response biases ("willingness to say yes"). Individual A may have been more willing to say that he recognized items and thus obtained a better score principally because of his response bias.

7. (True) You are limited to about seven pieces of information; however, if you chunk or group information into categories, you can hold a greater amount of information even though you are still limited to about seven chunks.

8. (False) The rehearsal buffer is located in short-term memory.

9. (True) Memory can be viewed as a continuum from the levels-of-processing approach, with the depth at which information is processed determining how well information is remembered.

10.   (False)   Retrieval in long-term memory is not always direct; frequently it is complex and may involve several stages.

11.   (False)   We may, in fact, encode the same nominal stimulus in different ways on subsequent occasions.

12.   (False)   Our ability to retrieve information effectively is very much dependent on the information being stored in an organized and systematic fashion.

Memory II: Organization, Forgetting, and Models of Memory

Chapter 5 continues our examination of memory. We first turn our attention to how information is organized in long-term memory, with an emphasis on the role of context in memory, constructive processes, semantic memory, and perceptual grouping. Other instances of organization in memory such as clustering in free recall, subjective organization, and imagery were discussed in chapter 3 on verbal learning and are not to be reexamined. Next we examine the important process of forgetting, focusing on decay, interference, and information-processing theories of forgetting. Then we take a brief look at models of memory, emphasizing the influential buffer model and the human associative memory model. Finally, we turn to the practical matter of study habits and memory and outline some practical ways in which you can improve your study habits.

Organization and Memory

We have already noted that an important characteristic of human learning and memory is organization. As we saw in chapter 3, the cognitive approach to learning assigns an important role to organizational processes and emphasizes the active role of the learner. The learner is viewed as actively processing the information to be learned, not simply passively registering the information. The organizational approach to learning and memory assumes that we attempt to organize information into some meaningful pattern, and that we devise strategies and plans and formulate hypotheses about information being encoded and stored in memory. Information which is stored in long-term memory is assumed to be highly organized in order to make use of the available storage capacity and to aid in the search and retrieval of information. As a result, incoming information is usually carefully rearranged so that the new information is integrated and made compatible with the existing organization in long-term memory. We have already looked at some of the evidence for organization in chapter 3, noting such evidence in clustering in free recall, subjective organization, coding, natural language mediation, and imagery. In this section we will examine a few more instances which illustrate organizational processes.

Context and Memory

Another way in which organizational processes are seen to operate in memory is by way of context effects in memory. The way information is encoded and stored in memory can be easily influenced by the context in which the to-be-remembered information is embedded. For example, the verbal context in which the word *jam* is encoded such as *strawberry jam* versus *traffic jam* will determine the kind of features encoded in memory. The role of context is thus to bias selectively certain features designated for encoding and storage. In short, the context serves to help organize particular features for placement in memory.

Context effects have been observed in studies of perceptual memory using such stimuli as geometric forms, random shapes, and semiabstract line drawings. Subjects shown ambiguous drawings, such as a pattern consisting of two circles connected by a straight line, encode the patterns differently as a result of different verbal labels given to the forms. Subjects shown such a pattern labeled Eyeglasses will tend to reproduce the pattern quite differently from subjects shown the same pattern labeled Barbells. Again, the prevailing verbal context is seen to bias the particular object as encoded in memory.

Instructions to learn also serve as contextual variables. James Jenkins and his students have examined the role of *incidental learning* instructions on memory for lists of words. In the typical experiment, different groups of subjects were given one of several kinds of instructions prior to being read a list of words to be remembered. These instructions serve as an orienting task in learning the list. In one case the subjects were asked to indicate whether or not each word contained the letter *e* as the word was read aloud. In a second case the subjects were asked to estimate the number of letters in each word, and in a third case subjects were asked to rate each word on a scale of "pleasantness to unpleasantness." The result of chief interest was that subjects who engaged in semantic ratings of the words recalled about 60 percent more words correctly than did the *e* checkers or letter counters. The point to note is that the orienting instructions served as a context which biased the level at which the words were processed. When the words were processed at a superficial level, fewer words were recalled; in contrast, when the words were processed at a deeper level, then substantially more words were recalled. Indeed, this type of finding is just what the *levels-of-processing* view describes.

In summary, contextual information can serve to bias the way in which to-be-remembered information is encoded. Thus, biasing at input is just one instance of organizational processes in memory.

Constructive Processes

Another feature of human memory is that it shows evidence for constructive activity. Not only do we recall information with some accuracy, but we also sometimes construct information, as shown in our memory for stories and jokes. In recalling a story we may tend to add new details to make it more meaningful and coherent; we may also drop features that seem unimportant. Sometimes elaborate detail may be added, which indicates that we may make up new features based on whatever limited information we can recall. In general, *constructive processes* refers to the actions by which we are somehow able to integrate or organize information in memory into a more or less coherent pattern called a *schema*. Once acquired, a schema can influence how new information gets integrated into long-term memory.

In an interesting study John Bransford and Jeffrey Franks demonstrated that humans recognize information even though it is *not* explicitly presented for study. They presented subjects with a list of simple sentences which if combined would represent a complex sentence containing several ideas. Consider the following sentence which represents a complex idea: The scared cat running from the barking dog jumped on the table. This complex idea can be broken down into four simple ideas as follows: (1) The cat was scared, (2) The cat was running, (3) The dog was barking, and (4) The cat jumped on the table.

During the study phase of the experiment the subjects were read a list of sentences containing one, two, or three simple ideas, but they never heard a sentence containing four ideas. If we use as an example the set of sentences just discussed, the subjects heard "The cat was scared" (one idea), "The scared cat was running from the dog" (two ideas), and so forth, but they did not hear the four-idea sentence. During the recognition test the subjects were presented the sentences that contained one, two, or three ideas and also the four-idea sentence which they had not heard and were asked to indicate which sentences they recognized and to rate the degree of confidence with which they recognized each sentence. Some of the sentences in the test were sentences actually heard and others were new sentences consistent with the ideas heard. Two findings are especially important. First, the subjects were just as confident that they had heard the new sentences as they were of hearing the old sentences, and second, subjects were actually more confident that they heard the four-idea sentences (never presented in the study phase) than the one-, two-, or three-idea sentences presented in the study phase. In brief, it appears that humans are willing to believe that they hear something even when it is never actually spoken.

Thus humans appear to construct information in the course of organizing it for storage or in preparing it for retrieval.

The fact that human memory can be constructive has important implications for anyone who accepts the automatic validity of eyewitness identification or eyewitness testimony. There has been a tradition for acceptance of such testimony in the courtroom on the grounds that humans are valid and reliable devices for memory and perception. Yet we know that our memory and perceptual systems are not perfectly valid in the sense that we do not perceive and remember perfectly everything we see or hear, nor do we exclude the products of constructive processes from memory. The fact that we can add information to whatever we encode in memory indicates that serious doubt about the credibility of testimony must be raised.

Semantic Memory

Another area in which we see evidence for organizational processes is the area of semantic memory. The study of semantic memory concerns such questions as: How do humans store the many words they use in speaking and understanding a language? What kind of network organization exists among words in memory? and What is the structure of semantic memory? The study of semantic memory concerns our natural memories, that is, our memories of semantic events which we acquire during our language experiences as distinct from memories of events acquired in the laboratory.

A popular view of semantic memory is that the various meanings of words are related to each other in memory by various nodes in a network. Consider the word *car* as a memory node; it is linked with other concept nodes in memory that help to define the concept of car. For instance, related concepts include properties like "tires," "brakes," "steering wheels," "gas tank," and so forth; other concepts include "recreation," "going to work," "visiting a friend," which describe functional features of cars. The network model of semantic memory views our memory as somewhat like a dictionary, but *not* organized alphabetically because an alphabetical organization is not conceptually useful. Not all the links among the related words are equally important. Those words more critically related or important to the meaning of the concept are thought to be more closely related than are other words. For example, the concept "human" probably has links to "people," "hands," "hearts," and "cavities," but they probably differ as defining properties of "human."

One test of such network models has been the inference task in which subjects are asked such questions as Are canaries yellow? and Do canaries fly? The length of time it takes a person to respond "yes" or "no" is taken. It is theorized that the search in memory for these questions requires activation of the nodes involved, such as *canary* and *yellow* and *canary* and *fly* and that this activation then spreads throughout the complex network of associated links. This particular version is called the spreading-activation theory of semantic memory as developed by Allan Collins and Elizabeth Loftus. If it is assumed that the link between *yellow* and *canary* is closer than the link between *fly* and *canary,* then the reaction time to the first question will be faster than the reaction time to the second question, which is what occurs. In short, the reaction time to such questions is regarded as a measure of the strength of the connection or the travel time between the two nodes.

Perceptual Grouping and Memory

An important idea stemming from the Gestalt theory of memory is that the way things are grouped perceptually will determine the way they are eventually organized in memory. Information in our environment is sometimes spatially or temporally organized so that we use this organization to encode and store the information. For instance, telephone numbers are grouped in digit sequences of three and four digits. Melodies have a particular temporal grouping which can facilitate our memory. More generally, the basic idea of perceptual grouping is that discrete stimuli in our environment are not responded to as such but are organized perceptually into some structured pattern or sequence.

One approach to studying perceptual grouping has been to present subjects strings of digits auditorially which are broken up into groups by pauses. A person might, for example, hear the digit sequence 418–35–9472–6257 in which the dashes represent pauses which break up the digits into groups or chunks. Only if the groups or chunks remain constant or identical on subsequent presentations can the digit sequence be learned. In contrast, if the grouping structure varies on successive presentations, such as 41–8359–4726–257 and 4183–5947–26–257, subjects show little mastery of the sequence. In short, humans must have some consistency in grouping or they will be unable to encode and store sequences. This generalization holds where the sequence to be learned has no obvious higher-order structure, that is, where the person is unable to detect a hidden sequence of digits or letters that would be easier to encode than the sequence presented in study.

In contrast, if the series to be learned does have a higher-order structure, then varied rather than constant groupings actually facilitate recall of the sequence. Consider, for example a letter sequence such as CU PN ET, which is derived from the word pair CUP-NET. If we are shown the letter sequence in varied fashion, such as CU PN ET,

C UPN ET, CU PNE T, etc., on successive presentations, our recall of the entire letter sequence is much better than if we are shown a constant grouping of letters. In this case you never actually see the intact words *cup* and *net*. Thus varied input in the form of varied spatial groupings allows us to organize the information more effectively, but *only* if there is some *overall structure* in the material to be learned. A more general implication of these findings may be that varied stimulus presentations provide for a deeper level of processing because we are forced to work harder with the information.

Forgetting

Once information is placed in long-term memory it is much more resistant to forgetting. Nevertheless, information in this system can also be forgotten despite the fact that long-term memory is a much more stable system than short-term memory. Therefore, a principal problem of long-term memory is to determine the cause(s) of forgetting after a prolonged period involving no additional practice.

A long-held view was that forgetting occurred because of *disuse*. If we failed to use the material learned, in the sense of no additional practice or rehearsal, then it was thought that disuse would bring about forgetting. A disuse theory implies that forgetting occurs because of the passage of time; however, the passage of time, that is, time per se, cannot be the cause of forgetting. Events do change in the course of time but it is not time that produces the change. Rather, *it is what happens during the passage of time that brings about forgetting.* Therefore, memory theorists have focused on processes that can produce forgetting.

Classical Theories of Forgetting: Decay and Interference

Memory psychologists have proposed two general kinds of theory for explaining forgetting: *decay* theory and *interference* theory. Decay theory contends that hypothetical memory traces, which are representations of events learned, decay or weaken automatically with the passage of time. The memory trace decays autonomously, that is, independently of any additional learning that takes place. This decay or weakening of the memory trace is seen as the result of some built-in property of our nervous system. Therefore, forgetting is the natural outcome of a trace-decay principle.

Interference theory, on the other hand, has emphasized that forgetting occurs because of the interfering effects of new learning and of prior learning. The primary task of this theory has been to formulate the various processes that bring about interference and to demonstrate that these processes do, in fact, account for forgetting. The central point to note about interference theory, without describing its details, is to remember that the reason we forget is because of new learning that interferes with memory traces, or because of old learning that gets in the way of remembering more recently learned events.

The advantage of interference theory is that it has led to experiments that ask how new learning affects our retention of previously learned events. Interference theory has the considerable advantage of being experimentally testable, whereas decay theory has been difficult to evaluate experimentally. Studies of interference theory have led to examination of the effects of events that occur during the retention interval, that is, events that occur between learning some task and the retention test. The study of these effects is known as *retroactive inhibition.*

Retroactive Inhibition

Retroactive inhibition refers to the fact that an event learned during a retention interval can lead to some forgetting of a previously learned event. Retroactive inhibition is simply the forgetting of an earlier-learned task produced by the effects of learning some interpolated task during the retention interval. Suppose you learned a list of Spanish vocabulary and then learned a list of French vocabulary. A test of your retention of Spanish would probably show some forgetting of Spanish vocabulary because of the interpolated activity of learning French. What you do during the interval between learning some task and being tested for retention can have powerful effects on what you remember.

The importance of events that occur during the retention interval as a factor influencing forgetting has long been known. For example, in one experiment researchers required human subjects to learn a serial list of nonsense syllables to a criterion of one perfect recitation. Following learning, half the subjects slept and half the subjects stayed awake. Subjects slept in the laboratory so that control over this activity was maintained. Subjects who were awake were allowed to leave the laboratory and to return at appropriate time intervals for a retention test. Both groups of subjects were given retention tests after varying amounts of time up to eight hours, using different lists for each retention interval. The same subjects were tested under both conditions. The retention test was a free-recall test requiring the subjects to produce as many items learned as possible. The results of this study are shown in figure 7, a plot of the percent retained for the sleep and waking conditions. While both conditions showed some forgetting, the sleep condition produced far less forgetting than did the awake condition. Forgetting continued to occur for the awake condition over the retention intervals employed,

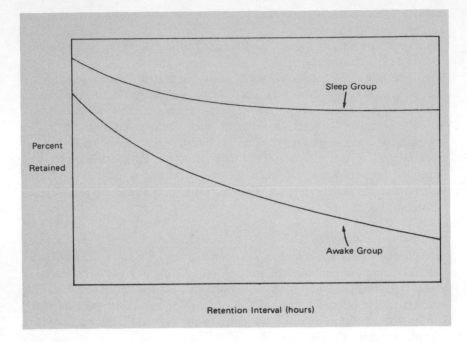

Figure 7. Temporal course of retention of verbal materials following sleep and waking conditions. The figure shows the usual superior retention when subjects sleep after learning a verbal task.

whereas retention was relatively stable after the two-hour retention interval in the sleep condition.

This study demonstrates that the normal activities that occur while we are awake can produce considerable forgetting. Sleep, on the other hand, prevents interfering activities from producing a comparable amount of forgetting. Why this is the case is not fully clear. Sleep may allow consolidation of the memory traces, protecting them from possible interference, whereas normal everyday activities may provide conditions for interference. In any event, the fact that the awake subjects continued to show forgetting and retained far less than the sleep subjects is evidence in support of an interference theory of forgetting.

The study of retroactive inhibition requires an experimental group and a control group. The *experimental* group learns an initial task, A, and then learns a second task, B, which is interpolated between the initial task A and the test of retention. The *control* group learns some unrelated or irrelevant task during the retention interval so that rehearsal of task A is prevented or minimized. The paradigm for retroactive inhibition is shown thus:

Group	Learn	Learn	Retention Test
Experimental	Learn task A	Learn task B	Retention of A
Control	Learn task A	Learn Unrelated task	Retention of A

The basic question is, Does the learning of the interpolated task, B, interfere with the retention of task A, compared with the retention shown by the control group? A comparison of the experimental and control groups in their performance on the retention task reveals the amount of forgetting due to the learning of task B. If the effect of learning task B is such that the experimental group retains less than does the control group, retroactive inhibition is then inferred. The logic of this paradigm assumes that the experimental and control groups are comparable or equivalent on the average in task A learning. Therefore, any differences in retention of A must be due to the interference effects of task B on the memory traces or representations of task A. The term *retroactive inhibition* does not literally mean that events act backward in time, which is a concept foreign to science. All that is meant is that the interpolated task acts to disrupt, change, or interfere with the current memory trace of task A. Moreover, the term *inhibition* refers merely to the forgetting that occurs. It is not a theoretical concept in the sense that it does not explain anything; it only describes an effect.

Usually the effect of the interpolated task is to produce interference in retention, that is, retroactive inhibition. It must be noted, however, that the relationship between tasks A and B can be of such a nature that the experimental group retains more than the control. In this case we speak of retroactive *facilitation*. In the vast majority of cases, interest in this paradigm has been in its interference and not in its facilitative effects. Before we look at the factors that produce retroactive inhibition, let us examine a second procedure for studying interference in retention.

Proactive Inhibition

The second procedure which is used for investigating interference effects in retention is one that produces proactive inhibition. *In general, proactive inhibition* is *the loss in retention produced by the effects of some previously learned task.* In this case, however, the effects are due to the learning of a task *prior to* rather than after the to-be-tested task. As shown below, the paradigm for studying proactive inhibition, like that for studying retroactive inhibition, requires a comparison of performance between an experimental and a control group.

The experimental group learns an initial task, B, *prior* to learning task A and is then tested for retention of task A. The control group learns only task A and is subsequently tested for retention of task A. The proactive inhibition paradigm is schematized below:

Group	Learn	Learn	Retention Test
Experimental	Learn Task B	Learn Task A	Retention of A
Control	Learn "Unrelated" Task	Learn Task A	Retention of A

The basic question is: Does the learning of the preliminary task B interfere with the subsequent retention of task A? A comparison of the experimental and control group's performance on retention of A reveals the amount of forgetting due to the learning of task B. If the experimental group remembers less of task A than does the control group, then proactive inhibition is inferred. In some fashion, the learning of B interferes with the retention of A.

Factors Influencing Retroactive and Proactive Inhibition

We have already noted that sleep during the retention interval is an important factor in preventing forgetting. Indeed, more recent experiments have continued to show superior retention following sleep with much less forgetting than was obtained in earlier studies. As we indicated earlier, we do not have a complete understanding of this process, although it is clear that sleep reduces the opportunity for interference effects. From a practical viewpoint, one way of minimizing forgetting is to sleep after learning a particularly important task, such as studying for an upcoming test.

A second factor that affects retention in the retroactive inhibition paradigm is the *degree of original learning,* that is, learning on the initial task. In general, the greater the degree of original learning, the greater is retention of the originally learned task. In short, if a task is to be made more resistant to forgetting, then ideally it should be well learned.

A related factor is the *degree of learning of the interpolated (interfering) task.* In general, the greater the degree of learning of the interpolated task, with degree of first-task learning held constant, the less is the retention of original learning. Similarly, in the proactive inhibition paradigm, as degree of learning on the prior task increases, forgetting of task A also increases.

Similarity between the two tasks also affects the amount of forgetting obtained in both retroactive and proactive inhibition paradigms. With materials low in meaningfulness, such as trigrams, we find that in general the more similar the two tasks, the greater will be the forgetting in both retroactive and proactive paradigms. With more meaningful materials, such as prose passages, far less interference is produced by similarity. This is especially the case where the test task is one of retention of the factual or substantive content of the passage. Presumably, more meaningful materials can be better organized by the learner so as to minimize or prevent interference.

Where the effects of stimulus and response similarity have been separately examined, the picture is more complicated. In the case of response similarity, forgetting increases with a decrease in response similarity where the responses belong to the same class. Consider the situation in which you learn two successive paired-associate tasks designated A-B and A-B'. The A-B task can be regarded as the original task and the A-B' as the interpolated task. If we now test for retention of the original A-B associations, we find that retention improves as the responses increase in similarity. If, however, the responses are drawn from *different* classes, as would be the case with an A-B and A-D arrangement, then the more dissimilar the response classes, the less is the forgetting of the initial A-B associations.

The effects of stimulus similarity on interference are also complex. In general, as the stimuli are increased in similarity, the less is the interference when the responses are the same. Where the responses are different, then an increase in stimulus similarity is accompanied by an increase in forgetting.

Contextual factors also influence interference. For example, if two tasks that are known to produce interference are learned in different environments, such as different rooms, then less interference is produced. This kind of finding indicates the importance of environmental or contextual cues and indicates that they can become effective or functional stimuli during learning. Indeed, for this reason students who study in the same room in which they will be tested tend to perform slightly better on tests.

Finally, *instructions* on what to expect can influence forgetting in interference situations. For example, if subjects are told that learning a second task will hinder their performance, they actually show less forgetting than subjects who are told that learning the second task will facilitate learning. This occurs despite the fact that both subjects receiving the two kinds of instructions learned the second task at the same rate. It is possible that subjects told that learning a second task would hinder performance developed some strategy, probably rehearsal of the first task, so as to retain it better than they normally would.

These, then, are some of the important factors in retroactive and proactive inhibition. They show the importance of interference factors in retention, and have led in turn to the development of interference theory. Let us now turn our attention to some of the salient features of this theory.

Interference Theory

The study of retroactive and proactive inhibition in long-term memory has led to the development of interference theory. Interference theory begins with the fundamental assumption that forgetting is the result of other learning which prevents what initially has been learned from being remembered. Interference theory emphasizes, however, that forgetting can be due to several factors and not just one process. Thus modern interference theory consists of a collection of several assumptions about processes that are viewed as underlying forgetting.

One aspect of interference theory that was formulated early in its development is the notion of *response competition*. According to this view, responses acquired in the original and interpolated learning tasks and attached to identical (or similar) stimuli, as in the A-B and A-D paradigm, remain available to the learner and compete with each other during the learner's attempt to recall the original (A-B) list. This simply means that the D responses may tend to intrude and displace the B responses at the time of A-B recall. Evidence for response competition is seen when your latency for correct responses is significantly lengthened, when incorrect (D) responses are given, or when response blocking occurs such that no response is given unless you are forced to respond. These intrusion errors, however, occur principally after the first few trials on the interpolated task, indicating that interference is not solely due to response competition.

It was therefore proposed that a second factor must be operating to produce forgetting in retroactive inhibition paradigms, the factor of *unlearning*. The concept of unlearning was viewed as analogous to the extinction of instrumental responses. The unlearning mechanism hypothesizes that the first-list responses in an A-B—A-D paradigm tend to be unlearned, or extinguished, during second-list learning. Theoretically, unlearning takes place in the following fashion: During A-D learning it is assumed that the B responses will tend to be elicited because they have already been associated with the A stimuli. When the B responses do intrude during A-D learning they are nonreinforced since the D responses are now the correct ones, and hence should undergo extinction in a manner analogous to that of classical and instrumental conditioning. Therefore, a later test for retention of the A-B associations should show some forgetting of the B responses to the extent that they have been extinguished.

The fact that unlearning does occur has been dramatically shown in an experiment by Jean Barnes and Benton Underwood. In their experiment, subjects first learned a list of paired associates and then learned a second list with varying amounts of practice on the second lists. The lists were arranged as an A-B and A-D paradigm. Following practice on the second (A-D) list, subjects were presented the A stimuli and asked to recall responses from *both* of the lists. They found that with increased practice on the A-D lists, subjects recalled fewer A-B associations. It was as if the A-B associations had undergone extinction during A-D learning.

It is important to note that this view of unlearning emphasizes the extinction of *specific* stimulus-response associations. Making a new response to an old stimulus leads to a weakening of the originally learned associative connections, with each specific association itself being weakened. If, however, we extend the analogy to extinction, it should follow that some *spontaneous recovery* of the A-B associations should occur, just as spontaneous recovery is shown in instrumental conditioning. Experimental tests for spontaneous recovery of the A-B associations after relatively long-term intervals have not shown consistent or dependable evidence for the phenomenon. Thus, the early conception of unlearning as the extinction of specific S-R associations has been questioned. More recently, the notion of unlearning has been modified by Leo Postman and colleagues.

Instead of specific S-R associations being necessarily extinguished, Postman has emphasized that unlearning in the sense of the relative unavailability of the originally learned associations following interpolated learning represents a "set" to respond in terms of the list most recently learned. This view emphasizes that the learner restricts himself to the responses of the most current list. Moreover, Postman's modification represents a shift in the locus of interference from individual responses or S-R associations to entire *systems of responses*. The critical feature of this view of unlearning is the shift in emphasis from the extinction of specific associations to the operation of a more central selector mechanism. It is as if the learner suppresses the entire set of first-list responses at the time of recall.

Interference theory has undergone a number of changes in response to increasingly demanding experimental tests. Its current status appears to be in disarray, primarily because recent additions and changes have according to many of its critics changed its fundamental character. In addition, alternative conceptions of forgetting, stemming from the information-processing approach to memory, which challenge interference theory are being developed.

Information-Processing Approach to Forgetting

A view of forgetting which has received increasing importance is the information-processing approach which focuses, as we saw earlier, on the processes of encoding, storage, and retrieval. An important difference between the explanation of forgetting as outlined by the information-processing approach and by the interference theory is the *limited* acceptance of a *decay* principle in short-term memory. As we saw in our discussion of interference theory, interference theorists have generally objected to a decay idea on the grounds that it is not necessary to explain forgetting and that the existing evidence on forgetting doesn't require such a principle. Theorists continue to debate the necessity of a decay principle, and the principle receives some acceptance by proponents of information-processing interpretations of forgetting.

In contrast, the decay notion receives little attention in accounts of forgetting in long-term memory because information-processing theorists generally accept the principle that long-term memory is essentially permanent. Forgetting from long-term memory is viewed as the result of *failure to retrieve* the desired information. Endel Tulving and others have distinguished between what they call *trace-dependent* and *cue-dependent* forgetting. Theories that describe forgetting in terms of decay are assuming that forgetting in long-term memory occurs because of a trace-dependent process. In contrast, theories which argue that forgetting occurs because of the inadequacy of retrieval cues emphasize a cue-dependent process. In the latter view, once information has been effectively encoded and stored in memory, the only problem is to retrieve that information. Since retrieval processes are importantly dependent upon cues, a major factor in forgetting is the loss of cue effectiveness. This approach to forgetting raises the issue of why formerly effective cues are no longer effective for retrieval. We cannot, of course, simply say that forgetting occurs because of loss of our retrieval cues because that simply raises another question, namely, Why do we forget our retrieval cues? Nevertheless, this approach to forgetting appears useful because it has raised some new and important issues.

In summary, forgetting from the viewpoint of an information-processing approach results from the failure to retrieve information. We fail to retrieve information in short-term memory because of the decay of the memory trace. We fail to retrieve in long-term memory because of the loss of cue effectiveness. The concepts of decay and loss of cue effectiveness stand in contrast to interference theory which emphasizes response competition and unlearning. Nevertheless, there are unsolved questions about the concept of loss of cue effectiveness which need to be worked out before we have a complete theory.

Models of Memory

In recent years psychologists have concerned themselves with models of memory. Models are somewhat formal, abstract descriptions of the way in which our memory systems are thought to operate. We have already described the essential features of many models of memory at a general level in the earlier discussion of stages of memory storage in chapter 4 in which the typical or "modal model" of memory from the information-processing viewpoint was described. This general viewpoint is a way of thinking and theorizing about the workings of the human mind and, specifically, in the case of memory attempts to describe the flow of information through our memory system. In this section we will briefly describe two models of memory which have had considerable influence.

Buffer Model

The buffer model was developed in 1968 by Richard Atkinson and Richard Shiffrin. Its general features were described earlier, in the section on stages of memory storage in Chapter 4, and now we shall outline its essential features in greater detail. Like many models of memory it postulates three storage systems: a sensory register, a short-term store, and a long-term store. The name buffer model is used because it assumes that information is maintained in an *active* state in the short-term store prior to being transferred to the long-term store. The short-term store thus serves as a buffer between the sensory register and the long-term store.

The buffer model consists of two basic components: *structural* features and *control* processes. The structural features of the model consist of the sensory register, the short-term store, and the long-term store, which are permanent features of the memory system. In contrast, the control processes are the nonpermanent aspects of the memory system and are transient processes under control of the human. The key feature of the model is the rehearsal buffer, as shown in figure 6 (chapter 4) in which information can be maintained via rehearsal. By rehearsing information in the short-term store, the buffer system keeps the information processed until it can be transferred to the long-term store.

When a stimulus is presented, an immediate registration occurs in the sensory register where the information is thought to be held in the form of a visual image. The second component of the system is the short-term store which is regarded as our working memory. Working memory has several functions. As we noted earlier, one function is to act as a buffer between the sensory register and long-term memory.

Information transferred from the sensory register to the short-term store is regulated by selective attention, which is a major control process. A second function is to handle information that has been retrieved from the long-term store. Finally, working memory acts to facilitate the transfer of information from short-term to long-term storage.

The control processes regulate the flow of information throughout the memory system. Besides selective attention, other important control processes include rehearsal, retrieval and search strategies, coding, organization, and mediation. The important control processes in the short-term store are rehearsal, coding, and search and retrieval of information, whereas organizational processes are the major mechanisms of control in long-term memory. We have discussed these processes in detail earlier in this chapter and will not elaborate further.

The buffer model, or some variation of it, is accepted by many psychologists. It furnishes a broad conceptual framework for memory. Its principal limitation is that it did not specify in detail the way information is organized in long-term memory. In recent years, models of memory have attempted to specify in great detail the nature of information in long-term memory in the form of elaborate networks, and we shall briefly examine one such model.

Human Associative Memory (HAM) Model

One type of network model of human memory which has gained prominence is the human associative memory model, also called HAM, developed by John Anderson and Gordon Bower in 1973. HAM describes memory as a vast collection of associations interrelated in a huge network. The basic unit of the model is called a *proposition* which is a meaningful or grammatical relation between encoded units of information stored in memory. The encoded units are known as nodes; thus, the basic unit or component of memory is some relation between memory nodes. The proposition is something like an English sentence, except that the proposition is a more formal and abstract representation. Moreover, propositions are not limited to linguistic information, but can also represent nonlinguistic information such as visual scenes.

A proposition, then, represents a set of associations in memory. Any given association represents the connection between two concepts, and HAM distinguishes four basic kinds of associations. One type of association involves contextual information and facts such as "On the porch was the newspaper." Another type of association specifies the relation between location and time such as "At the store yesterday. . . ." Other associations involve subject-predicate relations such as "John played tennis," and relation-object associations such as "Diane is taller than Joan." These four types of associations may be combined to form a single proposition. The proposition can best be represented in the form of a tree diagram as shown in figure 8. The figure shows how the various concepts can be combined to form a proposition. Consider the sentence On the playground the coach teaches the children. At the top of the tree we have the labeled proposition *A,* which is divided into two parts: a context subtree and a fact subtree. Going down the tree we see that the context node *(B)* is the association between the location *(D)* and the time of the event *(E)*, which is the present. Similarly, the fact node *(C)* represents the association between the subject *(F)* and

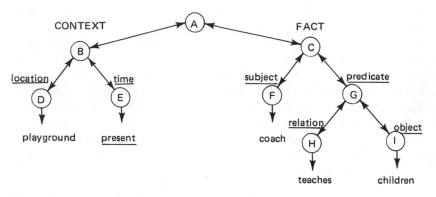

Figure 8. A tree diagram representing a proposition.

the predicate *(G)*. Similarly, the predicate node *(G)* can be further broken down into the relation node *(H)* and the object *(I)*. In summary, a proposition is composed of a context and a fact. The context is composed of location and time information, and the fact is composed of subject and predicate information. Finally, the predicate is composed of a relation and an object.

Now let us examine the architecture of HAM as shown in figure 9. Here it is somewhat like the buffer model in that it adopts an information-processing approach in which information is viewed as flowing through the memory system. Information enters the system through visual and auditory receptors and is stored in visual and auditory buffers which are limited-capacity systems. These are givens in the model about which little is said since the model is primarily concerned with long-term memory. In the next stage information in the visual and auditory buffers is analyzed by linguistic parsers and perceptual parsers. The function of the parser is to analyze the information and to produce a meaningful description of it suitable for transmission to and storage in long-term memory. The linguistic parser is designed to translate linguistic or verbal information into conceptual descriptions. Similarly, the perceptual parser tries to develop a description of the sensory information in the perceptual buffer. For example, consider the sentence, "Jimmy Connors played"; the linguistic parser would develop a memory representation such as "a major tennis star played in a tournament," whereas the perceptual parser would take the visual stimulus "Jimmy Connors played" and store a representation something like this: the pattern "Jimmy Connors" occurred to the left of the pattern "played." In either case the description of the phrase would be expressed in propositional terms.

At the next stage the outputs of the parsers are sent to working memory where they are compared with the information in long-term memory. If the purpose of the comparison is to recognize the input, that is, recognize the sentence as old or new, then a *match* process is initiated. The match process involves search of the long-term store followed by comparison of what is located with the input from the parsers. After the input is matched, it is then sent to the executive portion of the system which regulates the output from working memory. The executive portion has very general control over all information processing in the system. The final component is the language generator, which is used to output answers to questions or to request further information about the working memory output. The model says very little about this final process.

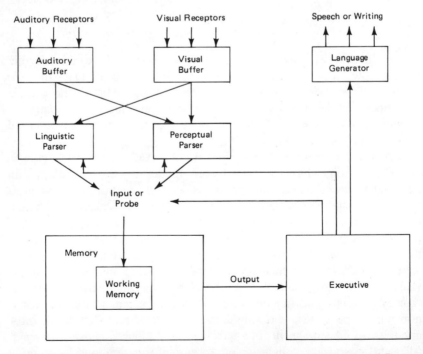

Figure 9. The architecture of HAM's mental system (from Anderson and Bower, *Human associative memory,* Hemisphere Press, 1973).

Study Habits and Memory

Let us now turn our attention to the matter of study habits and memory. A good deal of what has already been described has clear implications for the way in which you read, take notes, and prepare for examinations. A principal issue is how you can arrange your study activities so as to ensure maximum retention of the material. We shall focus on only a few basic points which are relatively straightforward and which derive largely from our discussion of learning and memory.

Understand the Objectives of What Is Being Studied

A major feature of good study habits is that you *understand the principal objectives or goals of whatever it is you are studying.* It is, therefore, good practice before reading a chapter to review the chapter outline if one is given in the table of contents. Note what topics are listed and the order in which they are discussed. In this fashion you will begin your reading of the chapter with fewer misconceptions of what to expect and with a clearer picture of the objectives of the author.

If a detailed chapter outline is not presented, then try to obtain some structure by careful reading of the introduction. In addition, read over the chapter, noting the topic headings, in order to get a feel of what the author is discussing. Sometimes a summary which may be profitably scanned before careful study of the chapter is undertaken is given at the end of the chapter. Regardless of how you achieve this overall picture, keep in mind that you are trying to get a good mental road map of the material before you study it in greater detail. By reading the major headings and the italicized sentences and words, you will obtain what David Ausubel has termed an "advance organizer," or what I term a mental road map of the assigned reading. At this stage do not try to understand details or fine points. Get the big picture. Just as it is much easier to travel to a new place if you have a good road map, it is much easier to comprehend materials when you have a general idea of what the chapter contains. This first step will provide you with a *preliminary organization* of what you will subsequently study more carefully.

Focus Attention on the Study Materials

Once you have decided to study a particular chapter, focus your attention on your task and eliminate irrelevant stimuli. Remove magazines and newspapers from your desk, turn off the television, ignore the poker or bridge game in the next room, and avoid getting in a bull session with friends. If you are to learn the material at hand, you must tune out irrelevant stimuli.

Students sometimes report that they have no understanding of what they have read after finishing several pages. A similar experience is that of holding a book in your hand staring at page after page without any clear comprehension of the material. Chances are in both instances that you have failed to *attend* to the material and perhaps are daydreaming about some unrelated activity. While daydreaming can be pleasant, it simply is a way of avoiding the task at hand.

The matter of daydreaming and thinking about irrelevant activities can be handled if you learn to *monitor* your reading and thinking. As we noted in an earlier chapter, a good practice is the habit of occasionally looking at your thoughts while reading. In this fashion you can detect if you have wandered off course and can redirect your attention to the materials that must be studied. Failure to do this may lead to hours of wasted effort in which you neither engage in effective study nor use the time in recreation or other important activities.

Arrange Contingencies of Reinforcement

The business of paying careful attention to what you are reading is a *learned habit*. That is, you can teach yourself to attend by periodically asking yourself questions about what you are reading. Moreover, you can schedule coffee breaks and other forms of rewards if you arrange these rewards so that they occur only *after* you have achieved some goal or subgoal of studying. For instance, you may require yourself to study and outline two chapters *before* you take a break for conversation with friends. By actually planning these contingencies, in the form of rewarding yourself *after* you have completed some agreed-upon segment of study, you will find yourself managing your study habits in a far more efficient fashion. This practice of arranging your study so that you reward yourself only after you have accomplished some subgoal or task is called self-management of contingencies. With practice in the management of reinforcement contingencies, a topic that was discussed in chapter 2 on conditioning, you can become increasingly effective in studying.

Organize the Materials

An important feature of efficient study habits is the matter of organizing the material into some kind of systematic, useful structure. Some texts will present materials in a reasonably organized fashion, just as some lectures will be highly systematic. In such cases little effort on your part to organize the material will be required. Other materials will be less well-organized. Regardless of the nature of the material, it is good practice to organize it into some kind of useful framework that will enable you to encode it in memory. Indeed, the best organization will be idiosyncratic. As we have already noted, the effectiveness of memory retrieval depends in part on how well the material is organized.

In our discussion of the topics of conditioning, verbal learning, and memory, you may have noted certain fairly consistent features of each chapter. Each of these topics has been dealt with in a reasonably consistent way and each has a structure or format that you may have detected. For any topic you may have noted that the discussion revolves around five central features: nature or characteristics of the concepts, methods of measurement or study, major processes and principles, some theoretical issues, and finally, implications and applications of the principles discussed. Therefore, a good way to ask yourself questions about any chapter for purposes of review is to focus questions around these five central features. In this fashion you organize your studying around identifiable issues and are more likely to avoid directionless study.

If structure is not immediaely evident in the material, you must then seek structure or *create* some kind of useful system for organizing the materials. This is simply to say that you must impose some kind of organization upon the materials if none is readily evident. Keep in mind that the organization that you develop or impose will be useful to the extent that it can provide efficient *retrieval* cues. Thus the usefulness of outlines, tables, charts, and so forth, that you construct in note-taking depend on how well these cues work in enabling you to recall the materials.

Practice Retrieval

We have already emphasized the importance of practicing retrieval, so we shall simply reemphasize this point. You must practice or rehearse *output* as well as concentrate on *input* of information. Too often students concentrate on how many pages were read as the index of their study effort. *The final and vital key to effective memory is direct practice in the retrieval process, that is, in producing the information.*

The importance of practicing retrieval activities cannot be over-emphasized. How is this accomplished? This requires that you try to anticipate and answer test questions. Moreover, you should construct questions and try writing answers to them as part of your study. In general, let part of your study involve practice in the very kinds of activities that a course exam requires.

Summary

In this chapter we have described some of the major processes of memory. Organizational processes were further examined, having been introduced in chapter 3 on verbal learning. The role of context, the importance of constructive processes, and the elements of semantic memory were described. The fact that human memory is constructive was seen to have several important implications for practical affairs.

Another important aspect of memory is forgetting. Forgetting in long-term memory was seen as the result of interference processes and the failure of retrieval. Forgetting is attributed to both retroactive and proactive sources of interference. Interference theory was seen as in a state of flux. Models of memory were seen as efforts to describe the structure and processes of memory as an integrated system. Two prominent models were examined: the buffer model and the human associative memory (HAM) model.

Our knowledge of principles of learning and memory have clear implications for effective study habits. Five features were emphasized: (1) understand the objectives of what you are studying; (2) focus attention on the study materials; (3) arrange contingencies of reinforcement; (4) organize the material; and (5) practice retrieval.

Multiple-Choice Items: Memory II: Organization, Forgetting, and Models of Memory

1. A witness in a trial contended that the defendant, facing a murder charge, was heard to say "I hate my business partner and intend to get rid of him." What, in fact, the defendant actually said was "I dislike my partner and plan to dissolve the partnership." This type of distortion in memory is an example of
   a. encoding variability
   b. forgetting
   c. retrieval
   d. constructive processes

2. Your memory of how to take the square root of a number would be an example of
   a. short-term memory
   b. semantic memory
   c. encoding
   d. levels of processing

3. Suppose that you are told to study for an essay examination in one course and for a true-false test in another course. Such instructions may affect the way in which you study, and thus would be instances of
   a. associationism
   b. semantic memory
   c. constructive processes
   d. context effects

4. In studying prose passages we may tend to remember a generalized abstraction or representation of the passage. This repre-

sentation is sometimes called a(n)

a. working memory
b. schema
c. trace
d. image

5. A basic difference between decay and interference theories of forgetting is that

a. decay theory assumes unlearning
b. decay theory is a two-factor theory
c. decay theory emphasizes autonomous processes
d. interference theory emphasizes neural consolidation

6. Interference theory makes the fundamental assumption that forgetting occurs because

a. of qualitative changes in the memory trace
b. we haven't had time to consolidate information in memory
c. of a conservation principle
d. of other learning

7. Retroactive inhibition is

a. an improvement in recall
b. forgetting due to new learning
c. forgetting due to old or prior learning
d. forgetting due to trace decay

8. Studying in the same place in which you will take a test can

a. be desirable because of the same context
b. produce proactive inhibition
c. be undesirable because of the same context
d. lead to autonomous decay of memory traces

9. A major change in the unlearning concept in recent years has been the

a. emphasis on specific associations
b. emphasis on suppression of sets of responses
c. emphasis on cue-dependent forgetting
d. strong evidence for spontaneous recovery

10. The buffer model of memory makes an important distinction between the structure of the memory system and its control processes. One example of a control process is

a. sensory register
b. levels of processing
c. decay
d. attention

11. The basic unit of the Human Associative Memory Model is the

a. predicate
b. sentence

c. proposition
d. association

True-False Items: Memory II: Organization, Forgetting, and Models of Memory

1. You may fail on occasion to write a good essay examination, not because you don't know the material, but because you have insufficiently practiced getting out (producing) the material.
2. A good way to practice retrieval of information is to reread the text and lecture notes just before a quiz.
3. A decay theory of memory emphasizes that the memory trace weakens with the passage of time.
4. Interference theory states that forgetting is due to disuse, that is, to failure to continue rehearsing the material.
5. The following schematic experiment represents the paradigm for proactive inhibition:

| Experimental | Learn A | Learn B | Recall A |
| Control | Learn A | Learn X | Recall A |

6. Eyewitness testimony is almost always valid.
7. You are likely to remember a story or anecdote because, in part, of the particular person who tells the story.
8. Going to sleep after a long study session is a good practice.
9. Cue-dependent forgetting means that you forget something because the memory trace has weakened over time.
10. One function of working memory is to hold and handle information that has been retrieved from long-term memory.
11. A proposition in HAM expresses a relationship at the highest level between a fact and an object.
12. Probably the most neglected feature of studying for most people is the failure to underline key concepts in the text.

Discussion Items: Memory II: Organization, Forgetting, and Models of Memory

1. Describe in some detail how the prevailing context can influence your memory of a person or an event.
2. How can constructive processes operate to reduce the trustworthiness of eyewitness testimony and/or eyewitness identification?
3. Distinguish between decay and interference theories of memory.
4. How could either retroactive or proactive interference affect

your ability to recall information for an examination in a specific course such as history, Spanish, or biology?

5.   What are the major objectives of models of memory?

6.   Outline in some detail a number of steps that you could take to improve your study habits, based on your knowledge of memory and learning principles.

Multiple-Choice Answers: Memory II: Organization, Forgetting, and Models of Memory

1.   (d)   This example illustrates the role of constructive processes in memory. The witness has distorted his memory of the actual spoken sentence into something quite different in both meaning and implied intent.

2.   (b)   Memory of how to extract the square root of a number is an instance of semantic memory, part of a verbal rule system that most people can learn.

3.   (d)   Instructions which may affect the way you study would serve as contextual stimuli for the occasion of studying.

4.   (b)   The generalized abstraction which we remember is called a schema and functions much like a concept.

5.   (c)   Decay theory assumes that forgetting is due to autonomous central processes. The memory trace is thought to weaken or decay with the passage of time.

6.   (d)   Interference theory assumes that the basic reason for forgetting is because new learning interferes with existing memory representations, or because old learning gets in the way of remembering more recently learned events.

7.   (b)   Retroactive inhibition is forgetting due to the influence of new learning. When you have learned task A, task B which follows may produce interference in your memory for task A.

8.   (a)   Studying in the same place in which you take a test can be desirable because the contextual cues remain the same or very similar. Because the context is essentially the same, you can benefit from having the same contextual cues because they provide for a greater likelihood of accessing the appropriate information during test taking.

9.   (b)   The unlearning concept is now thought to be the suppression of an entire set of responses in a list rather than the extinction of specific pairs in the list.

10.   (d)   Selective attention is a major control process in the buffer model and regulates what gets into the short-term store.

11.   (c)   The basic unit in the HAM model is the proposition,

which is an abstract relationship between contextual and factual information.

True-False Answers: Memory II: Organization, Forgetting, and Models of Memory

1.   (True)   Producing the material is retrieval, and the key to memory output is the matter of practicing the task of retrieving information as well as simply storing information.

2.   (False)   This practice still emphasizes input of storage. It fails to emphasize output or retrieval processes, which involve such things as practice in writing answers to questions.

3.   (True)   Decay theory stresses that memory traces weaken automatically in the course of time.

4.   (False)   Interference theory does not assume a principle of disuse. Rather, interference theory contends that forgetting is the result of other learning.

5.   (False)   This schematic experiment represents retroactive inhibition in which the effect of learning task B is to produce interference in the recall of task A.

6.   (False)   Eyewitness testimony can be invalidated as the result of several processes. One of the most important aspects of memory is that it is constructive, which means that information can become elaborated, distorted, and reorganized in memory.

7.   (True)   The person telling a story is part of the context and can well determine our memory of the story. For example, if the person is trustworthy we then tend to believe the story, whereas if we distrust the person we may simply dismiss the conversation.

8.   (True)   Going to sleep tends to prevent or minimize interfering activities so that we are less likely to forget the material studied.

9.   (False)   Cue-dependent forgetting refers to the case in which we have forgotten our cues for retrieval, not the memory trace itself.

10.   (True)   The notion of working memory is that it works, namely, it holds and handles information that has been retrieved from the long-term store.

11.   (False)   A proposition in HAM at the highest level of the tree structure expresses a relationship between a fact subtree and a context subtree.

12.   (False)   Probably the most neglected aspect of studying is practice in the business of retrieval.

Concept Learning

6

Human learning would be a complex and burdensome affair if you had to learn a particular response for every stimulus situation you encounter in life. If each new learning situation was essentially a matter of rote learning, you would be overwhelmed by a mass of specifics in a complex world. Fortunately, you are not reduced to treating each and every situation with such a high degree of specificity. Humans have the capacity to generalize from particular situations, which thus enables the learning of concepts.

Concepts provide you with a certain kind of stability in interaction with your environment. Concept learning allows you to rise above the specific and infinitesimal variability of your environment and to treat events that have common properties as members of a class. For example, young children, in learning the concept of dog learn to classify a variety of specific instances as members of a set. They learn that the label dog may be applied to specific instances, but more importantly they learn that dog refers to a *class of instances* which have certain properties or features in common.

If children apply the concept of dog *only* to a specific dog, such as their own, they then have not really developed the concept of dog. It is only when they can apply the term to a number of specific instances in a reasonably accurate fashion that one can say that they acquired the concept. Moreover, it is important not only that they apply the term appropriately in the presence of instances but also that they recognize other events or objects that are properly not part of the concept. Thus, for example, they must properly exclude instances such as cats, rabbits, and other animals. More generally, the formation of concepts refers to *both* the *selection* of appropriate instances and the *rejection* or exclusion of inappropriate instances.

The development and refinement of some concepts probably takes place over an extended time period. Moreover, it is true that the learning of many concepts involves progressing from some gross, diffuse state to a highly refined condition in which fine-grain distinctions can be made. Thus, it is reasonable to say that you may have only a general concept about some things or events and a quite precise concept about others. In addition, you may be in the process of refining some of your more vague concepts. It is known that in the course of formal learning, students' concepts of things such as "justice," "freedom," and "integrity" constantly grow and change as they are exposed to new experiences and knowledge. Similarly, you have probably experienced the condition in which your understanding of a particular concept has sharpened and expanded with additional experience, advanced training, or new knowledge.

A good deal of teaching is directed toward the development of concepts because concepts are necessary for more complex behaviors such as the learning of principles, problem solving, and symbolic activities such as thinking. One of the principal objectives of formal education is the teaching of basic concepts that enable individuals to function in our society, and to teach also the notion that concepts can be revised, altered, and amended on the basis of new knowledge and experience. The ability to handle concepts as they currently exist and to deal with them in a flexible and changing fashion is a joint objective of school learning.

Concept learning as a topic in the psychology of learning stands roughly midway between the simpler processes of stimulus discrimination, response learning, and association formation on the one hand and the more complex processes of thinking, reasoning, and problem solving on the other hand. It is the juncture at which one shifts from the development of simple one-to-one associations to the development of many-to-one associations. This feature will be amplified when we compare concept learning with paired associate learning.

Finally, concept learning represents no clear and sharp break from the simpler processes involved in verbal learning. Even in verbal learning tasks such as paired associate and free recall learning, you saw that humans may engage in conceptual activity. Indeed, it is doubtful that one can devise a learning situation that entirely prevents the human from forming concepts, adopting strategies, or engaging in thinking. Therefore, this chapter on concept learning in no way implies that you have not already been dealing with conceptual behavior. The thrust of this chapter, however, is most exclusively on these activities that are typically labeled conceptual.

Nature of Concept Learning

Concept learning has already been described in an informal way. More formally, however, *concept learning refers to any activity in which the learner must learn to classify two or more somewhat different events or objects into a single category.* The fact that you can learn to classify events in a reliable and consistent fashion is taken as evidence of the development of a concept. Thus, concept learning involves learning to make a common (classification) response to a group of stimuli which have some features or properties in common. This is *not,* however, all that is involved in knowing whether a person has acquired a concept.

What is a concept itself? A concept is the cognitive basis for assigning a category label or term, which in turn refers to a number of specific instances. For example, Jimmy Carter is not a concept; he is a particular instance of a concept. Nor is John F. Kennedy a concept. Carter, Ford, Nixon, Kennedy, Johnson, Eisenhower, and Truman are instances of the concept American President. The concept *President* includes Nixon, but it also includes those individuals mentioned as well as Washington, Jefferson, and all the other individuals. Thus, more generally, *a concept refers to a set of features or attributes sharing one or more common properties which are connected by a rule.*

Let us consider the difference between concept learning and paired associate learning. As we have seen, paired associate learning requires learning a particular response for a particular stimulus; that is, the ratio between stimuli and responses is one to one. Concept learning, on the other hand, involves learning a single response for two or more stimuli; that is, the ratio between stimuli and responses is several to one. This distinction is illustrated schematically below in which a paired associate task consists of six pairs, whereas a concept learning task contains two concepts (R1 and R2) and three stimuli for each response.

Paired Associate Learning	Concept Learning
S1-R1	S1 ↘
S2-R2	S2 → R1
S3-R3	S3 ↗
S4-R4	S4 ↘
S5-R5	S5 → R2
S6-R6	S6 ↗

It is possible, however, for someone learning a conceptual task to learn in a rote fashion. This is simply to say that one can treat the situation as if it were essentially a paired associate task rather than a classification task. Even though one can classify the stimuli S1, S2, and S3 as instances of the category R1, one may be doing so simply by learning each stimulus-response pair as a separate association. For concept learning to have genuinely occurred, we want to be able to say that the person has classified S1, S2, and S3 on the basis of some common feature, and that he treats them as an instance of a class. Therefore, the true test of concept learning is to present the learner with *new* instances of the concepts and determine if he appropriately classified them.

Consider, for example, teaching elementary color concepts to children. A child is shown a specific instance of a white object such as white paper and told that it is white. He is then instructed to repeat the response "white" in the presence of the sheet of white paper. This, of course, in no way ensures that he has learned the concept of white; he may simply be responding to the size or shape of the piece of paper or to some other property. Therefore, we continue to present the child other objects that contain the property of whiteness, such as a white sweater, piece of chalk, and so forth, requiring that he say "white" to each of the objects presented. Even though he correctly says "white" to all of the objects, you still cannot be sure that he has learned the concept. He may simply be learning associations between specific stimulus objects and the response of saying white.

To ensure that he has, in fact, learned the concept of white, two additional factors are necessary: (1) he must be presented with additional objects that are *instances* or exemplars of the concept to see if he appropriately classifies these as white, and (2) he must be presented *noninstances* or inappropriate exemplars to see if he excludes these as part of the concept. If he can *both* appropriately include instances and exclude noninstances, we then infer that he has learned the concept. In the actual practice of teaching concepts, one typically includes both instances and noninstances so that the concept becomes sharpened and well defined for the student. The test of whether one has learned the concept requires, as has been said, the presentation of *new* instances and noninstances.

Our discussion so far has indicated that one must come to classify events in terms of common features or properties if concept learning is to occur. This means that the learner responds to the relevant features of the set of events and comes to ignore other features. For example, in learning the concept of a circle, a child is shown a number of circles that differ in size, in color, and in other features that might be systematically varied. The child learns, however, that the *only relevant* feature is the round-circular property of the event, and that size and color are irrelevant properties or dimensions. By "relevant" is meant simply the feature or features that are pertinent to the concept.

In order to refine the concept further, other shapes such as triangles and squares are presented so that the child also learns that shape is the only relevant dimension that distinguishes circles, triangles, and squares. Again, he learns that size and color are irrelevant to these concepts. Thus, *concept learning requires that the learner come to respond to the relevant features of the concept and to ignore the irrelevant features in classifying events.*

Concept Learning, Generalization, and Discrimination

So far, our description of concept learning may make it appear as a special case of generalization and discrimination. Indeed, psychologists who adopt a stimulus-response associationistic approach to learning have characteristically viewed conceptual behavior as involving primarily the processes of generalization and discrimination. With this approach, *learning of concepts is seen as a combination of (1) discrimination between classes of events and (2) generalization within classes of events.*

An illustration of this viewpoint can be seen by examining how one might teach the concepts of "circle," "square," and "triangle." A child is shown several exemplars of each concept which vary not only in the relevant dimension (shape) but also in irrelevant dimensions (such as size and color). For example, the exemplars of square are very large, large, medium-sized, small, and very small; they also are colored differently; they may have shadings or hatch marks. In general, the exemplars vary in several ways. The same is true for the exemplars of circle and triangle. Children can be said to have learned the three shape concepts when they *generalize* within the exemplars for each class, that is, correctly categorize instances of each, and when they *discriminate* between each class. This is simply to say that they classify correctly all exemplars of square regardless of size, color, or other irrelevant dimensions. Likewise, they do this for the exemplars of circle and triangle, respectively.

This view of concept formation appears reasonable under conditions in which there is some element or dimension that is common to all the examples. In the illustration just given, the common element was shape. Children could thus be said to be discriminating among classes of shapes and generalizing within instances of the class. There are, however, other instances of concept learning in which no element or dimension is common to the instances. For example, tacos and ice cream belong to the class foods, but no obvious *elements* or physical dimensions are common to both. They are members of the same conceptual category because of what we do with them. Thus things may become members of the same conceptual category because we make *common responses* to the exemplars.

The development of a concept based upon some common response to the exemplars not directly attributable to some common dimension leads to a *mediational* view of concept learning. Here we postulate some intervening link between the external stimuli (the exemplars) and the overt response made to the stimuli. Mediational approaches to concept learning will be discussed subsequently and compared with a major alternative view, that of hypothesis testing. For the present, we need only note that concept learning is a process somewhat akin to generalization and discrimination and can be described as a special case of the two processes *when* the exemplars have clear-cut dimensions or attributes. When the situation becomes more complex, however, the analogy with these two processes is less straightforward. Alternative approaches emphasizing the cognitive information-processing character of the learner become useful.

Study of Concept Learning

Although the study of concept learning has been described in a general way, it is more fully understood by examining some of the details of laboratory experiments in concept learning. In this section we shall briefly describe the principal features of any concept learning experiment. Some of these features have already been illustrated in our examples cited.

Features of Concept Learning Tasks

As in other human learning tasks, the typical concept learning study involves *stimuli, responses,* and some form of *feedback* to the learner. Stimuli consisting of both positive instances (exemplars) and negative instances (nonexemplars) are presented to the subject. These vary in several *dimensions,* one or more of which are relevant to the concept, whereas others are irrelevant. Each dimension may take on two or more *values.* For example, we may have shape, size, and color as dimensions, with two values for each dimension: circle and square for shape, large and small for size, and red and green for color. This arrangement produces eight stimuli, as shown in figure 10.

The particular concept to be learned is arbitrarily determined by the experimenter. If the concept to be learned is "square," then the square instances enclosed by the dotted line are positive instances of that concept. If the concept to be learned is "green," then the green instances enclosed by the dotted line are positive instances of that concept. A similar arrangement could be made for the size concept. Moreover, various combinations could be used such as "small red" and "large green" things, which designate a more complex kind of concept.

The category response used in this case is quite simple. The experimenter can instruct the subject to give the category name or the subject may simply say "yes" or "no" in the presence of each instance.

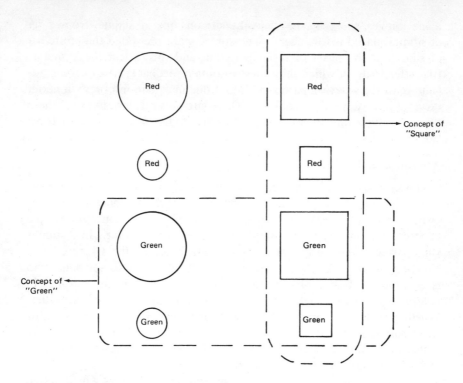

Figure 10. Schematic diagram showing instances of objects relevant to the concept "square" and to the concept "green."

Sometimes subjects press switches to designate whether the stimulus is an instance of the concept. Finally, the subject is given feedback as to the correctness of his responses.

Basic Paradigms

Psychologists have adopted two basic procedures in the laboratory investigation of conceptual behavior. The first of these employs the *reception paradigm* in which the stimuli are presented in some random or predetermined order by the experimenter and the subject attempts to classify each stimulus when it is presented. If only one concept is being learned, the subject classifies each stimulus as a positive or negative instance of the concept. As soon as the subject classifies a stimulus, he is given informative feedback. Usually only one stimulus is presented at a time, and thus subjects are required to depend upon their memory of the events over a series of trials.

The second procedure is known as the *selection paradigm*. As the name implies, the subjects select the stimuli, one at a time, from a set of stimuli placed before them. The subjects are presented the entire set of stimuli at the onset of the experiment and thus select the stimulus, trial after trial, on which they want to obtain feedback. An obvious advantage of the selection paradigm is that one may gain information about how subjects solve the problem. There are several variations of these two procedures, but most concept learning studies fall into one of these two categories.

Attributes and Rules

A concept has two critical features: attributes and rules. We have already seen that concepts possess *attributes,* which are those features or characteristics of the stimuli that are relevant to the concept. Simple concepts may involve only a single attribute, such as color. In a similar vein, "sweet" and "sour" are essential attributes of the Chinese dish, sweet-and-sour pork. The concept of "student" refers to someone who is engaged in study, either formally in the sense of being enrolled in course work or informally in the sense of self-directed study activities. Whether such a person is tall or short, or young or old, or has long or short hair are attributes irrelevant to the concept. The important thing is that in learning concepts you learn to focus on the relevant attributes and to disregard irrelevant features.

Attributes may be combined in several different ways which define a conceptual rule. In the preceding example, the Chinese dish consists of sweet-*and*-sour pork, that is, *both* the attributes of sweetness and sourness along with pork must be present. In this case we have an instance of a conjunction (joint presence) rule.

Other concepts may employ a disjunctive rule where the combination is *either/or.* For example, the concept of a "person" may refer to either a man or to a woman. The concept includes, of course, people of all ages. There are several rules for combining attributes of which conjunctive or disjunctive rules are instances. Thus, in describing a concept we must refer to its attributes and to how the attributes are combined (rules).

Classification of Conceptual Rules

There are a number of ways in which conceptual rules can be formed. Table 2 describes five basic types of rules that have been used in studies of concept learning. These rules do *not* describe how humans learn concepts; rather, they are logical rules which describe the relationships among attributes. They represent logically possible rules which conform to what humans may learn, but they do not conform to all the logical possibilities in everyday concept learning. Humans do not necessarily think of these rules, but the rules are a convenient way of describing relationships in an objective fashion.

A simple conceptual rule defines a concept simply by *attribution*. If the object possesses the simple attribute which defines the concept, the object is then an example of the rule. For example, if the correct attribute is redness, then all objects regardless of size or shape which are red are classified as instances of the concept. Thus a positive instance of the concept is any instance which shares the relevant attribute. A more complex concept is the *conjunctive* rule in which the concept is defined by the joint presence of two features. In the example in Table 2 the concept is illustrated by an object which is both red and square.

TABLE 2   Some Major Conceptual Rules

Rule Name	Verbal Description of Concept
Affirmation	All red objects are examples of the concept
Conjunction	All objects which are both red *and* a square are examples of the concept
Inclusive disjunctive	All objects which are red or square or both are examples of the concept
Conditional	If an object is red, then it must be a square to be an example of the concept
Biconditional	Red objects are examples of the concept if and only if they are squares; a red nonsquare on a nonred square is not an example

Another type of conceptual rule used is the *disjunction* rule. Assuming that the correct attributes are still red and square, then any object which is red *and/or* square is an instance of the concept. The important feature of this disjunction rule is the and/or relationship. We can distinguish between a conjunctive rule and a disjunctive rule by using real-life examples. A green car is an object which is *both* green and a car; hence, a green car is a conjunctive concept. An eligible voter might legally be defined as anyone who is a resident and/or a property owner; hence, an eligible voter is an instance of a disjunctive concept. Finally, conditional and biconditional rules are used in studies of concept learning. A *conditional* rule is one in which what counts as a correct (relevant) attribute depends upon the presence of another attribute. If an object is red, then the object must be square to be an instance of the concept. If the object is *not* red, it is automatically assumed to be an instance of the concept regardless of the shape of the object. A *biconditional* rule would be illustrated by the example of red objects if and only if they are squares. Similarly, in real life the behavior of turning on the air conditioner if and only if the weather is hot would be an instance of the rule.

Factors Which Affect Concept Learning

Let us now turn our attention to some important factors which influence concept learning. In general, these factors can be classified into two categories: *task* variables and *learner* variables. Instances of important task variables include positive and negative instances, relevant and irrelevant attributes, stimulus salience and abstractness-concreteness, feedback and temporal factors, and conceptual rules. In a parallel vein, examples of learner variables known to be important are intelligence and memory.

Positive and Negative Instances

A question of interest is whether humans learn concepts faster from positive instances than from negative instances. The issue focuses on the *nature* of the instances as a factor in concept learning. The answer to this question is somewhat complicated by the fact that at least in our society we are more accustomed to dealing with positive instances and are, therefore, more likely to learn concepts faster from positive than from negative instances. This, however, is not the complete picture.

Early studies of concept learning found that humans make little or no use of negative instances. This was the case, however, because the negative instances typically carried far less information than did the positive instances. In laboratory situations where the negative instances can be controlled or constructed so as to carry more information there is a corresponding increase in their use.

Another reason why humans tend to prefer positive over negative instances in concept learning tasks, as just noted, is that they are much more likely to encounter positive instances in their everyday experiences. Rarely are concepts in everyday life formed by negative instances alone. One close approximation is medical diagnosis, where a physician may judge a disease category by the absence of certain symptoms and by negative laboratory tests. This is because different diseases may have similar symptoms and the way they may be distinguished is by the absence of a particular symptom or pattern of symptoms. Thus, it is not surprising that humans generally learn faster from positive instances. Yet some parents try to teach the concept of "honesty" principally by identifying instances of "dishonesty"; such teaching may produce only limited effects. If, however, humans are trained to learn concepts from negative instances alone, they can learn to become almost as proficient as people who use positive instances alone. The fact that differences in the facility with which humans use positive and negative instances can be largely eliminated through training indicates that such differences are not immutable. Nevertheless, in your everyday experiences you are much more likely to use positive instances, principally because the number of negative instances is much larger than the number of positive instances and are, therefore, less useful in carrying information.

Relevant and Irrelevant Attributes

What happens to the efficiency of concept learning when the number of relevant and irrelevant dimensions is varied? First, in any concept learning task the number of irrelevant attributes or cues may be increased, which means that the proportion of relevant attributes will decrease given that the total number of attributes remains constant. *The larger the number of irrelevant attributes in a conceptual task, the more difficult is the task.* This is not hard to understand because increasing the number of irrelevant attributes makes it more difficult for the learner to discover the relevant attributes that are correlated with the correct response. Putting it simply, the more irrelevant cues that you must learn to discard or ignore, the longer it will take to latch on to the relevant cue.

Second, the number of relevant *redundant* attributes can be increased, thus increasing the relative proportion of correct cues. Relevant redundant attributes refer to features that are perfectly correlated so that either feature validly predicts the concept. For example, if every circle is blue, every square is red, and every triangle is yellow, and if these attributes are relevant to the concept to be learned, we then say that shape and color are redundant. Thus, in this example it is possible to obtain a solution for the concept on the basis of either shape or color or of both features. The principle regarding the role of number of relevant redundant attributes is quite simple: *The larger the number of relevant redundant attributes, the easier is concept learning.* Intuitively, this principle is easy to understand because by increasing the number of relevant redundant cues the likelihood that you will discover one or more of the cues is increased. This principle is recognized by many lecturers who repeat a point, but in a slightly different way, in order to ensure that the audience grasps the central idea.

Stimulus Salience and Abstractness-Concreteness

The salience or distinctiveness of the relevant cues determines in part the ease of learning concepts. Young children tend to learn color concepts more readily than form concepts which may, of course, be related to differences in previous experience with these dimensions. Similarly, concrete concepts such as, for example, "house," "dog," and "car," are learned more readily than abstract concepts that involve, for example, spatial form. The difficulty of abstract concepts is apparently related to the difficulty in giving them a mediating label and to the fact that you are less likely to have image-like mediators for them.

The salience or distinctiveness of the relevant cues is related to the degree of similarity among the cues. As the cues increase in similarity, which in effect reduces their distinctiveness, concept learning becomes more difficult. Moreover, since cues related to abstract concepts may be more similar to each other, the effect of greater difficulty in concept learning with more abstract concepts may be due to the greater similarity of such cues. For example, concepts such as "circle" and "elipse" may be more difficult to learn than concrete concepts such as "tree" and "house" because instances of the abstract concepts may be more similar or confusable. Even more abstract concepts such as "democracy" or "socialism" may be difficult to distinguish because of their several overlapping features.

Feedback and Temporal Factors

Feedback in the form of indicating whether a response is correct or not provides the learner with information about the correctness of his responses. Moreover, feedback can serve to guide subsequent responses in conceptual tasks. At one level feedback can be viewed as somewhat analogous to reward in instrumental learning situations if the learner's response is correct. At another level, feedback is important because of the *information* that it provides the learner, both with respect to what hypothesis seems to be correct and to the elimination of incorrect hypotheses. The learner must, however, utilize the information in the stimulus in conjunction with feedback in order to achieve an efficient solution to the problem. Merely being told that you are "right" or "wrong" on each trial is insufficient for concept learning unless you simultaneously attend to and use the information in the particular exemplars presented. This means, of course, that you must remember something about the particular exemplars, noting and remembering from trial to trial what feature(s) is present when the response is confirmed as correct.

One aspect of feedback that has been examined is the time delay between the learner's response and informative feedback. Although it might be expected that *delay of feedback* would exert a pronounced effect on concept learning, this factor has been found to have very little effect on performance. This finding stands in striking contrast to studies with lower animals, where delay of reward produces a marked effect on performance.

In contrast, another kind of delay called postfeedback delay produces a potent effect on performance. Postfeedback delay refers to the delay between feedback on one trial and the next presentation of a stimulus: *As postfeedback delay is lengthened, concept learning is facilitated.* This is not difficult to understand when you consider that by lengthening the postfeedback interval the learner is given more time to think about what was learned or to process the information that was obtained from that particular trial. On the other hand, simple delay of feedback, as described previously, exerts little effect apparently because the learner cannot process the information fruitfully until *after* he has been given feedback.

These effects of feedback can be intuitively appreciated if you think about them in the context of an ordinary conceptual game such as twenty questions. In this game you are allowed to ask twenty questions in order to solve a problem, asking only categorical questions (that is, questions that can be answered by yes or no). You ask one question at a time, trying to zero in on the correct concept. Each question is answered yes or no by the person with whom you are playing the game. The more time you are given to think about the information you have gained from your question following a yes or no response, the more rapidly you are likely to solve the problem. Indeed, for this reason the twenty-questions game is sometimes played at a particular pace so as to control the rate at which information is conveyed.

Conceptual Rules

The manner in which particular attributes are combined, that is, the conceptual rule, also determines the ease with which a conceptual task is learned. This is simply to say that there are several basic conceptual rules, and they differ in ease of learning. At the simplest level, concepts that merely *affirm* the presence of an attribute, thus conforming to an affirmation rule, are the easiest to learn. This rule simply means that all stimuli with a given attribute are members of that concept. For example, all people who currently breathe can be said to be alive. Conversely, people who have ceased to breathe (after some brief but specified time interval) are dead. The converse of an affirmative rule, which is the lack of a given attribute, is the negation rule.

Concepts which employ a conjunctive rule are also relatively easy to learn. *Conjunctive rules* refer to conditions in which both attributes must be jointly present, which can be described as A and B. For instance, a "black cat" is a conjunctive concept since these two attributes, "black" and "cat" must be jointly present. In contrast, concepts which employ *conditional* rules (if A, then B) and *biconditional* rules (if A, then B; if B, then A) are much harder to learn.

Memory and Intelligence

Conceptual learning depends not only upon characteristics of the task but upon characteristics of the learner as well. Both memory and intelligence are individual-difference variables which are known to affect the ease with which we learn concepts. The role of memory is reasonably obvious in conceptual tasks in which a series of instances are presented over successive trials. In order to achieve a particular concept, the learner must remember information over several trials because a single trial usually does not present sufficient information for the concept to be learned. Thus, memory for specific instances increases the ease with which concepts will be learned.

In a similar vein, it is most reasonable to expect that intelligence is an important factor in concept learning. Indeed, more intelligent children solve conceptual tasks consistently faster than do less intelligent children. The explanation of this relationship apparently lies in the greater ability of the more intelligent children to construct hypotheses and in their greater skill in using verbal mediating responses. Mediational responses are implicit responses that are in some way symbolic of or representative of the class of instances; these responses enable humans to respond to instances in terms of their common properties. Mediational responses may not necessarily be verbal, but may be perceptual in nature.

Theories of Concept Learning

Several general approaches have been taken in trying to account for the process of concept learning. One approach stems from stimulus-response associationistic conceptions of the learning process and adopts principles of conditioning to explain conceptual behavior. With this approach, concept learning is thought to develop in a manner like that of simple discrimination learning and is regarded as a special case of the processes of generalization and discrimination. In contrast to S-R association theory, a second approach to concept learning emphasizes the importance of hypotheses and strategies and adopts, therefore, a cognitive approach. Here emphasis is placed upon the active role of the learner in developing concepts and the manner in which he tests various hypotheses.

There is no single S-R theory and there is no single cognitive hypotheses-testing theory. Rather, there is a constellation of approaches that can be roughly classified as S-R and there are several approaches that adopt an hypothesis-testing emphasis. These approaches have been modified over time and are still evolving, and it is our intent therefore to characterize only their typical features. Many nuances of detail will, therefore, not be considered since the focus will be on the essential and characteristic features of these approaches, looking at them in bold relief.

S-R Association Theory

In general, S-R association theories of conceptual learning regard the process as akin to, or a special case of, discrimination learning. We have already noted certain features of this approach in the discussion of concept learning, generalization, and discrimination.

A conceptual task is seen as consisting of a series of instances or exemplars, each instance consisting of both relevant and irrelevant features of attributes. The learner must respond on each trial, sometimes being correct and sometimes being incorrect. Each response to a positive instance is reinforced by being given feedback. S-R theories contend that associative strength between the relevant dimension and correct response is gradually built up to some point at which a person can be said to have acquired the concept. In turn, response strength to the irrelevant dimension is gradually weakened because it is not consistently reinforced. Thus, concept learning is similar to discrimination learning in that a discrimination between relevant and irrelevant cues is gradually developed by differential reinforcement.

With this approach a concept is viewed as a learned association between a class of stimuli having some common element and an overt response. The associative strength is, however, between the common element and the response. For example, in learning the concept of "green," associative strength develops between the property of "greenness" in the various stimulus objects presented and the response "green" made to these various objects.

In this connection, the reader must be cautioned not to confuse the *manner* in which concepts are taught with *theory* about what is learned. Our previous illustrations about how concepts are typically taught may superficially look like theory. Theory refers to the conceptualization about *what* gets learned, which in this case is an association between stimulus elements and a response.

When a person responds to new stimulus objects that contain the relevant feature or cue, that person is said to generalize. Thus, once a concept has been acquired it may be applied in new situations. This occurs if the new situation contains the relevant features because of the built-in associative strength between the features and a response. Thus, if we refer back to our previous example, new objects that are green will tend to evoke the correct response by virtue of a generalization process.

S-R Mediational Theories

As we noted in a previous section, an S-R associative conception of concept learning is reasonable when the stimulus examples contain elements common to all of the examples. There are, however, many situations in which no element or dimension is common to the examples. As we noted, tacos and ice cream are members of the same conceptual class— namely, foods—not because of common dimensions but because we make responses common to these events.

Mediational S-R theories assume that concept learning develops because of mediating responses made to the stimulus instances. For example, the common response of "eating" is made to the following stimuli:

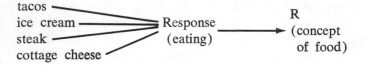

Thus, we don't *directly* identify tacos as an instance of the concept of food because of some physical dimension such as their color or of the fact that they may be hot, but because of our response to them. Thus, things that are edible are called *foods*. We may further require that these things have "food value," in the sense of having vitamins, minerals, or caloric value if they are to be called foods. This, however, represents simply a further refinement of the food concept. The point to note is that a mediational view emphasizes an association between a common response to a class of stimuli and the overt response.

The mediational response can be characterized in several ways. Frequently it is regarded as a verbal response or some kind of verbal label is given to the stimulus instances. It may also be regarded as some kind of perceptual response or attentional response that involves images. More generally, we may think of mediating responses as symbolic events that serve to represent particular aspects of external stimulus events.

The more general importance of mediational views of concept learning is that an intervening step is introduced between stimuli and responses. Instead of thinking of connections between the relevant attributes of stimuli and overt responses, we think of connections between mediating responses made to stimuli and overt responses. Mediational theories are therefore more complex than simple S-R association theories. Moreover, mediational theories are more flexible in their ability to handle certain kinds of conceptual behaviors.

Solution Shifts and Mediation Theory

Two basic types of *solution shift* problems are used in the study of concept learning. In one, called the *reversal* or *intradimensional* shift, the subject initially learns a particular solution to a problem and then must learn exactly the opposite solution with the same stimuli. This problem is illustrated in figure 11 in which two-dimensional stimuli varying in shape and color are shown. Shape is represented as a circle or square and color is represented as red (R) or green (G). In the training phase all red stimuli are assigned to Category A and all green stimuli are assigned to Category B. Once a subject acquires this concept, he is then shifted to a second task in which the rule is reversed. Now, all red stimuli are assigned to Category B and all green stimuli are assigned to Category A.

The second solution shift problem is called a *nonreversal* or *extra-dimensional* shift and is also illustrated in figure 11 using the same stimuli. The training phase remains the same as in the first example with all red stimuli assigned to Category A and all green stimuli assigned to Category B. The shift in the test problem differs from the reversal shift in that it involves a shift from color to shape as the relevant dimension; hence, the designation *extra*dimensional. Consequently, only half the category assignments are changed.

Association and mediation theories of concept learning can make different predictions about performance in the two solution-shift problems described. The prediction has to do with which shift is easier to learn. An association theory which views concept learning as the result of associations being formed between attributes of physical stimuli and overt responses would predict that the intradimensional shift is more difficult than the extradimensional shift. This is true because only half of the stimuli in the extradimensional shift are assigned to new response categories. In contrast, with the intradimensional shift all the stimuli are assigned to new response categories. Theoretically, this situation would require extinction of all the original associations and thus learning would be more difficult.

In contrast, a mediational theory such as the one proposed by Howard and Tracy Kendler would make just the opposite prediction. A mediational theory makes the assumption that during initial training the subject not only learns to attend to the colors red and green, but also establishes a *mediating response* to the color attributes. With an intradimensional shift, the mediating response established during training is the correct one during the test phase. The subject has only to

INTRADIMENSIONAL SHIFT

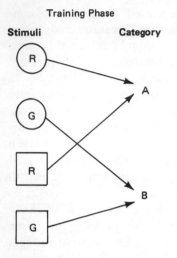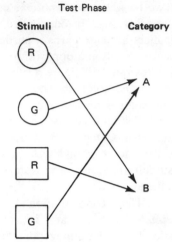

EXTRADIMENSIONAL SHIFT

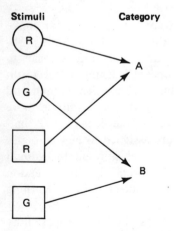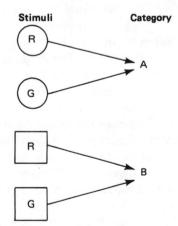

Figure 11. Illustration of intradimensional and extradimensional solution shift problems.

reverse the category responses as she continues to use the mediators established in training. In contrast, with the extradimensional shift, the initial mediational response based on color is no longer appropriate and must be withheld, while a new mediational response based on shape must be developed.

How do the predictions fare? With very young subjects whose verbal ability is not fully developed the extradimensional shift is easier. For subjects seven years and older who have reasonable language facility the intradimensional shift is easier. This result has been interpreted to indicate that the behavior of younger organisms, whose verbal capacity is not yet well developed, can be adequately described by association theory. The behavior of young children is comparable with the performance of lower animals who also show better performance with the extradimensional shift. In turn, as organisms become more verbal their behavior is better predicted by mediational theory according to the Kendlers.

It is possible, however, that a simpler interpretation of these results can be made. Rather than assume that the solution shift behaviors are due simply to verbal mediational processes, it is also possible to account for the results in terms of perceptual and attentional processes. If children are familiar with the stimulus dimensions, they then perform better on the intradimensional shift problems. If children are unfamiliar with the dimensions, they tend to perform better on the extradimensional problems. These results suggest that an intradimensional (reversal) shift is truly an intradimensional shift only for those subjects who recognize and understand the dimensions used in the task.

Hypothesis-testing Theories

Hypothesis-testing theories of concept learning emphasize the human as more active in the task in the sense that we are actively selecting and testing possible solutions. These theories emphasize the importance of the selection of hypotheses, of the decision-making character of the task, and are therefore cognitive theories in the sense that implicit decision processes are involved.

The essential difference between S-R and hypothesis-testing theories is that S-R theories emphasize that the human is under control of the properties of the stimulus environment or of mediating responses made to the stimuli. In contrast, hypothesis-testing theories emphasize an additional set of processes, namely, what the learner himself does in the conceptual task. The particular hypotheses and strategies that he may employ are seen as important.

Formal models of hypothesis testing, such as those proposed by Gordon Bower and Frank Restle, emphasize that the subject samples from some population of hypotheses on each trial. The population of hypotheses consists of both relevant and irrelevant hypotheses and the subject is viewed, theoretically, as sampling at random from such a population. If the subject samples an irrelevant hypothesis, this must eventually lead to an incorrect response, leading the subject to sample a new hypothesis. The subject continues to sample hypotheses until one leads to continuous correct responding.

Strategies and Hypothesis Testing

Humans may show a variety of strategies in conceptual learning tasks. One type of strategy is called *conservative focusing*. Consider the case in which a subject has just been told that a large red square is a positive instance of the to-be-discovered concept. Conservative focusing requires that the subject's initial hypothesis include all three attributes of the stimulus in his hypothesis. The subject might then select a large red triangle as the next stimulus. If he is told he is correct, he then knows that shape is an irrelevant dimension. He might then select a small red square; if he is again correct he knows that size is irrelevant, but that color is the relevant feature. Thus the important aspect of conservative focusing is that only one feature is changed at a time until the concept is identified. In general, humans do better with conservative focusing than with anything else.

A more risky strategy is seen in *focus gambling*. With focus gambling a person takes a chance and varies two or more attributes at a time in trying out hypotheses. If a person is successful with this strategy, learning can then take place quickly. Using the stimuli in the example just given our subject first selects a large red square; if he follows the strategy of focus gambling the subject might then select a small red triangle, changing both size and shape. If, in fact, blue is the relevant feature, the subject would have then learned the concept in one trial. On the other hand, if the subject fails in his gamble, learning is then slower.

Information-Processing Theories

Finally, theories have been developed which emphasize the information-processing character of concept learning. These theories derive from computer analogies and view concept learning in terms of a sequence of decisions made by the learner. The general idea is that of an analogy between man and a high-speed computer. Both are seen as accepting external information or stimuli, as processing the information in a variety of ways, and as producing some terminal response or behavior.

Information-processing theories assume hypothesis testing by the learner in which hypotheses are first generated and then tested.

One approach used in the development of information-processing theories is computer simulation. A computer program which is designed to simulate conceptual behavior is written. The computer program is written so that it attempts to describe the decisions that make up conceptual behavior. The computer then solves the problems of the same type given to human subjects, and a comparison of performance is made. If the performance of the computer simulation is similar to the performance of the human subject, the theorist may then begin to suspect that the decisions in the program may be like those of the human.

Some Practical Principles of Concept Learning

It is reasonable to ask what is known about concept learning that may be usefully applied by yourself. Psychologists know about many of the factors that affect concept learning and have formulated some principles regarding efficient concept learning. Therefore, it is appropriate to examine some of these factors and principles and note some of their potential implications. The focus of this section will be on only a few of these, with the objective of seeing how they might apply in familiar learning situations.

Think of New Examples of Concepts

A moment's reflection on your part may lead you to recognize that much of classroom instruction involves going from concepts to examples and from examples back to concepts. Frequently, an instructor introduces a concept by briefly defining it and then proceeds to illustrate the concept by giving one or two examples. After a few illustrations he proceeds to refine and clarify the concept, developing it to some level required by its inherent complexity. Similarly, many textbooks reveal this characteristic feature.

In order that a concept be fully grasped and understood, *it is important that you think of additional examples beyond those presented by your instructor.* The instructor typically has time to present only one or two examples, perhaps a few more at best, and depends upon these examples to provide you with sufficient information to abstract the essential features of the concept. Unfortunately, you may fail to understand the concept with only one or two examples, or at best you may achieve only a general idea of the concept. Your instructor, however, may expect you to achieve a much more detailed and elaborate concept, one that you cannot obtain unless you continue to think of additional examples that will aid you in refining and enriching the concept.

Obviously, your examples must be pertinent to the concept. If you are in doubt about the adequacy of your examples and hence about your full grasp of the concept, you must check these by talking with other students, or by continued reading in other sources, or by asking your instructor about the adequacy of your ideas.

Generating new examples not only helps to sharpen and refine the particular concept, but also provides practice in retrieval of information, a process important for memory. Test questions frequently ask the student to produce new examples or illustrations, as distinct from those given in a lecture. Thus, thinking of new examples not only sharpens, refines, and enriches the concept, but also provides practice in the important process of information retrieval.

Use Both Positive and Negative Instances

The sharpness and precision of a concept develops as we process both positive and negative instances of a concept. In learning a particular concept you must discriminate between instances of the concept and those instances which fail to fit the category. If all of your examples are positive instances of the concept, then you have certainly minimal opportunity to compare positive and negative instances and, hence, to zero in on the essential attributes or features.

Consider teaching a young child the concept of "dog" in which all the examples are positive instances. Assume that the child is shown pictures of a collie, fox terrier, miniature poodle, and German shepherd. To each of these the child learns to say "dog." But what are the relevant attributes of the concept? What features of these examples control his response? Obviously, we cannot be entirely sure in this situation. Moreover, if we show the child a picture of a cat or rabbit, we cannot be sure of the response unless we have additional information about the child's experience with these animals. Indeed, the child may well regard a picture of a cat as another instance of dog. It is for this reason that the inclusion of carefully selected negative instances is helpful in developing a concept.

In order to develop a sharply delineated concept, negative instances must contain toward some latter stage of training irrelevant attributes that are likely to be found in the positive instances. Both dogs and cats are four-legged animals, so the property of "four-leggedness" is an irrelevant feature. Cats are frequently smaller than dogs, but obviously not always. Hence size is not a predictable feature. Nor is the presence of a tail, paws, or coat of fur. It is clear that differences between cats and dogs are based on the presence and absence of several features in combination. Features like head shape and presence or absence of claws help to distinguish the two. Even with head shape we may have difficulty when we first show a child a picture of a Pekingese.

The more general point is that if you teach concepts only by the use of positive examples, or try to learn concepts with only positive examples, you may fail to respond to the *essential* features of the concept and respond instead to some superficial or unessential feature.

Use of a Variety of Examples

The previous sections implicitly emphasized the importance of a variety of examples in learning concepts. With only one example you may easily attend to some nonessential feature of the concept and erroneously assume that you have learned it.

How many examples should you use? No simple answer can, of course, be given to this question because concepts vary in difficulty and complexity. Perhaps the best answer is that examples should be selected so that they encompass the *range* of the concept. Practical limitations will prevent you from considering all possibilities, but by sampling examples along some range you are likely to include highly pertinent ones.

Highlight Relevant Features

From the viewpoint of teaching, a major task is to highlight or emphasize the relevant features of concepts. One objective is to make the relevant aspect or essential parts of a concept more distinctive than the nonessential features. In a similar vein, you can help to highlight the essential features of concepts by *verbalizing* these features to yourself. This effort can involve trying to define the concept in your own words, as distinct from memorizing formal definitions of concepts.

Relevant features of concepts can be made more distinctive by the *simultaneous presentation* of both positive and negative examples. This simply means that in the teaching of a particular concept, a positive instance as well as a negative instance should be presented to the learner at the same time, allowing him to compare the instances. For example, when the concept "lake" is taught a picture of a lake, a stream, a river, and an ocean are all shown together. Leaving all of the pictures in view minimizes the burden on memory and makes discrimination between the relevant and irrelevant features easier. This superiority of simultaneous over successive presentation of stimulus examples holds for simple discrimination learning as well as for concept learning.

Similarly, by comparing and contrasting concepts and principles, you can emphasize the feature of simultaneous presentation in your own study habits. Comparison of concepts stands clearly in contrast to concentrating on each idea as an isolated event.

Summary

This chapter has described some of the major characteristics of concept learning. Concepts serve to reduce the complexity of one's environment, provide one with tools for thinking and for learning principles, and reduce the necessity for constant learning in each new situation. One objective of formal education is concept learning coupled with the notion that concepts can be revised and amended with new experiences and knowledge.

Concept learning is any activity that requires you to classify two or more events or objects into a single class. A concept is a class of stimuli that share one or more common features. Concept learning differs from paired associate learning in that the ratio of stimuli to responses is several to one. Concept learning requires both learning to respond to one or more relevant aspects and learning not to respond to irrelevant features. At a simple level, concept learning is akin to generalization and discrimination.

Experiments on concept learning have three principal features: stimuli, responses, and feedback. Stimuli consist of positive and negative instances, and stimuli may vary in several dimensions. Each dimension in turn can have one or more values or attributes. Concept learning experiments employ typically either the reception or selection paradigm. A concept has two essential features: attributes and the rules by which the attributes are combined.

Factors which affect concept learning include both task and learner variables. Important task variables discussed were positive and negative instances, relevant and irrelevant attributes, stimulus salience and abstractness-concreteness, feedback and temporal factors, and conceptual rules. Learner variables described were memory and intelligence.

Theories of concept learning discussed were S-R theories and hypothesis-testing theories. S-R theories may be simple association theories and may include the process of mediation. Hypothesis-testing theories are cognitive-type theories emphasizing the importance of decision making by the learner.

Several practical principles for effective concept learning were described. These emphasized the importance (1) of thinking of new examples of concepts, (2) of using both positive and negative examples, (3) of having a variety of examples, and (4) of highlighting the relevant features of concepts.

Multiple-Choice Items: Concept Learning

1. A concept is
   a. just the label we assign to objects and events
   b. an association between many stimuli and many responses
   c. an association between one stimulus and many responses
   d. the basis for assigning or classifying things
2. Concepts have two important aspects
   a. attributes and rules
   b. attributes and knowledge
   c. knowledge and rules
   d. knowledge and thought
3. The conceptual rule which classifies all people as both the living and the dead is a(n) _____ rule.
   a. affirmation
   b. conditional
   c. conjunctive
   d. inclusive disjunction
4. Lengthening which interval tends to facilitate concept learning?
   a. delay of feedback interval
   b. memory interval
   c. postfeedback interval
   d. prefeedback interval
5. The importance of a variety of examples was emphasized as desirable in concept learning because stimulus variation increases the likelihood that the learner will respond to the
   a. redundant dimensions
   b. irrelevant dimensions
   c. relevant dimensions
   d. schema
6. Concept A has four irrelevant attributes, whereas concept B has seven irrelevant attributes
   a. A is easier to learn because it has fewer irrelevant attributes
   b. A is harder to learn because it has fewer irrelevant attributes
   c. B is easier to learn because it has fewer relevant attributes
   d. B is harder to learn because it has fewer relevant attributes
7. Stimulus-response mediational theories of concept learning emphasize responding to
   a. overt responses
   b. associations with covert responses
   c. nominal stimuli
   d. mediating responses which act as stimuli

8. An extradimensional solution shift problem is one in which
   - a. only half the stimuli are assigned to a new category
   - b. most of the stimuli are assigned to a new category
   - (c.) a new dimension becomes the fully relevant one
   - d. no change is made except to add one new dimension not present during training

9. The strategy of focus gambling is one in which a person
   - a. changes only one attribute at a time
   - b. assumes that the first hypothesis is correct
   - c. limits himself to only three hypotheses
   - (d.) varies two or more attributes at a time

10. An advantage of using both positive and negative instances in developing a concept is that
   - (a.) we increase the precision or defining limits of the concept
   - b. we can lengthen the postfeedback interval
   - c. we automatically present more positive instances
   - d. we downplay the role of memory

True-False Items: Concept Learning

T   1. Your understanding of abstract concepts such as "honesty," "democracy," and "cognition" and even of the concept of a "concept" can change, grow, and become refined as the result of new knowledge and experiences.

T   2. Classifying a set of facial photographs into the categories "attractive" and "unattractive" is an instance of concept learning.

T   3. Concept learning is defined as the process by which you learn both to include exemplars and to exclude nonexemplars of the concept.

T   4. Concepts are distinguished by their attributes and by the rules for combining the attributes.

F   5. Humans characteristically learn concepts from negative instances about as fast as they do from positive instances.

T   6. In general, the greater the number of relevant redundant attributes in a concept, the easier it is to learn the concept.

F   7. Concepts such as "justice," "fair play," and "gravity" are generally easier to learn than concepts such as "desk," "chair," and "house."

T   8. The longer the delay of feedback, that is, the interval between response and feedback, the harder it is to learn the concept.

T   9. Stimulus-response association theories differ from stimulus-response mediation theories of concept learning in that the latter are somewhat more complex.

F   10. Hypothesis-testing theories place considerable emphasis on conditioning principles in concept learning.

T 11. In learning to refine your concept of "learning," it is helpful to distinguish between instances and noninstances of the concept learning.

T 12. A variety of examples which illustrate the *range* of a concept are more likely to ensure that a concept is well learned.

Discussion Items: Concept Learning

1. Define concept and concept learning.

2. How does concept learning relate to generalization and discrimination? How does it differ?

3. Describe the typical procedure used in a concept-learning task.

4. Compare and contrast the major features of association, mediation, and hypothesis-testing theories of concept learning.

5. How would you go about teaching the concept of "justice" to a child? What factors would you consider in teaching this concept?

Multiple-Choice Answers: Concept Learning

1. (d) A concept is the basis for classifying things. It is not simply a label per se, but is a label assigned in accordance with a rule.

2. (a) Concepts are composed of attributes, which are the defining features, and a rule, which specifies how the attributes are combined.

3. (c) Since "people" is defined as both "living" and "dead," a joint-presence rule, "people" is treated in this case as a conjunctive concept.

4. (c) It is the postfeedback interval which is important, presumably because the longer interval gives a person more time to process the feedback presented.

5. (c) Many examples are desirable because they increase the likelihood that you will actually respond, or be under control of, the relevant dimension or dimensions.

6. (a) Concept A is easier to learn because there are fewer irrelevant attributes to gain your attention and fewer attributes that you must consider in forming an hypothesis about the correct concept.

7. (d) Mediational theories of concept learning emphasize that an association is formed between a common mediating response to a class of stimuli and the overt response. It is this *link* between stimuli and overt response that characterizes mediation theory.

8. (c) The formerly irrelevant dimension now becomes the relevant dimension. For example, if the stimuli vary only in size and shape and size is the relevant dimension during training, then shape becomes the relevant dimension during the test phase.

9.   (d)   Focus gambling means simply that instead of being conservative, varying only one attribute at a time, the person gambles and varies two or more at a time.

10.   (a)   We are more likely to sharpen the concept because we see both positive and negative instances.

True-False Answers: Concept Learning

1.   (True)   Concepts need not be fixed; they may be modified or amended as we gain additional information.

2.   (False)   The individual is presumably sorting the photographs on the basis of an already learned concept of attractiveness. Here he is *using* a concept, as distinguished from *learning* a concept.

3.   (True)   Concept learning involves both responding to instances and not responding to noninstances of the concept.

4.   (True)   The concept of "a red barn" is defined by its attributes ("redness" and "barn like" structure) and by the rule of joint presence, that is, the object must be both red and a barn.

5.   (False)   On the contrary, we typically learn concepts faster from positive instances.

6.   (True)   This is the case because with more relevant redundant attributes your likelihood of discovering any one attribute is greater.

7.   (False)   Abstract concepts are typically harder to learn than concrete concepts.

8.   (False)   Delay of feedback produces no systematic or marked effect on concept learning. This is distinguished, however, from the effect of postfeedback delay, whose increase tends to improve concept learning.

9.   (True)   Stimulus-response mediational theory introduces one additional step, that of a mediating link between the stimuli and responses.

10.   (False)   Hypothesis-testing theories emphasize what the learner does (e.g., uses strategies) in the task.

11.   (True)   Concept learning is facilitated when you can compare and contrast both positive and negative instances.

12.   (True)   With a greater number of examples, you are more likely to focus on the essential features of a concept.

Language

7

The one kind of behavior that most clearly distinguishes human beings from other animals is their facility with language. Although it can be demonstrated in the context of controlled laboratory situations that lower animals can think, learn concepts, and solve problems, language is frequently said to be a distinguishing human feature. Recent investigations of language behavior in chimpanzees suggest, however, that humans may not be the sole possessors of language. These animals have been shown capable of using language at a simple level. Language is closely related to thought and other cognitive processes such as problem solving.

Language clearly relates to thinking and problem solving, and a few comments on this relationship are pertinent at this point even though chapter 8 deals exclusively with the topics of thinking and problem solving. Thinking represents our most complex and advanced activity. This mental activity results from our ability to manipulate symbols and concepts and to use them in new and different ways in order to solve problems. The importance of thinking is clearly evident in our daily activities. Humans are urged to think carefully, sometimes to think fast, sometimes to think systematically or clearly, and sometimes just to think. Indeed, the widespread importance of thinking is reflected in the forceful motto Think! used by a major international corporation. In a similar vein, the importance of thinking is attested by the fact that it is a frequently expressed objective of education.

Teachers may exhort students to think clearly without, however, complete understanding of how one engages in this activity. Although teachers have a reasonably clear understanding of how to help one write systematically and speak clearly, it is more difficult to specify how one thinks logically. In part this is because thinking refers to *covert* activities, events that we do not directly observe or measure, whereas writing and speaking are overt language behaviors which are directly observable.

Much of your thinking is directed toward solving problems of practical importance. Certainly you are more likely to think when your old habits, skills, and routines are inappropriate for the particular task at hand. In such situations you are forced to search for and try out new solutions. Moreover, thinking ranges from relatively simple events to quite complex activities. If you play the game of categories and are asked to think of instances of the category tree, numerous examples come to mind immediately. This represents a case of the simplest kind of thinking which involves the direct association between some conceptual category and an instance. Only when you exhaust the immediately obvious instances do you begin a more careful search of the various possibilities. Perhaps you first think of subcategories such as evergreens, deciduous trees, and overlapping subcategories such as tropical vegetation, and then think of instances of each subcategory. This aspect of thinking involves a two-stage process in which specific words are produced only after you have thought of two or more categories that serve to mediate specific words. In summary, language, thought, and problem solving are intimately related activities.

Characteristics of Language

Language is the basic tool with which humans think. Jean Piaget, the distinguished Swiss psychologist, has made an interesting analogy in pointing out that language is to thought as mathematics is to physics. Just as we use mathematics as the language of physics, ordinary language bears a similar relationship to thought.

Language is composed of words combined according to certain rules. Words themselves represent symbols which are composed of basic vowel and consonant sounds. These sounds are called *phonemes* and represent the basic unit of language.

At a more general level, language represents the major system of *symbols* available to the human for communication. Other symbol systems are of course available. For example, the deaf communicate with sign language, small children count by raising their fingers, mathematical formulas convey information, and signs convey emotional feelings of the carrier. All of these are symbols in the sense that they convey meaning. They provide some kind of information which, in turn, allows some kind of response by other humans. The symbol ⊕ represents "peace," but the symbol is not peace itself. Rather, it stands for the concept of peace and for the hope of peace by the person who uses the symbol. It communicates a set of feelings and attitudes by the user of the symbol; it clearly conveys meaning.

Functions of Language

Language, as the most important symbol system for humans, serves at least four identifiable functions. (1) First, language can be *instrumental* in the sense that verbal behavior can lead directly to reward. For instance, young children may learn that by saying "please" they obtain a reward such as candy or a cookie from their parents. Commands such as "stop" and "be quiet" are instrumental in that they may lead to the cessation of unpleasant stimuli. (2) Language serves as *stimuli* or signals for other behaviors. This is to say that language aids us in thinking and in mediating behaviors that ultimately may achieve some kind of reward. (3) Language serves as a vehicle for communication with others. This communication may, of course, directly achieve some kind of reinforcement for the speaker. (4) Finally, language conveys meaning.

Basic Units of Language: Phonemes and Morphemes

All languages are made of basic sounds called *phonemes*. Adult humans can produce approximately 100 phonemes, and the English language is made up of about 45 phonemes. Languages vary in the number of phonemes, ranging from as few as 15 to as many as 85. One reason why it is difficult for some Americans to learn foreign languages is that different phonemes are used. For instance, Germanic and Slavic languages contains phonemes never used in the English language.

Phonemes are in turn composed of about twelve *distinctive features.* The linguist Roman Jakobson has constructed a classification of distinctive features by which phonemes differ. For example, a given phoneme (speech sound) may be sounded nasally or orally. Another feature is the explosive or tense character of some sounds as seen when you pronounce letters like *p* or *f.*

Another unit of language is the *morpheme,* which is the smallest meaningful unit in a language. Morphemes usually consist of combinations of two or more phonemes and roughly correspond to the most elementary words. The words *good, put,* and *go* are single morphemes. *Goodness, putting,* and *going* consist of two morphemes. Thus, single morphemes may be root words of a language; they may also consist of prefixes or suffixes.

At about two years of age the young child begins to combine two words to form the most rudimentary kind of sentence. The combination of words into sentences is referred to as *syntax.* A young child will frequently use sentences like "Want cookie," "Where ball?" or "Drink Mommy" which clearly convey meaning. These sentences are quite systematic, are usually understood by the parent, and are similar to adult English sentences with the unessential words omitted.

Higher Levels of Linguistic Analysis

We have just considered two of the most basic analyses possible of language. The study of the speech sounds which make up a language is called phonology and the study of how these sounds combine to produce morphemes is called morphology. However, psychologists are frequently interested in a more global analysis of language than is provided by phonology and morphology. Psychological investigations of language typically adopt words or phrases as the most fundamental unit of analysis, rather than more elementary speech sounds.

There are several levels at which these higher-order analyses can be made. First, one could analyze the *lexical* content of a sentence or of some other unit of language production. In performing a lexical analysis, you are simply asking, "What words were used in this sample of language? This was the basic approach of Thorndike and Lorge who tabulated the frequency with which different English words occurred in large samples of printed material. For example, these investigators reported the average frequency of occurrence per million words of text for each of a large number of common words such as *kitchen* (over 100 times per million) and rare words such as *rostrum* (only 1 time per million). Information gained from lexical analyses of language such as that by Thorndike and Lorge has proved to be very useful in predicting the ease with which different words can be learned in standard verbal learning paradigms.

At another level of linguistic analysis, the *syntactic* content of language text may be investigated. In the study of syntax, the concern is with the arrangement or ordering of words to form phrases and sentences. The question being asked in this type of analysis is, How is this phrase (or sentence) structured? Psychologists and linguists interested in syntactic theory have attempted to specify rules that will generate an infinite number of grammatically correct sentences and no incorrect sentences. The set of rules indicating how the elements of the language may be combined to make intelligible sentences is referred to as a *grammar*. Although a large number of different grammars have been proposed, linguists have not been able to write down the extremely complex system of rules which generates all the syntactically correct sentences of the English language, or of any other natural language. At present, there is little agreement about the necessary features of an adequate grammar. However, an important part of many of the proposed grammars is that of rules for phrase structure, which we will consider in the next section.

Perhaps the most important level of analysis of language is the one which considers the *semantic* content or meaning of a passage. This perspective on language results in the asking of questions such as What does the passage communicate? and What is the meaning of this particular sentence? Unfortunately, psychologists and linguists know less about the rules for determining the meanings of words and combinations of words than they do about the rules of syntax or morphology. The critical role of semantics, however, has been clearly demonstrated in a number of psychological investigations. For example, when subjects listen to passages of connected discourse, their recognition memory for sentences after a short delay is much more sensitive to changes in semantic content (e.g. subject-object reversal) than to changes in syntactic content (e.g., switching from active to passive voice).

Although we will not be able to consider theories of semantics in any detail, it is appropriate to point out the dramatic differences in approaches to theorizing in this area. On one hand, associationistic theories have been proposed in which meaning is viewed simply as a conditioned response. Thus the responses we make to a word are thought to be modifications of the unconditioned response we once made to the thing referred to by that word. In contrast to this S-R approach, more recent theories have suggested possible structures of the semantic memory necessary for the use of language. This latter approach has conceived of the human being as an information-processing system rather than as an association learner and has resulted in a number of computer programs which attempt to model the human's ability to deal with semantics. Certain of these programs provide persuasive demonstrations of their understanding of portions of the English language. For example, computer programs have been written which can respond in ordinary English to questions concerning the properties of objects or events which the computer has stored in its memory after being presented with a series of sentences describing those objects or events. Although the extent to which the analogy between a human's and a computer's semantic memory can be pushed has, of course, been questioned, the collaboration between computer scientists, psychologists, and linguists seems to offer one of the most promising approaches to the study of how we acquire knowledge of semantics.

Phrase Structure in Sentences

In order to understand language in the adult, it is necessary to examine the structure of sentences. At one level of analysis a sentence can be simply regarded as a string of phonemes. The single phoneme, however, is not a particularly useful way of analyzing sentences since this would be looking at a sentence as a series of isolated speech sounds. At another level, a sentence can be regarded as a series of morphemes, which are groupings of phonemes. From this viewpoint, however, the sentence is viewed as a string of words. Linguists have found it more useful to describe a sentence in terms of *phrases,* which are groupings of words.

Analysis of a sentence into its various phrases describes the *phrase structure* of a sentence. A sentence is regarded as composed of two basic phrases, a *noun phrase* and a *verb phrase,* which are in turn composed of subcomponents. Figure 12 shows the phrase structure of a simple sentence, The boy rode the bicycle. The noun phrase is composed of a determiner and a noun, and the verb phrase is composed of a verb and noun phrase; the latter noun phrase is also composed of a determiner and a noun. The relationship between the two phrases is portrayed in the tree diagram of figure 12. Our pauses in speech are defined by phrase marking. For example, we would be most likely to say "The boy —rode—the bicycle," pausing ever so briefly after *boy* and *rode.* We would not be likely to say "The—boy rode—the bicycle," grouping *boy* and *rode* or "The—boy rode the—bicycle," grouping *boy, rode,* and *the.* While in normal speech we may search and grope for a particular word, and thus alter the pauses, the listener would still tend to understand the message.

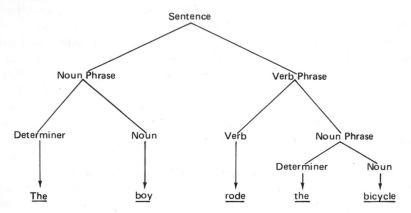

Figure 12. Phrase structure of the sentence "The boy rode the bicycle" represented by a tree diagram.

Surface Structure and Deep Structure

Linguists distinguish beteen surface structure and deep structure of sentences. The *surface structure* is the actual sentence as it is sounded and reflects simply the relationship among the parts of the sentence. In contrast, *deep structure* refers to the meaning of the sentence, that is, to the specification of the logical relations between the words in the sentence.

Consider the sentences John threw the ball and The ball was thrown by John. Both sentences convey the same meaning despite the fact that they sound differently. Hence their deep structure is the same.

But consider the sentence They are eating apples which can have two meanings. *Eating* may serve as a verb or it may modify the noun *apples*. Thus, the deep structure can vary with the same sentence depending on what meaning the speaker wishes to convey.

These illustrations indicate the necessity of distinguishing between surface and deep structure. The deep structure of a sentence conveys the basic or underlying information in the sentence. By applying certain theoretical rules of grammar, it is possible to link the surface structure of a sentence to its deep structure. Rules for the specification of this linkage process, called *transformational* rules, have been developed by Noam Chomsky and other linguists. These transformational rules are the rules by which ideas (deep structure) are transformed into understandable sentences (surface structure).

Transformational rules have clear implications about what features of sentences humans do store in memory. If the sentence is very simple, so that its deep structure approximates its surface structure, then features of the surface structure may be stored. As sentences become more complex, what is stored is some underlying base structure or schema, plus one or more "footnotes" that serve as rules necessary to regenerate the sentence in its original surface form. This is simply to say that what is stored is some coded representation of the complex sentence.

This brief description only begins to sketch some of the complexities of language. What is clear is that young children have an enormously complex task in learning to speak, read, and use language in a meaningful fashion. The fact that humans can acquire and use language emerges as a remarkable achievement.

Transformational Grammar

As we noted, phrases appear to be the way in which we naturally group information for thinking and memory. Information tends to be remembered in chunks, and chunking is one type of organization process. Some linguists such as Chomsky point out that a phrase structure analysis of language is nevertheless incomplete and that a complete analysis of language must have a transformational component. By making a distinction between the underlying structure of a sentence and the surface form of the sentence, transformational grammar provides a way to represent relationships among sentences which on the surface take quite different forms. Transformations are based upon rules which apply to sentences, and the transformation allows us to express the same idea in, say, either an active or a passive sentence. For example, The dog chased the cat and The cat was chased by the dog have quite different phrase structures as sentences, but both share a common underlying or deep structure.

The surface structure of a sentence is produced by the application of various transformational rules to the deep structure. For instance, the first sentence, The dog chased the cat, is an active-declarative transformation of the deep structure, and the second sentence, The cat was chased by the dog, is a passive-declarative transformation. A variety of different surface structures may be produced by the same deep structure. The basic idea of any sentence is to express a relationship between a subject, a verb, and an object; the idea is called a base marker from which many different sentences can be generated. The base marker having to do with the dog chasing the cat can be transformed into various forms (such as The cat was chased by the dog and Did the dog chase the cat?). While the surface structures may be different, they all relate to a common base marker.

Some Issues in Language

In this section we will examine a few selected issues in language. Included are the topics of language development, language and thought, language in animals, cultural differences in language, and language and the brain.

Language Development

Language development follows a fairly orderly course. The beginning of language is evidenced in babbling, which is an elementary type of vocalization. Children do produce sounds earlier than six months, but babbling, which is the repetition of speech sounds, is most clearly evident beginning around six months. Between six and nine months, infants are able to produce all of the basic speech sounds that make up a language.

The emission of speech sounds, even at this early age, can be controlled to some extent by an adult. For example, the rate at which infants emit speech sounds can be increased by having an adult repeat the sounds after the infant. These responses, called *echoic responses,* can be shaped in the sense of increasing their rate just like other instrumental responses. Language learning is not, however, simply the result of reinforcement of particular speech sounds and sequences. Language involves maturational processes as well as learning. Moreover, the structure of language is sufficiently complex to require principles beyond those of S-R formulations in order to account for its development.

Making speech sounds is only the first step in acquiring language. The sounds must come to represent objects, symbols, and events in the child's environment. This is simply to say that the sounds must acquire meaning for the child. Moreover, the child must learn to *associate* particular sound symbols with particular aspects of his environment. The child is familiar with many aspects of his environment before he learns to speak. His parents are familiar stimuli; toys, pets, siblings, and household objects are also familiar stimuli. His task, at this early stage of language development, is one of learning to associate particular environmental stimuli with particular responses. For example, he must learn to associate the sight of mother with the sound of *mama*. Similarly, the sight, feel, and taste of a cookie must become associated with the sound of *cookie*. Only when such associations are acquired can the speech sound come to represent or symbolize some object or event for the child. Thus, the development of meaning begins with the acquisition of associations between objects and events, on the one hand, and speech sounds, on the other.

The particular speech sounds a young child makes are shaped by cultural (e.g., parental) reinforcement much the same way other responses are shaped. First, whether a particular reward (such as parental approval) is given determines what responses will be strengthened. If, for example, a parent thinks it important for the child to say "please" when asking for something, the parent will arrange to reward the response when the child says "please" and will omit reward if the child fails to say "please." Thus, the particular responses that a child may make are under some control of external reinforcing events.

In a similar vein, properties of verbal behavior such as its loudness and rate are also influenced by reinforcement. If members of the family characteristically talk loud or fast, the child is likely to do the same. In addition, these properties of verbal behavior may be reinforced if the parent chooses to do so. For example, the parent may withhold a reward until the child speaks sufficiently loud, as judged by the parent. Moreover, as the child approximates a desirable pronunciation, the response may achieve rapid reward from the parent. Thus, properties of speech such as its loudness, rate, and quality of pronunciation can be shaped by their careful reinforcement.

The association of speech sounds to environmental stimuli is, of course, only a part of language development. Once the child has acquired a rudimentary vocabulary, he must then begin to form sentences. At first the young child will form quite simple sentences, usually consisting of two or three words, such as "Want drink." Even as his vocabulary expands, short sentences continue to be used.

Gradually, however, the child begins to construct more complex sentences that take on the characteristics of adult language. This is an enormously complex task, far more complicated than associating sounds with environmental stimuli. He must learn to construct increasingly complex sentences, many of which he has never heard. His task is not only that of understanding complex sentences, but also of constructing sentences that are grammatically correct in the sense of being understood by the listener.

What the child is now learning are sets of *grammatical rules* for constructing sentences. Usually, of course, the child is unable to verbalize the rules. Indeed, many adults who speak grammatically acceptable English are unable to specify the rules they employ. Thus, you learn to recognize and use (operate in accord with) grammar appropriately even though you are frequently unable to specify the rules.

It is at this level of language learning that principles of conditioning and reinforcement are less applicable. There are an enormous number of possibilities in constructing sentences, so many that we cannot regard sentence construction as resulting simply from some S-R associative process. Rather, humans learn grammatical rules in learning to use language, rules that enable them to generate a large number of different kinds of sentences.

Language and Thought

Language and thought are related events. The ability of children to handle concepts is related to their language development. Indeed, children who can verbalize relationships such as nearer than or larger than are better able to deal with problems involving relationships among stimuli than children who do not yet verbalize such relationships.

Nevertheless, language does not seem to be *essential* for complex mental processes, despite the fact that language facilitates problem solving. For instance, deaf children, who are deficient in language, are able to handle many concepts. Thus, although language is a facilitating factor in thought, it does not appear to be essential in some critical sense for the development of cognitive capacities. As noted, this is the case because deaf children can develop other modes of communication by acquiring symbol systems other than conventional language.

The most explicit attempt to relate language and thought is seen in the *linguistic relativity hypothesis* developed by Benjamin Whorf. Whorf's hypothesis contends that the structure of one's language leads one to conceive of the world in particular ways, ways that differ from someone using a different language. This is simply to say that a person's language imposes a particular view of the world. Presumably, cognitive processes are in some way inevitably affected by the structure of language. The notion of linguistic *relativity* is emphasized because thought is presumed to be relative to the particular language used.

Vocabulary differences provide one instance of how language is presumably related to thought. For instance, Eskimos have several different words for labeling snow, depending upon its characteristics, whereas only one is widely used in English. Skiers, of course, do distinguish between several kinds of snow. Some cultures have many words for the various colors, others have only a few. For Whorf, the range of words or labels available influences the range of cognitive activities with which humans may engage. If a person has a number of different descriptive labels that he can apply to a range of events, presumably he is able to think about these events in more alternative ways than one who has only a few labels.

There are two versions of Whorf's hypothesis. The *strong* version emphasized that language *invariably* influences thought, whereas the *weak* version emphasized that language affects thought when the particular task directly depends upon properties of the language system. There is little support for the strong version of the hypothesis, but a reasonable amount of support for the weaker version.

Language in Animals

Many people have raised the question, Do animals have language? The answer depends upon how one defines language. Animals clearly communicate with each other, and in this sense animals can be said to have language. But communication is not synonymous with language, although it is part of language. Language is composed of symbols which stand for other things. The word *dog* stands for the object dog; the word *joy* stands for an emotional experience. Words are used in accordance with complex rules of grammar, and the intent is to convey meaning.

Psychologists have made a number of attempts to teach language to chimpanzees. Early attempts were largely unsuccessful, with only limited evidence for language being learned. In one of the most famous studies the Kelloggs raised their son with a chimpanzee named Gua. The chimpanzee learned to understand a number of commands, but never produced a single word. In a similar study a chimpanzee raised by the Hayeses learned to speak only three identifiable words, *mama, papa,* and *cup,* and only after great difficulty and extended training. As a result of these failures many psychologists concluded that chimpanzees lack the vocal chord structures necessary for humanlike speech and that such efforts are doomed to failure.

Recognizing this vocal inability of chimpanzees, more recent attempts to teach chimpanzees language by Allen and Beatrice Gardner and David Premack have taken a different approach to the problem. Their approach has been to teach chimpanzees a *nonverbal* version of language. The Gardners have attempted to teach their subject, Washoe, the sign language used by the deaf, which consists of making signs for different words. Using her hands, Washoe eventually learned over one hundred fifty signs appropriately. Of even greater importance was that Washoe learned to string signs together to make up primitive sentences. The fact that Washoe was able to produce simple strings is suggestive of a very primitive form of language. Premack's approach was to teach another chimpanzee, Sarah, a form of sign language using colored plastic chips displayed on a board, where each chip stood for a word. For example, a red square stood for banana. Sarah learned to "write" by placing the chips on a magnetized board and with practice learned to construct simple sentences.

Do these studies allow us to conclude that chimpanzees possess language? For some the answer is yes because the animal has shown the ability to produce simple sentences, one criterion of language. For others the answer is no or doubtful because other features of language have not been shown. Some linguists contend that the uniquely human aspect of language is its *self-reflexive* quality, that is, the quality of referring to itself. Thus the problem of trying to answer the question of whether animals have language depends ultimately upon what constitutes an acceptable and agreed-upon definition of language. Even if the case is that only humans have true language, it would appear that the definition of true language has become more restricted. Meanwhile, the study of language in animals is suggestive of some continuity in behavior rather than a sharp and complete break in behavior.

Cultural Differences in Language

One of the fascinating issues in language is the question of how individual differences in language are to be explained. More specifically, one issue is the development of cultural, regional, and ethnic differences in language. Well-known regional variations in the dialect of American English include dialects associated with the South, New England, New York City, Texas, and the Midwest. The Midwestern dialect is frequently referred to as standard, and this accent is sometimes preferred for radio and television broadcasting. Indeed, some natives of the Outer Banks of North Carolina and Appalachia speak with a sixteenth-century English accent (similar to a cockney accent). It is not clear how all these variations maintain themselves other than the general conclusion that we each learn the language patterns typical of our particular culture.

Many black Americans speak a dialect which is different from the standard American English as spoken by Midwesterners and television announcers. Black American dialect is different in several ways from standard American English including slight differences in sound and important differences in grammar. For example, the expression "I do," "I did," and "I have done" are the accepted forms of the verb "to do" in standard English; however, a black child might say "I do," "I done," and "I have did." While these forms depart from standard English, linguists have recently recognized that such forms are grammatical.

Until quite recently the use of nonstandard English by blacks has been assumed by many white educators to be a reflection of the cultural deprivation of blacks. Some have felt that the use of nonstandard English may be the principal basis for blacks scoring lower than whites on the average on standard intelligence tests and for school performance of blacks to reflect slower progress than whites. While there may be a relation between language and scholastic performance, recent evidence argues that nonstandard English is logical, orderly, and grammatical. It has been proposed that if whites were required, for example, to take I.Q. tests based on black culture and language they would also show poorer performance.

This issue can be placed in another perspective. Is nonstandard black English like any other dialect, or is it a less optimal form of language that may possibly limit the intellectual functioning of those who use it? Although we do not have a full and complete answer to this and similar questions, the recent arguments of some linguists lead us increasingly to the position of regarding black English as a dialect in its own right, having its own rules and its own sense of time.

Language and the Brain

The human brain is divided into two hemispheres which are not functionally equivalent. Each hemisphere receives information from the senses, but the two hemispheres generally receive separate information. Information from our visual environment is usually divided, with information from our right visual field being projected to the left hemisphere and information from the left visual field being projected to the right hemisphere. Nevertheless, information which reaches each half of the brain is usually coordinated or integrated in some fashion.

The fact that the human brain is asymmetrical is especially important for language. For most human adults, the left cerebral hemisphere controls the functions of language which include both spoken and written language production and the comprehension of verbal information. In contrast, the right cerebral hemisphere is frequently unable to produce language or to comprehend abstract words. In turn, the right hemisphere is concerned with perceptual processes such as picture recognition and comprehension and learning of visual forms.

Our knowledge of this dual functioning of the brain stems from what is called the *split-brain* experiment. A split brain usually results from surgery which severs the corpus callosum, fibers connecting the two hemispheres, in order to alleviate symptoms of certain rare forms of epilepsy. Since the normal interaction between the two hemispheres is eliminated with this operation, it is possible to observe the function of each largely independent hemisphere. Important differences in how the two hemispheres are involved in language behaviors have been discovered. For example, when a split-brain patient held an object in his right hand, allowing sensory information to be sent to the left cerebral hemisphere, he was able to name and describe the object. In contrast, when the patient held the object in his left hand, allowing sensory information to go primarily to the right hemisphere, he was unable to describe the object verbally although he could match the object to an identical one in a recognition task. Similarly, if a split-brain patient was shown a picture of an object so that sensory information went to the right hemisphere, he was unable to label the object in the picture; in addition, he was able to select the object in a recognition test when it was presented with others.

A number of systematic studies have begun to reveal the functioning of the two hemispheres. This separation of language and perceptual functions is the beginning of an important line of work.

Theories of Language Learning

One issue which has been of some concern to language researchers is how we learn to speak and produce language. A popular view is that children simply imitate what they hear and if they make a mistake their parents correct them. At a general level this view captures the essence of the learning theory or *conditioning* approach to language. In this section we shall examine two approaches to language learning: the conditioning approach and the psycholinguistic approach.

Conditioning Approach

The conditioning approach to language learning makes the basic assumption that language is learned in accordance with the basic principles of conditioning. This simply means that the principles of conditioning derived from the study of lower organisms can be applied to the understanding of language learning. B. F. Skinner was among the early psychologists to advocate the study of language behavior from the viewpoint of conditioning. His view contends that children learn language in essentially the same way that they learn all other behaviors such as riding a bicycle and using kitchen utensils. The basic idea is that *verbal behavior* is like any other class of behavior and that it is acquired through *reinforcement* of appropriate verbal responses. In general, Skinner contends that children tend to imitate the verbal behavior they hear from the adults around them, and if they do so appropriately they tend to be rewarded, and if they do not, the adults may withhold reinforcement or even punish the behavior. For example, the young child is properly rewarded by her parents if she says "dog" in imitation of the parents. The parents reward the child with expressions of approval or maybe with a cookie. With older children parents may punish inappropriate verbal behavior with such statements as "You can't say that." The operation of conditioning principles is easily seen when the child learns a naming response such as "That is a cow" or "Mother's dress is blue."

The principles of generalization and discrimination also operate in conditioning theories of language learning. Consider the situation in which a young child learns to say "dog" in the presence of the family's pet collie. Subsequently the child may label other animals which he has not experienced, such as cats and cows, as dogs. In this case the label is misapplied because of stimulus generalization tendencies. Because the dog, cat, and cow share some similar features the child tends to overgeneralize to other animals. If this occurs, the parents may then attempt to teach the child to discriminate among these animals. When the dog label is reinforced when appropriate and reinforcement withheld when the label is inappropriate the child will come to apply the dog label to the appropriate set of stimuli.

Another class of verbal behavior that is presumed to be learned via reinforcement consists of behaviors which control the behaviors of others. Verbal behaviors in response to such as "Close the door" and "Give me a cookie" become strengthened presumably because they are reinforced by the listener. Remember that such behaviors don't always have to be reinforced to be strengthened, that is, such behaviors can be strengthened even if they are only partially reinforced.

Probably the most difficult problem of the conditioning approach to language is accounting for the fact that a set of rules apparently guides the production of language. Somehow we learn a set of fairly abstract grammatical rules which constrain our output of verbal behavior in a reasonably consistent fashion. In addition, the variability in reinforcing conditions from child to child might be expected to produce much wider variations in language development and behavior than is actually the case. Despite wide variations in social reinforcement and training experiences of children, the development of language in children across various cultures follows a rather general pattern. Indeed, very young children of deaf parents, who obviously have an atypical speech environment, show language development patterns similar to other children. Finally, as we have already noted, language development appears to be a constructive process in the sense that young children construct verbal statements that they may never actually hear from adults. In other words, language development is not simply an imitative process. For these and other reasons the majority of psychologists reject the conditioning approach as adequate for a full understanding of how language is learned.

Psycholinguistic Approach

The conditioning approach to language learning, especially as outlined by B. F. Skinner, has been challenged by alternatives which emphasize psycholinguistics and information processing. Noam Chomsky has strongly criticized Skinner's approach to language learning, arguing that a learning theory analysis of language is inadequate to deal with its richness and complexity. The basic assumption of the psycholinguistic approach is that children learn a complex set of rules in learning a language, even though they may not be able to verbalize or describe the rules. Moreover, children acquire these rules without necessarily having someone teach them in a formal sense, and they acquire these rules at a very early age. It is the use of these abstract rules, according to the psycholinguistic approach, which governs the production of language. Moreover, it is generally held by psycholinguists that the ability to develop an abstract set of rules for language production is unique to humans. Because of the general uniformity of language development across different cultures some psycholinguists stress the biological basis of language development. They emphasize that there is an innate ability underlying language development which determines its course.

The psycholinguistic approach emphasizes the distinction between surface structure and deep structure. The focus is on how humans are able to produce unique or original sentences which they have not actually heard or read. They can generate novel sentences because they have learned a set of rules for generating sentences. According to one type of psycholinguistic theory proposed by Chomsky, we learn two sets of rules, one dealing with the surface or superficial structure of language and the other dealing with the deep structure of the language. As we noted earlier, surface structure rules deal with the relationship among the components of a sentence such as nouns and verbs, whereas deep structure rules concern the semantic interpretation to be made of the sentence.

The psycholinguistic approach represents an important alternative to the conditioning approach. It is nevertheless incomplete as a theory of language development with many of its details yet to be specified. We can expect to see much development of this approach to language and many of its features worked out in greater detail in the near future.

Summary

This chapter has described some of the main features of language. Language was seen to have four functions: it achieves reward, it has stimulus value, it serves as a vehicle for communication, and it conveys meaning. The basic units of language are phonemes and morphemes. In order to understand adult language, sentence structure must be examined. Sentences possess both a surface structure and a deep structure which can be related by transformational grammar. Language development is a progressive and orderly process in which children learn general rules of language so that they can communicate.

The question of whether animals have language depends essentially on the definition of language. Cultural differences in language exist, and regional and ethnic variations can be quite grammatical in form. A basic question is whether cultural differences in language have serious effects on intellectual functioning. Language is dependent upon the left cerebral hemisphere, whereas perception is predominantly dependent on the right cerebral hemisphere.

Finally, recent developments in psycholinguistics have challenged the learning theory or conditioning approach to learning. Instead, psycholinguistic approaches have emphasized that language is a process of learning a fairly abstract set of grammatical rules.

Multiple-Choice Items: Language

1. The basic sound unit of all languages is the
    a. phoneme
    b. phrase structure
    c. distinctive feature
    d. morpheme
2. The deep structure of a sentence refers to its
    a. relativity
    b. plan
    c. similarity
    d. meaning
3. The linguistic system for relating the surface structure and deep structure of a sentence is called
    a. linguistic relativity hypothesis
    b. phrase-structure
    c. transformational grammar
    d. distinctive features
4. The phrase structure of sentences emphasizes the way we
    a. associate single words

    b. group information for thinking
    c. transform information from deep structure to surface structure
    d. derive meaning

5. Language development
    a. can be fully explained by S-R principles
    b. requires going beyond S-R principles to rules
    c. is a matter of simple imitation
    d. is largely a matter of association

6. The idea that our language leads us to perceive and think about the world in particular ways is called the
    a. linguistic relativity hypothesis
    b. distinctive feature hypothesis
    c. conditioning hypothesis
    d. cultural hypothesis

7. Split-brain studies have revealed that
    a. the right hemisphere is the primary locus of language
    b. perceptual functions are controlled primarily by the left hemisphere
    c. language functions are controlled primarily by the left hemisphere
    d. imagery processes are equally controlled by both hemispheres

8. The basic assumption of the conditioning or learning theory approach to language is that language is
    a. the result of the complex interaction of genetic and developmental factors
    b. a matter of learning complex rules
    c. unrelated to imitation
    d. verbal behavior which is learned like other behaviors

9. A basic assumption of the psycholinguistic approach to language is that language is
    a. the learning of a complex set of rules
    b. an associative process
    c. unrelated to biological processes
    d. developed quite differently in different cultures

10. The fact that a child produces sentences which he has never in fact heard is taken as support of which conception?
    a. learning theory
    b. linguistic relativity theory
    c. psycholinguistic theory
    d. verbal behavior approach theory

True-False Items: Language

T 1.   Languages are composed of basic sounds called phonemes.

F 2.   Phonemes are composed of morphemes.

T 3.   The deep structure of a sentence refers to its meaning, whereas the surface structure refers to the actual sentence as sounded.

F 4.   Language learning is principally a matter of associating speech sounds with environmental stimuli.

T 5.   The linguistic relativity hypothesis emphasizes that language influences the way we think.

T 6. F It is now clear that man is the only organism that possesses language.

F 7.   Black English is a less grammatical form of English.

T 8.   Split-brain studies suggest a separate locus for language and for perceptual functions.

F 9.   The idea that children learn language primarily through imitation is well accepted.

T 10. Adults as well as older children may speak with grammatical correctness even though they may be unable to describe the rules of grammar.

Discussion Items: Language

1.   Outline several features of language development.

2.   Suppose that you had language for only four colors of the visual spectrum, say, red, yellow, green, and blue. Speculate as to how this might affect the way you think about colored objects in your environment.

3.   What does it mean to say that the issue of whether animals such as chimpanzees have languages reduces essentially to the question of how we define language?

4.   Compare and contrast learning theory and psycholinguistic approaches to language.

5.   Even if various dialects are grammatical, are there advantages to learning standard English? Discuss.

Multiple-Choice Answers: Language

1.   (a)   The phoneme is the basic sound unit of all languages.

2.   (d)   Deep structure refers to the semantic or meaning aspect of a sentence.

3.   (c)   The surface structure of a sentence is produced by the application of various transformational rules to the deep structure.

Hence, it is transformational grammar which relates both surface and deep structures.

4.   (b)   Phrases appear to be the way in which we naturally group information for thinking as well as for memory. Our pauses in speech allow for the effective grouping or chunking of phrases in memory.

5.   (b)   Language development entails the development and use of abstract rules of grammar. These rules are not reducible to simple S-R principles.

6.   (a)   The idea that language influences our perceptual and cognitive processes is called the linguistic relativity hypothesis, developed by Benjamin Whorf.

7.   (c)   Language is regulated primarily by the left hemisphere, whereas the right hemisphere is primarily concerned with perceptual functions. The loci of these functions have been determined by split-brain experiments.

8.   (d)   The conditioning approach to language assumes that language is verbal behavior and is learned like other behaviors. In short, language is governed by reinforcement and undergoes acquisition and extinction like other behaviors.

9.   (a)   The psycholinguistic approach to language views language as the learning of a fairly abstract set of grammatical rules. These rules provide the basis by which humans can generate a great variety of sentences.

10.   (c)   The production of novel sentences is thought to occur as the result of using the rules of grammar. This assumption is basic to the psycholinguistic approach to language.

True-False Answers: Language

1.   (True)   The phoneme is the basic unit of all languages.

2.   (False)   Morphemes consist of combinations of two or more phonemes.

3.   (True)   Deep structure refers to the ideas conveyed by the sentence and surface structure to the sentence itself.

4.   (False)   This is part of language learning, but certainly not the whole picture. Language learning also involves learning sets of grammatical rules which may not necessarily be verbalized by the learner.

5.   (True)   This hypothesis contends that the structure of languages leads us to conceive the world in particular ways.

6.   (False)   There appears to be good evidence that at least chimpanzees do show language of a limited kind, in the sense that they

can compose simple sentences. Whether or not this is to be regarded as true language depends ultimately on what is an acceptable definition of language.

7. (False)   Some linguists now regard black English as a dialect whose grammatical form is quite acceptable.

8. (True)   Split-brain studies do suggest a separate locus for language and for perceptual functions, with language functions being regulated primarily by the left hemisphere and perceptual functions by the right hemisphere.

9. (False)   The imitation theory of language learning is not well accepted. The fact that children produce sentences which they have never heard points out that mere imitation is insufficient as an account of language.

10. (True)   Many people are able to speak correctly even though they are unable to verbalize the rules of grammar.

Thinking and Problem Solving

8

In this chapter we focus on some issues in thinking and problem solving. These topics are closely related to issues in concept learning and language and logically follow their treatment. In this chapter thinking is viewed as a covert process involving the symbolic manipulation of stimuli. Thinking is frequently studied in the context of problem-solving situations; therefore the bulk of the chapter focuses on problem-solving activities. A brief discussion of Piaget's theory of cognitive development is presented since it involves the developmental sequence of language, thought, and problem-solving skills.

Thinking and Problem Solving

In this section we turn our attention to important issues of thinking and problem solving. Consideration of the nature of thinking and problem solving, general features of problem-solving tasks, and factors influencing problem solving are given. Subsequent sections deal with theories of thinking and problem solving and some practical principles of problem solving.

Nature of Thinking and Problem Solving

Thinking refers to *covert* processes not directly observable by the psychologist. Thinking is something that psychologists *infer* from the behavior of individuals, but it is not something directly seen. In general, *thinking refers to a class of covert activities that involve the manipulation of symbols.* For humans the most important symbols are language and concepts.

You may observe thinking *indirectly* when you watch a young child at play attempting to construct some object, such as a swing. At each stage of construction you may observe some characteristic pause in which the child appears to be making decisions about the next stage. The pauses may be very brief, but they are typically followed by a burst of fairly continuous activity until the next phase of the task is completed. It is assumed that the child is thinking during these pauses between activity, and this inference is made, in part, because the child continues to carry out productive sequences in reaching the desired goal.

Like overt behavior, thinking ranges from simple to complex levels. As noted earlier, at a very simple level thinking involves little more than making an association to some conceptual category. If I ask you to think of an example of transportation, "automobile," or "plane" immediately come to mind. On the other hand, if I ask whether it is less expensive to fly or go by train from Chicago to Los Angeles, the answer depends upon several considerations. At a simple level you may directly compare the cost of air fare versus train fare. But then you must include the cost of meals and incidentals if you travel by train. Finally, you must weigh the cost of the added travel time if you go by train. Clearly, this problem requires more complex thinking than the first.

The term *thinking* refers to numerous kinds of situations. A small girl *decides* that if she is especially pleasant to her father he will buy her a desired toy; a small boy *figures out* how to reach the cookie jar; a student *works* a math problem; a teacher *organizes* a lecture; a housewife *plans* a shopping list. The terms *decide, figure,* and *plan* all refer to the activity of thinking; however, we can only infer that thinking has taken place when we observe an outcome. Whether the outcome is successful is not critical for inferring thinking. What must be observed is some change in behavior in relation to some specified set of conditions, such as instructions to do something, that were present prior to the change in behavior.

The study of problem solving typically involves observing the way in which a learner arrives at a solution to some particular task. Psychologists usually make no attempt to distinguish rigorously between problem solving and thinking because it is assumed that thinking occurs during problem-solving activity. Moreover, problem solving is one class of activities that allows the psychologist to infer the process of thinking. Finally, the two terms are frequently used synonymously, and therefore no attempt is made to distinguish them here. One activity appears to involve the other and to overlap to such a great extent that they will be used interchangeably in this book.

General Features of Problem-solving Tasks

The typical problem-solving task presents the learner with a situation in which he must discover a solution to some problem. The task frequently allows many alternative responses to be made, thus making problem solving relatively complex in the hierarchy of activities studied by psychologists. Whereas in concept learning and paired associate learning relatively few response alternatives exist, problem-solving tasks characteristically allow many response alternatives. Sometimes only one response is correct and sometimes several responses are correct in the sense that they are acceptable solutions to the problem.

A large number of experimental procedures have been used in the study of problem solving. Moreover, there is no standard problem-solving task in the sense that the paired associate task is standard in verbal learning. Laboratory problem-solving tasks do, however, possess certain common features. These can be more easily seen by examining several examples of problem-solving activities.

Stages of Problem Solving

An analysis of the typical problem-solving situation indicates that we go through several stages in solving problems. In solving many problems we may proceed through these stages in a matter of minutes. However, other problems may require days or weeks for solution. Psychologists have described a number of stages in problem solving, but they all seem to reduce to a basic few. These include recognizing and interpreting the problem, generating hypotheses about solutions, deciding among the alternative hypotheses, and testing or evaluating an hypothesis.

Suppose that you are trying to select a major area in your college career. Your problem is that you cannot decide on an appropriate major, so you flounder around taking general courses in the hope that a solution will appear. But how will you proceed to select an appropriate major? How will you solve this problem? Your first step is simply to recognize that the problem exists. You decide that you must select a major, and normally you must do this no later than the beginning of your junior year in college. In order to interpret this problem you must collect information about yourself; you need information about your abilities, aptitudes, interests, and goals. You need to decide what kinds of things you like as well as the kinds of things you dislike. You might also wish to be informed about the realities of the job market and the predicted future needs in various job areas. With this basic information gathered you can proceed to the next stage of generating hypotheses. You may have decided that the health sciences represent one of your major areas of interest and ability, and that an undergraduate major with a premedical emphasis is appropriate for entering professional programs of medicine or dentistry or graduate programs of clinical psychology. If more than one alternative is plausible such as premedical versus pharmacy or premedical versus medical technology, you must then decide among the plausible alternatives. Once you choose a particular plan, you must test the reasonableness of your choice; in other words, you must evaluate your choice which might require a time period equal to several semesters. You will pursue your program of, say, a premedical course as long as you do excellent academic work; however, a few instances of poor grades in biology and chemistry should lead you to reevaluate your decision and to consider other alternatives.

In this example we have illustrated the stages of problem solving in choosing a career goal, a problem which is usually not solved quickly and, indeed, may take years for many people. The same sequence of stages is generally seen even with problems which can be solved in a shorter duration. For instance, if you were to deal with the problem of where to live, where to go to obtain an undergraduate education, or what topic on which to prepare a term paper, you would tend to go through the four stages of problem solving, although you may make your decision much faster in, say, where to live than in what major to choose as an undergraduate.

Incubation in Problem Solving

When a person has tried all the possible hypotheses that he can think of and has still not found a suitable solution to the problem, he may temporarily withdraw from the problem and engage in other activities. The French mathematician Henri Poincaré described this process during the period leading to one of his important discoveries. During a period in which he was trying unsuccessfully to solve some mathematical questions, he temporarily abandoned his work to take a beach vacation. One morning during a walk, the solution to the mathematical question came to him almost spontaneously as he was thinking about other things. Poincaré's example raises the question of unconscious mental activities during the period in which the person has turned away from the immediate problem in question. This rest period is called the *incubation* stage in which problem-solving activity continues, but without conscious attention to the problem. Most of our evidence about incubation comes from introspective reports of mathematicians, artists, scientists, and other persons who report the sudden solution to a problem after a period of preoccupation with unrelated issues.

Why an incubation period seems to help in the effective solution of problems may be for several reasons. First, it may be simply a matter of rest which allows fatigue to dissipate. It might also be that incubation allows for forgetting of inappropriate sets and approaches to the problem, thus permitting new approaches to be more easily perceived. Also additional practice may occur during incubation even though many people report that they do not practice. For whatever the reason or reasons, incubation appears sufficiently useful that it is certainly recommended when you find yourself stalled in efforts to solve a problem.

Persistence of Set in Problem Solving

One type of problem-solving task examines the tendency of humans to persist in inappropriate or less adequate ways of solving problems when simpler, more direct ways exist. The *water jar* problem is an example of this type of task. This task requires a person to determine how to fill a jar of water in order to obtain a specified amount. All problems follow this general form: "You will be given three empty containers, A, B, and C, and your task is to describe how to obtain a specific quantity of water, Y."

Table 3 illustrates a typical problem sequence. Problem 1 is an illustrative problem. Here the solution is to fill jar A, then remove 9 quarts from it by filling jar B three times. Problems 2 through 6 are training problems in which the solution is always to fill jar B first, then from this jar fill jar A once and jar C twice, which leaves the exact quantity specified. All problems, therefore, have a general solution of the form Y (the quantity specified) = B — A — 2C. Problems 7 and 8 can also be solved this way; however, there is a much simpler and direct solution in which you fill jar A first and pour off into jar C once, leaving the exact amount required for problem 7, and add A and C for problem 8. Problem 9 requires the simpler solution. Go through the sequence of problems in Table 3 and actually solve the problems so that you can experience the task.

If humans receive no instructions about the change in problems 7 and 8, they tend to persist in solving these problems just as they did for problem sequences 2 through 6. This simply illustrates the more general principle, namely, that most humans have a strong tendency toward *persistence of set. Once you have learned a rule that works, you may tend to continue applying that rule even when a simpler solution is possible.* This means that our old habits continue to be used, even when they are less efficient, if we fail to perceive that the situation has changed.

Many instances of the persistence of set can be seen in everyday life. For example, you may continue to try to solve mathematics problems by a rule no longer appropriate to the situation. The math problem may require, for instance, a combination of two rules or principles while you may be using only one of them. Similarly, inexperienced chess players may continue to make the same type of moves even when the moves are no longer strategic or efficient. Only when they can break their set will they have the opportunity to consider a new mode of attack.

TABLE 3   Water Jar Problem

Problem		Size of Jars (in quarts)			Quarts of Water Desired
		A	B	C	Y
Example ⟶	1	29	3	—	20
Training Problems ⟶	2	21	127	3	100
	3	14	163	25	99
	4	18	43	10	5
	5	9	42	6	21
	6	20	59	4	31
Test Problems ⟶	7	23	49	3	20
	8	15	39	3	18
	9	28	76	3	25

Functional Fixedness

Another kind of problem-solving task which also measures persistence of set are tests of functional fixedness. *Functional fixedness* refers to the tendency to think of objects as functioning in one certain way and to ignore other less typical ways in which they might be used.

A typical problem is described here. The subject is given a set of objects and asked to arrange them as a stand capable, say, of supporting a vase of flowers. Some of the objects are appropriate to solving the problem, while others are inappropriate or irrelevant. The point of such a task is to require you to use a familiar object in a novel fashion. In this example, the objects consist of a rectangular piece of plywood which has a wooden bar wired to it, pliers, and two L-shaped metal brackets. The first step is to use the pliers to loosen the wire and detach the wooden bar. The wooden bar can be used as a support for the plywood board, but this in itself is not sufficient. The L-shaped metal brackets appear reasonable to many subjects, but they will not support the board. In order to solve the problem, the subject must use the pliers in an unusual way as legs for the plywood stand. This is accomplished by opening the pliers and placing them under the stand. The weight of the stand keeps the pliers steady at one end, while the wooden bar supports the stand at the other end.

As emphasized, the principal interest in this kind of task is to see if the subject will use the familiar object in a novel and unusual way to solve the problem. The ability of humans to solve this kind of problem is hampered to the extent that they tend to think of the pliers in terms of its typical function. In effect, you must be able to break an established set in order to deal with this type of problem. Like the water jar problem, here is another instance of negative transfer in the sense that persistence of old ways of doing things or viewing objects hampers problem-solving efficiency.

Set in Verbal Anagram Problems

A third class of problems that has received wide use is the anagram problem. The anagram is a scrambled series of letters such as BOLREMP which when rearranged makes at least one word such as PROBLEM. The subject may be asked to form only one word or may be given an anagram which allows several possible solutions and asked to produce as many words as possible. Usually the former procedure is used. Either the number of correct solutions achieved in a fixed time period or the time to obtain a solution is measured.

Anagram problems can be used in a fashion directly analogous to the water jar problem. Subjects can be given a series of anagrams such as the following:

Training Problems
- APMR
- OSYB
- AEVH
- OTAG
- AFIW

Test Problems
- LCAM
- OFRT

The first five of these anagrams can be solved by the formula 4-1-3-2, where 1-2-3-4 is the presented order of the letters. For example, unscrambling OTAG yields GOAT. During training the subject learns a particular rule, although he may not verbalize it. During the next part of the sequence, the subjects are given test anagrams which require a new rule for solution. The problems are presented in a continuous series so that the subject does not know, of course, that the rules have changed. Under this circumstance, subjects have a strong tendency to persist in trying to use the old rule, taking longer to discover the new rule than control subjects who do not undergo the initial training.

What is characteristic of all three of these laboratory problems (water jar, functional fixedness, and verbal anagrams) is that *humans may show strong persistence of old habits in new situations where they are no longer appropriate.* Indeed, the typical study of problem solving characteristically looks like a negative transfer situation in the sense that learned behaviors *interfere* with learning of new responses. Negative transfer refers to situations in which the effect of prior learning is to hinder new learning, whereas positive transfer occurs when prior learning aids new learning. What is observed is the ease with which humans can overcome interference. Problem-solving tasks can, of course, be constructed so as to reflect positive transfer from one task sequence to another. This amounts to arranging the situation so that the rule or principle learned in the first stage of the task transfers positively to the second stage, facilitating the learner's performance. Much more emphasis has, however, been placed on the interference aspects of problem-solving tasks.

These three tasks provide a small sample of a large number of problem-solving tasks that have been used by psychologists. No attempt is made, however, to catalogue the great variety of tasks employed.

Motivational Factors

A person can bring a particular level of motivation to a problem-solving task and the task itself may induce some motivational state in the person. These motivational states can in turn influence the efficiency of problem solving. The general principle noted in an earlier chapter still holds: As the task becomes more complex, less motivation is necessary for achieving optimal learning.

A second important principle is that the relationship between degree of motivation and problem-solving efficiency is U-shaped. *As the degree of motivation increases, problem-solving efficiency increases up to some optimal point beyond which increases in motivation produce a reduction in problem-solving efficiency.* This relationship is shown in figure 13, which presents a hypothetical curve showing the effect of degree of motivation on problem-solving performance.

What this means is that excessive motivation interferes with problem-solving efficiency. Moreover, if failure to solve a problem induces frustration, this motivational state will then further hamper your effectiveness. One important implication of this principle is that children must be taught to deal with problems without reacting in an overly emotional fashion which can be destructive of personal efficiency.

Theories of Thinking and Problem Solving

Three theoretical approaches have been developed in accounting for the events of thinking and problem solving. In general, theories of thinking and problem solving are less formal than are theories of the less complex processes of human learning. One class of theories involves the extension of stimulus-response associationistic conceptions to the processes of thinking and problem solving. This class of theories is very similar to stimulus-response theories of concept learning and adopts the same

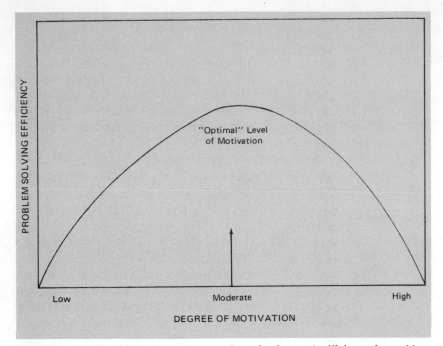

Figure 13. Relationship between degree of motivation and efficiency in problem solving.

fundamental assumptions. A second class of theories stems from Gestalt psychology and has emphasized the importance of insight in problem solving. This class of theories views thinking and problem solving as a matter of reorganizing one's perceptual world. Finally, a third class of theories use information-processing conceptions to understand thinking and problem solving.

Stimulus-response Theory

Stimulus-response conceptions of thinking regard it basically as an associative process. Thinking is viewed as *covert* or implicit trial-and-error behavior, just as there is overt trial-and-error behavior in many simple learning situations. It is assumed in any problem situation that the learner brings to the task a number of possible habits. These habits are assumed to be already available, in the sense of being associated to some degree of strength to the particular task situation. Not only do these habit tendencies vary in strength to the particular task situation, but they are also arranged in what Clark Hull termed a *habit-family hierarchy.* This is simply to say that the learner enters a given situation with a hierarchy of habits varying in strength.

The theory contends that in a problem-solving situation the available habits would be run off in the order of their strength until some particular response was successful. So far, this account is just like that of trial-and-error behavior of lower animals in solving simple problems. In order to account for thinking, however, S-R association theory does not need to assume that the responses are run off overtly. Rather, the theory assumes that these responses are run off *covertly* until one achieves success. The process is basically that of first trying (covertly) one response, then another, until you finally discover the correct response.

S-R theories, emphasizing covert activity, have been used to account for certain kinds of performances that require discovery of the optimal or correct response. Consider, for example, doing a complicated picture puzzle. According to S-R theory, your approach to the puzzle could be characterized as one of implicitly trying out several alternatives while holding a piece of the puzzle in your hand until you discover a solution that appears to work. The principal point is that your problem-solving behavior is interpreted as a matter of running off covert responses until you achieve a solution. In a similar fashion, S-R theory could characterize games such as chess as involving trying several alternative responses implicitly until you discover one that will optimize your position.

Gestalt Theory

Gestalt psychologists have approached thinking and problem solving from the viewpoint of how the organism perceives his world. Thinking is regarded, theoretically, as a matter of perceptual reorganization, that is, as the process of coming to see environmental stimuli in new and different ways. Thinking is thus viewed as some central perceptual-cognitive process. Like S-R theory, thinking involves covert activity; however, thinking is not conceptualized as a matter of running off available habits.

The characteristic approach of Gestalt psychologists such as Wolfgang Köhler has been to place a subject in a problem-solving setting and observe how he goes about solving the problem. A typical problem setting has been the *detour* task in which a barrier is placed between a subject and a goal object. Usually small children or animals such as chimpanzees or dogs are used as subjects, and the barrier is constructed so as to prevent the subject from *directly* obtaining the object. The animal or child must detour by going around the barrier to obtain the goal object. With this kind of problem, chimpanzees and dogs achieve fairly rapid solutions, whereas chickens tend to rush headlong into the barrier, usually failing to solve the problem. Presumably the performance of chickens represents their inability to perceive the stimulus features of the task that would enable a more insightful solution.

Other problem settings have required animals to use two sticks, joining them so as to form a rake for obtaining food. Descriptions of the behavior of animals solving problems emphasize such features as their observing the objects for some period of time followed by rapid solution of the problem. As the Gestalt psychologists contend, this rapid problem-solving activity implies that the animal was able to reorganize his perception of the world, thus achieving insight into the problem.

These examples can only briefly serve to illustrate the kind of tasks Gestalt investigators have used. These tasks usually allow the subject to perceive most aspects of the problem in its entirety. In contrast, problem-solving tasks used by S-R theorists have typically not been of this nature. Thus it is not too surprising that different theoretical conceptions should have developed. Stimulus-response and Gestalt conceptions of thinking have had a long and controversial history. Our concern is not with this history but with noting that different views of the process have in part stemmed from different experimental attacks on the problem.

Information-processing Approaches

Information-processing approaches to theorizing about psychological events are fairly new, with developments accelerating since 1960. Just as there are information-processing approaches to concept learning and memory, as noted in previous chapters, there are information-processing conceptions of problem solving, pattern recognition, language translation, perception, and learning.

Information-processing approaches to psychological events attempt to formulate a flowchart, or sequence of events, using the format of computer programs. A computer program consists of a series of steps or rules that tell the computer what to do. In a similar vein, the basic idea of information processing is to identify the steps involved in some psychological activity, list these steps in proper sequence, and then see if the computer can simulate these activities. To the extent that the computer can simulate the actions of a human the psychologist may gain some understanding of what must go into a theory designed to explain such actions.

Clearly, of course, a human being is much more than a computer. Basically all that is implied by information-processing approaches to behavior is that a program which can simulate some psychological process can, in turn, serve as a highly abstract model of the kinds of events that must make up the process. Thus, the theory of some process becomes essentially a statement of the rules of operations, restrictions placed on the rules, how the rules combine, and how much information the program must contain.

Several kinds of programs for problem-solving activities have been developed. An example of one type is seen in the letter-series completion tasks used by Herbert Simon and K. Kotovsky. These problems contain a series of letters and require that the subject fill in the next letter. A simple example is as follows:

B D F H __

Here the rule is very simple and can be solved by children seven or eight years old. Another series could take this form:

B T C T D T __

And a more difficult series could take this form:

P X A X O Y B Y N Z __

This type of task can be made even more difficult so that most college students are unable to solve the problem.

A problem-solving program of this type must contain a number of features. It must be able to recognize and distinguish letters. It must be able to detect regularities in the pattern by looking for repeatable periodicities in the sequence. More generally, it must be programmed to discover whatever regularity is intrinsically built into a particular letter series. Finally, if the program can successfully solve a given class of problems, then the psychologist gains some conception of the kind of rules that must be present in any theory of problem-solving activity.

Piaget's Theory of Cognitive Development

A concern of major interest to psychologists is the development of language, thought, problem-solving skills, and the like; collectively, such events are called cognitive processes. The understanding of cognitive development is a fundamental task in psychology. One of the major theorists in the area is Jean Piaget. In this section we shall briefly examine some of Piaget's ideas about cognitive development.

Piaget holds that two basic processes underly cognitive growth and development: *assimilation* and *accommodation*. *Assimilation* refers to the process by which a child incorporates objects or events which he has never previously experienced into his existing cognitive structure. When new information is assimilated, it is taken in and interpreted so that it makes sense and agrees with the existing cognitive structure. Sometimes the new information is altered or distorted so that it fits in with the existing cognitive structure. We have already noted in the memory chapters a quite similar process in our discussion of the constructive nature of memory. The second major process is accommodation, which involves changing the cognitive structure itself so that it can better incorporate new information. Thus the process of cognitive development allows for a change in the incoming information, assimilation, and a change in the cognitive structure itself, accommodation. The balance between the two processes provides the basis of the organism's adaptation to its environment.

Piaget contends that the initial response of a child to a new event or object is to interpret the experience in a way consistent with the existing cognitive structure rather than to change the structure itself. Ultimately, however, the process of assimilation is insufficient to deal with the experience. The child ultimately begins to recognize that the way he has perceived and encoded events contradicts other experiences, and as a result the process of changing the internal cognitive structure begins. Thus cognitive development is seen as a process of continuous assimilation and accommodation, with major changes in accommodation being viewed as changes in *stages* of cognitive development.

Using these ideas, Piaget has outlined four stages of cognitive development. These are the sensorimotor stage, the preoperational stage, the stage of concrete operations, and the stage of formal operations. At each stage Piaget identifies specific intellectual changes which occur in which the child engages in cognitive activities which he could not do previously.

Sensorimotor Stage

The *sensorimotor* stage operates from birth to roughly two years of age. During this stage the infant begins to interact with his environment, and out of this interaction are formed simple motor habits and perceptions of his environment. At this stage we find the earliest beginnings of the learning process which involve classical conditioning. Piaget identifies what he calls primary circular reactions which are the tendency of a child to repeat behaviors which he has mastered and secondary circular reactions which involve manipulations of the environment such as noise-making and moving toys. In either case, feedback from his responses is important to the child. Subsequently the child begins to perform intentional acts such as reaching which involve coordination of motor responses with visual perception of the environment. In addition, the ability to imitate begins to appear. Finally, sometime between the age of one and two, objects in the environment begin to acquire a kind of permanence for him. The child no longer acts as if objects are gone if they are not actually present, in sight. For example, when the mother removes an object from the child's view the child may attempt to find it, indicating that the child can hold a mental representation of the object.

Stage of Preoperational Thought

The second stage, that of *preoperational thought,* is from roughly two to seven years of age. During this stage there is a rapid increase in the use of language, symbols, and imagery. The child begins to form conceptual categories and show reasoning behavior, but he does not necessarily behave in a logically consistent fashion. At first, when the child learns that objects have a name, he regards the name as a real property of the object just as much as its color, shape, and other properties. Much later he realizes that the name or label is arbitrarily assigned to the object and is not part of the object. Thus names or labels have a kind of physical reality which only later become differentiated from physical attributes of objects. The child also has an immature idea of time, which is especially noticeable on long trips. The child may be told that it will take six hours to drive to the beach and yet after five or ten minutes of driving asks "Are we almost at the beach?" By the end of this stage the normal child has developed basic conceptual categories and can work with relations among them.

Stage of Concrete Operations

The stage of *concrete operations* is seen from approximately ages seven to eleven years. The child's thinking is now based on logical operations rather than on just perceptual or motor abilities. Although logical processes of thinking have developed, this stage is called concrete operations because the logical processes are not fully abstract. The child's thinking is still rather closely tied to concrete examples of the physical world. Thinking is logical as long as it is tied to concrete materials in the environment. Two important abilities which make logical thought more likely appear about age eight years: conservation and reversibility.

Conservation is the ability of a child to recognize that objects and some of their properties are still the same, or equivalent, even when viewed under different perceptual conditions. The child is able to maintain a concept of "equivalence" even though perceptual cues might lead to a breakdown of the concept. Conservation refers to the principle that material can be transformed or changed without changing the material itself. For instance, a child might be shown two containers of water, A and B, which are equivalent, as shown in figure 14. The child identifies the two containers as having the same amount of liquid. Then the water from container B is poured into the shallow container C and the child is asked if the amounts of water in A and C are the same. The child who fails to "conserve" fails to recognize that A and C contain the same amount of water even though the shape of the containers differs. When the child grasps the idea of conservation of volume he is able to recognize that the volume of any substance does not change when the shape of the substance changes. Presumably, the ability of the child to conserve occurs when he is able to defocus or decenter his attention on irrelevant features of the object.

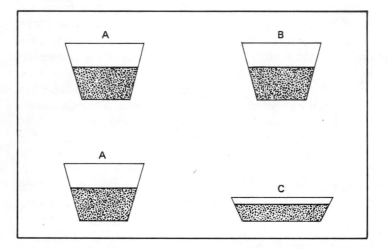

Figure 14. Problem to illustrate the principle of conservation.

Reversibility is the ability of the child to interrupt a sequence of thought, say, in problem solving, and return to the beginning of the sequence. The young child who is unable to show conservation in the example just cited is unable to recognize that the two containers, A and C, are equivalent because he is unable to think of C in its original state, B. The ability to think about some object in its originally presented state is the process of reversibility.

Stage of Formal Operations

The final stage of cognitive development is called *formal operations* and begins at about eleven years of age and is completed at about fifteen years of age. During this final phase the child moves into the world of abstract thought characteristic of normal adults. The child's thinking becomes more verbal and abstract and much less dependent upon the concrete features of objects. Here we see thinking which is tempered by reasoning and judgment and by the ability to weigh the appropriateness of alternative solutions to problems. Hypotheses can be developed and logical deductions from the hypotheses can be made. The ability to think in terms of formal, logical propositions is what allows for the most complex adaptive behaviors we see in the human adult. Some of our most creative, imaginative ideas are the result of thinking at the level of formal operations.

You should be cautioned that the normal adult does not, of course, spend all of his time in the rarefied atmosphere of abstract thought. Much of our day-to-day problem solving requires less than abstract thought. We maintain the cognitive skills that we learned at an earlier age and use them where they are appropriate. What we do see is that the cognitive development of humans is characterized by increasingly abstract abilities which allow them to deal with problems in a hypothetical, tentative fashion. It is this growth in cognitive development which allows us to adapt to the complexities of our everyday world.

Some Practical Suggestions

What can be summarized about thinking and problem solving that can be useful to you in everyday problem situations? In this section, five general principles that are useful in virtually all problem situations are outlined. Many additional practical rules of thumb can be cited, but these five principles focus on central aspects of problem solving.

Understand the Problem

Before you can solve a problem you must first be sure you understand it. Perhaps this appears so obvious as to sound trite. Yet all too frequently the basic difficulty you have in solving a problem is a failure to have a clear conception of its components. One of the frequent reasons that students do poorly on examinations is that in their haste to answer the question they fail to analyze and reexamine the question itself. An all-too-familiar experience of students is to discover that they have written an answer to a question other than the one asked. Thus, not until you understand a problem can you attempt to answer it. Moreover, once you have clarified a problem, it is good practice to check again to see if your initial understanding is still correct.

Remember the Problem

Another source of difficulty arises if you fail to remember the problem accurately. On occasion students produce incorrect answers on an essay examination because they fail to remember the problem as it is formulated. Somewhere in the course of writing an answer the student may veer away from the central issue and deal with irrelevant issues. You may, so to speak, shift in midstream from the main thesis to trivial, secondary, or utterly unrelated topics if you fail to keep the problem in mind. Therefore, periodically recheck your memory of the problem to ensure that you stay with the issue.

Identify Alternative Hypotheses

Problem solving requires, of course, that you produce hypotheses. Rather than fixate on one or two hypotheses, try to identify and classify several hypotheses that appear reasonable. It is generally advantageous to try the easier or simpler hypotheses first and if these fail then to shift to more complex hypotheses. Finally, avoid the premature selection of a particular hypothesis until you have had opportunity to evaluate reasonable alternatives, that is, generate a list of hypotheses.

Acquire Coping Strategies

Coping strategies refer to ways of dealing with difficulties, failure, and frustration encountered in problem situations. Frustration and difficulty are inevitable accompaniments of problem solving. Since frustration cannot in the long run be avoided under all circumstances, a major task is to learn how to *cope* with such difficulty.

Blind persistence in using old rules and excessive motivation, particularly in the form of frustration, are seen as barriers to successful problem solving. Therefore, you should attempt to recognize rigidity in yourself and to avoid inflexibility when solving problems. One way of doing this is to cultivate a general plan of using variable modes of attack as the situation demands. The colloquial expression *hang loose* captures much of the meaning of what is required for effective problem solving. Thus, it is important to remain open for new options, alternatives, and approaches.

Evaluate the Final Hypothesis

Once you have decided on a final hypothesis, reevaluate your choice. Consider the issue of implementing your choice. Even though it may be a good one on rational and logical grounds, is it practical and feasible? In summary, take one final look before you commit yourself to a particular sequence of action.

Summary

This chapter treated thinking and problem solving as interrelated topics. Thinking refers to a class of covert activities that involve manipulation of symbols. Problem-solving performance was seen as strongly dependent upon set and motivational factors. Typical problem-solving tasks were the water jar problem, tests of functional fixedness, and anagram problems. Problem solving was seen to involve several stages, and the possible role of incubation in problem solving was discussed.

Three theories of problem solving and thinking were described: S-R theory, Gestalt theory, and information-processing approaches. Piaget's theory of cognitive development was described in some detail. Finally, five practical principles for efficient problem solving were noted: understand the problem, remember the problem, identify alternative hypotheses, acquire coping strategies, and evaluate the final hypothesis.

Multiple-Choice Items: Thinking and Problem Solving

1. The concept of thinking is like the concept of learning in that
   a. they both are directly observable
   b. neither deal with nominal stimuli
   c. neither deal with covert or implicit responses
   d. they both are inferred, hypothetical processes
2. In the discussion of problem solving several stages were described. Which stage was *not* described?
   a. interpretation of the problem
   b. associating old ideas
   c. generating hypotheses
   d. testing hypotheses
3. The idea of incubation in problem solving comes from situations in which the problem solver
   a. shows immediate insight upon presentation of the problem
   b. solves the problem in systematic steps
   c. adopts clever strategies
   d. withdraws from the task for a period, followed by the solution
4. The water jar problem is designed to study the persistence of set in problem solving. Another way of describing this is
   a. flexibility
   b. accommodation
   c. rigidity
   d. retrieval
5. Suppose you have difficulty in visualizing or imagining old objects or stimuli as functioning in a novel fashion. This would exemplify

    a.   functonal fixedness
    b.   accommodation
    c.   assimilation
    d.   flexibility

6.   The Gestalt theory of thinking and problem solving has emphasized the significance of
    a.   insight
    b.   associations
    c.   computer models
    d.   language

7.   The process of incorporating objects and events into an existing cognitive structure is called
    a.   accommodation
    b.   functional fixedness
    c.   insight
    d.   assimilation

8.   According to Piaget, the stage at which the child begins to show logical operations in thinking which is still closely tied to the physical world is called
    a.   concrete operations
    b.   formal operations
    c.   preoperational thought
    d.   assimilation

9.   An important aspect of problem solving is learning how to handle frustration and difficulty. This process was described as acquiring
    a.   insight
    b.   perceptual reorganization
    c.   flexibility
    d.   coping strategies

10.   Incubation appears to help in solving problems for several possible reasons. Which one was *not* identified?
    a.   additional practice may actually occur
    b.   you have sufficient time to read further on the problem
    c.   incubation may allow for forgetting of inappropriate sets
    d.   the period of rest may allow for dissipation of fatigue

True-False Items: Thinking and Problem Solving

1.   Thinking is not a process that we can directly observe.
2.   Persistence of set refers to the fact that humans may tend to apply old rules or principles when they are no longer appropriate.
3.   You can have too much motivation for efficient problem-solving activity.

4. Stimulus-response theory of thinking regards it basically as a matter of perceptual reorganization.

5. Information-processing conceptions of behavior attempt to state the rules of operation (or steps) involved in some process.

6. One reason that humans fail to solve problems efficiently is that they fail to understand the problem in the first place.

7. Frustration may be a frequent accompaniment of problem solving; therefore an important task to be learned is developing adequate ways of responding to frustration.

8. Piaget views cognitive development as basically a matter of altering or changing information so that it fits in with our cognitive structure.

9. According to Piaget the ability to conserve normally appears during the early part of the preoperational stage.

10. An important feature of problem solving is being able to identify alternative hypotheses if more than one plausible hypothesis exists.

11. The persistence of an inappropriate set in problem solving is much like a negative transfer situation.

12. Growth in cognitive development according to Piaget means that we learn new strategies and cognitive skills while forgetting the skills learned at an earlier age.

Discussion Items: Thinking and Problem Solving

1. Select a particular problem such as deciding on a term paper topic and outline the stages of problem solving you might use.

2. Since persistence of an inappropriate set is a deterrent to problem solving, how might you teach yourself or someone else to become more flexible in your (their) approach to problems?

3. Discuss the principle that you can have too much motivation for efficient problem solving.

4. Outline in some detail the basic stages of cognitive development as described by Piaget.

5. How might you apply the five practical suggestions for effective problem solving to some problem of significance to you?

Multiple-Choice Answers: Thinking and Problem Solving

1. (d) Both thinking and learning are hypothetical processes. In both cases we do not directly observe the processes, but only infer their operation indirectly from various performance measures.

2. (b) Nothing was said about associating old ideas, although this process could occur as part of the stage of generating hypotheses.

3. (d) Incubation is basically a rest period in which the problem is set aside and you go about your affairs doing other things. A solution appears subsequently after you have withdrawn from the task.

4. (c) The persistence of set in water jar problems can be described as a form of rigidity, which is resistance to change or unwillingness to try new approaches or ideas.

5. (a) The persistence in visualizing old objects in their typical function is another type of rigidity or persistence of set. In this case it is called functional fixedness.

6. (a) Gestalt theory has emphasized the significance of insight in problem solving. Insight refers to some type of perceptual reorganization of one's environment in which relationships between objects and events are perceived in new ways.

7. (d) The process of assimilation is one in which objects or events are incorporated into an existing cognitive structure. In contrast, accommodation involves changing the cognitive structure itself.

8. (a) Thought begins to become logical in the stage of concrete operations, but it is still based on concrete examples of the child's physical environment.

9. (d) Learning how to handle frustration is a matter of acquiring appropriate coping skills and strategies.

10. (b) Incubation is a process where you withdraw at least at the conscious level from the problem. Thus further reading on the problem would not be part of incubation.

True-False Answers: Thinking and Problem Solving

1. (True) Thinking is a covert process; we infer that thinking has occurred, but we don't directly see thinking.

2. (True) The carryover of old rules or habits is called persistence of set.

3. (True) Problem solving efficiency bears a U-shaped relationship with motivation, indicating that beyond some level an increase in motivation can actually interfere with efficient performance.

4. (False) Stimulus-response theory of thinking regards it as implicit or covert trial-and-error behavior. Gestalt theory views thinking as perceptual reorganization.

5. (True) Information-processing conceptions formulate some kind of sequence of rules, usually in the format of a flowchart showing each step in the process.

6. (True) This is a common source of difficulty in problem solving.

7. (True) A major task is learning how to cope with frustration since it is likely to occur during problem-solving activity.

8. (False) Cognitive development is both a matter of accommodation and of assimilation.

9. (False) Conservation typically appears in the early part of the concrete operations stage.

10. (True) This is an important part of problem solving, especially if there are disadvantages to some of the alternatives which must be weighed.

11. (True) Persistence of set is the transfer of a strategy or solution which is inappropriate and hence is like a negative transfer situation.

12. (False) We not only learn new cognitive skills, but according to Piaget also maintain our earlier acquired skills.

Attention and Perceptual Learning

9

Most of us experience situations in which we are unable to process all of the information coming into our senses. An obvious example is talking on the phone while another person in the room either asks us a question or gives us messages to relay to the person on the other end of the line. In most instances we must listen to only one of the two speakers or run the risk of not understanding either or both of the messages. An inability to process information from different sources might also occur when we listen to a lecture. For example, if the instructor makes a point which is particularly interesting to us, we might reflect about the importance of the point for several minutes, only to realize that we haven't heard or understood what the instructor was saying while we were thinking. Although the first example has two external sources of information and the second example one external (lecture) and one internal (thinking) source of information, both examples demonstrate our limited capacity to process information.

This limited ability to process information is said to reflect our limited amount of total attention. In order to process information, we must give it attention, but we are limited in how many and what kinds of inputs we can attend to at any one time. Our *attentional capacity* thus refers to the maximum amount of information we can process. Thus, when we exceed our attentional capacity some of the incoming information will be lost.

Theories of attention differ in their assumptions about which psychological processes such as memory are dependent upon our attention. If a psychological process requires attention, then carrying out that process while we receive two simultaneous messages will result in a loss of information from the messages because the attentional capacity has been exceeded. In contrast, if the process requires no attention, it may then be carried out in the presence of two simultaneous messages without any loss of information (parallel processing). We will discuss the theories and their assumptions about which processes require attentional capacity after we have looked at the basic type of experiment in this area and some relevant experimental results.

Dichotic Listening and Attention

Experiments dealing with attentional capacity usually investigate which types of tasks tend to interfere with each other. A specific example is the *dichotic listening task*. In this type of experiment headphones are used to present two messages, one to each ear. The *primary message* is presented to one ear and contains the information to which subjects are instructed to listen. For instance, the primary message might consist of the experimenter reading a newspaper article or a prose passage to the subject. To ensure that subjects are actually listening they are instructed to *shadow* the primary message, in which shadowing consists of repeating each word in the primary message immediately after the speaker says it (much like a fast echo). The *secondary message* is presented to the other ear and might be a tone of one-second duration. Subjects would be told to shadow the primary message as accurately and quickly as possible, but any time they hear a tone they should press a button as quickly as possible. Interference in attention is measured by comparing the speed and accuracy of shadowing performance (and reaction time to the tone) when these tasks are performed separately versus when the two tasks are combined. If subjects' performance on shadowing is worse when they are also pressing the button to a tone, we may then infer that the demands on attention are greater than the available capacity. Thus, a decrement in shadowing performance would indicate that shadowing and responding to the tone share some process which can only be applied to one input at one time. It should be noted that such experiments are not limited to auditory presentation; however, it is the type most frequently used. The primary message in the previous example could just as easily have been monitoring a radar screen, while the secondary message could have been pressing a button whenever a light flashed in the subjects' visual field. We will now turn to some of the basic experimental results, most of which were investigated in the dichotic listening situation.

Some Experimental Findings

Many of the studies of dichotic listening have used the same basic procedure. Typically, a single primary message is presented along with one of several different secondary messages. The main variable of interest is the relatedness of the primary and secondary messages. For example, if the subjects are shadowing a prose passage, the secondary message might then be as follows: (1) another very similar prose passage, (2) a moderately similar prose passage, or (3) something unrelated to English. One study indicated that subjects noticed only certain things about the secondary message; when the same prose passage was played to both ears, subjects noticed a change in the secondary message when the voice changed from male to female and vice versa. In contrast, they failed to notice when the message switched from English to German or when the tape was played backward.

Other studies have shown that one's name is almost always noticed, even when it is presented in the secondary message. Most of us have experienced this personally; even in a crowded, noisy room we seem to hear our name if someone says it. In fact, we may even think that some-one said our name when he used only a similar-sounding word.

In an interesting series of experiments Donald MacKay examined the effects of the secondary message. The principal feature of these ex-periments was that the primary message contained ambiguity at one of the following three levels: (1) lexical (word ambiguity), (2) surface structure (part of speech), or (3) deep structure (actor, object). MacKay selected sentences for the primary message that were equally likely to be interpreted in either of two ways. In the lexically am-biguous situation the primary message was "They threw stones toward the bank yesterday." In this sentence *bank* can mean a place where money is kept or the bank of a river. At the same time that the word *bank* was presented in the primary message, either the word *money* or *river* was presented in the secondary message. In this situation, subjects' recognition judgments about which sentences had been presented shifted toward sentences with the meaning of *bank* implied by the word in the secondary message. Thus, the content of the secondary message influ-enced the interpretation or meaning of a word in the primary message. Therefore, we can infer that processing the sentences and the word did not exceed attentional capacity because the word in the secondary mes-sage had an effect on the interpretation of the sentence in the primary message.

In a similar situation the primary message was constructed to have ambiguous surface structure: "John looked over the fence" can mean John looked over the top of the fence or that John inspected the fence. At the same time that "looked over" was presented in the primary mes-sage, "phoned up" was presented in the secondary message. Since "phoned up" consists of a verb plus an adverb its use should bias the interpretation of the primary message toward meaning that the fence "was inspected." This is exactly what occurred. Subjects' bias for rec-ognizing the interpretation of "John inspected the fence" increased. This also indicates that attentional capacity is not exceeded when subjects jointly process a sentence and the surface structure of the secondary mes-sage, as evidenced by the influence of the secondary message on the in-terpretation of the primary message.

In the deep-structure situation subjects heard the primary message

"Flying planes can be dangerous," which means either that for you to fly a plane can be dangerous or that flying planes can present a danger to you even if you don't fly them. The secondary message, the phrase "growling lions," was presented at the same time as "flying planes." "Growling lions" means "lions that are growling" and should bias the interpretation of the sentence toward "planes that are flying." The secondary message, which attempted to bias deep-structure interpretation, had no effect on the interpretation of the primary message in this situation.

Thus, attempts to bias the interpretation of the primary message were successful in the case of lexical and surface-structure ambiguity, but not in the case of deep-structure ambiguity. This led MacKay to suggest that processing the primary message takes most or all of the attentional capacity and that the different secondary messages require different amounts of attention. In processing the lexical meaning or surface structure of the secondary message no attention is necessary. Therefore, subjects can process the primary message and the lexical or surface-structure information in the secondary message at the same time, thus biasing the interpretation of the primary message. However, processing the deep structure of the secondary message requires attentional capacity, but processing the primary message leaves insufficient capacity for this purpose. Thus, the deep structure of the secondary message has no effect on interpretation of the primary message.

Theories of Attention

We will now turn to several theories of attention. As was mentioned earlier, the theories differ in where they postulate the limited-capacity portion of the system. The first two theories we will discuss postulate some filtering at the sensory or perceptual level; the idea of filtering refers to the fact that information may be processed only at a certain level. Filters can operate early at input, at the sensory perceptual level, at intermediate levels, and at late levels involving memory.

Filter Theory

The first theory is called filter theory and was proposed by a British psychologist, Donald Broadbent. He proposed a processing system that might be thought of as a Y-shaped funnel. The arms of the Y represent sensory input channels, and the stem represents the limited-capacity portion of the system. Where the sensory channels meet is a flap that can move in either direction to shut off one of the channels. If we represent information in the system as marbles, then a marble coming in one sensory channel will hit the flap and close off the other channel, blocking any marbles coming in that side. Thus, the filter is *all or none* in the sense that information either gets all the way through the system or is filtered out completely at the sensory level. In Broadbent's theory sensory channels are assumed to be related to the physical characteristics of the stimulus. Thus, one channel might be for high frequencies and the other for low frequencies. In addition to the sensory channels based on physical characteristics of the stimulus, Broadbent also assumed that each sense organ, such as each ear, is also a separate sensory channel. The assumption that each ear is a separate input channel provides problems for the theory.

As we have seen, our name almost always is heard in dichotic listening experiments, even when it is presented as the secondary message. According to Broadbent's theory, the primary message coming in one ear should move the flap over so that inputs from the other ear cannot get through the system. However, our name is not filtered out as would be predicted by Broadbent's theory. The results of MacKay's experiments are also inconsistent with an all-or-none filter position. The fact that lexical or surface-structure information in the secondary message influences the interpretation of the sentence in the primary message indicates that the secondary message is not being filtered out at the sensory level.

Attenuated Filter Theory

Because of the difficulties encountered by the assumption of all-or-none filters, filter theory has been subsequently modified to produce the *attenuated* filter theory. This position says that the perceptual filters don't act in an all-or-none fashion, but serve to attenuate or decrease the amount of information coming in the secondary channel. Attenuated filter theory further assumes that the amount of attenuation of the secondary message decreases as the number of sensory channels carrying information increases. Therefore, the more sensory channels that are carrying information, the less effective is the filter in blocking out the irrelevant sensory channels. Having filters which only attenuate the secondary message is consistent with the fact that we hear our name when it is in the secondary message, if we assume that our name has a very low threshold. Even in attenuated form the input provides enough information for our name to exceed threshold, and thus we hear our name. However, attenuated filter theory is not completely consistent with MacKay's results. MacKay's experiments indicate that the nature of the secondary message is important. There is no reason for the theory to assume that the secondary message is not filtered when it is to be later analyzed for lexical and surface-structure information, but is filtered when it is to be analyzed for deep-structure information. Attenuated filter theory cannot predict that the secondary message will be filtered in the deep-structure situation alone. Thus, *attenuated* filter theory also fails to be consistent with all of the results we discussed earlier.

No Sensory Filter Theory

The final theory we will discuss differs from sensory filter theories in an important way; it proposes *no sensory* filtering at all. Instead, all stimuli are assumed to make contact with their representation in memory, which results in activation of the representation. Thus, there is no limit to the number of stimuli that can contact memory at any one time. The limitation on processing takes place *after memory contact*, with some types of further processing requiring more attention than others. Stimuli are selected for further processing based on their importance to the organism, where importance is based on past experience and other factors. Thus, our name is presumably important to us and will be further processed after memory contact, resulting in our ability to recognize that our name had been presented in the secondary message. In MacKay's experiments, we can assume that both the primary and secondary messages were important enough to receive further processing after memory contact was made by the individual words. However, the nature of the further processing might be such that processing the deep structure of the secondary message would require more attentional capacity than is available while also processing the primary message. In contrast, processing the lexical meaning or surface structure of the secondary message would require little or no attention and would be carried out at the same time as processing of the primary message. Thus, a theory postulating unlimited memory contact by incoming stimuli would be consistent with all of the results we discussed previously.

Perceptual Learning

Imagine trying to locate a friend in the midst of many people at a busy air terminal. You find yourself busily scanning a large number of unfamiliar faces, obtaining enough information to be confident that each face is not the friend until the friend is finally identified. This process of rapidly scanning various stimuli characterizes the typical search task which we engage in daily. Scanning the want ads in the newspaper, looking over the vegetables in the grocery, and searching for your car in a gigantic parking lot are all instances of scanning tasks. More important, the fact that we *improve* in our search skills is one kind of evidence for perceptual learning.

Also imagine the skillful automobile driver who has learned to make reasonably precise judgments about distance, objects in space, and speed of approaching vehicles, as a result of considerable practice. In a similar vein, some drivers become proficient in reading city maps as a result of practice. Novice map readers may experience difficulty in relating things on a map to city streets or freeways, whereas skillful map readers can quickly see the relationship between the map and where they actually are at some moment as well as where they want to be. In both instances perceptual judgments are observed to improve with practice. The fact that such perceptual judgments do improve with practice is another kind of evidence for the process known as perceptual learning.

There is considerable evidence which indicates that our perceptions are influenced by our past experience and that our perceptions can be modified or changed by various practice conditions. Thus, in a general sense, *the term perceptual learning refers to various changes in perception that can be brought about by learning.* Instances of perceptual learning are common in your everyday experience. You learn, for example, to recognize a particular melody even though it is played by different bands using different musical instruments. Indeed, you may recognize a Beethoven symphony when played by a rock band. The fact that you can pick out a common set of features (melody) regardless of large changes in musical context is one instance of the process called perceptual learning.

Another instance of perceptual learning is seen when you become skillful in identifying objects under a microscope. The beginning student occasionally has difficulty in seeing what she is supposed to see, and indeed may even describe her own eyelashes or some other irrelevant object. With practice, however, one becomes quite proficient in identifying objects and in describing their important features. Similarly, one learns to make certain perceptual adjustments when first wearing eyeglasses. This is particularly the case if one has to wear bifocals which require somewhat separate adjustments for close and distance viewing.

We have already referred to the significance of perceptual processes as they relate to learning in earlier sections of this book. For example, in paired associate learning the related processes of stimulus discrimination, stimulus selection, and stimulus coding were described. It was emphasized that if a particular stimulus was to become reliably associated with a particular response, the stimulus of the moment must come to be *perceived* in a relatively consistent fashion on each trial. This process called attention to the significance of perceptual processes in associative learning. Similarly, in our discussion of memory we emphasized the role of organizing materials in some fashion for purposes of efficient storage and retrieval. In order, however, for the learner to organize the material in some fashion, she must *perceive* some kind of structure by which the material can be organized or construct some sort of structure if it is not evidently apparent. In a similar vein, the use of concepts like stimulus discrimination in concept learning calls attention to processes akin to perception in concept learning. Thus, throughout this book perceptual processes have been seen to operate in learning. *This chapter focuses, however, on the manner by which learning influences perception as distinct from the way in which perceptual processes influence learning.*

Nature of Perceptual Learning

Perceptual learning has already been described in an informal way. As you saw, *perceptual learning refers to any modification of perception which can be attributed to learning.* Such a definition requires that both *perception* and *learning* be distinguished and the relationship between them described. Let us therefore turn our attention to some of the properties of the concept of learning and then distinguish it from perception.

At the beginning of this book learning was defined as a relatively permanent process that is inferred from performance changes due to practice. Four features of this definition are important: (1) *learning is an inference,* which means that it is not something directly observed. Thus learning is an inferred or hypothetical concept like gravity or electricity. We never see gravity directly; we observe falling objects and therefore infer that such a process exists. (2) *The concept of learning is tied to performance, but is not the same as performance.* Hence a distinction is made between learning and performance. Various performance indicators are employed to infer learning such as number of correct responses, errors, percentages of correct responses, response rate, response speed, and so forth. (3) *The concept of learning is tied to conditions of practice,* which serves to distinguish learning from performance changes attributable to other conditions such as fatigue, maturation, and drug states. This simply emphasizes that the conditions antecedent to learning are *practice* conditions as distinct from other kinds of conditions. (4) *Learning is a relatively permanent process,* an assumption which is useful in order to distinguish learning from other more temporary processes such as sensory memory or short-term memory.

Schematically, learning can be described as an intervening or inferred process as shown below:

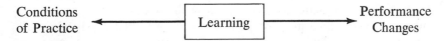

Conditions of Practice ◄——————— | Learning | ———————► Performance Changes

The phrase "conditions of practice" refers to the various conditions which might be varied in some experimental setting. These include, for example, such conditions as number of practice or training trials, reward and/or punishment conditions, feedback, distributed practice, intralist similarity, and meaningfulness. In general, they refer to the various training and task conditions which might be manipulated in order to see how they affect performance changes.

In a parallel vein, *perception is a process that is inferred from performance changes due to conditions of stimulation.* Thus perception, like learning, is an inferred or hypothetical process which is also tied to performance changes. A principal difference lies in the nature of the antecedent conditions; antecedent to perception are *stimulus* conditions whereas antecedent to learning are *practice* conditions. Some perceptual theorists may wish to make *additional* distinctions regarding the nature of the inferred process. We need, for present purposes, only emphasize the differences in antecedent conditions.

The fact that you detect a change in light intensity when you flick a light switch on is of course an instance of perception. Detection of an increase in brightness is a performance indicator, and "turning the light on" produces an increase in stimulus energy. Thus perception, like learning, is a relational concept inferred from both performance changes and stimulus input. The performance change in this example is going from a report of no detection to detection of the light.

The concepts of learning and perception can now be more formally compared as illustrated here. As the diagram shows, both concepts are tied to performance changes and both concepts are inferences from performance tied to some class of antecedent conditions.

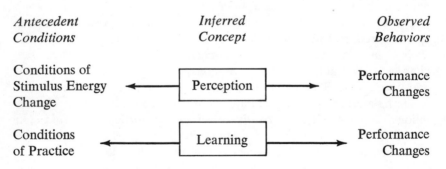

We can now define perceptual learning by showing how learning and perception relate. Consider first a simple instance of perception. Imagine that two points of pressure about the size of a pencil point are applied to your forearm. The points, which are initially very close together, are gradually moved apart at greater distances until you report at some stage in the test sequence that you feel two distinct points. This report defines what is called the *two-point threshold* for cutaneous sensitivity. In general, the minimal distance between two stimuli pressing on the skin which yields a report of "feeling like two" defines the two-point threshold. Here is an instance of *perception* which, by the above definition, involves a relationship between stimulus energy impinging on the skin receptors (varying the distance between the two points) and some performance indicator (a report of a feeling of "twoness").

Once a two-point threshold is determined, however, you may be given extended practice in making this perceptual judgment. With extended practice the threshold will gradually decrease, which is simply to say that you can detect progressively smaller distances between two points as you are given more practice in making this perceptual judgment. In this instance, decrease of the two-point threshold with practice would be an instance of perceptual learning. Thus the definition of *perceptual learning as a change in perception due to practice* becomes quite clear. It is a change in perception because the threshold value becomes smaller, and the observed change is due to practice factors. This does not, of course, specify what processes might operate during practice, but merely emphasizes that perception can become modified as a result of practice conditions.

This example is, of course, but one of many instances of perceptual learning. It serves principally to illustrate in fairly precise terms what is meant by the phrase "perception can become modified by learning."

Categories of Perceptual Tasks

The study of perceptual learning focuses on how practice conditions produce changes in perception. To get at changes in perception psychologists must have certain performance indicators or responses that presumably index changes in perception. A taxonomy of perceptual tasks relevant to perception has been developed in recent years, a taxonomy which categorizes the various kinds of behaviors observed in studies of perception and perceptual learning. The five basic response categories are *detection, discrimination, recognition, identification,* and *judgment.* Let us consider each of these briefly.

Detection

An observer watching for blips on a radarscope is engaged in the task of detection. Similarly, when you respond to the ring of the telephone you do so because you have detected a stimulus. *A detection task is one in which the observer reports the presence or absence of a stimulus.* The stimulus might be a brief flash of light, a tone, or a target stimulus embedded in a complex as found, say, in hidden puzzles. All that is required in a detection task is the reported presence or absence of some specified target stimulus. For example, is there a misspelled word in this sentence? Answer yes or no.

Discrimination

A wine taster reporting that he distinguishes between two wines is engaged in discrimination. He does not have to name or identify the wines to be engaged in discrimination; all that he must do is report that they are different. Similarly, being able to perceive the difference between identical twins is an instance of discrimination. Thus the term *discrimination refers to the reporting of a difference between two stimuli.* In an experimental setting a subject is presented two stimuli, either simultaneously or successively, and asked to report whether they are the "same" or "different." Noting that the warmed-over roast tastes different from when it was first cooked, that your girl friend has changed her hairstyle, or that a change in the temperature has occurred are all instances of discrimination.

Recognition

In recognition the observer must report if a particular test stimulus is old (familiar) *or new* (unfamiliar) *following a training series in which the observer looked at one or more stimuli.* Recognition differs from discrimination in that the judgment required is one based upon the familiarity of the stimulus. As we noted in a previous chapter, an example of recognition tests is the typical multiple-choice examination. The task of the subject is to designate which item he thinks he has previously seen or experienced.

Identification

An identification task goes essentially one step beyond that of recognition in that an identifying response must be made in the presence of a stimulus. This is simply to say that the *task of identification requires a unique response be made to each stimulus.* Producing the name of each individual shown in a photograph is an instance of identification. It is not necessary that a name be used as such because arbitrary labels, letters of the alphabet, or numbers could also be used as identifying responses.

Judgment

Judgment, as a perceptual response indicator, refers simply to the placing or ordering of stimuli along some scale. The subject is typically presented with a series of stimuli and asked to make judgments about them in accord with some scale. For instance, beauty contest judges are asked to rank contestants in accord with some scale of beauty. Similarly, observers may be given some visual patterns and asked to rate them in accord with some scale of complexity going from simple to very complex patterns.

Categories of Perceptual Learning

In this section we shall examine several representative categories of perceptual learning. We can do no more than illustrate a few of the various kinds of changes that have been studied, changes which illustrate the process of perceptual learning. Six categories of perceptual learning studies will be examined: (1) effects of practice on perceptual skills, (2) reward and punishment factors, (3) adaptation to transformed stimulation, (4) cross-modal transfer, (5) verbal labels and perceptual learning, and (6) schema learning.

Effects of Practice on Perceptual Skills

An earlier section illustrated one kind of improvement in perceptual skills with practice. The example described the reduction in two-point thresholds with practice. Other kinds of perceptual skills are also known to improve with practice. In general, improvements in all five perceptual tasks—detection, discrimination, recognition, identification, and judgment—do occur as a result of practice.

A typical example of improvement in perceptual skills associated with practice is seen in a search task. A typical search task requires you to scan a group of stimuli such as letters, numbers, or visual patterns and to detect some prespecified target stimulus or stimuli. For example, you might be shown a series of letters presented in scrambled order and asked to locate all the *m*'s. Similarly, you might be shown several paragraphs of prose material and asked to detect the number of words misspelled in which the misspelled words are experimentally built into the passage. An obvious real-life example is proofreading. In any event, the materials can be presented so that humans detect either single or multiple targets. Figure 15 shows the typical improvement in performance when humans are given search tasks on successive days. The figure shows that search time, that is, time to locate either single or multiple targets, progressively decreases with days of practice.

Not only does search time decrease with practice, but also the number of targets detected increases with amount of practice. In general, the improvement in search-task performance appears to be a phenomenon very much like learning to learn. The individual is learning something about efficient scanning habits, perhaps learning to reduce the search down to a few critical features of the stimuli in the case of multiple targets.

Similar kinds of improvements are seen in recognition and identification tasks. Here the task is to recognize or identify stimuli in successive tasks. Both recognition time and recognition accuracy, as well as identification accuracy, improve with sustained practice.

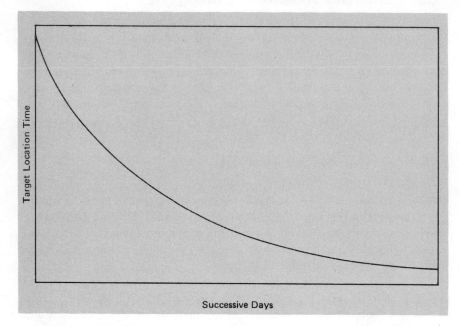

Figure 15. Gradual improvement in target location on successive days of practice.

Reward and Punishment Factors

What humans tend to perceive is governed in part by the conditions of reward and punishment. This is simply to say that under certain conditions we are more likely to perceive those stimuli which have been associated with reward. The role of reward factors has been demonstrated in studies using ambiguous stimuli, either of which can be perceived as a facial profile. In such studies, subjects have been shown each profile separately and rewarded when they responded to one profile and not the other. In the test situation, they are shown both profiles together and asked to report what they perceive. Typically, subjects report that they tend to perceive the rewarded profile more frequently than the nonrewarded profile. We cannot conclude, however, that perceptions themselves are being modified as such. It appears that what is being modified is the subject's *response bias,* that is, his likelihood of making a particular response. In this connection, you saw earlier in chapter 4 how response bias can influence recognition performance. Here again we have an instance of response bias which is separate from perception itself. Therefore, reward appears to affect response tendencies (performance), but not necessarily perception as such.

Similar kinds of effects have been found in studies of perceptual recognition. Subjects have been shown so-called taboo words such as *whore, kotex,* and *rape* intermixed with nontaboo words such as *apple* and *cigar.* The words have been presented for extremely brief durations and the task of the subject is to identify each word. Usually it takes somewhat longer for subjects to identify the taboo words, suggesting to some psychologists the operation of a *perceptual defense* mechanism. By this is meant that human organisms tend to protect themselves against stimuli that they perceive as potentially threatening. A simpler interpretation, however, is that humans are simply more likely to withhold responding until they are sure they have seen a taboo word, indicating that longer recognition times are a matter of response bias rather than any perceptual process as such.

Adaptation to Transformed Stimulation

Another type of perceptual learning is seen when one adapts to stimulation that is transformed in some fashion. For instance, you have learned to perceive the world in a particular orientation. If, however, you now wear eyeglasses constructed such that the world is perceived upside down you have the problem of readjusting to your perceptual world. The world, of course, has not changed, but your perception of it has. In particular, your ability to locate objects in space is seriously disturbed. The meaning of objects doesn't change, as people are still seen as people, houses as houses, and so forth, but one must learn to reorient oneself to this new stimulus input.

A simple example of adaptation to transformed stimulation requires that the subject manually locate a target while looking through a prism at his hand. The prism has the effect of displacing the image of his hand, and the subject is allowed to observe his hand movements alone, or the target alone, but not both together. The subject attempts to repeatedly localize the target under the condition of transformed stimulation and gradually improves in his performance. This type of task has been used most extensively by Richard Held and his associates, and the results indicate that perceptual learning in the form of improved localization skill depends upon active movement of the subject's hand rather than on no movement or passive movement by an experimenter.

Cross-modal Transfer

Cross-modal transfer refers to the fact that learning in one sensory system such as the visual mode can transfer to another sensory system such as the tactual mode. For example, if you learn a paired associate task consisting of visual patterns as stimuli, then such learning will transfer to a second task if the same stimuli are now presented tactually. In the second task you are not allowed to see the stimuli, but only to feel them. Such learning is an instance of perceptual learning and implies to some perceptual theorists such as James Gibson a kind of "unity of the senses." This notion implies that there are certain properties of stimuli such as shape which have invariant features regardless of the sensory system in which they are learned. Thus when you learn something about stimuli in one system you tend to automatically pick up some information in another system. Despite the fact that there is considerable evidence for cross-modal transfer, we understand very little about the mechanisms that produce the effect.

Verbal Labels and Perceptual Learning

A long-standing view in psychology has been that language or verbal labels can aid humans in distinguishing otherwise confusable or highly similar stimuli. The basic notion has been that if distinctive verbal labels are associated with confusable stimuli, this process will serve to make the stimuli more distinctive or less confusable. At the outset it should be noted that there is evidence indicating that if humans are trained to associate distinctive verbal labels with stimuli such stimuli become more recognizable, or are more easily learned in new situations, under *some* conditions. The point to note, however, is that the *mechanisms* by which such an effect occurs are not fully understood.

In these studies, subjects are usually trained to label stimuli in paired-associate fashion with distinctive verbal labels. Their performance is sometimes compared with subjects who are merely shown the stimuli without instructions to label or who are trained in labeling other stimuli which are unrelated (or irrelevant) to the stimuli used in the test task. Presumably, if the verbal-labeling task makes the stimuli more distinctive in some perceptual sense, they should then be more easily discriminated or recognized in a test task when compared with subjects who only look at the stimuli. The evidence indicates that verbal labeling does produce this effect, but principally when the stimuli are fairly complex. With simple stimuli there is usually little if any effect due to verbal-labeling practice. A simple stimulus is a visual shape, for example, with few sides or angles, whereas a complex shape is a many-sided figure.

The most complete explanation of such an effect lies presumably in relating stimulus complexity to the *codability* of the shapes. Henry Ellis has proposed that complex visual patterns are more difficult to code verbally, and therefore if subjects are given verbal labels which are representative of the shapes, such a label helps the person to more rapidly or efficiently encode the pattern. On the other hand, if the shape is simple and easily encoded, then association of a verbal label is unlikely to do much in addition to what the individual can do for himself. Simple shapes easily suggest verbal codes and hence are unlikely to benefit from the additional effects of labeling.

The effect of verbal labels on subsequent recognition memory of shape stimuli is thus seen, according to this formulation, as one of providing the subject with a rule or verbal instruction for encoding the visual shape. If the verbal label is representative of the shape, it tends to encourage the individual to attend to those distinctive features which are suggested by the label. In effect, the verbal label can suggest to the person certain features of the stimulus to which she should attend, thus allowing more rapid encoding of the stimulus.

Other investigations of verbal-labeling effects have been conducted in which common labels have been associated with different but similar stimuli. Here the object has been to see if associating a common response to different stimuli makes these stimuli less distinctive, an effect sometimes referred to as *acquired equivalence of cues*. In general, stimuli become less recognizable when common labels are attached to them. Again, this process seems to be the result of the common label encouraging the individual to look for common features, much as she might do in a concept-learning experiment.

Not only can verbal labels facilitate perceptual performance, but they may also mediate or bring about changes in the way in which humans respond to stimuli. For instance, learning to attach the same labels to dissimilar stimuli may make them less distinctive or more equivalent. Indeed, verbal labels serve to mediate or facilitate the learning of new responses to stimuli in a number of everyday situations. You may, for instance, respond to a particular person in a particular way because the person has been labeled a "conservative" or a "radical" without additional information about the individual's belief system. Or you may tend to regard an entire group of people in a particular way simply because they have been labeled in some specific fashion. The phenomenon of racial and other prejudices appears to be basically a matter of generalizing to a class of stimuli (in this case, people), that is, a matter of responding to groups of humans by virtue of the verbal labels associated with them.

Schema Learning

Another kind of situation in which perceptual learning appears to be involved relates to the tasks that fall under the rubric of schema learning. *A schema* is a kind of concept that presumably is abstracted (developed) from studying a series of similar or related stimuli. For example, you may be said to have acquired a schema for the human face, which refers to some abstracted representation derived from your experience with faces. Moreover, if you are asked to draw a representative American face, your representation will be different from that of a Chinese face, for instance. A schema, then, represents some abstracted central tendency of the sample of stimuli to which you have been exposed. In this sense, a schema is somewhat like an image in that it may represent some visual picture of a typical member of some class of events. Thus, we may have schema for a variety of events such as trees, houses, people, faces, cars and books. So far, this use of the term *schema* is basically that of an inferred concept, based upon the responses that are made to classes of stimuli. It remains hypothetical, unobserved, and something inferred from behavior.

More recently, however, investigations by psychologists such as Selby Evans and Michael Posner have attempted to *define* the schema in advance of an experiment rather than *infer* its existence. Visual patterns are generated in accordance with statistical rules such that the central tendency or average figure is determined. In this fashion the most representative figure of some population of visual figures is known prior to an investigation.

Schema-learning researchers have been interested principally in how humans acquire schemas and how they use them to classify additional stimuli once the schema is learned. In the latter case, subjects are shown visual patterns that belong to two or more classes (schema categories) and asked to sort them according to their own judgments. Subjects do learn to classify patterns in accordance with rules built into the stimuli, that is, they do learn to sort stimuli in accordance with the statistical schema. Moreover, they seem to do this without the benefit of external reinforcement in the form of knowledge of results.

What Is Learned in Perceptual Learning?

Let us now turn our attention to the issue of "what is learned" in perceptual learning. We have illustrated several kinds of situations in which perceptual learning occurs, but we need now to ask what gets learned in these situations. The most explicit attempt to identify what is learned in perceptual learning has been outlined by Eleanor Gibson, and the following description is a summary of her account. Gibson's description emphasizes three aspects: (1) increase in specificity of responding, (2) detection of distinctive features, and (3) detection of properties and patterns.

Increase in Specificity of Responding

First, perceptual learning is seen as involving an increase in the specificity of responding to stimuli. Perceptual learning is not the learning of responses per se, but is seen as the responding to variables of stimulation not previously responded to. At the onset of some learning situation there are many aspects of stimulation to which the learner may fail to respond. For instance, the wine taster may respond to only one or a few features at first, but later respond to many features such as body, aroma, clarity, and the like.

Detection of Distinctive Features

Closely related to the first process is what Gibson calls detection of distinctive features. Consider learning to distinguish between a pair of twin Siamese cats. Upon first contact they are difficult to distinguish on the basis of any single quality or characteristic. Indeed, many complex stimuli must be distinguished on the basis of a bundle of characteristics rather than of one alone. This detection of critically distinctive features appears to be another aspect of perceptual learning.

Detection of Properties and Patterns

Finally, Gibson has proposed that the detection of *regularities* is another aspect of perceptual learning. Consider the earlier example of recognizing a melody regardless of the context in which it is played. Here is an instance of detecting a pattern or regularity in stimulation. More generally, this process involves the detection of invariant properties of stimulation as they appear in various settings.

Some Practical Implications

The study of perceptual learning focuses attention on the *properties of stimuli* in learning tasks. Emphasis is placed on how initially confusable and complex stimuli become distinguished and on the role of structural characteristics of stimuli in learning. The most extensive application of perceptual learning principles has been made by Eleanor Gibson in the analysis of reading skills. Reading skills are seen to consist of at least four distinctive stages. The first phase, which lasts for several years, is learning to speak. This phase precedes the others, involves much response learning, but is part of the total skill of reading. Next the child must learn to discriminate among the printed letters because they are the smallest units of the writing system. While this may seem like a relatively simple task, imagine learning to distinguish the symbols in Chinese or Arabic languages. The third phase involves decoding the letters to sound, that is, learning letter-sound combinations. Finally, the learner must learn higher-order units such as whole words and then phrases or sentences.

Many other practical skills clearly involve perceptual processes. Map reading is an obvious example. Architects and engineers must learn to read and interpret three-dimensional drawings. Structural properties of mathematical concepts such as equality, symmetry, and transitivity are instances of concepts that must be made perceptible to the learner. How to make structure, order and equivalence distinctive events for the learner is a major task for perceptual-learning research, an endeavor which focuses its effort toward the stimulus properties of the learning task.

Summary

This chapter has described some of the principal characteristics of perceptual learning. Perceptual learning refers to changes in perception that can be brought about by learning. Although there is somewhat less agreement about the concept of perception than there is about the concept of learning, perceptual learning can be easily understood in functional terms.

Important categories of perceptual tasks are those of detection, discrimination, recognition, identification, and judgment. To a large extent the study of perceptual learning is the study of how changes in these performances are related to conditions of learning.

Six categories of perceptual learning studies were described. These were (1) effects of practice on perceptual skills, (2) reward and punishment factors, (3) adaptation to transformed stimulation, (4) cross-modal transfer, (5) verbal labels and perceptual learning, and (6) schema learning. An examination of what is learned in perceptual learning suggests at least three aspects: increase in the specificity of responding, detection of distinctive features, and detection of properties and patterns.

Applications of perceptual learning principles have been made most extensively to the reading process. Perceptual learning focuses attention on the properties of stimuli as important determinants of learning.

Multiple-Choice Items:
Attention and Perceptual Learning

1. The maximum amount of information we can process at a given time is called
   a. shadowing
   b. primary message
   c. attentional capacity
   d. filtering

2. The study of attention frequently uses the dichotic listening task. This requires that the subject _____ a primary message.
   a. shadow
   b. filter
   c. think
   d. ignore

3. MacKay's main finding in his study of attention was that subjects
   a. always shadow accurately
   b. process the deep structure of secondary messages
   c. process the deep structure of primary messages
   d. process the lexical and surface structure of secondary messages but not the deep structure

4. Three kinds of theories of attention were described. Which one was *not* described?
   a. all-or-none filter theory
   b. presensory filter
   c. filtering at the level of memory
   d. attenuated filter theory

5. The fact that humans can improve in their proficiency in locating hidden targets, objects, and other events in space is one example of
   a. mediation
   b. retrieval
   c. motor learning
   d. perceptual learning

6. The conditions antecedent to learning are various "conditions of practice" whereas the conditions antecedent to perception are
   a. stimuli
   b. thresholds
   c. attention
   d. performance

7. Being able to tell that two cola beverages, one in container A and the other in container B, are different is an example of
   a. identification
   b. recognition

    c. discrimination

    d. detection

8. When you can correctly label an orange as "Valencia" and an apple as "red delicious" it illustrates the process of

    a. detection

    b. discrimination

    c. recognition

    d. identification

9. A schema is most like a(n)

    a. rule

    b. label

    c. concept

    d. association

10. Verbal labels associated with visual patterns are most likely to aid in memory of the patterns when the patterns are

    a. difficult to encode

    b. easy to encode

    c. easy to verbalize

    d. simple

11. If identical labels are attached to somewhat different although similar stimuli, the stimuli may become harder to distinguish. This process has sometimes been referred to as

    a. schema learning

    b. acquired distinctiveness of cues

    c. acquired equivalence of cues

    d. codability

12. Gibson's theory of perceptual learning does *not* emphasize which feature?

    a. detection of distinctive features

    b. increase in specificity in responding

    c. detection of properties and patterns

    d. learning of responses

13. Perceptual learning places emphasis on what aspects of the learning process?

    a. responses

    b. stimuli

    c. associations

    d. labels

True-False Items: Attention and Perceptual Learning

1. The all-or-none filter theory best handles the results of dichotic listening experiments.

2. The secondary message does not bias the subjects' interpretation of the primary message.

3. Your perceptions of events, of objects in space, as well as of coded stimuli, may be modified as a result of learning.
4. The fact that perception can be modified by learning implies that learning is uninfluenced by perceptual processes.
5. Both perception and learning are inferred processes.
6. The antecedent conditions of perception are changes in stimulus energy.
7. The fact that you can barely hear a tone is an instance of detection, whereas recognition means that you can tell the difference between two tones.
8. Identification is similar to recognition except that in identification you are able to name or label the stimulus in some fashion.
9. The fact that your proficiency in locating hidden objects improves with practice is an instance of perceptual learning.
10. The fact that we tend to perceive with greater frequency events or objects which have been associated with reward means that our perceptions have been modified.
11. Verbal labels associated with visual stimuli can make the stimuli more distinctive in the sense of becoming easier to recognize.
12. A schema is very much like a concept.
13. Learning to recognize a melody regardless of the musical context in which it is played is best described as an instance of response learning.
14. Applications of principles of perceptual learning have focused largely on analysis of the stimulus properties of learning tasks.

Discussion Items: Attention and Perceptual Learning

1. On the basis of your own personal experiences, indicate how you think attention affects memory.

2. How might you go about improving your ability to pay attention?

3. Define perceptual learning.

4. How could the process of becoming a proficient coffee taster or tea taster be described as perceptual learning?

5. Cite an everyday example of each of the following: cross-modal transfer, reward in perceptual learning, and adaptation to transformed stimulation.

6. How might you go about teaching someone to pay careful attention to stimuli as in, say, a proofreading task? Here use concepts and principles that you have been exposed to throughout this book.

7. Similarly, how might you teach someone such as a lifeguard to pay careful attention to the swimmers in a pool?

Multiple-Choice Answers:
Attention and Perceptual Learning

1.   (c)   This is how attentional capacity is defined.

2.   (a)   The subject must shadow (verbatim repeat) the primary message.

3.   (d)   From MacKay's studies it is obvious that the subjects process the lexical and surface structure of the secondary message but not the deep structure.

4.   (b)   No discussion was made of any presensory filter.

5.   (d)   Improvement in the proficiency of locating hidden targets is a case of perceptual learning. The task is one of detection, a perceptual task whose proficiency is increased with practice.

6.   (a)   The conditions antecedent to perception are stimulus conditions. More generally, any change in stimulus energy can be an antecedent to the process of perception.

7.   (c)   Being able to distinguish two cola beverages is the process of discrimination. If you were able to *name* the colas, it would then be the process of identification.

8.   (d)   Correctly labeling a stimulus by its name is called identification.

9.   (c)   A schema is most like a concept. It is a generalized abstraction which is achieved as a result of experiencing a variety of stimuli.

10.   (a)   Verbal labels help most when the stimuli are initially difficult to encode. If the stimuli are already easy to encode, verbal labels may then still help, but their effect is more limited.

11.   (c)   Attaching identical (common) labels to similar stimuli reduces the distinctiveness of the stimuli, a process called acquired equivalence of cues. The process may result from common attentional responses being made to the stimuli, or possibly from the addition of common response-produced cues.

12.   (d)   Gibson's theory of perceptual learning does *not* emphasize the learning of responses per se. There is an increase in the specificity of responding to stimuli, but this is not response learning as such.

13.   (b)   Perceptual learning places emphasis on the stimulus features of learning tasks. How stimuli and stimulus structure affect learning is of paramount interest.

True-False Answers: Attention and Perceptual Learning

1.   (False)   The all-or-none theory has great difficulty handling any finding which shows that we process secondary messages. The

memory-contact theory does the best job of handling our current findings.

2. (False)   On the contrary, the secondary message can bias the subjects' interpretation of the primary message.

3. (True)   This is simply to say that the process of perceptual learning occurs.

4. (False)   The interaction between perception and learning is a two-way affair. Not only is perception modifiable by learning, but learning is also influenced by perceptual and attentional processes.

5. (True)   Neither are directly observed but are inferred from some relationship between performance changes and antecedent conditions. Thus both are relational concepts in that they are defined by the relationship between two classes of events.

6. (True)   Perception is dependent upon changes in light or sound intensity, contour information in patterns, contrast, and color, all of which are instances of changes in stimulus energy.

7. (False)   Barely hearing a tone is detection, but being able to tell the difference between two tones is an instance of discrimination.

8. (True)   Recognizing a stimulus only means that it is familiar; identifying the stimulus means that you can give its appropriate name or label.

9. (True)   Here you are learning something about efficient search habits, in effect, how to scan in a proficient fashion.

10. (False)   We cannot be sure that our perceptions have actually changed; all that may have occurred is a change in response bias.

11. (True)   This process does occur, but principally when the verbal labels are representative of the stimuli and when the stimuli are somewhat difficult to encode.

12. (True)   The basic difference is that a schema is usually not tied to a single feature or dimension but to a bundle or complex set of dimensions, some of which may not be easily specified. In contrast, a concept may be tied to a defined specific dimension such as the concept of redness.

13. (False)   Learning to recognize a melody regardless of the context is an instance of detecting an invariant pattern of stimulation.

14. (True)   Perceptual learning places its main emphasis on properties of stimuli.

Motor Skills Learning

10

Skill learning has played a major role in human history. The development of even elementary forms of society has depended upon our possession of fundamental skills. For example, human beings had to acquire the necessary skills for constructing clothing and shelter. Similarly, human beings learned to construct tools for agriculture, crafts, and warfare. Skills also make possible the enjoyment of many activities. Playing musical instruments, engaging in sports, reading, driving, and dancing are all instances of complex skills from which you may derive pleasure.

With the development of modern technology in the twentieth century, skills that were formerly important have become less so, whereas new skills have become increasingly important. For instance, it is no longer necessary for most of us personally to construct shelter or make clothing. Many crafts formerly produced by individuals are now machine produced. The rapid development of new devices, coupled with the increased concern with leisure-time activities, has led to a shift in the kinds of skills regarded important. The development of stereo systems, dishwashers, airplanes, automobiles, motorcycles, to mention only a few, provides for a host of new skills to be acquired by the user. With more time for leisure, interest in skill activities such as skiing, boating, surfing, scuba diving, and billiards has seen enormous growth in recent years. Old standbys such as golf, tennis, swimming, and other athletic activities have also grown in significance for many people.

Another trend in the changes required of human performance is a shift from activities required while standing, or in motion, to more sedentary activities. Many industrial and clerical tasks can be done while the individual is seated. The type of task that has become increasingly important is one that requires a person to keep track of several sources of information and to make appropriate decisions about rapidly changing informational inputs.

Piloting an airplane exhibits these kinds of demands. The pilot must attend to the dials which provide information about speed, altitude, location, other aircraft, and weather. Additional information such as radio messages must be processed. The pilot must keep track of this information and make decisions based on this input. Finally, it is necessary to distinguish between effects produced by manipulation of the controls and effects due to the weather, such as turbulance.

Definition of Motor Skills Learning

"Motor skills learning" refers to any activity in which the learner must acquire a sequence of precise motor responses. Motor responses refer to bodily movements. Sometimes the term *perceptual motor skills* is used to designate the fact that this class of learning requires coordination of input stimuli (perceptual activity) with motor responses. Driving is an excellent example of a perceptual motor skill because you must coordinate what you "see" with what you "do." Driving requires that you adjust your responses in accordance with a continuously changing input. You must accelerate, slow down, turn, and apply the brakes with respect to an array of environmental stimuli such as bends in the road, intersections, stop signs and approaching vehicles.

The terms *motor skills* and *perceptual motor skills* are used interchangeably in this book. Besides flying and driving, most athletic skills require the coordination of motor behavior with stimulus input. Racquet sports such as tennis, squash, and badminton require that you adjust your motor responses to the speed and anticipated location of the ball. Thus, motor skills learning is frequently called perceptual motor learning, and motor skills learning refers to the acquisition of a precise sequence of motor responses.

Study of Motor Skills Learning

Psychologists have used a wide variety of tasks in investigating motor skills learning. Physical education researchers have studied the acquisition of skilled performance in a variety of athletic activities ranging from swimming to gymnastics to learning to kick a football. Despite the wide range of tasks employed, all tasks can be classified into basically two types: tasks that consist of specific *discrete* responses and tasks that are *continuous*.

Some motor tasks are composed of discrete responses which are responses separated by intervals of nonresponding. In contrast, other responses are more or less continuous in nature. Kicking a football is an instance of a discrete response; running with a football is essentially continuous (until you stop). Turning the ignition of your car is a discrete response; driving the car is a continuous response (again, until you stop). The distinction between the two is somewhat relative and arbitrary. Nevertheless, you can easily recognize that some responses are discrete, whereas others are essentially continuous.

Both kinds of responses have been studied. A widely used laboratory task is the line-drawing task in which the subject must, while blindfolded, learn to draw a line of some arbitrary length. At the end of each trial the subject is given feedback in the form of being told "right" or "wrong." Sometimes he is told about the size of his error. Line drawing is an instance of a discrete task.

In contrast, a popular continuous task is tracking. A standard laboratory tracking task is the rotary pursuit which consists of a phonograph turntable that turns at some given rate such as 40 or 60 rpm. Set in the disk is a target about the size of a dime, and the subject must try to contact this disk with a metal stylus while the disk rotates. Performance is usually scored in terms of total or percent time on target.

This description of motor tasks is sufficient for an understanding of the two major classes of motor tasks investigated. Let us now turn our attention to some of the principal characteristics of skilled performance.

Characteristics of Motor Skills

There are four fundamental elements of skilled performance. Skilled performance (1) involves a sequence of motor responses, (2) requires coordination of perceptual input with these motor responses, (3) involves an organized sequence of responses, and (4) depends heavily upon feedback. Let us briefly consider each of these features.

Response Sequences

First, any highly developed motor skill represents at one level a sequence of motor responses. A simple example is tying your shoe. Each response (for example, pulling the shoestrings tight) serves as a stimulus for the next response (for example, crossing the strings) and the sequence consists of a chain of responses. Another example is starting a car. Swimming, diving, running, and jumping all involve chains of motor responses that make up the skilled performance. But as the sequence becomes highly organized, it becomes more than just a chain; it becomes a highly structured sequence of patterns.

Perceptual Motor Coordination

We earlier noted that motor skills typically involve the *coordination* of perceptual input with motor responses. This coordination of perception of events with motor activity is readily evident in sports such as tennis, baseball, and basketball and need not be further elaborated.

Response Organization

A third feature of skilled performance is that the sequence of responses must be organized into response patterns. If we analyze the task of swimming, it can be broken up into a series of subtasks or subroutines. Each of these subtasks can receive particular emphasis by a coach by being taught as a task itself. Arm strokes, proper breathing, and leg kicks are each subtasks of response chains themselves. Ultimately, these subtasks become organized into an integrated pattern of swimming.

The organization or patterning of such skilled activity involves both temporal and spatial factors. The act of driving is a complex skill involving many subroutines. Consider just one, pressing the accelerator. You must learn where precisely to place your foot, when to do so, and the force appropriate for a desired speed. Beginners may fumble in initial efforts in locating the pedal. Moreover, they may press too hard, causing the car to accelerate in a rapid and/or jerking fashion. Ultimately, however, this action becomes smoothly integrated and coordinated with other aspects of driving such as braking and shifting gears.

Feedback

Finally, motor skills performance is heavily dependent upon *intrinsic feedback. "Intrinsic feedback" refers to the fact that responses produce stimuli which have consequences for subsequent responses.* When you talk, you hear yourself talking; when you walk, you feel the movement of your legs; when you putt in golf, you see the consequences of your putt. The stimuli produced by responses are fed back into the organism in the sense of providing him information about what he is doing.

The only responses that appear to be free from the effects of feedback are those which are so brief in duration that there is insufficient time for the feedback to be processed. For all practical purposes, feedback is extremely important when a response is a few seconds or longer.

The effects of intrinsic feedback can be dramatically illustrated with the playback of delayed speech. A person speaks directly into a microphone and what she says is recorded on tape. Her voice is replayed only after a fraction of a second delay into earphones which effectively mask direct airborne sounds. She is then instructed to continue reading some material out loud while the playback of her voice continues. Under this circumstance her performance rapidly deteriorates; she stutters, reads in bursts, talks louder or faster, and finally grinds to a halt. Although you may be unaware of the importance of feedback when you talk, the powerful effects of a short delay in feedback attests to its significance.

Another illustration of the importance of intrinsic feedback from the muscles is seen in patients with neurological diseases in which certain sensory nerve tracts in the spinal cord have been destroyed. These patients have great difficulty in walking, even though their leg muscles are not damaged, because of the loss of sensory feedback from walking. Only when they look directly at their feet and gain a compensatory source of feedback are they able to walk. Thus, intrinsic feedback is a basic feature of motor skills learning.

Phases of Motor Skill Learning

Although skill learning by humans is largely a continuous process, psychologists distinguish three principal *phases* of motor skill learning. The distinctions among them are not sharp and rigid because one phase gradually merges into another as learning progresses. The particular classification system described here was developed by the late Paul Fitts, a distinguished contributor to our understanding of skilled performance. The three phases are (1) early or *cognitive* phase, (2) fixation or *associative* phase, and (3) final or *autonomous* phase.

Cognitive Phase

During the early or cognitive stage, the learner attempts to understand what it is that is required of him. He attempts to understand the task, to verbalize about the task, and to intellectualize the skill in the sense of conceptualizing its components. In turn, a good teacher or coach attempts during this phase to describe to the student the elements or components of the task, instructing the student in what cues are important and how responses should be executed. The coach avoids, however, burdening the student with excessive detail until the student is capable of processing the information.

For example, the early phase of foreign language learning is characterized by these features. In instructing proper pronunciation of vowels, consonants, dipthongs, and words, the language teacher first instructs students on how to make particular sounds. This is done, for example, by telling students where to place the tongue, and by illustrating whether the sound is nasal or guttural. Similarly, a father teaching his son how to catch the ball with a glove begins by showing him how to hold the glove, instructing him to keep his arm partly outstretched, to use both hands, and to keep his eye on the ball.

In learning to dance, the instructor first outlines the basic steps, one at a time, and then demonstrates the entire sequence. The learner's task is first that of execution of the basic responses. You may verbalize these responses by saying, for example, "left foot forward" and then "cross over with the right foot." Thus, during this early stage of skill learning, principal effort is devoted toward instructing the learner in the basic components of the task, first by describing the components, and then by requiring the learner to practice each response segment. The first stage is very similar to the *response* learning stage of verbal learning in which discrete responses are made available.

Associative Phase

During the second stage of skills learning, the particular responses learned become associated with particular cues, and the responses become integrated as a highly efficient chain. This stage bears considerable similarity to the associative stage of verbal learning, hence the designation *associative* phase.

The associative phase of motor skills learning can be illustrated by examining the task of typing. In this stage you must learn to touch a particular key in response to a particular letter without looking at the keyboard. Each keyboard response made to a particular letter sound produced by an instructor, or a particular letter in a typing manual is in fact a stimulus-response association that must be learned. The task is one of learning to make a particular response in the presence of a particular stimulus, which is characteristic of associative learning also.

During this stage you also learn to execute a smooth sequence of responses and to respond at a fairly stable rate. Instead of looking at each single letter in your typing manual, the entire word becomes the cue for responding. Indeed, typing instructors tell their students to think the entire word rather than to look at each letter as typing proficiency increases. The associative stage in typing ranges from first learning to associate each keyboard position with a letter stimulus to typing at a steady rate with errors at a minimum.

In contrast to the associative phase, the first or cognitive stage of learning to type occupies a relatively short time span. During this stage, the learner becomes generally familiar with the requirements of typing, analyzes the skills involved, and verbalizes about what will be learned. While the cognitive phase is relatively brief in a task like typing, it occupies an increasingly important role as the task becomes more complex. For example, in learning to drive an automobile or to pilot an aircraft, the cognitive phase is much more time-consuming.

Autonomous Phase

The final phase in motor skills learning is the autonomous phase, where performance becomes highly efficient so that it can be executed in more or less automatic fashion. The speed of performance continues to increase because new response patterns become strengthened, not because of simple repetition of the same responses. For example, the fact that a number of girls can now swim faster than Johnny Weissmuller did when he held national records in the 1920s attests to their development of response patterns different from the ones he used. Moreover, there appears to be no evidence for a permanent leveling off in performance as is found, say, in verbal learning. Motor skills learning appears unique in this respect. Despite continued practice on a specific skill for many years, performance records indicate that speed or efficiency continues to increase even though at a much slower rate. You are witness to this lack of a final plateau in motor skills when you note that athletic records are continually broken. Similarly, industrial production records show that various tasks with a heavy motor skills component continue to show improvement in performance. These improvements in performance are due, however, to new ways of carrying out the tasks, that is, to the development of newer, more efficient response patterns.

During this final stage, performance becomes increasingly immune to sources of interference. A typist continues to type while carrying on a brief conversation; we continue to talk while driving a car; we manipulate the dial on the car radio while driving and watching the road. Thus, we are able to carry out two or more tasks proficiently without serious disruption of the principal task.

Factors Which Affect Motor Skills Learning

Like other types of learning, motor skills learning depends upon both characteristics of the task and characteristics of the learner. In this section we shall examine some of the important factors influencing motor skills learning.

Feedback

Feedback is the single most important factor affecting motor skills learning. *Extrinsic feedback* refers to the information that is provided the learner about his performance on a given trial. Extrinsic feedback is often referred to as *knowledge of results,* which emphasizes the informational character of feedback. A distinction is made between extrinsic and intrinsic feedback. We saw earlier that intrinsic feedback refers to the response-produced stimuli that result when we make a response, such as the feel of the swing of a tennis racquet and the visual feedback we get when putting in golf. More generally, *"intrinsic feedback" refers to the feedback we directly obtain from our own experiences and actions.* In contrast, *"extrinsic feedback" refers to the information that is provided by another person or by some device.* For instance, the score displayed on a pinball machine is a case of extrinsic feedback.

Extrinsic feedback may be in the form of qualitative information, in which learners are informed that their performance is either correct or incorrect. For example, imagine that your task is to draw a set of lines while you are blindfolded, and the line to be drawn is between, say, 3 and 3¼ inches long. At the end of each trial in drawing the line, you are informed only if your response is correct or incorrect. This is precisely analogous to looking at a discrete temperature gauge on most American cars. You know only if your car is "cold," "normal," or "hot," not how cold or how hot. Similarly, in playing golf, either the putt went in the hole or it didn't.

In contrast, feedback may be in the form of quantitative information. In the line-drawing task you may be told how *much* discrepancy there is between your response and the correct response. Similarly, in older models of American cars, the temperature gauge was graded (continuous) so that you could see if your car was, in fact, approaching some point of heating up. Usually, humans prefer continuous information because it enables them to make more precise judgments about what they should do.

Feedback has two properties. *First, feedback has information value to the organism, enabling him to direct his performance toward some desired objective. Second, feedback can have reinforcing properties in that it serves to reward performance.* Seeing that you made a strike when bowling not only provides you with information about your performance, but may also reinforce your skill in the sense of strengthening that class of responses produced just prior to the strike. Unfortunately, it is difficult to separate the informational and reinforcing aspects of feedback; thus, we are not always knowledgeable about their relative roles in affecting performance.

Importance of Feedback

With the information just given as background, we can focus on two kinds of questions: (1) Is feedback necessary for acquisition of skilled performance? (2) Does the type of feedback (discrete qualitative information versus continuous quantitative information) make a difference?

The evidence points overwhelmingly to the importance of feedback as a necessary variable in influencing performance. Where humans have been required to learn motor tasks without feedback, no appreciable evidence of improvement in the sense of achieving some criterion of learning imposed externally is found. Humans do, however, become less variable in their performance without external (extrinsic) feedback because they come to adhere more closely to some subjective criterion of performance which they adopt during learning. Thus, in one sense, response changes can occur without *external* feedback.

Intuitively, it is easy to see why feedback is so important for im-

provement. For example, imagine trying to learn to bowl without knowing the consequences of your actions. Conceive of a situation in which
you cannot see what you have hit (if anything), receive no score from
an outside observer, hear no noise which might allow some judgment
about your performance, and are prevented from even seeing the direction of the bowling ball once you have released it! If you manage to
show any improvement in the absence of feedback, such improvement is
likely to be the result of adopting a subjective criterion which corresponds inadvertently with the center of the lane.

With respect to our second question, humans achieve superior performance in motor learning tasks when they are given quantitative information about their performance. Quantitative knowledge about the
discrepancy between your performance and some task objective allows
you to reduce this discrepancy more effectively than if you are merely
told that you are right or wrong.

The effectiveness of quantitative over qualitative feedback can be
readily illustrated in several ways. Consider learning to play pool: In
one case imagine being informed only if your shots were good in the
sense of making a pocket or bad in the opposite sense. In this hypothetical situation you are prevented from seeing your shots and know
only what you are told. In a second hypothetical situation, imagine
being told precisely how far each miss is from a pocket. Here, of course,
you are given more information about your performance. In this latter
situation, your skill at playing pool would develop much more rapidly.

Withdrawal of Feedback and Subjective Reinforcement

Suppose that feedback is immediately withdrawn after it has been given
for a number of trials. How would this affect your performance? What
is observed is a gradual drop in performance, but not to the performance
level observed at the beginning of training. More generally, the effect
of withdrawal of feedback depends upon the level of ongoing performance. *If a level of training is low or moderate, withdrawal of feedback
produces a deteriorating effect on performance. After extended training,
however, little or no performance decrement occurs.* Thus, withdrawal
of feedback in humans does *not* act precisely as does withdrawal of reinforcement in instrumental learning of lower animals. This points to the
inadequacy of simply equating feedback with reinforcement since their
effects are not entirely comparable.

The fact that humans can maintain some of their training benefits
after withdrawal of feedback has suggested to some psychologists that
self-reinforcement may play an important role. The basic idea is that
after some period of practice in which you receive external feedback,
you begin to internalize the standards for a correct response and thus are
able to inform yourself about the adequacy of a response based on your

own standards. This notion of subjective or self-reinforcement should be thought of as a form of internal feedback that is developed over a series of trials with external feedback. It is as if you can learn to discriminate proprioceptive (internal) cues that aid you in defining the correctness of a response.

Many motor tasks are such that you can gradually acquire a feel for a good response and thus can distinguish a good response from a poor one. For instance, divers generally detect when they have executed a poor dive by the way they feel or sense body movements before they strike the water. Similarly, experienced golfers and tennis players can frequently judge the quality of their swing or stroke by how it feels to them. What they are learning is to judge the pattern and intensity of proprioceptive cues so that they gradually acquire subjective standards as to what feels appropriate.

Delay of Feedback

Another feature of feedback concerns the effect of the time delay between the learner's response and informative feedback. This interval is called the *delay of feedback*. Just as in investigations of conceptual learning, delay of feedback exerts virtually no effect on some types of motor skills acquisition. This finding differs, as noted earlier, from results with lower animals, where delay of reward produces a substantial effect on performance. This generalization is based on studies using relatively short delays and is the case with discrete motor tasks such as ball tossing and line drawing. In contrast, delay of feedback does seriously degrade performance in tasks such as continuous tracking. An example of this can be seen in the continuous task of driving. Suppose you were not allowed to see the consequences of your steering wheel movement for 5 to 10 seconds after it occurred. Under such conditions driving error would be very large. Since many motor tasks are continuous, it is best to keep delay of feedback to a minimum as a practical rule.

In contrast, another type of delay known as *postfeedback* delay does exert an effect on performance. Postfeedback delay is the interval between feedback on one trial and the beginning of the next trial. *In general, increasing the postfeedback interval up to some point brings corresponding improvement in performance*. Again, just as in conceptual learning, the critical interval is the postfeedback delay, because this appears to be the period in which one processes the information obtained on a particular trial. In effect, as this interval is lengthened you are given more time to think about how to execute the next response.

Distribution of Practice

When any motor skill is learned, the training conditions can be arranged so that rest intervals are interspersed between trials. In contrast, some

distributed, intro. of rest intervals thru-out
practice, course of acq.

tasks can be arranged such that they are continuous, lacking rest intervals during the course of acquisition. *Distributed practice* refers to the introduction of rest intervals throughout the course of acquisition, whereas the term *massed practice* refers to more or less continuous performance.

Distributed practice is an important factor in motor learning, and the general rule is that *distributed practice facilitates the acquisition of motor skills*. Most attempts to account for the facilitating effects of distributed practice have assumed the buildup of some fatiguelike or inhibitory process during massed practice. Such theories assume an *inhibition* process that accumulates during acquisition that reduces the tendency to respond. Presumably, during rest intervals this inhibition can weaken or decay, whereas during massed practice opportunity for such inhibition to decay does not occur. Therefore, the increase in inhibition during massed practice produces less rapid learning than occurs during distributed practice. Space limitations allow only a brief discussion of this inhibitory process. (A quite detailed discussion of this process, described in the context of a theory of classical conditioning, is provided in Frank Logan's *Fundamentals of Learning and Motivation,* a companion volume in this series.)

Stress and Fatigue

As you might expect, both stress and fatigue produce decrements in motor skills performance. Stress has been characteristically defined in at least two ways. In one definition, stress refers to a state of the organism usually characterized as motivational and/or emotional. Thus we sometimes speak of emotional stress of an individual when burdened or faced with unpleasant circumstances.

In the second definition, stress refers to the task demands made upon an individual. Thus, if you have to keep track of three events while carrying out some task, you are faced with a greater stress load than if you must keep track of only one event. This second meaning is sometimes called *information overload,* referring to how much information you must attend to while carrying out a task. For instance, consider driving an automobile alone along a quiet country road as compared with driving on an unfamiliar freeway in a large metropolis at the five o'clock rush hour with a car full of unruly children, one of whom is demanding to go to the bathroom. Clearly, the amount of information impinging upon you is considerably greater in the second situation.

With either meaning of stress, the relationship of stress and motor performance is similar to that observed in verbal learning and problem solving. *As the amount of stress increases, motor skills performance improves up to some optimal point beyond which increases in stress pro-*

duce a reduction in performance. Thus, the relationship between stress and performance is U-shaped, indicating some optimal level of stress.

Perhaps the notion of optimal stress may sound strange, but a moment's reflection will make this principle clear. A little stress alerts you to the demands of a given task and, indeed, facilitates performance. Most of you have experienced the fact that listening to music may help in carrying out a routine repetitive task such as washing dishes. On the other hand, as the task becomes more complex, less stress is desirable for optimal performance. For example, less stress in the form of overload is desirable when landing an airplane as compared, say, to tossing a page of rough draft into a wastebasket.

Theories of Motor Learning

Traditional theories of motor learning have viewed the process as essentially analogous to, or identical with, instrumental learning. This tradition stems from Thorndike, who viewed motor learning as instrumental in character, dependent upon the classical law of effect. A motor learning task, such as learning to draw a line of a particular length, was viewed as requiring the learner to make a series of discrete motor responses, each being followed by reinforcement in the form of knowledge of results or feedback. As a response approximated the correct or desired response, it achieved reinforcement and was thus strengthened by some amount. In turn, incorrect responses gradually weakened in the course of training because they were not reinforced.

Psychologists have not developed powerful theories of motor learning. As just emphasized, theoretical considerations have treated motor learning as a special case of instrumental learning governed by the principle of reinforcement. Only in the past few years has any serious effort been made to extend theories of motor learning. Most of these recent developments have tended to view motor learning as more than just instrumental learning, emphasizing the *problem-solving* and *cognitive* character of motor learning tasks. One of the better developed of these theories is proposed by Jack Adams.

Adams assumes that motor learning is best viewed as a problem to be solved and proposes a theory which contains elements of both S-R and cognitive conceptions of learning. The essential feature of this theory is that it is a *closed-loop theory,* which is a notion borrowed from engineering and servomechanism concepts. Before the theory is described, a few comments on closed-loop systems are in order.

The basic idea of any closed-loop system is that responses of a given system feed back into the system, thus making it ultimately self-regulating. A simple example of a closed-loop system involves the thermostat and heating unit found in many homes and buildings. The thermostat is set to some desired temperature. If the actual temperature is below the setting, this discrepancy is detected and the information is given to the heating unit which, in turn, is activated. The room or building is thus heated to the value set by the thermostat. The essential point to note is that a closed-loop system allows for the detection of a discrepancy, called *error,* and responds to this error in an adjusting or self-correcting fashion.

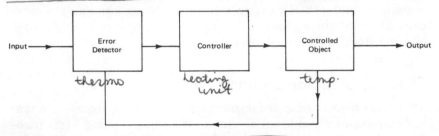

Figure 16. Block diagram of schematic closed-loop system.

Figure 16 portrays the basic components of a closed-loop feedback system. It contains, first, an *error detector* whose task is to detect the discrepancy between some current state of the system and feedback from the final component of the system. The thermostat in the preceding discussion is an example of an error detector. The discrepancy or error information goes to the next component, the *controller,* which is some regulating device in the system. The heating unit in the example is an instance of a controller. Finally, there is a *controlled object,* something to be acted upon, which in this case is the temperature of the room.

The input to the error detector refers simply to some setting of the thermostat, continuing the analogy. The feedback loop goes back to the error detector from the controlled object, informing it of the discrepancy between the output of the controlled object and the setting of the error detector. Thus you can see that a closed loop feedback system is dynamic in the sense of responding to error discrepancy and is self-regulating.

The theory outlined by Adams views motor learning as a problem to be solved in which the learner first tries a movement, is then given feedback, tries again on the next trial, and so on, using the information obtained from feedback to gradually acquire the desired response. According to the theory, the learner gradually acquires a *perceptual trace* of the motor movements he makes, where the trace is conceived much like an image. On each trial the learner receives proprioceptive (internal) cues from muscle movements and attempts to match these cues to the perceptual trace. Here the perceptual trace is viewed as some reference standard which must be acquired itself as a result of gradual experience in detecting feedback. In short, when a response is judged correct, the learner develops a standard for what proprioceptive cues feel correct. His memory of these cues, as distinct from those which are associated with incorrect responses, becomes his reference standard. This standard, of course, is not static and changes as it gradually approximates what is necessary for desired behavior.

In addition, the theory proposes a second mechanism, the memory trace. The memory trace is an additional memory system whose function is to select and initiate a response on a given trial before the perceptual trace is used. The reasons for using both a perceptual and memory trace are too complex to treat here. The principal point to note is that the learner initiates a given response after some amount of practice on the basis of his memory trace and then uses the perceptual trace for momentary judgment of how far to move.

At present the theory is somewhat informal, with details yet to be developed. Its principal feature is its emphasis on closed-loop assumptions. The more formal relationships between perceptual and memory traces have yet to be fully developed. Its virtue lies in its emphasis upon the importance of feedback and the dynamic, self-regulating character of motor learning. It should be noted that these features are being increasingly incorporated in other theories of learning and are certainly not unique to theories of motor learning.

Some Practical Principles

In this section we shall turn our attention to a brief discussion of some principles that are important in the acquisition of motor skills. Most of these principles are applicable to other categories of learning and have received some emphasis in previous chapters.

Understand the Task

At the onset of skills learning your initial objective is to understand what is required. It is good practice to observe the performance of skilled individuals, particularly teachers who can break the skill into its component parts. For instance, competent dancing instructors can show the individual components of a dance sequence as well as the highly integrated series of responses. Here your task is to verbalize about the skill, trying to identify its component parts.

Practice on Specific Components

As the task increases in complexity, you should focus your practice on specific components of the task. For example, swimmers may concentrate on one feature such as leg kicks, arm strokes, or breathing during a given training session and later concentrate on coordinating these features. Similarly, in playing pool, you may concentrate on bank shots to the temporary exclusion of other kinds of responses. Finally, in learning to drive a car with a manual transmission, you may focus your efforts on learning to shift gears as a component task before integrating this activity into the total pattern of driving. In general, where motor tasks are simple, they may be directly practiced in their entirety; however, with increasing complexity, motor tasks may more profitably be learned by practicing their component parts.

Obtain Feedback

Feedback is the most important factor in achieving skilled performance. Feedback may be both intrinsic and extrinsic. The importance of feedback is that it allows you to evaluate your performance by comparing it against some standard.

Practice Under Varied Conditions

Stimulus variation was earlier noted as an important factor in memory. Likewise, practice under varied circumstances facilitates motor performance. Athletic coaches have long observed that basketball players often show some performance decrement when playing in a new or different gymnasium. Changes in the size of the gymnasium or other features may temporarily influence well-practiced habits. Similarly, swimmers who are familiar with one pool may show some performance deterioration when first swimming in a new pool that is, say, longer. For this reason, varied context in training helps adapt your performance to potential environmental changes.

Sustain Practice

Proficiency in skills obviously requires sustained practice. The emphasis is not repetition per se since one can learn inappropriate responses as well as desirable ones. It is practice in conjunction with understanding the skill objectives, observing skilled performance, and obtaining feedback that is important.

[handwritten margin notes:
3 phase
1) cognitive
2) associative
3) autonomous (final)

4 features — Skilled performance
1) chain of motor responses
2) perceptual motor coordination
3) response organization
4) dependency upon feedback]

Summary

This chapter has outlined some of the major characteristics of motor skills learning. Despite the automation of many human activities, skill learning was seen as an increasingly important feature of leisure-time and recreational activities.

Motor skills learning refers to any activity which requires the learner to make a series of precise motor responses. Motor skills tasks may consist of either discrete or continuous responses. Although typical laboratory tasks have emphasized line drawing and pursuit rotor tracking, a quite wide variety of tasks have been employed in the study of motor learning.

Skilled performance consists of four essential features: (1) a chain of motor responses, (2) perceptual motor coordination, (3) response organization, and (4) dependency upon feedback. Three phases of skill learning were described: (1) cognitive phase, (2) associative phase, and (3) autonomous or final stage. These stages were observed to blend into each other rather than to be rigidly distinctive.

The most important factor influencing motor skills learning is feedback, sometimes called knowledge of results. Feedback may be either qualitative or quantitative, extrinsic or intrinsic, and may have both informational and reinforcing properties. Feedback appears to be essential for motor skills learning, and quantitative feedback is more effective than qualitative feedback.

The withdrawal of feedback produces its most detrimental effect only with low or moderate levels of training. With extensive training, feedback withdrawal produces virtually no effect primarily because humans come to depend upon their own subjective reinforcement. The postfeedback interval is the critical period for efficient motor skills learning because humans are able to process feedback information during this period.

Other important variables are distribution of practice, stress, and fatigue. An important feature of current theories of motor skills is the adoption of a closed-loop model by which humans are viewed as comparing feedback cues of the moment with some memory of past performance.

Several practical principles for efficient motor skills learning were described. These emphasized the importance of (1) understanding the task, (2) practicing on specific components, (3) obtaining feedback, (4) practicing under varied conditions, and finally (5) practice itself.

Multiple-Choice Items: Motor Skills Learning

1. Four main characteristics of motor skill learning were identified. Which is *not* one of the features?

  a. feedback
  b. response sequences
  c. perceptual motor coordination
  (d.) associations

2. Kicking a football and being praised for your skill provides you with _____ feedback for a _____ response.
  (a.) extrinsic, discrete
  b. extrinsic, continuous
  c. intrinsic, discrete
  d. intrinsic, continuous

3. Attempts to verbalize or describe a particular motor skill is characteristic of which stage or phase?
  a. associative
  b. autonomous
  c. continuous
  (d.) cognitive

4. Being able to carry out two or more tasks simultaneously at a high level of proficiency is characteristic of the _____ stage of motor skills learning.
  a. continuous
  b. cognitive
  (c.) autonomous
  d. associative

5. The most important factor affecting motor skills learning is
  (a.) feedback
  b. stress
  c. distribution of practice
  d. association

6. The two properties of feedback described were
  a. information value and punishment
  b. stress and reinforcement
  c. information value and stress
  (d.) information value and reinforcement

7. Delay of feedback does degrade or limit performance when the motor task is
  a. discrete
  (b.) continuous
  c. cognitive
  d. associative

8. A closed-loop system is called such because
  a. there is feedback directly from the error detector
  (b.) there is feedback to the error detector
  c. the controller receives input from the controlled object
  d. the system ignores attentional processes

9. Practice of skills in varied contexts was seen as desirable because it

(a.) helps you adapt to potential changes in the environment
b. provides you with immediate feedback
c. reduces stress in the form of information overload
d. is similar to massed practice
10. Which task is most desirable to practice by breaking up the task into subcomponents?
a. coloring drawings in a book
b. pouring a glass of milk
c. pulling a wagon
d. riding a bicycle

True-False Items: Motor Skills Learning

T 1. Discrete motor responses are responses separated by periods of nonresponding.
T 2. A response chain refers to a sequence of responses in which one response serves as a stimulus for another response.
F 3. The way a motor response is practiced is less important than sheer frequency of practice.
F 4. The information a swimming coach provides swimmers about their performance is an instance of intrinsic feedback.
F 5. The first stage of motor skills learning is the cognitive phase.
F 6. In a swimming race, seeing that you are ahead of all the other swimmers provides you with a source of extrinsic feedback.
F 7. Feedback has information value, but does not have reinforcing properties.
T 8. Being given quantitative feedback is more advantageous for motor skills learning than simply being told that you are right or wrong.
F 9. Motor skills learning differs from concept learning in that increasing the postfeedback delay interval does facilitate concept learning, but does not influence motor skills learning.
T 10. Listening to the radio is more likely to disrupt performance when you are planning and writing a term paper than when you are reading a magazine.
T 11. Closed-loop theory of motor skills learning emphasizes the manner in which learners use feedback from their movements.
T 12. If the motor task is fairly complex, it may be desirable to practice components of the task at first and then the entire task.

Discussion Items: Motor Skills Learning

1. Select a specific motor skill with which you are familiar such as typing, driving, or swimming and describe the cognitive, associative, and autonomous phases of learning the skill.
2. Why is feedback seen as so important in motor skills learning?

3.   How does the effect of feedback depend upon the type of motor task learned?

4.   How does stress in the form of information overload affect motor skills learning?

5.   Describe the basic features of a closed-loop system. How have these features been incorporated in one theory of motor learning?

Multiple-Choice Answers: Motor Skills Learning

1.   (d)   Associations are *not* one of the four main characteristics of motor skills learning. There is, of course, an associative *stage* of motor learning, but it is a different matter.

2.   (a)   Being praised is a case of extrinsic feedback and kicking a football is a discrete response.

3.   (d)   Verbalizing or describing the features of a particular motor skill is characteristic of the cognitive phase. Here, you are trying to understand the essential features of the skill.

4.   (c)   Carrying out two or more tasks simultaneously is characteristic of the autonomous stage of motor skills learning. Here performance becomes highly proficient, and skilled sequences can be carried out in a more or less automatic fashion.

5.   (a)   Feedback is the single most important factor in motor skills learning.

6.   (d)   The two important features of feedback are that it has information value and provides reinforcement. The information is called knowledge of results and the reinforcing properties can serve to reward performance.

7.   (b)   Delay of feedback can degrade performance of a continuous task because such tasks are dependent on moment-to-moment feedback.

8.   (b)   A closed-loop system has a feedback loop from the controlled object to the error detector. The feedback loop to the error detector informs the system of any discrepancy between the output of the controlled object and the setting of the error detector.

9.   (a)   Practice in varied context is desirable because it helps you adapt to varied situations. For example, playing on different golf courses and playing on different tennis courts can prepare you for facing new courses or courts better than playing on the same course or court repeatedly.

10.   (d)   Riding a bicycle is the most desirable of the tasks to break up into components because it is the most complex of the tasks listed. Such components might be sitting on the seat, pedaling, and steering as with a tricycle and, finally, riding the bicycle itself.

True-False Answers: Motor Skills Learning

1. (True)   Discrete responses are produced for some period followed by a period in which the response does not occur. For example, diving into a pool is a discrete response, whereas swimming 200 meters is a continuous response (until you stop); jumping the broad jump is a discrete response, whereas running a mile is continuous (again, until you stop).

2. (True)   A chain of responses consists of a sequence in which each response serves as a stimulus for another response.

3. (False)   You can practice a response frequently and yet practice incorrectly. Learning the proper response pattern is an important feature of motor skills learning.

4. (False)   This is an instance of extrinsic feedback. Intrinsic feedback refers to the swimmers' own internal response-produced cues which provide them with information.

5. (True)   It is in this stage that the learner attempts to understand the task.

6. (True)   Knowledge that you are in the lead provides you with extrinsic feedback in the sense of enabling you to compare your momentary performance with that of the other swimmers.

7. (False)   Feedback may also have reinforcing properties in that it can serve to strengthen a particular response or class of responses.

8. (True)   Quantitative feedback is generally superior to qualitative feedback because it provides you with more information about your performance.

9. (False)   Increasing the postfeedback delay interval facilitates both concept and motor skills learning.

10. (True)   As the task becomes more complex, stress in the form of additional input is more likely to be disruptive. In this case planning and writing a term paper is more complex behavior than reading a magazine.

11. (True)   Closed-loop theory contends that the learner receives proprioceptive cues from muscle movements which he attempts to match with a perceptual trace or reference standard.

12. (True)   Where the task is complex, practice on specific components at first is desirable. These components can then be integrated into the entire skill after each component has been reasonably well learned.

Transfer of Training

11

American visitors to England may experience some confusion in driving on the left side of the road because of their established habit of driving on the right. What happens is the tendency, especially under conditions of stress, to revert momentarily to driving on the right side of the road even though the rules of driving in England are clearly understood. Momentary confusion in which the driver vacillates between driving on the right or left has also been reported. In this illustration we see that previously learned habits can affect our performance in new situations, which is an instance of transfer of training. Similarly, a common experience of many individuals just learning to drive a car with an automatic transmission, *after* having driven only cars with a standard transmission, is to attempt to depress a nonexistent clutch pedal. Alternatively, if a person first experiences driving a car with an automatic transmission and then shifts to a car with a standard transmission, he may on occasion fail to use the clutch pedal when shifting gears. Here again, we see that earlier learned habits and skills can affect the way we perform in new situations.

Instances of transfer occur in more formal learning situations as well as in everyday experiences. For example, having thoroughly mastered the principles of algebra we find it easier to grasp concepts in advanced mathematics. Similarly, having mastered one foreign language such as Spanish, we find it somewhat easier to master a second and related language such as French. Proficiency in one athletic skill can affect performance in other athletic skills. For example, the experienced tennis player usually reports that playing squash hurts his tennis game. This can occur because tennis requires the player to maintain a stiff wrist, whereas squash requires flexible wrist movements. This example emphasizes that the concept of transfer applies regardless of whether prior learning aids or hinders new learning. Another instance of transfer is seen when skill in playing one musical instrument helps in learning to play a new instrument. The influence of transfer is pervasive throughout your life and is found not only in intellectual activities and athletic skills, but also in emotional reactions and attitudes of individuals.

246

A good deal of teaching is based upon the assumption that what is taught in the classroom will transfer to new learning situations. Students may be taught basic physics with the assumption that portions of what is taught, such as elements of the scientific method, will transfer to the solution of problems in biology, perhaps to the social sciences, and to advanced topics in physics itself. Similarly, students may be taught psychology with the similar assumption that at least certain features of the subject matter, such as scientific method and the development of some systematic way of viewing behavior, will transfer to more complex studies. Sometimes, of course, less than the desired transfer occurs. For example, students of mathematics may fail to recognize relationships among equations that are critical for their understanding of the topic. Likewise, similarities among languages may remain undetected, resulting in less than maximal transfer in foreign language learning.

Despite instances in which transfer is minimal, the assumption of transfer underlies much of what is taught in the classroom. Obviously, there must be some transfer or every new learning situation would involve starting from scratch. Since we frequently do not start from scratch in each new learning situation, but rather benefit (or suffer) considerably from much of our prior experience, our interest is focused on the factors that affect such transfer. Therefore, the issue is not *if* transfer occurs, but rather the *conditions* under which transfer occurs.

The phenomenon of transfer is extremely important. From a very early period in life much new learning is affected in some way by previous learning. For example, the responses that young children make when entering a new school may be influenced by previous experiences in school. Similarly, the attitudes of college students toward a particular course may be determined in a large part by their previous experience with similar courses and with the kinds of expectations they have about the course. Indeed, it is difficult to think of any adult learning that is not at least in some minimal way influenced by earlier learning.

Concept of Transfer

"Transfer of training" refers to the influence of prior learning on performance in some new situation. Transfer effects may be positive or negative, or there may be no observed effect, which defines zero transfer.

Positive transfer occurs in situations in which prior learning aids or *facilitates* subsequent performance. An instance of positive transfer is seen when mastery of Spanish facilitates your learning of French. What is meant is that you are able to master French faster or more skillfully as a result of having learned Spanish. *We frequently see instances of positive transfer where the learner first masters an easier task and then moves on to a more difficult task.* For instance, young children exhibit positive transfer when having first learned to ride a bicycle with training wheels; they then readily learn to ride skillfully when the training wheels are removed. Similarly, young children become skillful in discriminating among difficult letters, such as *d* and *b,* by seeing distinguishing features of the letters exaggerated, perhaps color coded, or made more discriminable in some fashion during his early training.

Negative transfer, in contrast, refers to situations in which prior learning *interferes* with new learning. An instance of negative transfer is seen when playing squash interferes with performance in playing tennis because of the different kinds of wrist activity required. *A general principle is that negative transfer results when you have to make a new response to an old stimulus situation, especially if the responses are incompatible or antagonistic to each other.*

Zero transfer, a third outcome, is one in which there is no effect of prior learning on new learning. Zero transfer can occur either as a result of prior learning having no effect on subsequent performance or as a result of combined effects of positive and negative transfer which cancel. The latter situation emphasizes that sources of *both* positive and negative transfer operate in many learning situations and that what is observed is some *net* effect.

Study of Transfer

Although transfer has been described in a general way, the concept of transfer is more fully understood by looking at the way in which it is studied. Consider the question, Is there transfer from having a mastery of French to becoming skillful in Spanish? Offhand you might suspect that there would be some positive transfer from French to Spanish based on the similarities between the languages. Suppose, however, that you want to know if such transfer occurs. The procedure for answering this question is quite straightforward and is outlined here.

Design of Transfer Experiments

One group of subjects, an *experimental* group, is first given extensive training in French until they reach some level of proficiency; they then are given the second task of learning Spanish. A second group, identified as *control* subjects, receives no training in French but learns Spanish. The two groups are then compared on their performance in learning Spanish. Some measure of achievement is obtained such as, for example, how long it takes to learn Spanish to some arbitrary level of proficiency. If those subjects who studied French learn Spanish at a faster rate than the control subjects we then conclude that there is positive transfer from

French to Spanish. On the other hand, should those subjects who studied French actually learn Spanish slower than the control subjects, this would then be evidence for negative transfer. Should this latter outcome occur, we would conclude that in some way the study of French interfered with the subsequent learning of Spanish (or at least interfered *more* than it aided).

The study of transfer can be schematized as shown here. The experimental group learns an initial task, Task A, and then learns a second task, Task B. The control group learns only Task B, without experiencing the initial task.

	Initial Task	*Transfer Task*
Experimental Group	Learn Task A (French)	Learn Task B (Spanish)
Control Group		Learn Task B (Spanish)

As just noted, we compare the experimental and control groups in their performance on Task B. If performance of the experimental group is superior to that of the control group, in the sense of fewer errors, more correct responses, faster rate of learning, and so forth, this defines positive transfer from A to B. If on the other hand the experimental group's performance is inferior to the control group, then this defines negative transfer. Finally, if the two groups are equivalent in Task B performance, we then define zero transfer.

This schematic illustrates the study of *gross* transfer. It tells us only whether there is transfer from A to B. It does not tell us anything about what processes are involved in such transfer, but only that a transfer effect does or does not occur. Similarly, in our example of transfer from French to Spanish, if the experimental group does perform better than the control, all we would know is that positive transfer was obtained. We would know that a gross transfer effect occurred, but we would be unable to specify what factors were responsible for transfer. For example, positive transfer from French to Spanish could be due to *specific* similarities between the languages. For instance, some words common to both languages have very similar spellings. On the other hand, there can be positive transfer as a result of *general* language skills acquired in studying French that transfer to Spanish. Study habits, modes of organizing the material, and so forth, may thus provide a source of positive transfer.

In many transfer studies, the interest of the psychologist is in distinguishing between *general* and *specific* sources of transfer. In the preceding example, if we wish to know if there are *specific* factors producing transfer from French to Spanish, as distinct from general factors, we would need another kind of control group. In this case, we would have control subjects learn some unrelated language such as Chinese or Navajo prior to learning Spanish. In this fashion, we have a control for the processes that are involved in learning how to learn a language in general, as distinct from transfer effects specific to the relationship between French and Spanish. Schematically, this new control group (Control Group 2) is shown below, in which the control subjects learn Task X prior to learning Task B. In general, Task X represents some task that is minimally related to Task B, but does provide for practice in learning how to learn tasks of the same class.

	Initial Task	*Transfer Task*
Experimental Group	Learn Task A (French)	Learn Task B (Spanish)
Control Group 2	Learn Task X (Chinese)	Learn Task B (Spanish)
Control Group 1		Learn Task B (Spanish)

The same comparisons are made as before, but now we have more information. Previously, we had only information about a gross transfer effect. Now, we can determine if transfer from A to B (or French to Spanish, as in our example) is *specific* to the similarities between tasks A and B. Returning to our example, only if the experimental group performs superior to this new type of control can we conclude that transfer from Franch to Spanish is *specific* to communalities and similarities between Spanish and French.

If, on the other hand, there is as much transfer from Chinese to Spanish as from French to Spanish, and both groups are superior to a control group that learns only Spanish (Control Group 1), then whatever is transferring from French to Spanish is *not* specific to the two tasks, but is some general kind of activity that occurs simply as a result of studying another foreign language.

Now that the concept of transfer and the procedures for studying transfer are clear, let us turn our attention to the study of paired associate transfer.

Basic Transfer Paradigms

The study of transfer in verbal learning typically employs the paired associate task. This is so because the paired associate task permits independent manipulation of stimulus and response factors in transfer. Subjects can be given an initial paired associate task, followed by a second paired associate task in which variations in stimuli alone, responses alone, or both are mainpulated by the experimenter. Variations in the relationships between the two tasks describe what are called *transfer paradigms*. *A paradigm is simply a schematic or shorthand way of describing the task relationships.*

In the A-B—C-D paradigm, as in all other paradigms, the subjects learn two successive paired associate lists. The first list is designated as A-B, where A represents the stimulus terms of the list and B represents the response terms. The second list is identified as C-D, where C refers to the stimulus terms and D the response terms. This designation means simply that there is no obvious similarity between the stimulus terms of the two lists (A and C) and no obvious similarity between the response terms of the two lists (B and D). Since both terms refer to verbal units, they are of course similar in this sense. What is meant by no similarity is that neither the stimulus terms of the two lists nor the response terms are formally similar or meaningfully similar.

The A-B—C-D transfer paradigm is illustrated here, using three pairs in each list:

Initial List	*Transfer List*
A-B	*C-D*
CAR-lip	CIGAR-ice
DOG-sea	APPLE-cow
BICYCLE-rug	PENCIL-sky

The important thing to observe is that the C-D list is essentially unrelated to the A-B list. No obvious or evident similarities exist between the two lists. The stimulus terms of the first list are unrelated to those of the second list. The same holds true for the response terms. Therefore, the A-B—C-D paradigm serves as a baseline measure for *general* transfer effects since specific similarities between the two tasks are removed or at least minimized. Any transfer from A-B to C-D is therefore due to general transfer effects against which specific factors can be assessed using other paradigms.

With an *A-B—A-D paradigm,* the task of the subject is to learn to associate new responses (D) to the same stimuli (A). The subject learns an initial list (A-B) of paired associates and then learns a second list (A-D) which contains the same stimuli, but new and dissimilar responses. The A-B—A-D paradigm produces negative transfer. *More generally, learning to make new responses to old stimuli is a basic condition for producing negative transfer.* There is at least one exception to this rule which we shall discuss later; this occurs when the stimuli are very difficult to discriminate. The A-B—A-D paradigm is illustrated here, again using three pairs in each list.

Initial List	Transfer List
A-B	A-D
CAR-lip	DOG-cow
DOG-bat	BICYCLE-sky
BICYCLE-rug	CAR-ice

With an *A-B—C-B paradigm,* the task of the subject is to learn to associate the same response terms (B responses) to new stimulus terms (C). Whereas the previous paradigm varied the responses and kept the stimuli constant, the A-B—C-B paradigm varies the stimuli and keeps the responses constant. Both positive and negative transfer are found with this paradigm. Whether positive or negative transfer occurs depends largely on the *meaningfulness* of the responses. In general, if the responses are low in meaningfulness positive transfer occurs, whereas if the responses are high in meaningfulness negative transfer occurs. Although this may strike you as strange, it is easily understood. With low-meaning responses, subjects have to spend considerable effort just learning the responses themselves before they can associate the responses with their appropriate stimuli. As a result, when subjects learn the transfer task, the response learning component of the task has been largely achieved, producing a positive-transfer effect. With high-meaning responses, the response learning component is unimportant since the responses are already familiar.

The A-B—C-B paradigm is illustrated here, again using three pairs in each list.

Initial List	Transfer List
A-B	C-B
CAR-lip	CIGAR-lip
DOG-sea	APPLE-sea
BICYCLE-rug	PENCIL-rug

Finally, with an *A-B—A-Br paradigm,* we can arrange the lists so that the subjects must re-pair the same responses with the same stimuli. In the second list, the subject is presented the same stimuli and responses; however, they are completely re-paired, thus requiring him to learn new associations. Hence the designation *Br,* where *r* indicates that the responses are re-paired. *This paradigm is notable because it produces massive negative transfer.*

The A-B—A-Br paradigm is illustrated here:

Initial List	Transfer List
A-B	A-Br
CAR-lip	CAR-boy
DOG-boy	DOG-rug
BICYCLE-rug	BICYCLE-lip

Although it is a bit difficult to think of any everyday situation in which this case might arise, you can easily imagine the negative transfer that might result if our traffic signals *were* reversed. Suppose that instead of stopping the car when the traffic light is red, we have to go when the light is red and stop in the presence of a green light. Confusion and accidents are quite predictable.

Comparison of Paradigms

How do the transfer paradigms compare with respect to their relative transfer effects? The relative ordering of the paradigms are shown in figure 17. In this figure, an *A-B* list is initially learned, followed by one of the four transfer lists. The transfer effects (second-list learning) are shown in the performance curves plotted. The figure shows that all paradigms produce some negative transfer compared to the *C-D* control condition, with the *A-Br* producing the greatest negative transfer and the *C-B* paradigm producing the least. The *absolute* level of the curves can change, for example, and the *C-B* paradigm actually yields positive transfer when the responses are low in meaningfulness. Nevertheless, the relative positions of the paradigm remain as shown in figure 17.

Expansion of Paradigms: Similarity Factor

Keep in mind that the paradigms are simply shorthand conventions for describing the relationship between first- and second-list learning. As we have described them, the stimuli, responses, or both are changed or kept the same. These paradigms may be expanded if we now vary the *similarity* of either stimuli or responses. For example, in the A-B— A-D paradigm the responses are quite unrelated. We can, however, vary the similarity of the response terms along some continuum of similarity, and thus produce what is known as the A-B—A-B' paradigm, where B and B' represent highly similar responses. Moreover, you can visualize a continuum of response similarity going from B', where the responses are highly similar to B, to B'', where they are less similar to B, to D, where they are unrelated to B. In a parallel fashion, you can visualize a similar continuum of stimulus similarity going from A', to A'', to C, which is completely dissimilar.

It should now be clear that a number of task relationships can be studied in transfer paradigms. The basic paradigms, which represent

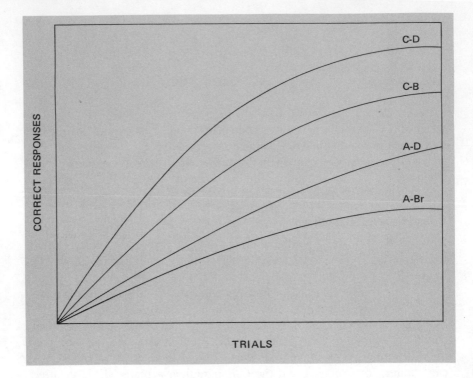

Figure 17. Transfer performance curves for the four basic paradigms.

extremes of the similarity continuum, can be expanded to include the dimensions of stimulus and response similarity. If you have difficulty remembering all this shorthand, remember the general point that in paired associate transfer tasks (1) the stimuli in the second list may be changed, (2) the responses may be changed, (3) both stimuli and responses can be changed, and (4) stimuli and responses can be varied along a similarity continuum. With an understanding of how transfer is studied, in particular of the basic transfer paradigms, we can now turn our attention to general and specific transfer.

Components of Transfer

We have already noted that transfer effects can be due to either general or specific sources. They may, of course, be due to the joint operation of both. Let us examine the concepts of general and specific transfer in greater detail.

General Transfer

It is frequently observed that individuals improve in their ability to learn new tasks or skills more proficiently as a result of prior practice on a series of related tasks. For example, parking lot attendants can quickly learn to operate a particular car even if they have never driven that make or model based on their long experience in driving various kinds of cars. Similarly, the skilled card player can readily learn a new card game based on a backlog of experience with previous games. Some of this transfer is due to specific similarities between the tasks, but much of it is due to general effects of practice.

The progressive improvement in ability to learn a series of new tasks (that is, at an increase in the rate with which the tasks are learned) is a form of transfer known as *learning to learn.* Learning to learn is observed in a variety of tasks ranging from verbal learning to problem solving and thinking and is one case of general transfer.

Humans show clear evidence of learning to learn paired associate verbal materials. If we learn successive lists of paired associates, say one new list each day for several days, we will gradually improve our performance in terms of the number of trials required to learn the list. This is simply to say that it will require fewer trials for us to learn each successive list. Figure 18 indicates such a relationship, one in which humans are given a number of successive lists over successive days of practice. The figure indicates that we require fewer trials to learn each list on successive days, and that performance begins to level off after extended practice. In other words, some level is reached at which very little improvement over the previous day's practice occurs. New and quite different lists of materials, conforming to successive C-D paradigms, are used each day so that the improvement in performance is not due to specific items in the list.

Similarly, learning to learn is seen in tasks of discrimination learning. For example, we can present young children with a task requiring them to respond to one of two stimuli such as a circle and a triangle. Arbitrarily, we arrange the situation such that a response to one of the stimuli, say the circle, is rewarded by giving the child a small toy or piece of candy. A response to the other stimulus is followed by no reward. This task will be readily learned by the child. Now, if we increase the difficulty of the task by making the stimuli very similar, or by using stimuli with several dimensions, such as size, shape, and color, with only one dimension being relevant (followed by reward), then the task becomes more difficult to learn. If we give the child practice in a series of such tasks, we will nevertheless observe that the child will learn successive discriminations faster, even if we use new stimuli on subsequent series of tasks. Again we have an instance of

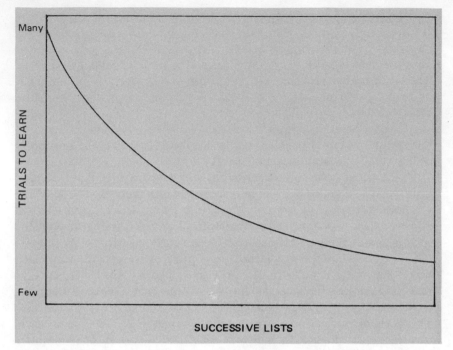

Figure 18. Ease of learning paired associate lists as a function of practice on successive lists. Curve shows steady improvement in performance, that is, progressively fewer trials to learn the successive lists.

learning to learn. Our ability to transfer general modes of attack, to adopt appropriate sets in new learning situations, and to use appropriate strategies provides the basis for learning to learn.

A second source of general transfer is *warm-up*. Warm-up is related to learning to learn; however, *the basic difference between the two is that warm-up is a much more transitory or short-lived effect.* Whereas learning to learn effects are long term, warm-up effects are quite brief in duration, usually no longer than an hour. Warm-up refers to postural adjustments and general attentive adjustments that carry over from one task to another and facilitate learning. The facilitation of performance due to warm-up effects is readily seen in a variety of situations. After you have played several games of pool in immediate succession, the next game in the series benefits from the general motor and postural adjustments necessary for optimal performance. Similarly, once you have started studying, you benefit from warm-up effects when you shift to studying new materials. If, however, you take an extended break, you will lose some of the benefits associated with warm-up because of its rapid dissipation over time.

Specific Transfer

Transfer depends not only upon general sources which we have just described, but also upon the presence of certain specific sources. For example, the stimuli in the initial and transfer tasks may be highly similar, the consequence of which is to produce positive transfer if the responses are new. Thus, transfer in this case would be dependent upon the specific factor of stimulus similarity. Likewise, transfer may also depend upon the relationship between the responses in the two tasks.

Transfer can depend upon many specific sources. The similarity of the two tasks is an example of a major specific source of transfer. For example, the fact that there are international traffic symbols makes it relatively easy to obey traffic signs when traveling in foreign countries using these signs, even though you may be unable to read the language. The international stop sign is a hexagonal (six-sided) sign. It is not, therefore, necessary to know the Spanish word for "stop" (which is *alto*) when traveling in Mexico. All you need do is recognize that any hexagonal sign means stop.

We shall briefly examine a few specific sources of transfer. They will all be illustrated in the context of paired associate transfer paradigms. These sources stem directly from "what is learned" when one learns a paired associate list. In chapter 3 we noted that several processes operate when we learn paired associates. These included discrimination among the stimuli, response learning, and establishment of both forward and backward associations. Once these processes are achieved during first-list learning, their effects can transfer to second-list learning, depending upon the particular paradigm involved. Let us see how this is the case.

Transfer of Stimulus Discrimination

Recall that during A-B learning, that is, the learning of a paired associate list, that part of what the learner must achieve is the discrimination among the stimulus terms. If the stimuli are highly similar, this process then requires more time for completion than if the stimuli are low in similarity.

Now, what happens if the learner transfers to an A-D list where the stimuli are identical to those of the first list? Since the stimuli were discriminated during first-list learning, then the learner should profit from already having learned to distinguish among the stimuli. The learner could thus begin the second task with this aspect of learning already achieved. This source of transfer, known as the transfer of stimulus discrimination, produces a source of positive transfer. Although the A-B—A-D paradigm usually produces *overall* negative transfer, *as the stimuli increase in intralist stimulus similarity, then relatively greater positive transfer of stimulus discrimination will result.*

This process can be illustrated by considering a hypothetical situation. Suppose that you have to learn arbitrary names to a set of facial photographs consisting of highly similar people. Assume that all photographs are brunette women about the same age, with the same hair style, and with similar facial features. Once you have learned to identify each person by giving her correct name, A-B learning is completed. Now, suppose that you have to learn to identify the same photographs with a new label, such as a letter of the alphabet. This, of course, is the analogue to A-D learning. Having already learned to discriminate the highly similar photographs, the learned discrimination among them would transfer to second-task learning.

It should be emphasized that the stimuli must be difficult to distinguish, that is, high in intralist stimulus similarity, for stimulus discrimination to be a potent source of transfer. If the stimuli are initially easy to distingush, then there will be virtually no transfer from this source. For instance, if the stimuli are familiar and already discriminable events, such as primary colors, discrimination of the stimuli will be an unimportant part of the total set of processes that operate in initial paired associate learning and hence provide for little transfer effects.

It also follows that a parallel process on the response side occurs. *If the responses are difficult to discriminate, then, there will be a source of positive transfer to the second task when the responses are identical.* Thus, we find in the A-B—C-B paradigm a source of positive transfer, called the *transfer of response differentiation,* when similarity among the response terms is high.

Transfer of Response Learning

Another specific source of transfer is due to response learning. Recall that one component of A-B learning is response learning. This is the process by which the responses become integrated as a unit so that they are available for recall. We noted that if the responses are low in meaningfulness or are difficult to pronounce, much of your effort will be devoted to integrating the responses into available recallable units. Thus, *response learning* refers to making the response terms available as recallable units, whereas *response differentiation* refers to the reduction in confusability of initially similar responses.

Now, what happens if you transfer to a C-B list where the responses are identical to those of the first list? Since the responses were made available during first-list learning, you should profit from the response learning that has already occurred. You begin the second task with this aspect of learning already achieved. This source of transfer, known as the *transfer of response learning,* produces a source of positive transfer. More generally, *the less meaningful the responses, thus requiring more response learning, the greater is the source of positive transfer due to response learning when the same responses are required.*

Transfer of Forward Associations

Whenever you learn an A-B association, this association can transfer to the second association and produce interference or negative transfer. This is the case when the stimuli are the same, but the responses are new or re-paired. Thus negative transfer in the A-B—A-D and A-B—A-Br paradigms can result because of the carryover of now inappropriate association. In other words, the old association would intrude and momentarily displace the appropriate association.

In verbal paired associates, however, actual intrusions of the B responses during A-D learning are infrequent. Rather, the arrangement appears to produce a suppression of the B responses during A-D learning. It is as if one sets aside the first-list responses during second-list learning in the sense of regarding these responses as now coming from an inappropriate list.

Transfer of Backward Associations

We have also seen that during A-B learning you may acquire *backward* associations as well as forward associations. Backward associations are weaker than forward associations, but they also serve as a source of negative transfer.

Consider the A-B—A-Br paradigm. We have already seen that interference is produced by the transfer of forward associations. In a similar vein, the backward association acquired during A-B learning, which we designate as the *B-A* association, can interfere with the *Br-A* backward association of the second list. Since we have interference stemming from *both* forward and backward associations in this paradigm, we would expect a large amount of negative transfer, which is the case.

In summary, we have examined four specific sources of transfer. Two of these, stimulus discrimination (as well as response differentiation) and response learning produce positive transfer. The remaining two, forward and backward associations, produce negative transfer.

Transfer and Task Similarity

We have already noted that similarity between two tasks is a major factor in producing transfer. Throughout this chapter we have seen instances of transfer based upon the similarity of the two tasks involved.

Transfer from French to Spanish, from tennis to squash, and from driving one car to another are all examples that we noted. In these examples we have not attempted to deal systematically with the separate effects of stimulus and response similarity between the two tasks. We have merely noted that when two tasks possess some similar requirements or features we may expect some positive transfer from one to the other.

Now, let us examine a more restricted example, one in which we can more closely look at the effects of stimulus similarity alone. Imagine that the laws governing traffic lights in the United States were suddenly changed so that we no longer stopped our car when the traffic light was red, but stopped when the light was orange. Would this change be likely to produce difficulty? Most likely not. What we have done is to require our driver to make the *same* response of stopping to stimulus events that are *highly similar*. Given the similarity of red and orange, it would be relatively easy to learn to stop at an orange light. You may recognize this example as an instance of an A-B—A'-B paradigm. The initial association is red-stop (A-B) and the new association is orange-stop (A'-B). This, of course, is a condition for positive transfer.

Now, recall our hypothetical example on an A-B—A-Br paradigm, in which the traffic signals are reversed. Imagine that you must now stop in the presence of green and go in the presence of red. Such a condition, as we noted, will lead to considerable interference, or negative transfer. The negative transfer may, however, occur mainly in the first or first few trials following this change.

Let us now reexamine our example of negative transfer from squash to tennis. Here we observed that tennis players might experience some difficulty with their game after playing a few sessions of squash. We noted that in this situation the task required a *new* set of wrist responses, responses incompatible with those of squash. What can we say about the stimulus events in the two games? Although there are some obvious differences in size of the courts, rules, and speed with which the ball moves, the essential and common stimulus event in both situations is that of a ball moving toward a player. In other words, both games have a common or highly similar stimulus event, but require different responses. If we ignore for purposes of analysis the differences between the stimuli and concentrate on the critical stimulus feature, a ball moving rapidly toward a player, this *aspec*t of the relationship between tennis and squash *approximates* that of an A-B—A-D paradigm, or at least of an A-B—A'-D paradigm, depending on whether we wish to regard the stimuli as identical or as highly similar. In real life, of course, it is sometimes difficult to analyze complex situations and reduce them to an appropriate paradigm. Everyday examples, because of their complexities, may only approximate laboratory paradigms. Moreover, we are less likely to discover stimulus situations that can really be regarded as identical.

These illustrations emphasize the significance of similarity in transfer. Before we examine the relationship between similarity and transfer we shall again look at the concept of similarity.

Concept of Similarity

Obviously, if we are to understand how similarity affects transfer, we must first have some reasonable understanding of what is meant by similarity. In chapter 3 we distinguished between formal similarity, meaningful similarity, and conceptual similarity of verbal materials. The basic issue is, How does one measure the similarity between two events? Three general approaches to this problem have been made.

One way of specifying the similarity of events is to measure the *number of elements that two events have in common.* This approach is useful when the stimuli or responses contain two or more elements. For example, the formal similarity of trigrams is defined by counting the number of letters held in common by two trigrams. TRM and TRH are high in formal similarity because they share two letters in common; TRM and BKM are somewhat less close in formal similarity because they share only one element in common; TRM and KJC are dissimilar because they share no common elements.

Whereas it is relatively easy to measure the similarity of some laboratory tasks by counting the number of elements in common, it is more difficult to accomplish this with everyday tasks. Nevertheless, you can get an intuitive grasp of the notion of common elements by considering the languages French, Spanish, and Chinese. French and Spanish possess many more common elements than do French and Chinese or Spanish and Chinese. French and Spanish are derived from a common language, Latin; they have many words that are similar in spelling and use the same alphabet. In summary, one way of measuring the similarity of complex events is to count the number of elements in common.

Many stimulus events vary along some *continuous dimension* such as size, brightness, color, and so forth. Lights can vary in brightness and color; tones can vary in intensity and pitch; objects can vary in size. The closer two lights are in brightness, the greater is their similarity. Likewise, the closer two objects are in size, the greater is their similarity. Responses can also vary along continuous dimensions such as speed or force. When relatively simple stimuli or responses are dealt with, the measurement of physical attributes is a convenient way of defining similarity.

Since studies of human learning usually use more complex stimuli and responses, common element definitions of similarity are used more frequently than physical dimensions. Only in relatively simple studies of human learning, where the stimulus events vary along a physical dimension, is similarity defined in terms of some measured attribute.

Not only may events vary in terms of physical features, whether this be in terms of common elements or dimensions, but events may vary in their *degree of learned similarity*. For example, words that are meaningfully similar become so not because they have a number of common elements, but because they define the same objects or events. The words *icy* and *cold* acquire similarity because they describe the same events. Words that are conceptually similar, in the sense of belonging to the same category, are so because of learned similarity. More generally, stimuli and responses acquire similarity when they are associated with some common event.

Stimulus Similarity and Transfer

Let us now look more closely at the effects of stimulus similarity on transfer. There are two general cases that we must consider. First, we can vary the similarity between the first- and second-task stimuli, keeping the responses identical in the two tasks. Second, we can vary the similarity of the stimuli while simultaneously changing the responses.

In the first case, *where stimuli are varied and the responses kept identical, positive transfer increases with increasing stimulus similarity.* This generalization is illustrated in figure 19, which shows transfer as a function of stimulus similarity. We note that as the similarity between the stimuli increases, the amount of transfer also increases. The stimuli vary along a continuum of similarity beginning with A, which represents identity between first- and second-task stimuli, to A', which represents high between-list similarity, to A'', which represents moderate similarity, to C, which represents dissimilar stimuli.

A simple illustration will amplify the principle. Consider the games of checkers, Chinese checkers, chess, and three-dimensional chess. We would expect considerable positive transfer from checkers to Chinese checkers. It would be quite easy to learn Chinese checkers, having learned checkers, because of the high similarity of the conditions of the games. The many features of similarity include similar, although not identical, playing boards, only one type of object (checker piece or marble), identical jumping rules, etc. We would also expect positive transfer from checkers to chess, again because of some common features of both games. Both use a common board and similar number of

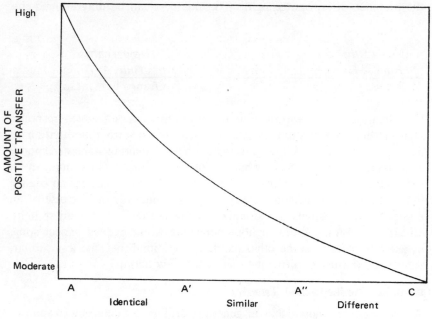

Figure 19. Transfer as a function of degree of stimulus similarity with responses kept identical.

pieces (sixteen in chess and twelve in checkers per player), and the *concept* of capturing pieces is similar, although the specific rules of capturing differ. The transfer from checkers to chess would, however, be less than our first example because the pieces differ and different playing rules are used. Finally, we would expect even less positive transfer from checkers to three-dimensional chess because the stimulus conditions are even less similar than in the first two examples.

When stimulus similarity is varied and responses also change, we have *a restriction* on the general rule that similarity aids transfer. The rule is: *If the responses in the transfer task are different from those in the first task, then the greater the similarity of the stimuli the less is the transfer.* Indeed, as the stimuli became highly similar, the effect shifts from positive to *negative* transfer.

A practical although hypothetical example will help make this principle somewhat more obvious. Suppose that the rules governing traffic lights in our society were now changed so that we no longer stopped our car in the presence of a red light and had to learn to go in the presence of an orange light. The situation can be diagrammed this way:

Old Traffic Rule A-B	New Traffic Rule A'-D
Red light: Stop	Orange light: Go

The situation amounts to making a new (in this case opposite) response D to a very similar stimulus A'. Thus we can regard the situation as like that of an A-B—A'-D paradigm, that of making a new response to a similar stimulus. Now, what is likely to happen? We would, in all likelihood, find it a bit confusing to learn to go when we saw an orange light. We would have some tendency to continue to stop because of an earlier learned response of stopping in the presence of a similar light. Since orange and red are highly similar, we would indeed expect some negative transfer. On the other hand, as the stimuli became less similar, we would find it less difficult to learn the new habit.

Response Similarity and Transfer

We have already noted that in general learning to make new responses to the same stimuli is a basic condition for negative transfer. This, of course, is what happens in the A-B—A-D paradigm. We may, however, vary response similarity and ask how this affects transfer.

If we keep the stimuli identical in the initial and transfer tasks and vary response similarity, positive transfer will increase with increasing response similarity. For example, let us compare the transfer from tennis to badminton with tennis to baseball. We would expect greater transfer in the former case because the responses are more similar than in the latter case. Both tennis and badminton are played with racquets, use rectangular courts, and require the habit of keeping your eye on the ball. Tennis and baseball are less similar, although they do have some features in common, such as the desirability of keeping your eye on the ball.

Theories of Transfer

Several kinds of transfer theory have been developed. These range from stimulus-response association theory based upon the principle of generalization to cognitive theories of transfer. In this section we shall examine several types of transfer theory.

Generalization Theory

One of the earliest theories of transfer was based on the idea of generalization. The concept of generalization was borrowed from conditioning theory and extended to human verbal learning. The theory deals with both stimulus and response generalization as explanatory mechanisms. Basically, the generalization theory says that the *amount* of transfer depends upon the stimulus similarity and the *direction* of transfer (positive or negative) depends upon response similarities or differences (response compatibility). We shall first examine the notion of stimulus generalization.

Consider the A-B—A'-B transfer paradigm which is known to produce positive transfer. In this situation the same set of responses are learned to new but similar stimuli. If we assume that during the learning of A-B associations there is some tendency for similar stimuli (A') to develop associative connections with the B responses, then we see that two things are happening. First, the A-B associations are learned and, second, A'-B associations are also strengthened but to a weaker degree. Therefore, when the second list (A'-B) is begun, the learner begins with some of this learning already accomplished by virtue of generalization. Thus she is able to proceed with A'-B learning quite rapidly.

This mechanism can be illustrated with a simple example. Let the stimuli consist of geometric symbols such as rectangles, triangles, and so forth. During A-B learning, the individual learns to associate a particular geometric figure with a particular response. For example, he learns △ - Happy, and ☐ - Increasing as two of several pairs. If we assume the process of stimulus generalization

A - B	*A' - B*
△- Happy	△ - Happy
☐ - Increasing	☐- Increasing

during A-B learning, then he learns not only the △ - Happy association, but learns to respond in a similar manner to other triangular-shaped stimuli to a weaker degree. Thus the second-list association of △ - Happy benefits from considerable transfer based upon stimulus generalization and is learned with relative ease. Similarly, having learned the association ☐ - Increasing, the second association ☐ - Increasing is quite easy to learn because the stimuli are similar, permitting stimulus generalization from one to the other.

A parallel mechanism of *response generalization* can be used to account for the effects of response similarity on transfer. The process of response generalization is seen when, having learned to make a particular response to a particular stimulus, responses similar to the learned response also acquire some strength. For example, having learned to type with a characteristic force, we also acquire some tendency to type with somewhat less and somewhat greater force.

Now consider the A-B—A-B' paradigm in which new but quite similar responses are learned to the same stimuli. As noted previously, this situation leads to positive transfer. In this case, assume that during A-B learning some strengthening of similar responses (B') occur so that both A-B and A-B' associations develop some associative strength. The A-B' associations are weaker, of course, because they are never directly reinforced. Nevertheless, when the second list (A-B') is begun, the learner begins with some of this learning already achieved. Thus, the new associations are readily learned because of response generalization.

The use of stimulus generalization and response generalization as explanatory mechanisms of transfer stems from the study of conditioned responses in lower animals. In these studies the stimuli are quite simple events like tones and lights and thus vary along only a single dimension of similarity such as loudness or brightness. In studies of human learning the stimuli are usually much more complex, involving at least several components or features. The use of generalization to explain transfer effects due to similarity is therefore most applicable when the stimuli vary along clearly defined physical dimensions. In addition, when the stimuli are formally similar, the generalization explanation is useful. When, however, we deal with *meaningful* and *conceptual* similarity, a second mechanism, *mediation,* is needed to account for some of the findings.

Mediation

It is possible in situations where the response terms are similar, as in the A-B—A-B' paradigm, or where the stimulus terms are similar, as in the A-B—A'-B paradigm, for transfer to occur on the basis of *mediation* rather than on simple generalization. Consider an A-B—A-B' paradigm in which the response terms are conceptually related, such as *table* and *chair*. We first learn the association CEJ-table and then learn CEJ-chair. Considerable positive transfer will result.

But how is the positive transfer produced? We know from word association tests that table and chair are common associates. Since most people already have this association, they can most likely use it in learning the second list. In the first list, the CEJ-table association is established. The second list is easily learned if we use table as a mediating stimulus to think of chair. In effect, we may develop the mediating chain of A-B-B', that is, CEJ-table-chair. Very little new learning is required for the second list if we think about and use the already available associative connection. Thus the process of mediation can account for the effects of similarity on transfer, particularly when the responses or stimuli are meaningfully or conceptually similar. Mediation theory is a type of stimulus-response theory, but it is more flexible than generalization theory because it assumes the operation of *implicit* processes which intervene between environmental stimuli and overt responses.

Cognitive Theory

Cognitive theories of transfer deal with the way humans acquire and then transfer rules, principles, strategies, and knowledge. These theories assume that humans learn strategies and/or acquire knowledge rather than stimulus-response associations. Cognitive theories differ from stimulus-response theories by emphasizing the active efforts of the learner to comprehend rules and strategies and to apply these rules and strategies to new learning situations. An important aspect of cognitive theories is the assumption that learning is some kind of higher-order mental structure or organization which is then used in a problem-solving fashion in new situations.

Let us see how a cognitive theory deals with *rules* in a paired associate task. Suppose subjects were given a paired associate list where the stimuli and responses were of the same class, such as geographical locations, digit pairs, and so forth. The basic rule is, "Like goes with like." Rule and nonrule pairs are illustrated here:

Rule Pairs	Nonrule Pairs
Spain - Nigeria	Spain - 35
79 - 35	79 - Banana
L - G	L - Nigeria
Apple - Banana	Apple - Belt
Shoes - Belt	Shoes - G

The rule pairs are much easier to learn that the nonrule pairs. Moreover, if subjects in both conditions are given a second list consisting of rule pairs to learn, we would expect some positive transfer from subjects having initial experience with the rule pairs. Presumably, subjects would have learned the general rule, Like goes with like, and would transfer this rule to the learning of the second list. Thus a cognitive interpretation can be given to an associative learning task.

Consider another example of the cognitive approach to transfer. The learning of arithmetic is assumed to transfer to such tasks as making change and balancing a checkbook. A cognitive explanation of this transfer emphasizes that what transfers to the new situation is a general understanding of rules involving arithmetic. Similarly, students learning algebra will hopefully be able to generalize to word problems, and the transfer will again occur presumably because the students understand the general principles.

More generally, cognitive theory sees effective transfer as due to the active role of the learner in applying rules, strategies, and knowledge. Negative transfer is viewed as the result of inappropriate application of old strategies in new situations, whereas positive transfer is the result of appropriate application of such strategies and knowledges.

Some Practical Applications of Transfer

We will now turn our attention to some of the major factors that affect transfer and discuss their implications for the teaching-learning process. From your viewpoint, an important issue is how to study so as to maximize the possibilities for transfer. Similarly, the instructor is concerned with how to teach for transfer. It is useful, therefore, to focus on how knowledge of principles of transfer and of the factors that produce transfer can be applied in educational and daily life activities. We can do no more than state some general guidelines; therefore, the present set of practical suggestions must be viewed as only suggestive of a larger number of possible applications.

Task (Stimulus) Variation

In order to maximize transfer, should you practice extensively on a single task or, alternatively, should you practice on a variety of tasks of the same class? *A factor of considerable importance for producing positive transfer is practice under varied task conditions.* For example, practice in driving different kinds of cars will make it easier to learn to drive a new car compared with an equal amount of practice on only one kind of car. Varied training with different kinds of cars provides experience with different stimulus situations, thus making new learning easier.

In a similar vein, you will find that your understanding of a topic can be improved not so much by repeated rereading of the same text, but by reading another text on the same subject matter. Getting a different slant on the topic, looking at another approach to the issues, and seeing the same ideas presented in a somewhat new context all serve to strengthen your understanding of a topic.

The importance of varied context and examples cannot be overemphasized. Regardless of whether you are learning simple discriminations or more complex concepts, stimulus variation can be helpful. For instance, several examples of a concept will serve to strengthen your understanding so that you are more likely to see potential applications in new learning situations. In contrast, with only one example, you may attend to features unessential to the concept and thus fail to transfer appropriately because of failure to learn the concept in the first place.

Transfer from Easy to Difficult Discriminations

An important principle of transfer is that transfer is more likely if one first begins with the easier aspects of a task and then shifts to the more difficult aspects. The principle is especially important in discrimination learning, where you must distinguish between two or more stimuli.

Consider the kinds of discriminations that a young child must make in learning the alphabet. To each letter the child must learn to respond with a distinctive speech pattern. At a simplified level, the child must learn twenty-six paired associates, a speech pattern for each visual symbol. Many of the letters are easy to distinguish, whereas others are more difficult, especially *b* and *d*. Two things are important in teaching the child this set of discriminations. First, it is wise practice to begin with the easier-to-distinguish letters such as *a* and *b*. Only after the child has mastered a number of the easier ones should you teach the more difficult ones. Second, when you begin with the more difficult ones, especially *b* and *d,* you should use letters that have been exaggerated or made more distinctive in some fashion. Subsequently you can teach the *b-d* discriminations with the letters as they normally appear.

The importance of this principle is seen in many situations. For example, in learning to type by the touch method, you first learn the easier discriminations and then move on to the more difficult ones. In learning to discriminate colors, it is best to distinguish the primary colors first and then to distinguish among the more subtle differences in varying shades of color. We are, however, unable to specify how easy the initial discriminations should be in order to optimize transfer. This is simply to say that we cannot specify the exact optimal level of difficulty for ensuring transfer. The work of Frank Logan suggests, however, that the "easy" discrimination should not be extremely easy, and that the transfer should be progressive but rapid. Thus the principle of going from easy to more difficult discriminations is a good rule of thumb, given your awareness of these qualifications.

Degree of Original Learning

Variations in the degree of original or first-task learning affect the amount of transfer produced. The effects of degree of learning are somewhat complicated because they depend on the transfer situation or paradigm. With the A-B—A-D and A-B—C-B paradigms, the effect of increasing the degree of learning is first to increase the amount of negative transfer and then to decrease the amount of negative transfer with additional practice. A general rule of thumb is that of a U-shaped function relating degree of learning and transfer. In contrast, with the A-B—A-Br paradigm, negative transfer increases with increasing amounts of original learning.

In situations where one learns successive tasks of the same class, greater positive transfer occurs when extensive practice occurs with the early tasks in the series. Therefore, a good practical rule is to ensure adequate practice with the original task so as either to minimize interference during second-task learning or to maximize positive transfer.

Task Similarity

We have seen that similarity between tasks is a fundamental condition for transfer. From a practical viewpoint this means that one should ideally learn under conditions that at least approximate the ultimate testing conditions. But how can this be achieved? How, for example, is it possible to study under conditions that approximate what is required of you during test situations? There are a number of ways that this objective can be accomplished.

Consider the matter of test preparation. If you know, for example, that the test will consist of short essay questions that require both recall of factual information and integration of materials from several sources, then your preparation must include these features. Indeed, you might even practice certain features of this task by asking and *writing* answers to essay questions. You might ask a friend to ask questions of you to which you *write* the answers. By writing short essays, as distinct from merely thinking about or discussing issues, you directly practice the very behaviors required by the test.

In a similar vein, if your examination consists of true-false and multiple-choice questions, you could agree among a small group of friends for each to construct a sample set of test items. The test items could be circulated and you could take the practice test. This has the double advantage not only of practicing an event similar to the forthcoming test, but also of forcing you to think about the important principles and ideas on which you will be examined.

Summary

In this chapter we have emphasized that prior learning can affect the way we perform in subsequent learning situations. The influence of previous learning on performance in some new situation defines transfer of training. Transfer effects may be positive, negative, or zero.

The study of transfer involves the comparison of experimental and control group performance on some transfer task. If the experimental group performs superior to the control, we have positive transfer; if the reverse occurs, we have negative transfer; if the two groups are the same, we have zero transfer. The study of paired associate transfer revolves around four basic paradigms: A-B—C-D (new stimuli and responses), A-B—A-D (old stimuli and new responses), A-B—C-B (new stimuli and old responses), and A-B—A-Br (responses re-paired). Transfer paradigms are simply shorthand expressions for describing the relationship between first- and second-list learning. They may be expanded to include the effects of variations in stimulus and response similarity.

Transfer effects can be analyzed into general and specific sources. General transfer includes learning-to-learn and warm-up effects. Specific transfer refers to transfer based upon similarities between the two tasks. Four sources of specific transfer examined included stimulus discrimination, response learning, forward associations, and backward associations.

Similarity was seen as a major factor producing transfer. Three approaches to defining similarity were noted: common elements, dimensions, and learned similarity. Formal similarity of verbal materials was seen as an instance of common elements; conceptual and meaningful similarity of verbal materials were seen as instances of learned similarity. We saw that the effects of similarity depended upon changes in stimuli and responses: (1) Where stimuli are varied in similarity between tasks and the responses kept identical, positive transfer increases with increasing stimulus similarity. (2) If the responses in the transfer task are different from those in the first task, then the greater the similarity of the stimuli, the less will be the transfer. (3) If the stimuli are kept identical in the two tasks and the responses varied, positive transfer will increase with increasing response similarity. Three kinds of transfer theories were discussed: generalization, mediation, and cognitive theory.

Some practical points in studying for transfer were noted: (1) practice under varied task of stimulus conditions, such as studying several instances of a concept, is an important factor for positive transfer, (2) arrange learning so as to begin with the easier features of a task before moving on to more difficult features, (3) make sure that sufficient practice with the initial task is obtained before you expect much transfer, and (4) study under conditions that at least approximate those of the ultimate testing conditions, that is, where possible, maximize similarities between study conditions and the ultimate testing situation.

Multiple-Choice Items: Transfer of Training

1. The concept of transfer means that prior learning _____ subsequent learning
   a. interferes with
   b. has an effect on

    c. facilitates

    d. does nothing for

2. A pilot learns that to push a lever up means "flaps up" in one plane, whereas in another plane pushing the lever up means "flaps down." In the second task he is most likely to encounter

    a. extinction

    b. positive transfer

    c. zero transfer

    d. negative transfer

3. Which transfer paradigm typically produces massive negative transfer?

    a. A-B—A-D

    b. A-B—C-D

    c. A-B—C-B

    d. A-B—A-Br

4. In the transfer of stimulus differentiation, the relative importance of stimulus learning is greatest when the stimuli are _____ in intralist stimulus similarity.

    a. high

    b. moderate

    c. low

    d. unrelated

5. The importance of a variety of examples in teaching for transfer appears to reside in the fact that such variety provides for

    a. more extinction

    b. more recovery

    c. less proactive interference

    d. superior learning or understanding

6. A comparison of the four transfer paradigms, rank-ordering them from least to most negative transfer, is as follows

    a. C-D, C-B, A-Br, A-D

    b. C-D, A-Br, C-B, A-D

    c. C-D, C-B, A-D, A-Br

    d. C-B, C-D, A-D, A-Br

7. A basic difference between warm-up and learning to learn is that

    a. learning to learn is transitory

    b. learning to learn is nonassociative

    c. warm-up is cognitive

    d. warm-up is transitory

8. In general, the effect of increasing the similarity of list-one and list-two stimuli while keeping the responses identical is to

    a. decrease positive transfer

    b. increase negative transfer

   c. decrease negative transfer
   d. increase positive transfer
9. Transfer in the A-B—A'-B paradigm can be attributed to
   a. stimulus generalization
   b. response generalization
   c. stimulus association
   d. stimulus satiation
10. A logical analysis of the A-B—A-Br paradigm reveals at least one
   source of positive transfer despite the fact that the paradigm yields
   overall negative transfer. The source of positive transfer stems
   from
   a. forward associations
   b. backward associations
   c. warm-up
   d. response learning
11. Cognitive theories of transfer stress the learning of
   a. associations
   b. rules
   c. mediators
   d. connections or bonds
12. A theory of transfer based on response generalization would be
   concerned with which paradigm?
   a. A-B—C-B
   b. A-B—A'-B
   c. A-B—C-D
   d. A-B—A-B'

True-False Items: Transfer of Training

1. Transfer of training refers only to situations in which prior learning
   aids subsequent performance.
2. The transfer design that employs a control condition in which subjects do not learn an initial task fails to control for nonspecific
   (general) transfer effects.
3. The A-B—C-D transfer paradigm is a control condition for measuring transfer effects in other paradigms.
4. Both the A-B—A-D and A-B—C-B paradigms characteristically
   produce positive transfer.
5. Learning to learn is one form of general transfer.
6. Specific transfer refers to transfer effects that depend upon similarities between the tasks such as stimulus and/or response similarity.
7. Increasing the similarity of the stimuli in the two lists while keep-

ing the responses identical leads to increasing amounts of positive transfer.

8. The three principal theories for explaining transfer are generalization, warm-up, and associations.
9. In order to ensure maximum positive transfer, the training (or teaching) conditions should concentrate on keeping stimulus conditions constant.
10. We might expect greater positive transfer from studying biology to psychology than from biology to mathematics.
11. In order to maximize the likelihood that your study habits will transfer to examination performance, as part of your studying you should include some sort of practice in writing examination questions.
12. Learning to make a new incompatible response to the same stimulus is a general condition for positive transfer.

Discussion Items: Transfer of Training

1. Illustrate the concepts of positive and negative transfer from several everyday experiences.
2. Distinguish between general and specific transfer and between warm-up and learning to learn.
3. Outline in detail how you might maximize the similarity between some training session or program and the ultimate test situation so as to ensure positive transfer. You might begin by asking how the similarity between your studying for an examination and your taking an actual examination could be increased. Then consider a motor learning task.
4. Compare and contrast generalization and mediation theories of transfer.
5. How might a cognitive theory of transfer apply to your ability to transfer knowledge and strategies? Cite a specific example.

Multiple-Choice Answers: Transfer of Training

1. (b)   Transfer means simply that prior learning has an effect on subsequent learning. The result may be either facilitative (positive transfer) or interfering (negative transfer).
2. (d)   This situation would produce negative transfer because it amounts to making a new opposite response to the same stimulus situation.
3. (d)   The A-B—A-Br paradigm typically produces massive

negative transfer. This is so because the subject must re-pair the same stimuli and responses.

4. (a) Stimulus learning becomes most pronounced when the stimuli are high in intralist similarity. This is the case because having to distinguish difficult-to-discriminate stimuli leads to greater transfer of stimulus discrimination effects.

5. (d) A variety of stimuli or examples is desirable because your understanding of the task or material is likely to be superior. The better the task is understood the more likely you will be able to transfer what you have learned.

6. (c) The C-D is the basic control paradigm. This is followed by C-B, which may sometimes yield positive transfer. Next is the A-D paradigm, which generally yields negative transfer. Finally, the A-Br paradigm yields large negative transfer effects.

7. (d) Warm-up is a relatively transitory phenomenon usually lasting no more than one hour in verbal learning tasks.

8. (d) As the stimuli increase in similarity, and the responses kept identical, positive transfer increases.

9. (a) This transfer can be attributed to stimulus generalization because the stimuli (A and A') are similar.

10. (d) The positive transfer stems from response learning. This occurs because the responses in the two lists are identical; thus you benefit from having already learned the list of responses when you learn list two.

11. (b) Cognitive theories of transfer stress the learning of rules. The learner applies or uses rules, principles, and strategies in cognitive theories.

12. (d) A response generalization theory of transfer would be concerned with the A-B—A-B' paradigm. This is so because B and B' responses are, by definition, similar.

True-False Answers: Transfer of Training

1. (False) Transfer refers to whatever effect prior learning has upon subsequent performance. Prior learning may aid or interfere with later learning; moreover, there may be both facilitation and interfering effects in the same task which cancel each other, producing zero transfer.

2. (True) In such transfer studies, we are unable to interpret the results in any analytical sense because even if positive transfer is obtained we are unable to estimate how much effect (if any) is due to specific transfer and how much is due to general transfer.

3.   (True)   The A-B—C-D paradigm allows for general transfer effects alone since both the stimuli and responses in the transfer task differ from and are unrelated to those of the initial task. Hence, any transfer from A-B to C-D is due to general practice effects.

4.   (False)   The A-B—A-D paradigm typically produces negative transfer, whereas the A-B—C-D paradigm is an occasional condition for positive transfer.

5.   (True)   The progressive improvement in performance when one learns a series of tasks of the same class is an instance of general transfer. In such tasks, neither the stimuli nor responses are identical or similar in terms of common elements; hence the transfer effects cannot be due to specific similarities among the successive tasks.

6   (True)   Specific transfer refers to transfer effects that occur in situations in which one or more features of the initial and transfer tasks are related, such as identical stimuli and responses, similar stimuli and responses, and so forth. For example, transfer of response learning is a specific transfer effect because it occurs when responses in the two tasks are identical; having learned the responses in the first task, the person begins the transfer task with this component of learning already achieved.

7.   (True)   Stimulus similarity is a basic condition for producing positive transfer when the responses are kept identical. Moreover, the limiting case of similarity is identical stimuli in the two tasks. With identical stimuli and identical responses, we have a continuation of the same task.

8.   (False)   The three important theories are generalization, in which there can be either stimulus and/or response generalization, mediation, which is the development and use of linkages between items, and cognitive processes such as the learning of rules or principles.

9.   (False)   On the contrary, stimulus variation is an important factor in facilitating positive transfer. In general, varied experience or practice and contextual variability provide for greater transfer than does training under constant conditions.

10.   (True)   We would expect somewhat more transfer from biology to psychology because these two areas are more similar than biology and mathematics. Biology and psychology are both life sciences, use some of the same concepts, and are concerned with the behavior of organisms.

11.   (True)   This example illustrates the principle of attempting to maximize the similarity between the training conditions and the ultimate test of performance.

12.   (False)   This is a characteristic condition for negative transfer.

Individual Differences
in Learning and in Memory

Consider the case of two children who are presented with a series of tasks which require them to learn a principle for discriminating among a number of similar-appearing figures. Both children are of the same age. One child reflects on each set of figures for over a minute before venturing an answer regarding which of the figures is different from the others in the set. In contrast, the second child responds very quickly to each problem after scarcely looking at the figures. By the end of the series of tasks, the first child is doing well on each problem while the second is still performing quite poorly. What are we to conclude? Does this indicate that the first child is more intelligent than the second? Or is the second child just as capable but has an approach or style which prevents his underlying abilities from manifesting themselves? Whatever our answers to these questions, this example illustrates a principle which is apparent to us all, namely, individuals differ markedly in how they learn.

As another example, consider the familiar topic of studying. College students obviously differ in how they approach the problem of learning course materials. One student takes exhaustive notes on class lectures, methodically outlines the readings, and depends heavily on these written materials. Another takes very few notes and seems to benefit most from talking about the material. A third student reports trying to remember facts for the course by generating mental pictures which suggest important principles. These three people might all get As in the course, but *how* they learned the material clearly varies.

Up to this point, we have talked very little about differences in the way people learn. Implicit in much of what has been said in earlier chapters is that there is a general, average learner who reacts in certain characteristic ways, depending upon conditions of learning. And it is true that the facts discussed represent *typical* performance under varying conditions. However, there is considerable variability among individuals in many learning tasks, sometimes in the final level of performance and sometimes in the manner in which the task is mastered. It is the case that preexisting differences among people are sometimes more predictive of their performance in learning and memory tasks than is the particular

12

"treatment condition" imposed by the experimenter. It is to a consideration of the nature of these differences among learners that we now turn.

Nature of Individual Differences

The reality and value of human diversity is obvious. But what system of
concepts is most useful for thinking about these differences? Perhaps the
most obvious approach is to sort people into *types*. This is like the kind
of classification made repeatedly by societies throughout history on the
basis of such things as occupation and parentage. Classification into psychological types also has a long history. Although they have no scientific
support, certain classifications based on the contours of the human skull
or on the position of the stars when a person was born, have achieved
popularity.

However, twentieth-century scientists have generally focused on one
aspect of individuality at a time and attempted to develop a relatively
continuous scale for measuring this *trait,* instead of classifying the person
as a whole into one of several classes. A trait may be characterized as a
relatively broad and stable disposition to behave in certain ways and implies a dimension along which individuals may be ordered. The focus is
on human characteristics that are reasonably consistent from one situation to the next, rather than on temporary states of the individual. An
example of a state rather than a trait is the kind of anxiety which fluc-
tuates drastically from day to day.

Of course, there is a vast variety of traits such as values, attitudes,
and interests with respect to which people differ. Our primary concern
in this chapter is with traits relevant to learning and memory. First, let
us consider some of the history which forms the background of current
work in this area.

Historical Antecedents

In recent years much attention has been focused on the differences in the
ways individuals learn and remember. Although this area was largely
neglected until recently by learning theorists, its history is as old as that
of any other topic discussed in this text. As early as 1000 B.C. the
Chinese were using tests of aptitudes in such areas as archery and arithmetic to screen candidates for positions in their government. Although
early European culture did not stress the importance of the individual,
the assessment of individual differences was given great impetus around
1700 by the growth of Protestantism with its emphasis on the individual
and the growth of science with its emphasis on measurement. Perhaps
the single most important factor leading to the widespread scientific in-

terest in individual differences was the development of the theory of evolution and the associated emphasis on the principle of variation. In fact, the measurement of differences among individuals in psychological characteristics is typically traced to Darwin's half-cousin Sir Francis Galton. But Galton's pioneering work was much different from current efforts to study differences in cognitive abilities. At his Anthropometric Laboratory in London, a person's "intellectual abilities" were evaluated by measures of handgrip strength, tests of motor skills, and measures of visual and auditory acuity.

An important conclusion which may be drawn from a study of this history is that the science of individual differences has long been closely tied to the technology of mental testing. For example, the first modern intelligence test was developed by Alfred Binet in 1904 at the request of French school officials. Binet was commissioned to produce an instrument that would allow segregation of those who would be the slowest learners in the Paris schools. In general, Binet's tests were more complex than Galton's and they had much less emphasis on sensory characteristics and motor skills. Another noteworthy feature of Binet's tests is that in response to practical demands he structured his test to yield *one* score representing an individual's general intelligence. It was not until later that workers concentrated on special abilities like those relevant to a smaller range of tasks, such as clerical and mechanical skills.

We will return shortly to a more detailed discussion of the nature of intelligence. But first let us move to a consideration of some of the issues involved in measuring individual differences.

Study of Individual Differences

The rise of the study of individual differences in traits has been closely related to developments in statistics and computer technology which have facilitated work with large amounts of data. Although it is possible to formulate the important ways in which people differ simply by theorizing about the nature of personality, this armchair approach has been rejected by those researchers associated with the scientific study of individual differences. Instead, these researchers have chosen to proceed by administering a number of tests to each of a large group of subjects. If the domain being investigated is learning ability, the set of tests to be analyzed might be measures of performance on a number of different tasks and paradigms discussed earlier in this book. Once the basic scores are obtained, a statistical technique known as factor analysis is used to extract more fundamental traits or factors from the original test scores, with the analysis typically being carried out using a computer. The logic of factor analysis is that by analyzing the complex interrelationships among a number of tests one may arrive at a smaller set of factors which may be interpreted as the basic dimensions of individual differences in that domain.

With this brief introduction in mind of how individual differences are studied, we can now highlight certain of the features of this approach. First, we see that a psychologist interested in discussing individual differences in some characteristic must begin with some type of measurement or mental test of that characteristic. Hopefully, the test used is one which yields consistent (reliable) measures of a single trait and which is valid in the sense of yielding scores which are closely related to real-life indicators of the trait the test was designed to measure. Consider the example of a psychologist interested in studying artistic ability. If a test of this ability were formulated, the reliability of this test could be estimated by obtaining two scores from each of a group of persons. The scores could be obtained by administering the test twice or by administering two slightly different forms of the test, with a short time interval between test administrations. If the ordering of individuals according to test scores on the first administration is the same as that based on the second administration, the test is said to be *reliable*. If there is no correlation between the two forms of the test, something is obviously wrong, and the test is unreliable. Now let us consider the validity of a test. In this example test validity might be assessed by investigating the relation of scores on the test to judges' ratings of the test takers artistic performance. The basic approach taken in assessing validity is to select a *real-world criterion* which the test should measure and then to determine the relation between this criterion and the test. If there is a high degree of relationship the test is said to be *valid*.

A second feature characterizing much of the work on individual differences is that it has been "long on data and short on theory." While they have successfully avoided the dangers of armchair psychology through stressing empirical observations, researchers in individual difference have more frequently been guided by practical concerns than by theory in their investigations. The result in some cases has been a proliferation of mental tests which have uncertain relationships to each other and to theoretical ideas.

A final feature of this type of research we will note is its quantitative emphasis. The focus on quantification has resulted in a technology of mental testing which allows precise statements to be made about an individual's performance relative to others on a well-specified task. Some critics argue, however, that the quantification has been premature and excessive. They maintain that our notions of things like intelligence are not sufficiently developed to embark on refined measurement, and that techniques such as factor analysis yield hundreds of numbers that are difficult to interpret and far removed from meaningful, naturalistic observation.

Some Individual Differences Important in Learning and in Memory

Of the very large number of distinguishing features of individual learners, we will discuss only four of the most important cognitive traits influencing learning and memory. First, because of the popular ideas concerning the relation of I.Q. and learning ability, we must consider the notion of intelligence. Also to be discussed are cognitive styles, learning strategies, and memory ability.

Intelligence

The individual difference tests that get most public attention are, of course, those which yield I.Q. scores. In the 1920s these tests were heralded as extremely useful. Supporters of the eugenics movement in the United States felt then that only persons with at least moderately high I.Q.s could be permitted to reproduce if a general deterioration of the mental abilities of the population were to be avoided. More recently, these same tests have been viewed as instruments supporting prejudice.

Part of the reason for both the fame and notoriety of intelligence tests has been confusion concerning what is being measured. Some testers have conceptualized intelligence as the ability to learn quickly. Others view intelligence as indicating the level of difficulty of problems a person of a given age is able to solve. Sometimes the definition is much broader and stresses a global capacity of an individual, for example, "the overall ability to act purposefully, to think rationally, and to deal effectively with one's environment." Still other testers go in the reverse direction as far as generality is concerned and prefer a totally operational definition of intelligence, for example, "the capacity to do well in an intelligence test or on whatever the test tests."

Whatever intelligence is, it is probably most important here to indicate something that it is not. Namely, it is *incorrect* to say that intelligence is *the* ability to learn. Studies of learning rate have indicated that several learning factors are required to adequately predict an individual's learning of various tasks. The number and specific types of factors needed depend upon the kinds of tasks—motor skills, verbal learning, concept learning and so forth—used in a particular study. In short, we may say that since there is no single learning ability it is inappropriate to interpret an I.Q. score as reflective of that ability. The fact that one person learns a task more quickly than a second person does not mean that their learning rates will be comparable when these people are faced with a different task. A mechanically minded student might learn how to operate a complex piece of machinery more rapidly than an academically oriented counterpart, yet lag considerably behind the academic friend when it comes to learning French.

It should be noted that I.Q. scores correlate significantly with measures of *school* learning. Tests fashioned in the Binet tradition are still effective in identifying children who have difficulties achieving in traditional schools. We must note that this fact does not necessarily imply that level of intelligence is the causal factor determining level of achievement. One could reverse the argument and say that the more a child achieves in school the higher his or her I.Q. will tend to be. In fact, children who learn more in school do tend to increase their tested intelligence over several years. The important point for our purposes is not which, if either, of these variables is the cause of the other as no final answer is possible. Rather, it is important to know there is some moderately strong relationship between the two variables. This means that knowing an individual's level of intelligence will allow us to predict with some degree of accuracy the level of academic achievement, and vice versa.

Up to this point in our discussion we have not explicitly questioned using a single I.Q. score as an adequate measure of an individual's intelligence. Most psychologists would say that a single I.Q. score requires considerable amplification and qualification in order to present an accurate assessment of an individual's potential. As Leo Kamin and others have stressed, for certain ethnic and racial minority groups I.Q. scores cannot be considered valid measures of intellectual potential. In addition, a single number should not be taken as an adequate representation of any individual's intellectual abilities. Humans are simply too complex for a single score to be representative, and it is necessary to focus on tests of special abilities as well as on general intelligence. Psychologists such as L. L. Thurstone and J. P. Guilford have long researched the area of tests of special abilities. As one of the first psychologists to use factor analysis techniques, Thurstone initially identified seven factors or special abilities which he referred to as the Primary Mental Abilities. Although these have been elaborated on by others, the number of primary mental abilities has never approached the one hundred twenty independent abilities hypothesized by Guilford in his structure of the intellect model. Certain of these abilities may be thought of as vocational aptitudes. For example, Thurstone's spatial thinking factor may be interpreted as a measure of the mechanical aptitude required for many jobs in an industrialized society. A final comment that should be made regarding these special abilities is that, although they are distinct, they tend to correlate with general intelligence to a certain extent.

Although tests based on factor analyses have found extensive use in classification and assignment of personnel to jobs in military and industrial settings, until recently these tests had not been employed to any significant degree by experimental psychologists interested in learning and memory. The renewed interest in memory and cognition, stressed repeatedly in this book, has prompted some investigators to wonder how such processes are related to the underlying abilities identified by psychometric tests. For example, John Carroll and William Estes have each attempted to analyze psychometric tests in terms of the cognitive processes required by the various subtests of psychometric tests. Such efforts indicate promise of constructive interaction between individual difference psychology and experimental psychology which in the past have been viewed as quite separate disciplines.

Cognitive Styles

Closely related to the problem of aptitude for learning is cognitive style. An individual's aptitude may be viewed as indicating a level of intellectual performance, whereas *cognitive style* refers to the manner of performance or how one attacks intellectual tasks. For example, individuals differ in their preferences for, or ability to learn from, specific sensory modalities. Some people learn best from written materials, while others learn more efficiently from auditory processing of the same content via lectures or videotapes.

Another example of a cognitive style variable related to performance is that of reflection/impulsivity. Individual differences along this dimension are assessed by a perceptual task called the matching familiar figures test which requires choosing the one of six very similar drawings which is exactly like a target figure. Only a minute detail in the figures distinguishes the right and wrong answers. Measures of response time for each individual are taken as well as accuracy scores. Persons who are slower than average and who make fewer errors than average are classified *reflectives,* whereas persons scoring above average in speed of responding and in number of errors are classified *impulsives*. Although this classification does include most test takers, it does not include all. Some individuals make many errors even though they go slowly, while other individuals are able to work quite quickly through the task without making many errors.

Research on impulsives and reflectives has focused primarily on elementary school children. In that age range, reflective children are found to obtain higher scores on measures of intelligence and school achievement. Also, children who fail one of the first three grades tend to be impulsive. Thus, some have hypothesized that individual differences in tempo of responding may underlie the difficulty some children have in school learning.

A question of great interest is to what extent cognitive styles are modifiable and to what extent changing someone's style will bring about changes in other behaviors. Preliminary results have been encouraging. For example, simply requiring children to wait several seconds before responding to questions from an intelligence test results in significant gains in performance.

Numerous other cognitive styles have been suggested and investigated. For example, differentiations in style have been made based on the extent to which an individual reacts to a complex stimulus as a whole rather than on analyzation of component parts (field dependence and field independence) and the extent to which an individual tends to ignore changes in incoming stimulation over time (leveling and sharpening). What is typically found is that a person's cognitive style is related not only to how he learns, but also to significant decisions such as choice of a vocation or college major.

Learning Strategies

In addition to differences in relatively global characteristics that influence learning, an important determinant of an individual's performance on a given task is the specific strategy adopted for that task. Different strategies have been extensively investigated in various learning and memory tasks.

In paired associate learning, for example, different strategies are typically discussed under the rubric of mediation or elaboration techniques. One of two methods is typically used for studying individual differences in this context: the subjects in the experiment either are simply queried as to the strategy they use or are given explicit instructions to use a specific strategy and differences in their ability to implement that strategy are noted. In the former procedure, possible strategies are typically specified by the experimenter prior to the start of the experiment and are ranked according to their degree of complexity. For example, in paired associate learning, a strategy which requires construction of a sentence linking the stimulus and response term might be ranked as the most complex strategy, while rote repetition might be viewed as requiring the least processing by the subject and thus be ranked least complex. The basic finding is that subjects who report on the average using more complex strategies tend to perform better on the paired associate task.

Studies using the second procedure have attempted to determine the effects of instructions to use a particular type of strategy on different individuals' learning. Frequently, imagery and verbal mediation strategies have been compared with each other and with instructions to use rote repetition. Both imagery or verbal mediation instruction result in significantly faster learning than rote instructions and no specific instructions. Imagery instructions also seem to have a greater impact than verbal instructions, although the effect is small relative to the difference between either of these and the other conditions. Discussion of studies which have combined these instructional treatments with assessments of individual difference variables are considered in the next section.

Individual differences in strategies in free recall have also been investigated recently. From the earlier discussions of verbal learning and memory, you can probably anticipate that an important difference among subjects in this type of task is their ability to subjectively organize material. Not only are people who subjectively organize material in free recall superior to those who do not in terms of number of words recalled in a free recall task, but their performance is also superior in paired associate learning, serial learning, and recognition memory tasks.

As mentioned in the chapter on concept learning, individual differences among learners have an impact on the rate with which such learning occurs. The selection of different strategies used in this context, such as conservative focusing and focus gambling, is related to the subject's memory ability and general intelligence. The selection paradigm for concept learning is typically employed to observe the use of these qualitatively different strategies.

Memory Ability

Individuals differ not only in their ability to acquire information, but also in their ability to retain whatever information they do acquire. Within the last few years, psychologists have begun to investigate these differences in memory ability and to relate these differences to measures of intelligence. Some of the most interesting of this work has been done by a team of researchers headed by Earl Hunt, an experimental psychologist, and Clifford Lunneborg, a psychometrician. The basic approach taken by Hunt and Lunneborg has been to test college students on a variety of memory tasks. The students are selected for inclusion in the study on the basis of their extreme scores on intelligence tests. They define this as students who are in the top fourth or bottom fourth of their class in both composite verbal and composite quantitative scores on a battery of entrance examinations. Hunt and Lunneborg's studies revealed two basic findings, one concerning the implications of differences in verbal ability and the other concerning the quite different implications of variations in quantitative ability. Basically, the distinction seems to be in the type of memory functions to which these abilities are related.

First, high *verbal* ability typically implies greater efficiency of short-term memory. For example, consider what happens when subjects are presented with a set of digits and are then asked after a very brief delay whether a particular digit is in the memory set or not. (This is basically the Sternberg paradigm mentioned in the discussion of reaction time as a method of studying memory in chapter 4.) High- and low-quantitative-ability subjects do not differ in how rapidly they answer in this task. However, high-verbal-ability subjects have significantly faster reaction times (or faster search rates) than low-verbal-ability subjects. This fact, together with similar findings in a number of other tasks, suggests that high verbal ability is associated with greater speed of information processing, particularly in situations emphasizing short-term memory.

Second, high *quantitative* ability typically implies greater resistance to forgetting caused by interference. For example, consider performance on the Peterson and Peterson task, which is used to assess the effects of a distracting task on short-term memory. Relative to low-quantitative subjects, high-quantitative subjects demonstrate much higher recall of the information which was presented prior to the distracting task. This resistance to interference also shows up on tasks requiring long-term retention of information. For example, although verbal ability is the better predictor of how long it will take to acquire the verbal information typically used in these tasks, it is quantitative ability which does the better job of predicting how much of this information will be retained five weeks later. Thus, by knowing a person's verbal ability, you can estimate that person's learning rate, while knowledge of quantitative ability allows an estimate of retention.

These results are of interest because the intelligence tests and the cognitive tasks used here are quite different in their demands on the subject. This is particularly striking in the case of verbal ability. The questions on college entrance examinations used to assess verbal ability basically pertain to the content of long-term memory. For example, like most standardized tests, there are questions concerning the definition of words and the content of prose passages. Basically, these tests are probing the content of long-term memory. In contrast the cognitive tasks, on which high- and low-verbal subjects differ, depend primarily upon the rate of processing of information in short-term memory, rather than upon specific information stored in long-term memory. One could hypothesize, though it is by no means proved, that it is this more efficient processing of incoming information by high-verbal subjects which results in their apparently larger base of knowledge in long-term memory.

Unusually Good Memory

Before leaving the topic of individual differences in memory ability, let us briefly consider the incredibly good memory possessed by a very few individuals. At least two such individuals have been extensively observed by psychologists. One of these, referred to as VP, was tested on the tasks we have been discussing. This work was also reported by Earl Hunt and colleague Tom Love. Perhaps the best known "mnemonist," though, is S who was observed for more than twenty-five years by the Russian psychologist A. R. Luria. Amazingly, both VP and S were reared in the same region of the same eastern European country.

Both VP and S performed unbelievable memory feats, yet they do so in quite different ways. For example, both VP and S were capable of memorizing a matrix of forty-eight numbers in a very few minutes and then reciting it rapidly either forward or backward, column by column or row by row. Luria's S did so by forming a mental picture from which he could read the numbers at will. In fact, S's memory was entirely dependent on imagery. Frequently he would remember lists of words using the method of loci, visualizing the object referred to by each word in front of successive houses on a familiar street. Luria reported that one of the few memory errors S made involved being unable to recall the word *snowball* in a serial list. S explained that when initially presented the list he had visualized the object in front of a house with a white fence. When he scanned his memory he had been unable to see the snowball against the white background!

On the other hand, VP reported very little imagery ability and in fact failed one memory test which required imaging patterns of dots. Nonetheless, VP was able to play as many as sixty games of chess by correspondence without consulting written records. He explained that he did not attempt to visualize the chessboard, but instead remembered the function of every piece involved in the game.

As you can imagine, such near-perfect memory is not without disadvantages. Luria's S was not able to determine if something should be forgotten rather than remembered and was thus somewhat disorganized and distracted by trivial details. VP's reported personal problems were not as serious as S's. Although his verbatim recall of conversations was not always a blessing, VP was able to capitalize on his memory in learning multiple foreign languages and in attracting crowds to exhibitions in which he played several simultaneous chess games, blindfolded.

Attribute-by-Treatment Interactions

A major concern of most research on individual differences in learning has been the practical implications of such work. While it is true that differences in how people learn are of theoretical importance, in that they place limits on the laws of learning, these differences can be of crucial significance in practical situations where the concern is to optimize what an individual learns.

It seems intuitively plausible that in practical educational situations a learner will do better when working on materials whose characteristics are matched with the learner's own characteristics than when they are mismatched. This notion lies at the core of individualized instruction. When in fact different learners perform more efficiently under different conditions, an *attribute-by-treatment interaction* (ATI) is said to occur.

Let us spend a moment analyzing the components of an ATI. First, *attribute* refers to any individual difference measure of the learner. For example, cognitive style and preferred sensory modality are attributes that have been investigated by ATI research. Perhaps most frequently, though, the attribute refers to a specific aptitude such as verbal ability. Second, the treatment in ATI research can most frequently be interpreted to mean the specific method of instruction such as programmed instruction or traditional classroom instruction. Finally, *interaction* has a statistical meaning which corresponds roughly to the common meaning of the word. Here, interaction means that the effect of a specific treatment is different in different types of learners, that is, in learners possessing different attributes.

This ATI research may be viewed as an attempt to integrate the two disciplines of individual difference and experimental psychology just mentioned. Individual difference psychologists have been concerned only with attributes by themselves and have developed an elaborate methodology of mental testing and factor analysis. Experimental psychologists, on the other hand, have frequently viewed differences among individuals as a nuisance or as "error variance" which is to be reduced as much as possible. Individual variation for the experimentalist is an indication that perfect control of behavior has not been achieved; the various treatments do not totally determine performance. ATI research involves the simultaneous investigation of attributes and treatments and as such represents the concession, first, by differential psychologists that treatment variation, as well as individual variation, is important and, second, by experimentalists that the performance of the average student may not be representative of individuals.

What then has been discovered by ATI research? It must be acknowledged that a relatively modest proportion of the research efforts designed to investigate ATI has actually obtained evidence for the hypothesized interactions. However, several examples of ATI can be cited. Several studies have addressed the issue of the possible interaction of the cognitive style dimension mentioned previously of field dependence and field independence with various treatments. Some of the most interesting work has evaluated the implications of matching or mismatching teacher-student pairs. Students who are placed in classrooms with teachers of similar cognitive styles tend to describe each other very positively along dimensions of attraction, competence, and desirability of personal characteristics. Students and teachers who are mismatched, that is, have different cognitive styles, evaluate each other negatively along these dimensions.

One of the factors underlying these differences in subjective evaluation seems to be subtle differences in communication mode which interfere with attempts to learn from an individual of a different cognitive style. For example, consider a perceptual discrimination task where the subject is required to select one photograph from a set of photographs on the basis of a verbal description from another subject. Subjects receiving descriptions from other subjects of the same cognitive style perform significantly better than those subjects receiving descriptions from subjects of different cognitive styles. That is, field-dependent subjects who have the target photograph described by field-dependent subjects, as well as field-independent subjects who receive descriptions from field-independent subjects, are able to identify the right photograph significantly more often than subjects of either cognitive style who receive descriptions from someone of the opposite cognitive style. Thus, research seems to support the commonly held belief that different students learn more efficiently from different teachers. It should be mentioned, however, that not all educators recommend the matching of students and teachers simply on the basis of cognitive styles, even if this could be easily implemented. Although matching may lead to faster learning, the answer is less clear to the more general question of whether exposure to alternative styles is desirable. Indeed there is some evidence that stimulus variability is desirable from an educational viewpoint, in that exposure to different stimuli (instructional procedures) enhances understanding, as well as adaptability to new situations.

Another area of ATI research that has received considerable attention recently has to do with the interaction of learning or mediation strategies with certain special abilities. Although there is little overall difference between the effects of instructions to use imagery mediation and instructions to use verbal mediation strategies, such difference is not the case when one considers separately subjects of different ability groupings. One approach to the problem has been to attempt to isolate tests which will assess the abilities required by different mediation strategies. The specific tests used have typically been taken from batteries of tests developed by people like Thurstone and Guilford to measure specific intellectual abilities. For example, typical tests used to measure imagery ability require subjects to visualize the rotation in space of certain geometrical forms. One test presents pictures of flat sheets of paper with lines and the test taker has to determine what three-dimensional figure would emerge if the sheet were folded along the lines.

The tests of verbal ability which have been used are more directly related to standard verbal learning tasks. To illustrate, an experimenter might attempt to assess subjects' verbal fluency by asking them to list as many synonyms as possible for each of a set of common words.

A detailed analysis of the results would indicate certain exceptions to the following rule. However, the general finding is that imagery ability interacts with type of mediation instructions, as does verbal fluency. Although you might think that the mediation instructions would serve a remediation function and have their greatest effect on subjects low in that ability, this is *not* the basic finding. Instead, the tests do assess one's ability to employ a particular strategy when instructed to do so. Thus, high-imagery-ability subjects perform much better, for example, in paired associate learning tasks when told to use imagery mediation than when told to use verbal mediation. Just the reverse is true for subjects who are low relatively speaking in imagery ability. An analogous result holds for individual differences in verbal fluency.

These and other aptitude-by-treatment interactions are of potentially great importance in educational settings. For example, it has been found that instructing elementary school children to "make up pictures in their minds" as they read a story generally improves their recall of the content of the story. However, closer examination reveals that the technique is effective only for those students who are high in imagery ability. Individualized systems of instruction can greatly improve the typical level of performance of a class by adapting these differences in students' abilities to learn, using alternative strategies.

Summary

In this chapter we have discussed the role individual differences play in learning and memory. The study of individual differences was introduced as the study of traits, and the long history of efforts in the area was sketched. The notions of reliability and validity were introduced as key concepts in the assessment of individual differences. The methodology used to investigate these differences was characterized generally as emphasizing mental testing, as being empirically oriented, and as being rigorously quantitative.

Next, four specific types of variations among people which determine performance in learning and memory tasks were selected for discussion. First, differences in I.Q. scores, while related to school learning, were said *not* to predict how quickly a person will learn every task. Intelligence was also viewed as a multifaceted concept involving several different dimensions. Second, cognitive styles were introduced as a modus operandi for attacking intellectual tasks. Third, certain specific learning strategies which typify how different individuals approach verbal learning and concept learning tasks were mentioned. Finally, individual differences in memory ability were described. Differences between high- and low-verbal subjects and high- and low-quantitative subjects, as well as two individuals with extraordinary memory, were considered.

An attribute-by-treatment interaction was said to describe any situation where different individuals learn more efficiently under different conditions. The fact that such research represents an integration of differential and experimental psychology was noted. Finally, two examples of attribute-by-treatment interactions were discussed, the first involving differences in cognitive styles and the second concerning differents in learning strategies.

Multiple-Choice Items:
Individual Differences in Learning and in Memory

1. The approach taken in this chapter emphasizes that individual differences
    a. are unimportant in most situations
    b. have been studied only in the last ten years
    c. are the major variable in studies of learning and memory
    d. are generally present in some amount
2. The modern study of individual differences focuses on the study of
    a. types
    b. traits
    c. the gifted
    d. the mentally deficient
3. Three features of the individual-difference approach to psychology were described. Which feature was *not* mentioned?
    a. empirical orientation
    b. emphasis on mental testing
    c. quantitative emphasis
    d. biological determinism
4. A test is said to be *reliable* if
    a. it correlates well with some real-world performance measure
    b. it correlates well with another administration of the test
    c. scores from the test correlate high with I.Q. scores
    d. it correlates zero with another form of the test
5. The fact that individuals may differ in their general approach to intellectual tasks refers to
    a. cognitive style
    b. intelligence

    c.   emotion
    d.   memory

6.   Subjects with high-quantitative ability have been noted to show
    a.   faster reaction time
    b.   photographic memory
    c.   efficient short-term memory
    d.   greater resistance to forgetting

7.   In the study of attribute-by-treatment interactions, the term *attribute* refers to
    a.   some trait of the person
    b.   an experimental factor manipulated
    c.   a feature of the experimental task
    d.   some measure of intelligence

8.   Measures of intelligence are best seen as
    a.   measures of general learning ability
    b.   exclusively the result of inheritance
    c.   predictors of academic success
    d.   predictors of job success

True-False Items:
Individual Differences in Learning and in Memory

1.   The contemporary study of individual differences sorts people into types.
2.   The scientific study of individual differences is of very recent origin.
3.   Early studies of individual differences focused on sensory-motor capacities.
4.   Validity of a test refers to how well it predicts some real-world performance.
5.   Intelligence is best defined as the ability to learn.
6.   Students characterized as reflective tend to be slower in responding to test problems on a perceptual task.
7.   Subjects classified as high in verbal ability typically show greater speed of processing information.
8.   Luria's subject S showed poor mental imagery.
9.   It is the general rule that low-imagery subjects show greater gains in performance than high-imagery subjects when instructed to use imagery mediation.
10.   The different mediational approaches a person might take in a learning task are called learning strategies.

Discussion Items:
Individual Differences in Learning and in Memory

1. Why is the trait concept more useful than the notion of types?

2. A reliable test is not necessarily valid, but a valid test must be reliable. Why?

3. Discuss some of the uses and limitations of intelligence tests.

4. How might differences in cognitive styles of instructors and students affect the performance of students in specific courses such as English, mathematics, science, and history?

5. Speculate on how an unusually good memory might be disadvantageous as well as advantageous.

6. Speculate on how individual differences in cognitive styles might arise.

Multiple-Choice Answers:
Individual Differences in Learning and in Memory

1. (d)   The emphasis has been that individual differences are usually present to some degree or amount.

2. (b)   The focus is on traits because a trait is something which varies along some dimension.

3. (d)   Biological determinism was not a feature described.

4. (b)   Reliability means consistency; thus, a reliable test is one which correlates well with another administration of the same test.

5. (a)   Differences in modes of attack on intellectual tasks refers to cognitive styles.

6. (d)   High-quantitative subjects show greater resistance to forgetting. They are less subject to interference from distraction tasks typically used in short-term memory.

7. (a)   An attribute simply refers to some trait or characteristic of the person.

8. (c)   Intelligence test scores are best viewed as predictors of school success.

True-False Answers:
Individual Differences in Learning and in Memory

1. (False)   The current approach focuses on traits, not on types.

2. (False)   The scientific study of individual differences began in the middle-1800s.

3. (True)   Early studies of individual differences did focus on

sensory-motor capabilities, whereas later investigations shifted to intellectual functioning and cognitive abilities.

4.   (True)   A test is said to be valid if it predicts real-world performance. For example, if a test of clerical aptitude predicts performance in clerical tasks then the test is valid.

5.   (False)   Tests of intelligence do not do a good job of measuring learning ability, in part because there are several different kinds of learning ability.

6.   (True)   Reflective students are somewhat slower in these kinds of tests.

7.   (True)   In general, high-verbal ability is associated with greater speed of information processing.

8.   (False)   On the contrary, Luria's subject showed excellent mental imagery.

9.   (False)   It is the case that high-imagery subjects show the greatest benefit from instructions to use imagery mediation.

10.   (True)   Differences in mediational approaches or elaboration techniques are called learning strategies.

Concluding Remarks

13

The objective of this book has been to present an elementary but coherent picture of the current state of human learning, memory, and cognition. It was written with the conviction that students can be introduced to these areas of knowledge through a systematic oversimplification so that the essential principles of human learning, memory and cognition are revealed in bold relief. This approach means that many nuances, details, and qualifications are left untouched. Nevertheless, it is my belief that students will gain from having a framework of principles on which details and qualifications may be attached in their subsequent learning. Indeed, without some kind of organizational framework, it would be difficult to integrate new facts and ideas about human learning, memory, and cognition.

This book attempts to bridge the gap between the old and new in human learning, memory, and cognition. The traditional and well-developed topics of human learning must be integrated with the newly developing topics. The area of human learning, memory, and cognition is rapidly changing, and this book should therefore be viewed as an attempt to describe the current state of these areas as distinct from any final description. Thus, in some sense this book must be regarded as a momentary state-of-the-science report rather than as a final picture of these areas.

Despite the attempt at simplification, enabling students to obtain a reasonably coherent picture of human learning, memory, and cognition, an effort has also been made to provide students with an image of the vitality, controversy, and excitement in these areas. Old views are being revised, new views are still emerging, and mergers of the old and new are in various stages of progress. The psychology of human learning, memory, and cognition has begun to come of age, freed from the constraints of a narrow behavioristic psychology of the forties. Mental imagery, organizational process, storage and retrieval systems, search processes, and strategies all attest to a growing concern for the fact that human beings can think. More generally, there is a strong renewed interest in the *cognitive* capacities of the human organism and a willingness of psychologists to grapple with the complex process of human behavior.

In no sense, however, does a cognitive revolution (or renaissance?) imply that older established concepts of human learning must be rejected. Concepts such as generalization, discrimination, mediation, and interference, developed within the framework of a more traditional psychology, are very much alive and useful and may well be integrated within the framework of the new cognitive psychology. Indeed, psychologists such as Patrick Suppes have indicated that it is possible to deal with complex cognitive processes in terms of stimulus-response conceptions without resort to more complex theoretical processes. The issue is not, however, a matter of whether stimulus-response or cognitive conceptions of behavior are correct, true, or more meaningful, but rather which set of conceptions will more efficiently account for the facts of human behavior. These issues, which lie principally in the domain of theory, have been largely bypassed in this introductory treatment. Theoretical controversy is to be resolved in terms of how well given theories handle the data of learning, memory, and cognition, not in terms of how intuitively appealing they may appear. These issues are left, however, for future study by students.

What does emerge is a vigorous psychology of human learning, memory, and cognition, a psychology that examines a wide range of human capabilities. Psychologists are busy exploring the panorama of activities from human conditioning to problem solving and thinking in an effort to discover regularities and lawfulness in behavior. Moreover, there is an active concern with the applicability of these principles and regularities to problems of everyday life. This enterprise is one of continuous development and evolution, and it can be expected to move in new directions, prodded by the stimulus of new research findings and new theoretical conceptions.

Glossary

Accommodation: Process underlying cognitive development in which the cognitive structure itself is altered so that it can better incorporate new information.

All-or-none principle: Principle which asserts that verbal associations gain their entire strength in a particular trial or none at all.

Assimilation: Process underlying cognitive development in which new information is taken in and interpreted so that it is consistent with an existing cognitive structure.

Associative stage: In verbal learning the stage in which particular responses become hooked up with particular stimuli; sometimes referred to as the hook-up stage.

Attention: The ability to focus selectively on some parts of the environment while ignoring other aspects.

Attribute: Feature or characteristic of a stimulus. In concept learning, attribute refers to some stimulus feature related to the concept.

Backward association: An association formed, as in paired associate learning, between a response and a stimulus item so that the response item acquires some tendency to elicit the stimulus item.

Behavior modification: An approach to therapy based upon principles of conditioning and learning.

Buffer model: An information-processing model of memory which assumes that information is held in an active state in the rehearsal buffer prior to being transferred to the long-term memory store.

Clustering: One instance of an organizational process; the tendency to order or organize items during recall into some grouping or sequence that differs from the order present during original learning.

Coding: The process by which an item is transformed into some modified or new representation.

Cognition: A class of processes that refer to symbolic, mental, and hence inferred events. Cognition refers to such processes as thinking, problem solving, concept learning, and reasoning, those activities emphasizing the active role of the learner.

Cognitive development: The process of intellectual growth with emphasis on language, thought, conceptual behavior, and problem-solving skills.

Cognitive theory: A class of theories which deals with knowing and understanding. Emphasis is placed on the learning of rules, strategies, and principles.

Concept: A class of stimuli or events that share in one or more common characteristics.

Concept learning: Any activity in which a learner must learn to classify or categorize two or more somewhat different events or objects as members of a common class.

Conceptual rule: Rule or principle by which attributes are combined in conceptual tasks.

Conditioning, classical: A procedure in which an initially neutral stimulus, a conditioned stimulus, is paired with an unconditioned stimulus so that the conditioned stimulus comes to elicit a response normally elicited by the unconditioned stimulus.

Conditioning, instrumental: A procedure in which the learning of a response is contingent upon reinforcement. The response is not freely available because discrete-trial procedures are used.

Conditioning, operant: A procedure in which the subject is allowed to respond freely, the rate of occurrence depending upon how reinforcement is scheduled.

Constructive processes: The tendency of human beings to construct or reconstruct information in memory, altering the information to make it more consistent with some schema.

Contiguity: Condition in which two or more events occur together in time or space.

Decay theory: A theory of forgetting which contends that forgetting is due to some autonomous decay of memory traces.

Deep structure: The meaning of a sentence.

Detection: The report of the presence or absence of a stimulus contingent upon its presentation.

Discrimination: Perceptual task in which the subject reports the perception of a difference between two stimuli (*see also* Stimulus discrimination).

Encoding: The process by which material to be learned is placed in some state such that its storage is possible.

Extinction: The reduction in the strength of a response following nonreinforcement of the response.

Feedback, extrinsic: External knowledge of results given to a learner following his response.

Feedback, intrinsic: Responses by the organism that produce stimuli which are fed back into the organism.

Forgetting: The amount of material that is inaccessible after some retention interval.

Forgetting, cue-dependent: Forgetting due to the loss of cue effectiveness.

Forgetting, trace-dependent: Forgetting due to weakening of the memory trace.

Forward association: An association formed, as in paired associate learning, between a stimulus and a response item as evidenced by the tendency of that stimulus to elicit its response mate.

Free recall: Task requiring the learner to recall the items in any order.

Generalization, response: The tendency to make response similar to the response learned in the conditioning session.

Generalization, stimulus: The tendency to respond to stimuli similar to the training stimulus employed in conditioning.

Human associative memory: An associative network model of long-term memory in which the basic unit of memory is the proposition.

Identification: A perceptual task in which the observer makes an identifying (labeling) response appropriate to some stimulus.

Imagery: Process in which we represent information in some perceptual-sensory mode.

Incremental principle: Principle that verbal or other associations gain associative strength gradually over a series of trials.

Information-processing approach: An approach which views the human as an active processor of information. Information is thought to flow through the memory system.

Interference theory: A theory of forgetting which contends that events are forgotten because other learning interferes with or prevents these events from being remembered.

Judgment: A perceptual task in which the observer orders or ranks stimuli along some scale.

Learning: A relatively permanent process that is inferred from performance changes due to practice.

Learning to learn: A progressive improvement in the ease with which some new task is learned as a result of practice with a series of related tasks.

Levels of processing: Principle that the degree, or depth, to which information is processed determines its accessibility in memory.

Linguistic relativity hypothesis: Hypothesis proposed by Benjamin Whorf contending that the structure of man's language leads one to conceive of the world in a particular way.

Meaningfulness: Scaled property of verbal materials which predicts the ease with which materials are learned. Refers to the number of associations elicited by an item in some standard period of time.

Mediation: The process by which organisms link items by way of implicit verbal responses.

Memory, codes: The stored representation of some event in memory.

Memory, long-term: A more permanent system of memory in which the information stored has been rehearsed or processed in some fashion so that it remains more accessible.

Memory, semantic: The study of our "natural memories," that is, memory of semantic events.

Memory, sensory: The brief period in memory in which a stimulus trace persists.

Memory, short-term: Limited-capacity system of memory in which items must be processed in some way or they drop out of the memory system.

Memory, working: An active system of memory where information is assembled and organized prior to recall.

Morpheme: Smallest meaningful unit in a language, consisting of two or more phonemes (*see also* Phoneme).

Motor skills learning: Any learning activity in which the learner must make a series of precise motor responses or learn to coordinate perceptual input with motor responses (sometimes called perceptual motor learning).

Negative instance: Any instance or example that does not represent the concept in question.

Organizational processes: Those activities engaged in by human beings which involve some kind of restructuring of the materials to be learned.

Paired associate learning: Verbal learning task in which stimulus and response terms become associated.

Partial reinforcement effect: The principle that resistance to extinction is greater following partial reinforcement rather than continuous reinforcement.

Perception: An inferred process in which changes in performance such as detection, discrimination, recognition, identification, and judgment are produced by changes in stimulus energy conditions.

Perceptual learning: Various changes in perception that are due to or brought about by learning.

Phoneme: Basic unit of language consisting of a fundamental vowel or consonant sound.

Phrase structure: Structural feature of a sentence consisting of a noun phrase and a verb phrase.

Positive instance: Any instance or example that represents the particular concept in question.

Proactive inhibition: The forgetting of some currently learned material produced by interference from some previously learned material.

Programmed instruction: Instructional technology in which material to be learned is broken into small steps called frames. Learner must respond to each frame and is given immediate knowledge of results.

Recall: A measure of memory in which you produce the required response(s).

Recognition: A measure of memory in which you select items that are familiar and reject items that are unfamiliar .

Recognition learning: Learning task requiring a subject to recognize items.

Rehearsal: The repeating of some information to yourself.

Rehearsal buffer: A function of the short-term memory system which maintains information.

Rehearsal, elaborative: The repeating of information to yourself, with an effort to elaborate or embellish the information.

Reinforcer, positive: Any event which increases the likelihood of a response when it is presented.

Reinforcer, negative: Any event which increases the likelihood of a response when it is removed.

Reinforcer, secondary: An event that functions as a reward by being associated with primary reinforcing events.

Response bias: Preferences or response tendencies that subjects have prior to entering an experiment or that they may develop during an experiment.

Response chain: A sequence of motor responses in which one response serves as a stimulus for the next response.

Response competition: The tendency of responses acquired during original and interpolated learning and attached to identical (or similar) stimuli to remain available and compete with each other at the time of recall.

Response differentiation: The process by which a response, or particular aspect of a response such as speed or force, becomes strengthened through differential reinforcement.

Response learning stage: In verbal learning, the stage in paired associate learning in which the responses becomes recallable or available as units.

Retention: The amount of material still retained after some retention interval.

Retrieval: Process of getting events out of memory storage.

Retrieval cues: Stimuli that humans use to help in retrieving information.

Retroactive inhibition: Process in which an event learned during a retention interval causes some forgetting of a previously learned event.

Savings: A measure of memory in which you are required to relearn some task.

Schema learning: Learning in which the human acquires some central tendency or average representation of some group of stimuli.

Serial learning: Verbal learning task in which the units are presented in the same order from trial to trial.

Serial position effect: The tendency to make the largest number of errors just beyond the middle of a serial list and fewest at the beginning and end of the serial list and the learner must learn the particular order.

Similarity: Degree to which materials possess common elements (formal similarity) or are meaningfully or conceptually related.

Solution shifts: A type of discrimination-learning problem in which the relevant cues are shifted or changed in the second phase of the task.

Spontaneous recovery: A response that reoccurs some time after an extinction session.

Stimulus coding: The process of changing some nominal stimulus into some new state or representation.

Stimulus discrimination: The process in verbal learning of learning to distinguish among the stimulus terms of a list; in conditioning, the process of learnng to respond differently to somewhat similar stimuli (*see also* Discrimination).

Stimulus selection: The tendency of humans to select only a part of a nominally presented stimulus and use it to cue a response.

Storage: Process by which materials are placed in memory and held.

Subjective organization: Tendency of humans to organize verbal materials in accord with some self-developed mode of organization.

Surface structure: Property of a sentence referring to the sentence as it is sounded.

Thinking: A class of covert activities involving manipulation and use of symbols and concepts.

Transfer, cross-modal: Transfer which occurs when learning in one sensory system carries over to another sensory system.

Transfer, general: Transfer effects due to learning to learn and warm-up.

Transfer paradigm: A schematic or shorthand description of the task relationships in a transfer study.

Transfer of response learning: Source of positive transfer due to the responses having become available.

Transfer, specific: Transfer effects due to specific features or properties of the task relationships.

Transfer of stimulus discrimination: Source of positive transfer as a result of discrimination among the stimulus terms.

Transfer of training: The influence of prior learning on the learning of some new task.

Transformational grammar: A way of relating the deep structure of a sentence to its surface structure.

Unlearning: The loss or weakening of first-list associations during the learning of a second list. Now viewed as list suppression.

Verbal conditioning: An operant conditioning procedure applied to verbal behavior. A verbal response or response class is selectively reinforced, thus strengthening the response.

Verbal learning: Any learning situation in which the task requires the learner to respond to verbal stimulus materials or to respond with verbal responses.

Warm-up: The transitory facilitation in learning some task as the result of prior practice with another task.

Suggested Readings for Further Study

Adams, J. A. *Learning and memory.* Homewood, Ill.: Dorsey, 1976.

Anderson, J. R., and Bower, G. H. *Human associative memory.* Washington, D.C.: Winston, 1973.

Bourne, L. E., Ekstrand, B. R., and Dominowski, R. L. *The psychology of thinking.* Englewood Cliffs, N.J.: Prentice-Hall, 1971.

Brown, J. (Ed.) *Recall and recognition.* New York: Wiley, 1976.

Crowder, R. G. *Principles of learning and memory.* Hillsdale, N.J.: Erlbaum, 1976.

Deese, J. *Psycholinguistics.* New York: Allyn & Bacon, 1970.

Ellis, H. C. *The transfer of learning.* New York: Macmillan, 1965.

Gibson, E. J. *Principles of perceptual learning and development.* New York: Appleton-Century-Crofts, 1969.

Hulse, S. H., Deese, J., and Egeth, H. *The psychology of learning.* New York: McGraw-Hill, 1975.

Kausler, D. H. *Psychology of verbal learning and memory.* New York: Academic, 1974.

Logan, F. A. *Fundamentals of learning and motivation.* Dubuque, Iowa: Brown, 1976.

Marx, M. H. (Ed.) *Learning: Processes.* New York: Macmillan, 1969.

Marx, M. H., and Bunch, M. E. *Fundamentals and applications of learning.* New York: Macmillan, 1977.

Melton, A. W., and Martin, E. (Eds.) *Coding processes in human memory.* New York: Winston, 1972.

Murdock, B. B., Jr. *Human memory: Theory and data.* Hillsdale, N.J.: Erlbaum, 1974.

Norman, D. A. *Memory and attention.* New York: Wiley, 1976.

Norman, D. A., and Rumelhart (Eds.) *Explorations in cognition.* San Francisco: Freeman, 1975.

Paivio, A. *Imagery and verbal processes.* New York: Holt, Rinehart and Winston, 1971.

Tulving, E., and Donaldson, W. *Organization of memory.* New York: Academic, 1972.

References

Introduction To Human Learning, Memory, And Cognition

Types of human learning

Melton, A. W. (Ed.) *Categories of human learning.* New York: Wiley, 1964.

Representative texts

Anderson, B. F. *Cognitive psychology.* New York: Academic, 1975.
Horton, D. L., and Turnage, T. W. *Human learning.* Englewood Cliffs, N.J.: Prentice-Hall, 1976.
Kintsch, W. *Learning, memory, and conceptual processes.* New York: Wiley, 1970.
Klatzky, R. L. *Human memory.* San Francisco: Freeman, 1975.
Saltz, E. *The cognitive bases of human learning.* Homewood, Ill.: Dorsey, 1971.

Theoretical issues

Boneau, A. Paradigm regained? Cognitive behaviorism restated. *American Psychologist,* 1974, *29,* 297-309.
Segal, E. M., and Lachman, R. Complex behavior or higher mental process: Is there a paradigm shift? *American Psychologist,* 1972, *27,* 46-55.
Seligman, M. E. P. On the generality of the laws of learning. *Psychological Review,* 1970, *77,* 406-418.
Solso, R. L. (Ed.) *Contemporary issues in cognitive psychology: The Loyola Symposium.* Washington, D.C.: Winston, 1973.
Solso, R. L. (Ed.) *Theories in cognitive psychology: The Loyola Symposium.* Washington, D.C.: Winston, 1974.

Elements of Conditioning

General

D'Amato, M. R. Instrumental conditioning. In M. H. Marx (Ed.), *Learning: Processes.* New York: Macmillan, 1969, pp. 35-118.

Gormezano, I., and Moore, J. W. Classical conditioning. In M. H. Marx (Ed.), *Learning: Processes.* New York: Macmillan, 1969, pp. 121-123.

Grant, D. A. Classical and operant conditioning. In A. W. Melton (Ed.), *Categories of human learning.* New York: Academic, 1964, pp. 1-31.

Keller, F. S. *Learning: Reinforcement theory.* New York: Random House, 1969.

Kendler, H. H., and Spence, J. T. *Essays in neobehaviorism.* New York: Appleton-Century-Crofts, 1971.

Kimble, G. A. *Hilgard and Marquis' conditioning and learning.* New York: Appleton-Century-Crofts, 1961.

Logan, F. A. *Fundamentals of learning and motivation* (2nd ed.). Dubuque, Iowa: Brown, 1976.

McGuigan, F. J., and Lumsden, D. B. (Eds.) *Contemporary approaches to conditioning and learning.* Washington, D.C.: Winston, 1973.

Classical conditioning (general)

Pavlov, I. P. *Conditioned reflexes.* London: Oxford University Press, 1927.

Prokasy, W. F. (Ed.) *Classical conditioning.* New York: Appleton-Century-Crofts, 1965.

Stimulus intensity

Grice, G. R., and Hunter, J. J. Stimulus intensity effects depend upon the type of experimental design. *Psychological Review,* 1964, *71,* 247-256.

Eyelid conditioning

Cerekwicki, L. E., Grant, D. A., and Porter, E. C. The effect of number and relatedness of verbal discriminanda upon differential eyelid conditioning. *Journal of Verbal Learning and Verbal Behavior,* 1968, *7,* 847-853.

Semantic conditioning

Maltzman, I. Theoretical conceptions of semantic conditioning and generalization. In T. R. Dixon and D. L. Horton (Eds.), *Verbal behavior and general behavior theory.* Englewood Cliffs, N.J.: Prentice-Hall, 1968, pp. 291-339.

Instrumental conditioning (general)

D'Amato, M. R. Instrumental conditioning. In M. H. Marx (Ed.), *Learning: Processes.* New York: Macmillan, 1969, pp. 35-118.

Operant conditioning (general)

Honig, W. K. (Ed.) *Operant behavior: Areas of research and application.* New York: Appleton-Century-Crofts, 1966.

Reynolds, G. S. *A primer of operant conditioning.* Glenview, Ill.: Scott, Foresman, 1968.

Verbal conditioning

Greenspoon, J. The reinforcing effect of two spoken sounds on the frequency of two responses. *American Journal of Psychology,* 1955, *68,* 409-416.

Kanfer, F. H. Verbal conditioning: A review of its current status. In T. R. Dixon and D. L. Horton (Eds.), *Verbal behavior and general behavior theory.* Englewood Cliffs, N. J.: Prentice-Hall, 1968, pp. 254-290.

Responses as reinforcers

Premack, D. Toward empirical behavior laws. I. Positive reinforcement. *Psychological Review,* 1959, *66,* 219-233.

Secondary reinforcement

Egger, M. D., and Miller, N. E. When is a reward reinforcing?: An experimental test of the information hypothesis. *Journal of Comparative and Physiological Psychology,* 1963, *56,* 132-137.

Extinction

Williams, C. D. The elimination of tantrum behavior by extinction procedures. *Journal of Abnormal and Social Psychology,* 1959, *59,* 269.

Partial reinforcement

Jenkins, W. O., McFann, H., and Clayton, F. L. A methodological study of extinction following aperiodic and continuous reinforcement. *Journal of Comparative and Physiological Psychology,* 1950, *43,* 155-167.

Generalization (general)

Mednick, S. A., and Freeman, J. L. Stimulus generalization. *Psychological Bulletin,* 1960, *57,* 169-200.

Spatial generalization

Brown, J. S., Bilodeau, E. A., and Baron, M. R. Bidirectional gradients in the strength of a generalized voluntary response to stimuli on a visual-spatial dimension. *Journal of Experimental Psychology,* 1951, *41,* 52-61.

Discrimination

Brown, J. S. Generalization and discrimination. In D. I. Mostofsky (Ed.), *Stimulus generalization.* Stanford: Stanford Universtiy Press, 1965, pp. 7-23.

Differentiation

Herrick, R. M. The successive differentiation of a lever displacement response. *Journal of Experimental Analysis of Behavior,* 1964, *7,* 211-215.

Conditioning principles, personality, and therapy

Kanfer, F. H., and Phillips, J. S. *Learning foundations of behavior therapy.* New York: Wiley, 1970.

Krasner, L., and Ullman, L. P. *Research in behavior modification.* New York: Holt, Rinehart and Winston, 1965.

Mehrabian, A. *Tactics of social influence.* Englewood Cliffs, N. J.: Prentice-Hall, 1970.

Ullman, L. P., and Krasner, L. (Eds.) *Case studies in behavior modification.* New York: Holt, Rinehart and Winston, 1965.

Instructional technology

DeCecco, J. P. (Ed.) *Educational technology.* New York: Holt, Rinehart and Winston, 1964.

Glaser, R. (Ed.) *Teaching machines and programmed learning. 2: Data and directions.* Washington: National Education Association, 1965.

Pitts, C. E. *Introduction to educational psychology: An operant conditioning approach.* New York: Crowell, 1971.

Skinner, B. F. Teaching machines. *Scientific American,* 1961, *205,* 90-102.

Taber, J. I., Glaser, R., and Schaefer, H. H. *Learning and programmed instruction.* Reading, Mass.: Addison-Wesley, 1965.

Child development and learning

Bijou, S. W., and Baer, D. M. *Child development: Readings in experimental analysis*. New York: Appleton-Century-Crofts, 1967.

Mussen, P. H., Conger, J. J., and Kagan, J. *Child development and personality*. New York: Harper & Row, 1969, pp. 99-145.

Verbal Learning

Scope of verbal learning

Underwood, B. J. The representativeness of rote verbal learning. In A. W. Melton (Ed.), *Categories of human learning*. New York: Academic, 1964, pp. 47-78.

Wickens, D. D. The centrality of verbal learning. In A. W. Melton (Ed.), *Categories of human learning*. New York: Academic, 1964, pp. 79-87.

Concept of association

Kendler, H. H. Some specific reactions to general S-R theory. In T. R. Dixon and D. L. Horton (Eds.), *Verbal behavior and general behavior theory*. Englewood Cliffs, N.J.: Prentice-Hall, 1968, pp. 388-403.

Postman, L. Association and performance in the analysis of verbal learning. In T. R. Dixon and D. L. Horton (Eds.), *Verbal behavior and general behavior theory*. Englewood Cliffs, N. J.: Prentice-Hall, 1968, pp. 550-571.

Problems with associationism

Asch, S. E. The doctrinal tyranny of associationism: Or what is wrong with rote learning. In T. R. Dixon and D. L. Horton (Eds.), *Verbal behavior and general behavior theory*. Englewood Cliffs, N. J.: Prentice-Hall, 1968, pp. 214-228.

Scaling

Archer, E. J. A re-evaluation of the meaningfulness of all possible CVC trigrams. *Psychological Monographs,* 1960, *74,* (10, whole no. 497).

Noble, C. E. An analysis of meaning. *Psychological Review,* 1952, *59,* 421-430.

Serial learning

Young, R. K. Serial learning. In T. R. Dixon and D. L. Horton (Eds.), *Verbal behavior and general behavior theory*. Englewood Cliffs, N. J.: Prentice-Hall, 1968, pp. 122-148.

Serial position curve

Murdock, B. B., Jr. The serial position effect in free recall. *Journal of Experimental Psychology,* 1962, *64,* 482-488.

Paired associate learning

Battig, W. F. Paired-associate learning. In T. R. Dixon and D. L. Horton (Eds.), *Verbal behavior and general behavior theory.* Englewood Cliffs, N.J.: Prentice-Hall, 1968, pp. 149-171.

Cofer, C. N., Diamond, F., Olsen, R. A., Stein, J. S., and Walker, H. Comparison of anticipation and recall methods in paired-associate learning. *Journal of Experimental Psychology,* 1967, *75,* 545-558.

Free recall

Tulving, E. Subjective organization and effects of repetition in multi-trial free-recall learning. *Journal of Verbal Learning and Verbal Behavior,* 1966, *5,* 193-197.

Recognition learning

Underwood, B. J., and Freund, J. S. Errors in recognition learning and retention. *Journal of Experimental Psychology,* 1968, *78,* 55-63.

Recognition and paired associate learning

Ellis, H. C., and Tatum, B. C. Stimulus encoding and the relationship between stimulus recognition and association formation. *Journal of Verbal Learning and Verbal Behavior,* 1973, *12,* 174-184.

Martin, E. Relation between stimulus recognition and paired-associate learning. *Journal of Experimental Psychology,* 1967, *74,* 500-505.

Verbal discrimination learning

Underwood, B. J., and Freund, J. S. Relative frequency judgments and verbal discrimination learning. *Journal of Experimental Psychology,* 1970, *83,* 279-285.

Meaningfulness

Cieutat, V. J., Stockwell, F. E., and Noble, C. E. The interaction of ability and amount of practice with stimulus and response meaningfulness (m, m') in paired-associate learning. *Journal of Experimental Psychology,* 1958, *56,* 193-202.

Underwood, B. J., and Schulz, R. W. *Meaningfulness and verbal learning.* Philadelphia: Lippincott, 1960.

Meaningfulness and encoding

Martin, E. Stimulus meaningfulness and paired-associate transfer: An encoding variability hypothesis. *Psychological Review,* 1968, *75,* 421-441.

Mental imagery

Bower, G. H. Mental imagery and associative learning. In L. Gregg (Ed.), *Cognition in learning and memory.* New York: Wiley, 1972.

Paivio, A. Mental imagery in associative learning and memory. *Psychological Review,* 1969, *76,* 241-263.

Intralist stimulus similarity

Runquist, W. N. Functions relating intralist stimulus similarity to acquisition performance with a variety of materials. *Journal of Verbal Learning and Verbal Behavior,* 1968, *7,* 549-553.

Two-process theories of paired associates

Polson, M. C., Restle, F., and Polson, P. G. Association and discrimination in paired-associates learning. *Journal of Experimental Psychology,* 1965, *69,* 47-55.

Underwood, B. J., Runquist, W. N., and Schulz, R. W. Response learning in paired-associate lists as a function of intralist stimulus similarity. *Journal of Experimental Psychology,* 1959, *58,* 70-78.

Multiprocess theory of paired associates

McGuire, W. J. A multi-process model for paired-associate learning. *Journal of Experimental Psychology,* 1961, *62,* 335-347.

Stimulus discrimination

Gibson, E. J. A systematic application of the concepts of generalization and differentiation to verbal learning. *Psychological Review,* 1940, *47,* 196-229.

Stimulus selection

Postman, L., and Greenbloom, R. Conditions of cue selection in the acquisition of paired-associate lists. *Journal of Experimental Psychology,* 1967, *73,* 91-100.

Stimulus selection and overtraining

James, C. T., and Greeno, J. G. Stimulus selection at different stages of paired-associate training. *Journal of Experimental Psychology,* 1967, *73,* 509-516.

Stimulus coding

Underwood, B. J., and Erlebacher, J. S. Studies of coding in verbal learning. *Psychological Monographs*, 1965, *79*, (13, whole no. 606).

Contiguity and association formation

Spear, N. E., Ekstrand, B. R., and Underwood, B. J. Association by contiguity. *Journal of Experimental Psychology*, 1964, *67*, 151-161.

Association formation

Estes, W. K. Learning theory and the new "mental chemistry." *Psychological Review*, 1960, *67*, 207-223.
Underwood, B. J., and Keppel, G. One-trial learning? *Journal of Verbal Learning and Verbal Behavior*, 1962, *1*, 1-13.

Backward association

Ekstrand, B. Backward (R-S) associations. *Psychological Bulletin*, 1966, *65*, 50-64.

Organizational processes

Mandler, G. Organization and memory. In K. W. Spence and J. T. Spence (Eds.), *The psychology of learning and motivation: Advances and theory*. Vol. *1*. New York: Academic, 1967, pp. 328-372.

Clustering

Bousfield, W. A., Cohen, B. H., and Whitmarsh, G. A. Associative clustering in the recall of words of different taxonomic frequencies of occurrence. *Psychological Reports*, 1958, *4*, 39-44.
Cofer, C. N. On some factors in the organizational characteristics of free recall. *American Psychologist*, 1965, *20*, 261-272.

Subjective organization

Tulving, E. Subjective organization in free recall of unrelated words. *Psychological Review*, 1962, *69*, 344-354.

Organization, storage, and retrieval

Tulving, E., and Pearlstone, Z. Availability versus accessibility of information in memory for words. *Journal of Verbal Learning and Verbal Behavior*, 1966, *5*, 381-391.

Coding (general)

Miller, G. A. The magical number seven, plus or minus two: Some limits on our capacity for processing information. *Psychological Review*, 1956, *63*, 81-96.

Response coding

Underwood, B. J., and Keppel, G. Coding processes in verbal learning. *Journal of Verbal Learning and Verbal Behavior,* 1963, *1,* 250-257.

Mediation

Jenkins, J. J. Mediated association: Paradigms and situations. In C. N. Cofer and B. S. Musgrave (Eds.), *Verbal behavior and learning.* New York: McGraw-Hill, 1963, pp. 210-245.

Schulz, R. W., and Lovelace, E. Mediation in verbal paired-associate learning: The role of temporal factors. *Psychonomic Science,* 1964, *1,* 95-96.

Connected materials

Bower, G. H., and Clark, M. C. Narrative stories as mediators for serial learning. *Psychonomic Science,* 1969, *14,* 181-182.

Deese, J. From the isolated verbal unit to connected discourse. In C. N. Cofer (Ed.), *Verbal learning and verbal behavior.* New York: McGraw-Hill, 1961, pp. 11-38.

Incidental learning

McLaughlin, B. "Intentional" and "incidental" learning in human subjects: The role of instructions in learning and motivation. *Psychological Bulletin,* 1965, *63,* 359-376.

Anxiety and learning

Spence, K. W. A theory of emotionally based drive (D) and its relationship to performance in simple learning situations. *American Psychologist,* 1958, *13,* 131-141.

Memory I: The Processing of Information

Memory and learning

Murdock, B. B. Jr. Short-term memory and paired-associate learning. *Journal of Verbal Learning and Verbal Behavior,* 1963, *2,* 320-328.

Information processing approaches

Atkinson, R., and Shiffrin, R. Human memory: A proposed system and its control processes. In G. H. Bower (Ed.), *The psychology of learning and motivation.* Vol. *2.* New York: Academic, 1968.

Broadbent, D. E. Flow of information within the organism. *Journal of Verbal Learning and Verbal Behavior,* 1963, *2,* 34-39.

Lindsay, P. H., and Norman, D. A. *Human information processing.*
New York: Academic, 1977.

Norman, D. A. *Memory and attention.* New York: Wiley, 1976.

Recall

Ekstrand, B. R., and Underwood, B. J. Paced versus unpaced recall in
free learning. *Journal of Verbal Learning and Verbal Behavior,*
1965, *4,* 390-396.

Recognition

Kintsch, W. An experimental comparison of single-stimulus tests and
multiple-choice tests of recognition memory. *Journal of Experimental Psychology,* 1968, *76,* 1-6.

Murdock, B. B., Jr. An analysis of the recognition process. In C. N.
Cofer and B. S. Musgrave (Eds.), *Verbal behavior and learning.*
New York: McGraw-Hill, 1963, pp. 10-22.

Reproductive memory

Perkins, F. T. Symmetry in visual recall. *American Journal of Psychology,* 1932, *44,* 473-490.

Comparison of measures

Bahrick, H. P. The ebb of retention. *Psychological Review,* 1965, *72,*
60-73.

Response bias in recognition memory

Egan, J. P. Recognition memory and the operating characteristics. Technical Note No. AFCRC-TN-58-51. Hearing and Communication
Laboratory, Indiana University, 1958.

Kintsch, W. Memory and decision aspects of recognition learning. *Psychological Review,* 1967, *74,* 496-504.

Continuous recognition

Shepard, R. N., and Teghtsoonian, M. Retention of information under
conditions approaching a steady state. *Journal of Experimental
Psychology,* 1961, *62,* 302-309.

Recognition and implicit associations

Underwood, B. J. False recognition produced by implicit associative
responses. *Journal of Experimental Psychology,* 1965, *70,* 122-129.

Sensory memory

Sperling, G. A model for visual memory tasks. *Human Factors,* 1963,
5, 19-31.

Short-term memory

Melton, A. W. Implications of short-term memory for a general theory of memory. *Journal of Verbal Learning and Verbal Behavior,* 1963, *2,* 1-21.

Peterson, L. R., and Peterson, M. J. Short-term retention of individual items. *Journal of Experimental Psychology,* 1959, *58,* 193-198.

Arguments for a dual memory system

Glanzer, M., and Cunitz, A. R. Two storage mechanisms in free recall. *Journal of Verbal Learning and Verbal Behavior,* 1966, *5,* 351-360.

Waugh, N. C., and Norman, D. A. Primary memory. *Psychological Review,* 1965, *72,* 89-104.

Arguments against a dual memory system

Craik, F. I. M., and Lockhart, R. S. Levels of processing: A framework for memory research. *Journal of Verbal Learning and Verbal Behavior,* 1972, *11,* 671-684.

Melton, A. W. Implications of short-term memory for a general theory of memory. *Journal of Verbal Learning and Verbal Behavior,* 1963, *2,* 1-21.

Wickelgren, W. The long and the short of memory. *Psychological Bulletin,* 1973, *80,* 425-438.

Encoding

Craik, F. I. M., and Lockhart, R. S. Levels of processing: A framework for memory research. *Journal of Verbal Learning and Verbal Behavior,* 1972, *11,* 671-684.

Crowder, R. G. Visual and auditory memory. In J. F. Kavanaugh and I. G. Mattingly (Eds.) *Language by ear and by eye.* Cambridge, Mass.: M.I.T. Press, 1972.

Ellis, H. C. Stimulus encoding processes in human learning and memory. In G. H. Bower (Ed.), *The psychology of learning and motivation.* Vol. 7. New York: Academic, 1973.

Frost, N. Encoding and retrieval in visual memory tasks. *Journal of Experimental Psychology,* 1972, *95,* 317-326.

Wickens, D. D. Encoding categories of words: An empirical approach to meaning. *Psychological Review,* 1970, *77,* 1-15.

Rehearsal and short-term memory

Bernbach, H. A. The effect of labels in short-term memory for colors with nursery school children. *Psychonomic Science,* 1967, *7,* 149-150.

Chunking and memory

Miller, G. A. The magical number seven, plus or minus two: Some limits on our capacity for processing information. *Psychological Review,* 1956, *63,* 81-97.

Retrieval cues

Tulving, E., and Pearlstone, Z. Availability versus accessibility of information in memory for words. *Journal of Verbal Learning and Verbal Behavior,* 1966, *5,* 381-391.

Dependence of retrieval upon storage

Tulving, E., and Osler, S. Effectiveness of retrieval cues in memory for words. *Journal of Experimental Psychology,* 1968, *77,* 593-601.

Retrieval

Anderson, J. R., and Bower, G. H. Recognition and retrieval processes in free recall. *Psychological Review,* 1972, *79,* 97-123.

Thompson, D. M., and Tulving, E. Associative encoding and retrieval: Weak and strong cues. *Journal of Experimental Psychology,* 1970, *86,* 255-262.

Tulving, E., and Thompson, D. M. Encoding specificity and retrieval processes in episodic memory. *Psychological Review,* 1973, *80,* 352-373.

Memory II: Organization, Forgetting, and Models of Memory

Organization

Bower, G. H. Organizational factors in memory. *Cognitive Psychology,* 1970, *1,* 18-46.

Bower, G. H., and Winzenz, D. Group structure, coding, and memory for digit series. *Journal of Experimental Psychology Monographs,* 1969, *80,* No. 2, Part 2, 1-17.

Tulving, E., and Donaldson, W. *Organization of memory.* New York: Academic, 1972.

Context

Light, L. L., and Carter-Sobell, L. Effects of changed semantic context on recognition memory. *Journal of Verbal Learning and Verbal Behavior,* 1970, *9,* 1-11.

Constructive processes

Bartlett, F. C. *Remembering: A study in experimental and social psychology.* New York: Cambridge University Press, 1932.

Bransford, J. D., and Frank, J. J. The abstraction of linguistic ideas. *Cognitive Psychology,* 1971, *2,* 331-350.

Cofer, C. N. Constructive processes in memory. *American Scientist,* 1973, *61,* 537-543.

Perceptual grouping and memory

Bower, G. H. A selective review of organizational factors in memory. In E. Tulving and W. Donaldson (Eds.), *Organization of memory.* New York: Academic, 1972.

Bower, G. H., and Winzenz, D. Group structure, coding, and memory for digit series. *Journal of Experimental Psychology,* 1970, *80,* No. 2, Part 2, 1-17.

Ellis, H. C., Parente, F. J., Grah, C. R., and Spiering, K. Coding strategies, perceptual grouping, and the "variability effect" in free recall. *Memory and Cognition,* 1975, *3,* 226-232.

Ellis, H. C., Parente, F. J., and Walker, C. W. Coding and varied input versus repetition in human memory. *Journal of Experimental Psychology,* 1974, *102,* 619-624.

Language and memory

Ellis, H. C. Transfer of stimulus predifferentiation to shape recognition and identification learning: Role of properties of verbal labels. *Journal of Experimental Psychology;* 1968, *78,* 401-409.

Ellis, H. C., and Daniel, T. C. Verbal processes in long-term stimulus recognition memory. *Journal of Experimental Psychology,* 1971, *90,* 18-26.

Loftus, E., and Palmer, D. Reconstruction of automobile destruction: An example of the interaction between language and memory. *Journal of Verbal Learning and Verbal Behavior,* 1974, *13,* 585-589.

Semantic memory

Anderson, J. R., and Bower, G. H. *Human associative memory.* Washington, D.C.: Winston, 1973.

Collins, A. M., and Loftus, E. F. A spreading activation theory of semantic memory. *Psychological Review,* 1975, *82,* 407-428.

Collins, A. M., and Quillian, M. R. Retrieval time from semantic memory. *Journal of Verbal Learning and Verbal Behavior,* 1969, *8,* 240-247.

Forgetting

Ekstrand, B. R. To sleep, perchance to dream (about why we forget). In C. P. Duncan, L. Sechrest, and A. W. Melton (Eds.), *Human memory.* New York: Appleton-Century-Crofts, 1972.

Keppel, G. Retroactive and proactive inhibition. In T. R. Dixon and D. L. Horton (Eds.), *Verbal behavior and general behavior theory.* Englewood Cliffs, N. J.: Prentice-Hall, 1968.

Underwood, B. J. Interference and forgetting. *Psychological Review,* 1957, *64,* 49-60.

Decay theory

Brown, J. Some tests of the decay theory of immediate memory. *Quarterly Journal of Experimental Psychology,* 1958, *10,* 12-21.

Interference theory

Postman, L., and Stark, K. Role of response availability in transfer and interference. *Journal of Experimental Psychology,* 1969, *79,* 168-177.

Postman, L., and Underwood, B. J. Critical issues in interference theory. *Memory and Cognition,* 1973, *1,* 19-40.

Rehearsal

Craik, F. I. M., and Watkins, M. J. The role of rehearsal in short-term memory. *Journal of Verbal Learning and Verbal Behavior,* 1973, *12,* 599-607.

Rundus, D. Analysis of rehearsal processes in free recall. *Journal of Experimental Psychology,* 1971, *89,* 63-77.

Models of memory

Anderson, J. R., and Bower, G. H. *Human associative memory.* Washington, D.C.: Winston, 1973.

Atkinson, R. C., and Shiffrin, R. M. Human memory: A proposed system and its control processes. In K. W. Spence and J. T. Spence (Eds.), *The psychology of learning and motivation.* Vol. *2.* New York: Academic, 1968.

Norman, D. A. *Models of memory.* New York: Academic, 1970.

Structure of memory

Cofer, C. N. (Ed.) *The structure of human memory.* San Francisco: Freeman, 1975.

Kintsch, W. *The representation of meaning in memory.* Hillsdale, N.J.: Erlbaum, 1974.

Concept Learning

General

Bourne, L. E. *Human conceptual behavior.* Boston: Allyn & Bacon, 1966.

Glaser, R. Concept learning and concept teaching. In R. M. Gagné and W. J. Gephart (Eds.), *Learning research and school subjects.* Itasca, Ill.: Peacock, 1968, pp. 1-36.

Concept materials

Underwood, B. J., and Richardson, J. Some verbal materials for the study of concept formation. *Psychological Bulletin,* 1956, *53,* 84-95.

Concept and paired associate learning

Underwood, B. J., and Richardson, J. Verbal concept learning as a function of instructions and dominance level. *Journal of Experimental Psychology,* 1956, *51,* 229-238.

Basic processes

Haygood, R. C., and Bourne, L. E. Attribute- and rule-learning aspects of conceptual behavior. *Psychological Review,* 1965, *72,* 175-195.

Neisser, U., and Weene, P. Hierarchies in concept attainment. *Journal of Experimental Psychology,* 1962, *64,* 644-645.

Paradigms

Bourne, L. E., Ekstrand, B. R., and Dominowski, R. L. *The psychology of thinking.* Englewood Cliffs, N. J.: Prentice-Hall, 1971, pp. 189-193.

Positive and negative instances

Freibergs, V., and Tulving, E. The effect of practice on utilization of information from positive and negative instances in concept identification. *Canadian Journal of Psychology,* 1961, *15,* 101-106.

Hovland, C. I., and Weiss, W. Transmission of information concerning concepts through positive and negative instances. *Journal of Experimental Psychology,* 1953, *45,* 175-182.

Attributes and positive instances

Haygood, R. C., and Devine, J. V. Effects of composition of the positive category on concept learning. *Journal of Experimental Psychology,* 1967, *74,* 230-235.

Conceptual rules and instances

Bourne, L. E., Learning conceptual rules. II. The role of positive and negative instances. *Journal of Experimental Psychology,* 1968, *77,* 488-494.

Stimulus salience

Suchman, R. G., and Trabasso, T. Color and form preference in young children. *Journal of Experimental Child Psychology,* 1966, *3,* 177-187.

Stimulus redundancy

Bourne, L. E., and Haygood, R. C. The role of stimulus redundancy in the identification of concepts. *Journal of Experimental Psychology,* 1959, *58,* 232-238.

Feedback

Bourne, L. E., and Bunderson, C.V. Effects of delay of information feedback and length of the postfeedback interval on concept identification. *Journal of Experimental Psychology,* 1963, *65,* 1-5.

Bourne, L. E., Guy, D. E., Dodd, D. H., and Justensen, D. R. Concept identification: The effects of varying length and informational components of the intertrial interval. *Journal of Experimental Psychology,* 1965, *69,* 624-629.

Use of conceptual rules

Bourne, L. E. Learning and utilization of conceptual rules. In B. Kleinmuntz (Ed.), *Memory and the structure of concepts.* New York: Wiley, 1967.

Memory

Trabasso, T., and Bower, G. H. Memory in concept identification. *Psychonomic Science,* 1964, *1,* 133-134.

Intelligence and anxiety

Denny, J. P. Effects of anxiety and intelligence on concept formation. *Journal of Experimental Psychology,* 1966, *72,* 596-602.

S-R theory

Bourne, L. E., and Restle, F. Mathematical theory of concept identification. *Psychological Review,* 1959, *66,* 278-296.

S-R mediation theory

Kendler, H. H., and Kendler, T. S. Mediation and conceptual behavior. In K. W. Spence and J. T. Spence (Eds.), *The psychology of learning and motivation.* Vol. *2.* New York: Academic, 1968.

Kendler, H. H., and Kendler, T. S. Vertical and horizontal processes in problem solving. *Psychological Review,* 1962, *69,* 1-16.

Hypothesis testing theory

Restle, F. The selection of strategies in cue learning. *Psychological Review,* 1962, *69,* 320-343.

Trabasso, T., and Bower, G. H. *Attention in learning.* New York: Wiley, 1968.

Information processing

Hunt, E. B. *Concept learning: An information-processing problem.* New York: Wiley, 1962.

Language

General

Brown, R. W. *Words and things.* Glencoe, Ill.: Free Press, 1958.

Carroll, J. B. *Language and thought.* Englewood Cliffs, N. J.: Prentice-Hall, 1964.

Jakobson, R., and Halle, M. *Fundamentals of language.* The Hague: Mouton, 1956.

Langacker, R. W. *Language and its structure.* New York: Harcourt Brace Jovanovich, 1973.

Lenneberg, E. *Biological foundations of language.* New York: Wiley, 1967.

Staats, A. W. *Learning, language, and cognition.* New York: Holt, Rinehart and Winston, 1968.

Phonemes and Morphemes

Bourne, L. E., Ekstrand, B. R., and Dominowski, R. L. *The psychology of thinking.* Englewood Cliffs, N.J.: Prentice-Hall, 1971, pp. 308-14.

Miller, G. A., and Nicely, P. E. An analysis of perceptual confusions among some English consonants. *Journal of the Acoustical Society of America,* 1955, *27,* 338-52.

Phrase structure

Fodor, J., and Bever, T. The psychological reality of linguistic segments.

Journal of Verbal Learning and Verbal Behavior, 1956, *4,* 135-39.
Garrett, M., Bever, T., and Fodor, J. The active use of grammar in speech perception. *Perception and Psychophysics,* 1966, *1,* 30-32.
Johnson, N. F. Linguistic models and functional units of language behavior. In S. Rosenberg (Ed.), *Directions in psycholinguistics.* New York: Macmillan, 1965.

Surface and deep structure

Mehler, J., and Carey, R. Role of surface and base structure in the perception of sentences. *Journal of Verbal Learning and Verbal Behavior,* 1967, *6,* 335-338.

Transformational grammar

Chomsky, N. *Aspects of the theory of syntax.* Cambridge, Mass.: M.I.T. Press, 1965.
Chomsky, N. *Syntactic structures.* The Hague: Mouton, 1957.

Language development

Brown, R. W., and Fraser, C. The acquisition of syntax. In C. N. Cofer and B. S. Musgrave (Eds.), *Verbal behavior and learning.* New York: McGraw-Hill, 1963.
Ervin-Tripp, S. Language development. In L. W. Hoffman and M. L. Hoffman (Eds.), *Review of Child Development Research.* (2nd ed.) New York: Russell Sage Foundation, 1966.

Language and thought

Glucksberg, S., and Weisberg, R. W. Verbal behavior and problem solving: Some effects of labeling in a functional fixedness problem. *Journal of Experimental Psychology,* 1966, *71,* 659-664.
Ranken, H. B. Language and thinking: Positive and negative effects of naming. *Science,* 1963, *141,* 48-50.

Linguistic relativity hypothesis

Whorf, B. L. *Language, thought, and reality.* (Ed. J. B. Carroll). New York: Wiley; Cambridge University Press, 1956.

Language and perceptual recall

Glanzer, M., and Clarke, W. H. Accuracy of perceptual recall: An analysis of organization. *Journal of Verbal Learning and Verbal Behavior,* 1962, *1,* 288-299.

Language and perceptual recognition

Ellis, H. C., Bessemer, D. W., Devine, J. V., and Trafton, C. L. Recog-

nition of random tactual shapes following predifferentiation training. *Perceptual and Motor Skills,* 1962, *10,* 99-102.

Ellis, H. C., and Muller, D. G. Transfer in perceptual learning following
stimulus predifferentiation. *Journal of Experimental Psychology,*
1964, *68,* 388-395.

Thinking and Problem Solving

General

Bourne, L. E., Ekstrand, B. R., and Dominowski, R. L. *The psychology
of thinking.* Englewood Cliffs, N.J.: Prentice-Hall, 1971.

Bruner, J. S., Goodnow, J. J., and Austin, G. A. *A study of thinking.*
New York: Wiley, 1966.

Dominowski, R. L. Problem solving and concept attainment. In
M. H. Marx (Ed.), *Learning: Interactions.* New York: Macmillan,
1970, pp. 107-191.

Duncan, C. P. *Thinking: Current experimental studies.* Philadelphia:
Lippincott, 1967.

Kleinmuntz, B. (Ed.) *Problem solving: Research, method, and theory.*
New York: Wiley, 1966.

McGuigan, F. J. *Thinking: Studies of covert language processes.* New
York: Appleton-Century-Crofts, 1963.

Persistence of set

Adamson, R. E. Functional fixedness as related to problem solving:
A repetition of three experiments. *Journal of Experimental Psychology,* 1952, *44,* 288-291.

Luchins, A. S. Mechanization of problem solving: The effect of Ein-
stellung. *Psychological Monographs,* 1942, *54* (6, whole no. 248).

Problem solving and transfer

Schulz, R. W. Problem solving behavior and transfer. *Harvard Educational Review,* 1960, *30,* 61-77.

Anxiety and problem solving

Russell, D. G., and Sarason, I. G. Test anxiety, sex, and experimental
conditions in relation to anagram solution. *Journal of Personality
and Social Psychology,* 1965, *1,* 493-496.

Motivation and problem solving

Svedfeld, S., Glucksberg, S., and Vernon, J. Sensory deprivation as a
drive operation: Effect upon problem solving. *Journal of Experimental Psychology,* 1967, *75,* 166-169.

S-R theory

Maltzman, I. Thinking: From a behavioristic point of view. *Psychological Review,* 1955, *66,* 367-386.

Gestalt theory

Kohler, W. *The mentality of apes.* New York: Harcourt Brace, 1925.

Information processing

Miller, G. A., Galanter, E., and Pribram, K. *Plans and the structure of behavior.* New York: Holt, Rinehart and Winston, 1960.

Simon, H. A., and Kotovsky, K. Human acquisition of concepts for sequential patterns. *Psychological Review,* 1963, *70,* 534-546.

Attention and Perceptual Learning

Attention (General)

Norman, D. A. *Memory and Attention.* New York: Wiley, 1976.

Broadbent, D. E. *Decision and stress.* New York: Academic, 1971.

Keele, S. W. *Attention and human performance.* Pacific Palisades, Calif.: Goodyear, 1973.

MacKay, D. G. Aspects of the theory of comprehension, memory and attention. *Quarterly Journal of Experimental Psychology,* 1973, *25,* 22-40.

Treisman, A. M. Verbal cues, language, and meaning in selective attention. *American Journal of Psychology,* 1964, *77,* 206-219.

Perceptual Learning (General)

Bevan, W. Perceptual learning: An overview. *Journal of General Psychology,* 1961, *64,* 69-99.

Epstein, W. *Varieties of perceptual learning.* New York: McGraw-Hill, 1967.

Gibson, E. J. *Principles of perceptual learning and development.* New York: Appleton-Century-Crofts, 1969.

Postman, L. Perception and learning. In S. Koch (Ed.), *Psychology: A study of a science.* Vol. 5. New York: McGraw-Hill, 1963.

Vanderplas, J. M. Perception and learning. In M. H. Marx (Ed.), *Learning: Interactions.* New York: Macmillan, 1970.

Perceptual tasks

Bush, R. R., Galanter, E., and Luce, R. D. Characterization and classification of choice experiments. In R. D. Luce, R. R. Bush, and E. Galanter (Eds.), *Handbook of mathematical psychology.* Vol. *1.* New York: Wiley, 1963.

Vanderplas, J. M. Associative processes and task relations in perceptual learning. *Perceptual and Motor Skills,* 1963, *16,* 501-509.

Wohlwill, J. F. The definition and analysis of perceptual learning. *Psychological Review,* 1958, *65,* 283-295.

Perceptual learning materials

Attneave, F., and Arnoult, M. D. The quantitative study of shape and pattern perception. *Psychological Bulletin,* 1956, *53,* 452-471.

Brown, D. R., and Owen, D. H. The metrics of visual form: Methodological dyspepsia. *Psychological Bulletin,* 1967, *68,* 243-259.

Fitts, P. M., Weinstein, M., Rappaport, M., Anderson, N., and Leonard, A. J. Stimulus correlates of visual pattern recognition. *Journal of Experimental Psychology,* 1956, *51,* 1-11.

Effects of practice on perceptual skills

Gibson, E. J. Improvement in perceptual judgments as a function of controlled practice or training. *Psychological Bulletin,* 1953, *50,* 401-431.

Neisser, U. Visual search. *Scientific American,* 1964, *210,* 94-101.

Neisser, U., Novick, R., and Lazar, R. Searching for ten targets simultaneously. *Perceptual and Motor Skills,* 1963, *17,* 955-961.

Reward and punishment factors

Epstein, W. *Varieties of perceptual learning.* New York: McGraw-Hill, 1967, chap. 7.

Rock, I., and Fleck, F. S. A re-examination of the effect of reward and punishment in figure-ground perception. *Journal of Experimental Psychology,* 1950, *40,* 766-776.

Schafer, R., and Murphy, G. The role of autism in a figure-ground relationship. *Journal of Experimental Psychology,* 1943, *32,* 335-343.

Adaptation to transformed stimulation

Harris, C. S. Perceptual adaptation to inverted, reversed and displaced vision. *Psychological Review,* 1965, *72,* 419-444.

Held, R., and Hein, A. Adaptation of disarranged hand-eye coordination contingent upon re-afferent stimulation. *Perceptual and Motor Skills,* 1958, *8,* 87-90.

Held, R., and Schlank, M. Motor-sensory feedback and the geometry of visual space. *Science,* 1963, *141,* 722-723.

Cross-modal transfer

Gaydos, H. F. Intersensory transfer in the discrimination of form. *American Journal of Psychology,* 1956, *69,* 107-110.

Holmgren, G. L., Arnoult, M. D., and Manning, W. H. Intermodal transfer in a paired-associates learning task. *Journal of Experimental Psychology,* 1966, *71,* 254-259.

Pick, A. D., Pick, H. L., and Thomas, M. L. Cross-modal transfer and improvement of form discrimination. *Journal of Experimental Child Psychology,* 1966, *3,* 279-288.

Shaffer, R. W., and Howard, J. The transfer of information across sensory modalities. *Perception and Psychophysics,* 1974, *15,* 344-348.

Verbal labels and perceptual learning

Ellis, H. C. Transfer of stimulus predifferentiation to shape recognition and identification learning: Role of properties of verbal labels. *Journal of Experimental Psychology,* 1968, *78,* 401-409.

Ellis, H. C., Bessemer, D. W., Devine, J. V., and Trafton, C. L. Recognition of random tactual shapes following predifferentiation training. *Perceptual and Motor Skills,* 1962, *10,* 99-102.

Ellis, H. C., and Muller, D. G. Transfer in perceptual learning following stimulus predifferentiation. *Journal of Experimental Psychology,* 1964, *68,* 388-395.

Katz, P. A. Effect of labels on children's perception and discrimination learning. *Journal of Experimental Psychology,* 1963, *66,* 423-428.

Verbal labels and generalization effects

Malloy, T. E., and Ellis, H. C. Attention and cue-producing responses in response-mediated stimulus generalization. *Journal of Experimental Psychology,* 1970, *83,* 191-200.

Schema learning

Attneave, F. Transfer of experience with a class-schema to identification-learning of patterns and shapes. *Journal of Experimental Psychology,* 1957, *54,* 81-88.

Evans, S. H. A brief statement of schema theory. *Psychonomic Science,* 1967, *8,* 87-88.

Oldfield, R. C. Memory mechanisms and the theory of schemata. *British Journal of Psychology,* 1954, *45,* 14-23.

Vernon, M. D. The functions of schemata in perceiving. *Psychological Review,* 1955, *62,* 180-192.

Theoretical issues

Gibson, J. J., and Gibson, E. J. Perceptual learning: Differentiation or enrichment? *Psychological Review,* 1955, *62,* 32-41.

Postman, L. Association theory and perceptual learning. *Psychological Review,* 1955, *62,* 438-446.

Applications

Gibson, E. J. Perceptual learning in educational situations. In R. M. Gagné and W. J. Gephart (Eds.), *Learning research and school subjects.* Itasca, Ill.: Peacock, 1968.

Motor Skills Learning

General

Adams, J. A. Motor behavior. In M. H. Marx (Ed.), *Learning: Processes.* New York: Macmillan, 1969, pp. 481-507.

Bilodeau, E. A. (Ed.) *Acquisition of skill.* New York: Academic, 1966.

Fitts, P. M. Perceptual-motor skill learning. In A. W. Melton (Ed.), *Categories of human learning.* New York: Academic, 1964, pp. 243-285.

Fitts, P. M., and Posner, M. I. *Human performance.* Belmont, Cal.: Brooks/Cole, 1967.

History

Irion, A. L. A brief history of research on the acquisition of skill. In E. A. Bilodeau (Ed.), *Acquisition of skill.* New York: Academic, 1966, pp. 1-46.

Response chains

Gagné, R. M. *The conditions of learning.* New York: Holt, Rinehart and Winston, 1965, chap. 4, especially pp. 87-92.

Response organization

Vince, M. A. The part played by intellectual processes in a sensory-motor performance. *Quarterly Journal of Experimental Psychology,* 1953, *5,* 75-86.

Feedback (general)

Gould, J. D. Differential visual feedback of component motions. *Journal of Experimental Psychology,* 1965, *69,* 263-268.

Phases of skill learning

Fitts, P. M. Perceptual-motor skill learning. In A. W. Melton (Ed.), *Categories of human learning.* New York: Academic, 1964, pp. 243-285.

Fitts, P. M., and Posner, M. I. *Human performance.* Belmont, Cal.: Brooks/Cole, 1967, chap. 2.

Intrinsic feedback

Smith, K. U., and Smith, W. M. *Perception and motion.* Philadelphia:
Saunders, 1962.

Extrinsic feedback

Elwell, J. L., and Grindley, G. C. The effect of knowledge of results on
learning and performance. I. A coordinated movement of the two
hands. *British Journal of Psychology,* 1938, *29,* 39-53.

Quantitative and qualitative feedback

Trowbridge, M. H., and Cason, H. An experimental study of Thorndike's theory of learning. *Journal of General Psychology,* 1932, *7,*
245-260.

Withdrawal of feedback

Bilodeau, E. A., Bilodeau, I. M. D., and Schumsky, D. A. Some effects
of introducing and withdrawing knowledge of results early and late
in practice. *Journal of Experimental Psychology,* 1959, *58,* 142-
144.

Delay of feedback

Bilodeau, E. A., and Ryan, F. J. A test for interaction of delay of knowledge of results and two types of interpolated activity. *Journal of
Experimental Psychology,* 1960, *59,* 414-419.

Distribution of practice

Kimble, G. A., and Bilodeau, E. A. Work and rest as variables in cycli-
cal motor learning. *Journal of Experimental Psychology,* 1949, *39,*
150-157.

Informational stress

Miller, J. G. Adjusting to overloads of information. In D. M. Rioch and
E. A. Weinstein (Eds.), *Disorders of communication.* Research
Publications, Association for Research in Nervous and Mental
Disorders, 1964, *42,* 87-100.

Motor learning theory

Adams, J. A. A closed-loop theory of motor skills learning. *Journal of
Motor Behavior,* 1971, *3,* 111-149.

Transfer of Training

General

Ellis, H. C. *The transfer of training.* New York: Macmillan, 1965.
Ellis, H. C. *Transfer and retention.* In M. H. Marx (Ed.), *Learning Processes.* New York: Macmillan, 1969, pp. 381-478.
Ellis, H. C., and Hunt, R. R. Transfer. In M. H. Marx and M. E. Bunch (Eds.) *Fundamentals and applications of learning.* New York: Macmillan, 1977, pp. 293-315.

Measurement

Murdock, B. B. Jr. Transfer designs and formulas. *Psychological Bulletin,* 1957, *54,* 313-326.
Runquist, W. N. Verbal behavior. In J. B. Sidowski (Ed.), *Experimental methods and instrumentation.* New York: McGraw-Hill, 1966, pp. 487-540.

Design problems

Twedt, H. M., and Underwood, B. J. Mixed vs. unmixed lists in transfer studies. *Journal of Experimental Psychology,* 1959, *58,* 111-116.

Paradigms

Postman, L. Differences between unmixed and mixed transfer designs as a function of paradigm. *Journal of Verbal Learning and Verbal Behavior,* 1966, *5,* 240-248.

Learning to learn

Postman, L., and Schwartz, M. Studies of learning to learn. I. Transfer as a function of method of practice and class of verbal materials. *Journal of Verbal Learning and Verbal Behavior,* 1964, *3,* 37-49.

Warm-up

Hamilton, C. E. The relationship between length of interval separating two tasks and performance on the second task. *Journal of Experimental Psychology,* 1950, *40,* 613-621.

Transfer of stimulus discrimination

Ellis, H. C., and Muller, D. G. Transfer in perceptual learning following stimulus predifferentiation. *Journal of Experimental Psychology,* 1964, *68,* 388-395.
Ellis, H. C., and Shaffer, R. W. Stimulus encoding and the transfer of

stimulus differentiation. *Journal of Verbal Learning and Verbal Behavior,* 1974, *13,* 393-400.

Underwood, B. J., and Ekstrand, B. R. Differentiation among stimuli as a factor in transfer performance. *Journal of Verbal Learning and Verbal Behavior,* 1968, *7,* 172-175.

Transfer of response learning

Jung, J. Effects of response meaningfulness (m) on transfer under two different paradigms. *Journal of Experimental Psychology,* 1963, *65,* 377-384.

Forward and backward association

Harcum, E. R. Verbal transfer of overlearned forward and backward associations. *American Journal of Psychology,* 1953, *66,* 622-625.

Martin, E. Transfer of verbal paired-associates. *Psychological Review,* 1965, *72,* 327-343.

Stimulus similarity and transfer

Bruce, R. W. Conditions of transfer of training. *Journal of Experimental Psychology,* 1933, *16,* 343-361.

Response similarity and transfer

Barnes, J. M., and Underwood, B. J. "Fate" of first-list associations in transfer theory. *Journal of Experimental Psychology,* 1959, *58,* 97-105.

Underwood, B. J. Associative transfer in verbal learning as a function of response similarity and degree of first-list learning. *Journal of Experimental Psychology,* 1951, *42,* 44-53.

Transfer processes

Martin, E. Transfer of verbal paired associates. *Psychological Review,* 1965, *72,* 327-343.

Osgood, C. E. The similarity paradox in human learning: A resolution. *Psychological Review,* 1949, *56,* 132-143.

Transfer and generalization

Underwood, B. J. Associative transfer in verbal learning as a function of response similarity and degree of first-list learning. *Journal of Experimental Psychology,* 1951, *42,* 44-45.

Transfer and mediation

Horton, D. L., and Kjeldergaard, P. M. An experimental analysis of associative factors in mediated generalization. *Psychological Monographs,* 1961, *75* (11, whole no. 515).

Transfer and task variation

Duncan, C. P. Transfer after training with single versus multiple tasks. *Journal of Experimental Psychology,* 1958, *55,* 63-72.

Transfer from easy to difficult discrimination

Lawrence, D. H. The transfer of a discrimination along a continuum. *Journal of Comparative and Physiological Psychology,* 1952, *45,* 511-516.

Degree of original learning

Postman, L. Transfer of training as a function of experimental paradigm and degree of first-list learning. *Journal of Verbal Learning and Verbal Behavior,* 1962, *1,* 109-118.

Cognitive view of transfer

Mandler, G. From association to structure. *Psychological Review,* 1962, *69,* 415-427.

Associative view of transfer

Jung, J. Comments on Mandler's "From association to structure." *Psychological Review,* 1965, *72,* 318-322.

Theory

Greeno, J. G., James, C. T., and DaPolito, F. J. A cognitive interpretation of negative transfer and forgetting of paired associates. *Journal of Verbal Learning and Verbal Behavior,* 1971, *10,* 331-345.

Martin, E. Stimulus encoding in learning and transfer. In A. W. Melton and E. Martin (Eds.), *Coding processes in human memory.* Washington, D.C.: Winston, 1972.

Martin, E. Stimulus meaningfulness and paired-associate transfer: An encoding variability hypothesis. *Psychological Review,* 1968, *75,* 421-441.

Individual Differences in Learning and in Memory

Nature and study of individual differences

Buss, A. R., and Poley, W. *Individual differences: Traits and factors.* New York: Gardner Press, 1976.

Tyler, L. E. *Individual differences: Abilities and motivational directions.* Englewood Cliffs, N. J.: Prentice-Hall, 1974.

History of the study of individual differences

Galton, F. Statistics of mental imagery. *Mind,* 1880, *5,* 301-318.

Methodology

Nunnally, J. C. *Psychometric theory.* New York: McGraw-Hill, 1967.

Inappropriate uses of I.Q. scores

Kamin, L. *The science and politics of I. Q.* Hillsdale, N.J.: Erlbaum, 1974.

Intelligence and learning

Estes, W. K. Learning theory and intelligence. *American Psychologist,* 1974, *29,* 740-749.

Glaser, R. Some implications of previous work on learning and individual differences. In R. M. Gagné (Ed.), *Learning and individual differences.* Columbus, Ohio: Merrill, 1967, pp. 1-18.

Scott-Salapatek, S. Learning, intelligence and intelligence testing. In M. H. Marx and M. E. Bunch (Eds.), *Fundamentals and applications of learning.* New York: Macmillan, 1977, pp. 429-454.

Zeaman, D., and House, B. The relation of I.Q. and learning. In R. M. Gagné (Ed.), *Learning and individual differences.* Columbus, Ohio: Merrill, 1967, pp. 192-212.

Intelligence and special abilities

Guilford, J. P. *The nature of human intelligence.* New York: McGraw-Hill, 1967.

Resnick, L. B. (Ed.) *The nature of intelligence.* Hillsdale, N. J. Erlbaum, 1976.

Thurstone, T. G. Primary mental abilities in children. *Educational and Psychological Measurement,* 1941, *1,* 105-116.

Learning strategies and verbal learning

Cohen, S. R. Influence of organizing strategies and instructions on short-term retention. *Journal of Educational Psychology,* 1973, *64,* 199-205.

Earhard, M. Free recall transfer and individual differences in subjective organization. *Journal of Experimental Psychology,* 1974, *103,* 1167-1174.

Montague, W. E., and Wearing, A. J. The complexity of natural language mediators and its relation to paired-associate learning. *Psychonomic Science,* 1967, *7,* 135-136.

Learning strategies and concept learning

Bourne, L. E., Ekstrand, B. R., and Dominowski, R. L. *The psychology of thinking.* Englewood Cliffs, N.J.: Prentice-Hall, 1971, especially chap. 11, pp. 223-253.

Bruner, J. J., Goodnow, J., and Austin, G. A. *A study of thinking.* New York: Wiley, 1956.

Cognitive styles

Goodenough, D. R. The role of individual differences in field dependence as a factor in learning and memory. *Psychological Bulletin,* 1976, *83,* 675-694.

Kagan, J. Impulsive and reflective children. In J. Drumboltz (Ed.), *Learning and the educational process.* Chicago: Rand-McNally, 1965, pp. 133-161.

Witkin, H. A. Cognitive style in academic performance and in teacher-student relations. In S. Messick (Ed.), *Individuality in learning.* San Francisco: Jossey-Bass, 1976, pp. 38-72.

Memory ability

Carroll, J. B. Psychometric tests as cognitive tasks: A new "structure of intellect." In L. Resnick (Ed.), *The nature of intelligence.* Hillsdale, N. J.: Erlbaum, 1976, pp. 27-56.

Hunt, E. B., Frost, N., and Lunneborg, C. E. Individual differences in cognition. In G. Bower (Ed.), *The Psychology of Learning and Memory,* Vol. 7. New York: Academic, 1973, pp. 87-122.

Hunt, E. B., Lunneborg, C. E., and Lewis, J. What does it mean to be high verbal? *Cognitive Psychology,* 1975, *7,* 194-227.

Individuals with extraordinary memory

Hunt, E. B., and Love, T. How good can memory be? In A. W. Melton and E. Martin (Eds.), *Coding process in human memory.* Washington, D.C.: Winston, 1972, pp. 237-260.

Luria, A. R. *The mind of a mnemonist.* New York: Basic Books, 1968.

Attribute-by-treatment interactions

Bracht, G. H. Experimental factors related to aptitude-treatment interactions. *Review of Educational Research,* 1970, *40,* 627-645.

DiVesta, F. J., and Sunshine, P. M. The retrieval of abstract and concrete materials as functions of imagery, mediation and mnemonic aids. *Memory and Cognition,* 1974, *2,* 340-344.

Lesser, G. S. Matching instruction to student characteristics. In G. S. Lesser (Ed.), *Psychology and educational practice.* Glenview, Ill.: Scott, Foresman, 1971, pp. 530-550.

Subject Index

Name Index